The Jews

EUROPEAN PERSPECTIVES

EUROPEAN PERSPECTIVES

A Series in Social Thought and Cultural Criticism

Lawrence D. Kritzman, Editor

European Perspectives presents English translations of books by leading European thinkers. With both classic and outstanding contemporary works, the series aims to shape the major intellectual controversies of our day and to facilitate the tasks of historical understanding.

The Jews

History, Memory, and the Present

Pierre Vidal-Naquet

Translated and Edited by David Ames Curtis

WITH A FOREWORD BY PAUL BERMAN
AND A NEW PREFACE BY THE AUTHOR

Columbia University Press
NEW YORK

SSCCA

Columbia University Press

New York   Chichester, West Sussex

Copyright © 1996 Columbia University Press

Les Juifs, la mémoire et le présent © Éditions la Découverte 1991. Rev. ed. 1995 in one volume.
Translation copyright © Columbia University Press, 1995.

Columbia University Press wishes to express its appreciation for assistance given by the
government of France through Le Ministère de la Culture in preparation of the translation.

Columbia University Press wishes to thank its friend Bruno A. Quinson for his gift toward
the costs of publishing this book.

Library of Congress Cataloging-in-Publication Data

Vidal-Naquet, Pierre.
    [Juifs, la mémoire et le présent. English]
    The Jews : history, memory, and the present / Pierre Vidal-Naquet
  : translated and edited by David Ames Curtis : with an introduction
  by Paul Berman and a new preface by the author.
        p.   cm. — (European perspectives)
    Includes bibliographical references and index.
    ISBN 0-231-10208-9 (alk. paper).
    1. Jews—History—168 B.C.–A.D. 135   2. Jews—France—History.
  3. Jewish-Arab relations.   4. Holocaust, Jewish (1939–1945)—
  Historiography.   5. France—Ethnic relations.   I. Curtis, David
  Ames.   II. title.   III. Series.
  DS102.5.V3513   1996
  944'.004924—dc20   95–20960
                                                                       CIP

Printed in the United States of America
c 10 9 8 7 6 5 4 3 2 1

For Benjamin Cohen,
Charles Malamoud,
and Richard Marienstras

Contents

Translator's Note

DAVID AMES CURTIS

P ierre Vidal-Naquet's fascinating anthology, *Les Juifs, la mémoire et le présent*, was published in France in two volumes in 1981 and 1991 and reissued as one volume in 1995. The author and I, with the generous help of Olivier Nora, past president of the French Publishers' Agency in New York, compiled a representative selection from those two books for this English-language edition. We have also added, at Vidal-Naquet's initiative, a few more recent essays not published in the original French volumes, but which will appear in a forthcoming third volume in France. In translating the texts we selected, I encountered few difficulties. Fortunately, I was able to consult Pierre Vidal-Naquet directly, and I thank him for his patient answers as well as for his overall support.

We grouped these essays topically, following the section titles from the original French-language anthology. Within each section, moreover, the essays follow the chronological order in which they were written, and the sections themselves (with the sole exception of the "Conclusion," where Pierre Vidal-Naquet offers his own moving autobiographical overview of many of the themes broached in the previous four sections) also are ordered chronologically, following the successive periods of Jewish history Vidal-Naquet has chosen to examine. Because history is such an important element of this work and because the relations and contrasts between history and memory are so central to it, we decided the English-language edition would include the word *history* in the subtitle.

Three significant French words posed particular, though not very serious, translation problems. The first, *récit*, appears throughout this anthology of writings on Jewish history. Like the other two words I shall mention below, *récit* may variously be translated in English, depending upon the context; I have used "narrative," "account," "narrative account," "tale," even, on one occasion, "recital." And as with the other two words, my particular choice in each specific context may be open to question or challenge, or at least may be seen as partial and not always entirely satisfactory. I signal this problem here so that the reader will be aware that varying choices have been made for the successive translations of one and the same key term. Let us note here in passing that, while his critical examinations of various forms of "narrative" entail the introduction of a variety of literary-theory techniques into the field of historical analysis, Vidal-Naquet does not fall victim to current fashion, which treats "narrative" as all-encompassing, nor does he try to convince us that we are somehow beholden to, or must at all costs escape from, one or several "grand narratives." His historiographical enterprise is critical and discriminating, not a form of intellectual blackmail characterized by gross overgeneralizations. "Fiction," Vidal-Naquet notes categorically, "especially when it is deliberate, and genuine history constitute, no less, two extremes that never shall meet."

Related to the first term and obviously quite central to this historian's work, the second French word I wish to highlight is *histoire*. In Greek, *historia* (ἱστορίη in Herodotus's Ionian dialect) originally meant "inquiry" or "research," critical investigations as to the truth of what did or did not occur at a particular time. Over the past twenty-five-hundred years, other meanings, of course, have become attached to this word: history as a source for the learning of lessons, history writ large with a capital H, history as a fated or determined process, history as "bunk" (Henry Ford), and history as open-ended human creation (Cornelius Castoriadis), to cite a few examples. As Vidal-Naquet himself notes, "In French, the word *histoire* is wonderfully equivocal. It can designate everything from the nursery-rhyme story all the way to the most scholarly historical study, from the true tale to erudite or novelistic fiction." Forced to choose in English, I have often placed *histoire* in brackets in the text in order to indicate the inevitable loss of equivocality these choices have entailed or I have adopted a compromise translation that retains both "story" and "history." Vidal-Naquet's attitude toward fiction and genuine history rightly is one of "never the twain shall meet." It does not follow, of course, that the ambiguities of everyday language should be suppressed.

The final French word to bring to the reader's attention is *témoignage*.

This term has both the general historical (and sometimes even legal) connotation of oral or documentary "testimony" and the specific connotation of an "eyewitness account" or "testimonial," sometimes relating specifically to events surrounding the Second World War and the great premeditated massacre of Jews, Gypsies, and others. Many such accounts were published in France soon after the war and some have recently been republished, as Vidal-Naquet notes. For the French, Marc Bloch's *Strange Defeat* and Anne Frank's *Diary* are two such *témoignages*. The *Journal* of Pierre Vidal-Naquet's father, discussed by him in part three, is another. In her book on *The Theme of Nazi Concentration Camps in French Literature* (Paris and The Hague: Mouton, 1973), Cynthia Haft has simply left *témoignage* in the original French. For my part, I have again felt obliged in each case to choose one of the English-language terms mentioned above, as the context (or a mere desire for variety) best suggested to me one alternative or another.

I end by dedicating this translation to my late father, Grant Edward Curtis. Before becoming one of the pioneers of college financial aid, he was a student of history. For him, too, historiography is a critical, secular attempt to learn from the past as part of a present-oriented effort to remake the world. In addition to offering this commemorative dedication (for a book that examines memory as well as history), I thank those who generously helped me make this translation a reality: Olivier Nora, for his thoughtful early contribution; publisher Jennifer Crewe; series editor Lawrence D. Kritzman; Miranda Spieler, for her diligent and conscientious work tracking down several final bibliographical references; Paul Berman, who kindly accepted my invitation to write an introduction; as well as Linda Cardinal, Robert DuToit, Henry Louis Gates Jr., Clara Gibson Maxwell, Mary Maxwell, S. Thompson Moore, and Yves Ternon.

Paris, April 1995

Foreword

PAUL BERMAN

It was my very good fortune to encounter Pierre Vidal-Naquet during the early 1980s as the result of a transatlantic political controversy which, at the time, seemed relatively minor. For who in those innocent days would have predicted a resurgence of ethnic persecutions in Europe—and not just there? Who could have pictured the old-fashioned movements of the ultra-right clambering up from their caskets of disgrace and obloquy and once again striding around the modern world, winning votes and sometimes power and doing as they pleased? The likelihood that "ethnic cleansing" would take place in the Balkans, that concentration camps would be constructed to lock up and murder Europeans who cling to a non-Christian religion, that neo-Fascists would help form a government in Italy, that extreme-right movements with Axis nostalgias would prosper in so many places, that neo-Nazi German skinheads would conduct arson and murder campaigns—all of that, our reality in the 1990s, seemed so remote, so difficult to imagine, ten or fifteen years earlier. And yet, in the early 1980s one modest sign of such a future did loom into sight. It was a small but unusual movement to exonerate Hitler.

There had always been little groups, marginal ones mostly, of nostalgic Fascists and extreme-rightists. But until the Faurisson Affair in France, the little groups had always seemed incapable of big successes. Robert Faurisson was the French professor who proclaimed a more-or-less sympathetic view of the wartime Nazis. He did his best to argue that Hitler was innocent of genocide, that killing the Jews was never a Nazi program, and that extermination in the gas chambers was a Zionist hoax, concocted as part of a gigantic Jewish conspiracy to defraud the German people and expropriate the Palestinians. Faurisson, in short, was someone who ought to have been doomed to life in the shadows. Paranoia and looniness radiated from his every syllable. Yet in the late 1970s a group of French ultra-leftists decided, on the basis of their own harebrained left-wing interpretation of evil among Hitler's enemies, to discover all kinds of unsuspected virtues in Faurisson and his cause.

The ultra-leftists were extreme without being marginal. Some of them were well known from the student uprisings of 1968. Noam Chomsky, the linguist, was their comrade and fellow-thinker in America. They were the publishers of some of Chomsky's political writings in French translation. Chomsky's prestige in France, because of his brilliance in linguistics together with his courage and energy in opposing America's war in Vietnam, was enormous. His role in the affair proved to be crucial. On behalf of his French comrades, Chomsky wrote a harebrained essay of his own, instantly notorious, defending Faurisson as "a sort of relatively apolitical liberal" free of anti-Semitism (in the course of making further arguments, entirely unobjectionable, in favor of free speech). And by the early 1980s, there were respectable intellectuals in France who began to suggest that perhaps Faurisson deserved a hearing; Faurisson might well be a legitimate scholar; Faurisson might have contributions to make to our understanding of the Second World War; genocide might never have occurred.

Newspapers featured debates on the matter, as if there were anything to debate. And to anyone who stopped to ponder the implications of what was going on, it became obvious that the wildest of conspiracy theories and neo-Nazi extravagances could be accepted surprisingly easily by people in the mainstream of a modern democratic society, and Fascist beliefs from the past could very well make a comeback, and were doing exactly that before our eyes, and would continue doing so—unless somebody knowledgeable, forceful, and sober stood up at once to analyze the delusions and outright lies that had suddenly begun to pass as scholarly research.

As it happened, in France a good number of people did stand up, and Pierre Vidal-Naquet, the great classics scholar, was chief among them, and the corrective effect he had on intellectual opinion was large. The notion that Nazi gas chambers were anything but historical fact faded rather quickly—among the more serious intellectuals and journalists. Yet the world of the intellectuals and the mainstream press is not the same as the world of the demagogues. Faurissonism, defeated among the more sophisticated writers and journalists, began to prosper among the leaders of the

extreme-right National Front in France, who themselves began to flourish at the polls. And Faurissonism turned out to be merely the French version of a far larger phenomenon. For all over Europe, and not just there,
a variety of nationalist and ultra-right-wing ideologues were soon enough
standing up to articulate any number of bizarre justifications for ethnic
bigotry, not only against the Jews. The voices advocating those several theories grew louder, and by the 1990s in Europe and elsewhere words began
to congeal into violent deeds (against the Turks of Germany, the Gypsies,
and how many others—even apart from the massacred Muslims of
Bosnia), until by now we would need ten thousand Vidal-Naquets all over
the world merely to identify the horrific uses to which ethnic conspiracy
theories and myths and pseudohistory have been put. But we do not have
ten thousand Vidal-Naquets.

The Faurisson Affair was a transatlantic matter partly because of
Chomsky's disastrous intervention, partly because Faurisson's theories
found an echo and support among the white-supremacist organizations in
the United States. The American connection caught the eye of a number
of journalists and commentators in the United States, myself among
them. And so I sat down to read what Vidal-Naquet had written about the
affair. I studied the essays that have appeared in English under the title
Assassins of Memory: Essays on the Denial of the Holocaust. I struck up an
acquaintance with the author, then a correspondence, which blossomed
into mutual exchanges of French and American writings on anti-Semitism
and related themes, which blossomed into friendship. And having examined his writings on the theme of Holocaust denial, I dug a bit deeper and
began to read him on any number of other themes.

I read his essays on the Roman Jewish historian Flavius Josephus—brilliant essays, truly a tour de force of historical analysis, which figure among
the pieces in this present volume. I read his famous study of French atrocities during the Algerian War; his book about the false accusations against
the Resistance hero Jean Moulin, with its remarkable discussion of the history of heroes and monuments from Antiquity to the present; his books
on Ancient Greece, *The Black Hunter* and *Myth and Tragedy in Ancient Greece*
(written with Jean-Pierre Vernant). I followed his arguments on hunting,
sacrifice, and military strategy among the Greeks, on Sophocles and the
tragedians, and on a dozen other topics whose home is Athens, Sparta, and
Thebes. I read him on the Catholic theologian Jacques Maritain and Maritain's complicated relation with Judaism. As any reader would be, I was
hugely impressed. I was struck by the immensity of his learning and by his
willingness to take on topics of all sorts. His combative spirit appealed to

me. But I was struck, most of all, by a quality, something undefinable but undeniable, that can be described only as moral authority.

Where does that quality come from? It is not the product of one or another rigid intellectual system. In his work on Ancient Greece, Vidal-Naquet tends to make use of what is called structural analysis, an anthropological approach. But structural analysis has never been for him a dogma. When he turns to historical and political topics of more recent times, he dispenses with the structural approach altogether. His political instincts have always identified him as a man of the left. But in political matters, too, he has never been drawn to the doctrinaire. His generation of intellectuals were children during the Second World War, and when they came of age a great many of them were drawn to the Communist movement, as party members or fellow travelers. But not Vidal-Naquet. The anti-Stalinist and dissident left was more his style. He kept his independence.

He made his reputation as a political fighter because of the position he took, a very courageous one, against France's role in the Algerian War. Just as Chomsky, the young linguist, was one of America's leading intellectual opponents of the Vietnam War, Vidal-Naquet, the young classicist, was one of France's leading intellectual opponents of the war in Algeria. He campaigned against America's role in Vietnam, too, and in that respect he was not only Chomsky's equivalent but his comrade. But when Chomsky made his strange endorsement of Faurisson's ideological bona fides (and his equally strange decision over the years to stand by what he had originally written), how many other veterans of the antiwar movement chose to bite their tongues, out of a lingering respect or affection for Chomsky or, most commonly, out of a self-enforced lack of knowledge? But not Vidal-Naquet.

On the topic of neo-Nazism and of retrospective defenses of Vichy France and of the Nazis, he has always been, of course, a one-man Resistance movement. Yet he has never hesitated to criticize Israel for its treatment of the Palestinians, and in the sharpest terms, especially during the period of Likud rule, though not only then, as readers of the present book will discover. On the other hand, in 1991 after Saddam Hussein had conquered Kuwait, the same Vidal-Naquet who had rebuked the Israelis and had opposed the previous foreign interventions by France and the United States took the position of supporting, regretfully but forcefully, the Allies' war against Saddam. For say what you will about these various political positions (myself, I say hurrah—others are free to dissent), Vidal-Naquet has always thought his own thoughts, without regard to party affiliation or to ideological orthodoxies of any sort or to the authority that parties and ideologies might confer.

That moral authority of his, then—where does it come from? In my judgment, it derives from his sense of vocation as historian. As a classicist, Vidal-Naquet has always been fascinated by the division in Greek culture between the world of man and the mythic world of the gods. The search for that division characterizes almost everything he writes. He does not compose his essays in order to seduce or enchant the reader. He wants to distinguish history from legend, and he performs that task by establishing facts, comparing texts, defining what is known, and the limits of what is known. His vision of history is strictly antilyrical (which does not inhibit him from invoking Proust as a model of how to understand memory). Since ours is increasingly an age of nationalist mythologies, ethnic slanders, conspiracy theories, legends and mythologies of every kind, this antilyricism of his is supremely useful. It is a demonstration of the mental discipline that can help all of us keep our own feet on the ground and our own heads out of the fantastic clouds of mythology that are always drifting by.

But there is something more. It was an old principle of the American pragmatist philosophers that serious scholarly thought and research contain, as an aspect of their intellectual method, an implicit embrace of reason and democracy. Vidal-Naquet's work as historian seems to me a perfect example of that principle—with an unusual extra trait. For in his own approach to historical inquiry and analysis, the implicit dedication to reason and democracy takes on flesh and life and becomes, at last, visible and explicit. His professional commitment to the Greeks has something to do with that. The historian of Ancient Athens is, after all, also the historian of the origins of both philosophical reason and of democracy. A clear blue Attic light falls across everything he undertakes. Thucydides is virtually his friend. Even in this present book, which is concerned more with Jerusalem and the Jews than with Athens and the Greeks, Thucydides appears and reappears from one essay to the next, like a beloved house guest who keeps poking his head into Vidal-Naquet's study to make one more pertinent comment.

But beyond the inspiration from Athens, yes, you do find, especially in these present essays, an inspiration from Jerusalem. Vidal-Naquet is a French intellectual in the grand national tradition; but he is also the heir to a specific intellectual and political tradition of the French Jews. It is the tradition that derives from the French Revolution, a tradition of rigorous adherence to the principles of republican citizenship. It is a secular rationalist tradition, a tradition that, during the nineteenth century, took Greek classical studies as one of its scholarly ideals—yet never lost sight of its own origins in Judaism. It is a tradition of Jewish patriotism for France—yet which has always recognized that French national impulses can follow republican paths or paths of nationalist prejudice and oppression. The tradition is, in a word, Dreyfusard. It is the tradition of the French Jews who saw in Captain Dreyfus at the end of the nineteenth century a model of patriotism in the face of a false nationalism; of honesty in the face of lies; of dignity and firmness in the face of hatred and persecution—anyway, of as much firmness as could reasonably be demanded of a flesh-and-blood man and not a bronze statue. And it is a tradition that, during the years of Vichy rule and German occupation, had to undergo the extreme suffering—persecutions, arrests, deportations, Auschwitz, nothing was left out—of which Captain Dreyfus's experience was only a foretaste.

The essays that make up *The Jews: History, Memory, and the Present*, translated with scrupulous exactitude by David Ames Curtis, touch on the Jewish Revolt against the Romans, on the culture of the French secular Jewish bourgeoisie in the nineteenth century and its heritage in the twentieth, on the Dreyfus Affair, on the massacre of the Armenians, on the Nazi era in France and in the camps, on the modern Israelis and other themes. Certain of the essays call on Vidal-Naquet's shrewdness and skill as textual investigator, others on his judgment as political analyst. In still others we see him as an historian who has had to call on his own personal memories as well. The same scholar who begins his book by evaluating the primary texts that have come down to us from some of the worst moments of Roman Jerusalem ends by offering us a searing memoir of his own, recalling the supremely grim experience of a Jewish schoolboy in France during the time of Hitler—fully aware that, in the future, other historians will weigh and make use of his own testimony exactly as he himself weighs and makes use of Flavius Josephus's.

The result is a book with more dimensions than may at first be obvious. The reader will see in these pages sundry aspects of mostly Jewish history; will see some exhilarating examples of historical analysis and criticism; will see a discriminating political intelligence at work. The reader will see several of the values of the high intellectual culture of the secular French Jews, which Vidal-Naquet has made it his mission to express and preserve. And the reader will see a great soul: always curious, always informed, always animated by a passion for justice. Always and forever heartbroken, because of what happened during the war. Yet always fair, disciplined, scholarly, and precise. Always—no matter how terrible the circumstances or painful the memories.

Preface to the English-Language Edition

I concluded my preface to the 1981 volume *Les Juifs, la mémoire et le présent* as follows: "Stretched between the Israel of the first century and the Israel of today, between the victims and the executioners, between the misfortune of yesterday and the lies of today, this book is a torn fabric." In 1991 a second volume succeeded the first and a third one, now in preparation, is scheduled for publication before the end of 1995. The present American volume incorporates texts from all three of these French volumes. If it finds a receptive public, nothing obliges one to think that it will remain the only one of its kind.

This book contains reflections on Jewish history from the era of the second reconstruction of the State, in the second century B.C.E., to the most recent times. Not that there is on my part any hope or possibility of dominating all of Jewish history. That was the ambition of the great historians of the nineteenth century and the beginning of the twentieth, a Graetz or a Dubnow. It was also the ambition of Salo W. Baron, who gave his name to the chair my illustrious colleague Yosef Yerushalmi now occupies at Columbia University. These examples notwithstanding, I do not believe that such a synthesis is possible, for I know that in Jewish history the Same is constantly mixed with the Other, and one would therefore have to have all of universal history at one's command in order to dominate Jewish history.

In fact, my texts concentrate on three quite specific areas of study. And each one of these areas, it turns out, is marked by the decisive presence of the Other.

My first area of study in Jewish history was the State. When the Maccabees reconstituted the State in the second century B.C.E., they could not help but imitate an already existing model. Whatever their intentions might have been in setting up this State, the unavoidable model was that of a Hellenistic kingdom. And the same may be said for modern Israel. Herzl was conscious of this fact when he wrote his *Altneuland*, but the pioneers who created the modern State of Israel had to fit themselves into a context that was all the more difficult as it contained an unmistakably colonial dimension. Under these circumstances, it became very difficult to create a just and righteous State, the messianic State many had dreamed of creating.

My second area of study concerned the process of Jewish emancipation. The entire second part of the present volume is devoted to this topic. The French Revolution created, for the Jews, a new kind of liberty that allowed them either to envisage the dissolution of their communities within the "Grande Nation" or to create for themselves their own national model along the lines of the strongly nationalist movements of eastern Europe. America alone has, in large part, escaped this dilemma.

Finally, I could not avoid taking an interest in one other form of contact with the Other. This last form concerns the attempt, inspired by Hitlerism, to destroy European Judaism.

I have attempted to study all three of these areas from both the historical and the historiographical points of view. In this endeavor I am indebted to a great human example, that of Arnaldo Momigliano.

I came to Jewish studies late in life. By training, I am a historian and a specialist in the study of the ancient Greek world. Taking a broad overview—that is to say, adopting a long-term perspective on the French Jewish intellectual bourgeoisie, of which I am a member (as will be seen by reading, in the third part of the present volume, my presentation of the *Journal* my father kept during the Occupation)—there is nothing surprising about this. Classical studies were, for this section of the bourgeoisie, one way of becoming integrated into the French Republic. Quite recently, in October 1994, I happened upon an amusing example of this tendency. In the library of one of my cousins, who married an American diplomat and who now lives in Washington, D.C., I found a beautiful edition of Abbé Barthélémy's *Voyage du jeune Anacharsis en Grèce*. Starting in 1788 when it was first published, and for more than a century afterward, this book introduced the ancient Greek world to several successive generations of the French bourgeoisie. The copy I came across in Washington bore the following inscription, signed by a certain Armand Lévy: "To my dear student, Alfred Dreyfus, on the occasion of his bar mitzvah" (16 April [18]75). Here we have a book of ancient Greek history given to a young man on the occasion of his integration into the Jewish community. The Alfred Dreyfus mentioned in the inscription is none other than the hero of the Affair, which I discuss in the second part of the present volume. Again in this second part, I offer the example of the Reinach brothers: Joseph, Salomon, and Théodore. The two younger brothers were great archaeologists and great Hellenists, the eldest one of the actors in and the historian of the *Affaire*. But Salomon, like Théodore, eventually left the field of classical studies to explore Jewish history in detail as well as in general terms.

These examples seem designed expressly to humble me. Allow me simply to recall that when I came to Jewish history in 1976 while writing a long introduction to the French translation of Flavius Josephus's *The Jewish War*,[1] it certainly was not entirely unavailing that I had devoted much time to working on Greek tragedy (which helped me to understand certain modern tragedies) and on mythology (which taught me not to take contemporary myths literally, no matter who had developed them). The case of Masada, which I discuss in the first part of the present volume, is rather exemplary in this respect, since I—and the critical-historical method along with me—have sometimes been accused of being a follower . . . of the French negationist, Robert Faurisson![2]

Nor was it entirely unavailing that I have been an involved party and committed witness of events in the contemporary world, in particular during the dramatic period of Algeria's decolonization. A number of texts from the three French volumes, some of which have been translated for the present English-language edition, were written in the heat of the Arab-Israeli or Palestinian-Israeli conflict as reportages or thought pieces. In speaking of this volume as a "torn fabric," I do not mean to say that it is torn between the historian of the past and the journalist of the present, reacting day to day. I hope to have surpassed this dichotomy. When dealing with the past, I have always remembered that the past must be read in the present and that, to borrow a phrase from Raymond Aron, all history is contemporary. When dealing with the present, I have always striven to situate this present in its historical context and to take the necessary distance with regard to it.

As concerns the conflict in the Near East, I have done my best since 1967 to hasten the day when mutual recognition would take place between two nationalist movements that could not have avoided a mutual confrontation. I have nevertheless always also been conscious of the two logics of exclusion at work there: the exclusion of Palestinians by Israel, whose State was conceived by Jews and for Jews, and the existential rejection of Israel by the Arabs of Palestine, who find it difficult to accept the idea that another nationalism has come to take root on their land.

One can easily imagine the immense joy with which I greeted the Accords concluded in Oslo in September 1993 and then made official in Washington, D.C. Thenceforth everything seemed possible, including the existence of two States, both of them democratic, since the Palestinian people are, intellectually as well as socially speaking, the most highly developed people in the Arab East. Now, it turns out that not everything was, and not everything yet is, possible. Without wanting to create any false symmetries, I note that both engines have continued upon their respective launch paths, each still dreaming of bringing about the other's destruction. In making Yasser Arafat the head of a Palestinian Authority that for the moment is limited to Jericho and Gaza, the Israelis have attempted to divide their adversaries rather than speak to them face to face. And since Yasser Arafat is a tyrant rather than a democratic leader, the game is a rather easy one. In blocking on the customs level the aid promised to the Palestinians—nay, in auctioning off donations that have reached their borders—the Israelis are sabotaging the most precious thing they themselves have created. The Likud government deliberately played the Hamas card against the "secular" PLO; in multiplying its mean-spirited ploys as it implements the Accords, the Rabin government risks unconsciously pursuing the same policy.

I write these lines on the day after the January 22 suicide-bombing attack which killed nineteen at Netanya.[3] This massacre follows upon many others and it has its counterpart, alas, on the Israeli side (as I discuss at the end of the fourth part of the present volume). This counterpart has had extremely serious consequences: without harking back to Deir Yassin in 1948, how can one avoid mentioning here Sabra and Shatila, as well as Hebron? During the latest attack, Mr. Rabin once again proclaimed that Israelis and Palestinians have to be "separated" from each other. This logic, alas, is rather summary and incomplete, for how is one going to prevent the three segments of the Palestinian people—the Arabs of Israel, those inhabiting the occupied territories, and those now living outside Palestine—from reuniting and from sometimes even rallying together? The Palestinians' dream of a "massive return" to Palestine is not one the Israelis should be ignoring. And above all, how can one fail to see the most blindingly self-evident fact? The principal obstacles to peace and separation are the colonial settlements now dotting the Palestinian territory, including

those located in the immediate environs of Arab Jerusalem. The very presence of these colonies reduces to nothing all of the Palestinians' hopes,
each time even a glimmer of a solution begins to appear. One must have
the courage to say up front and without equivocation: Either the government of Israel will brave the colonists' anger by dismantling the colonies
or it will render difficult, if not downright impossible, even mere coexis-
tence with Palestine.

A historian is not a prophet. But perhaps it will be understood that, if
this book is indeed a torn fabric, that is because the situation itself is
torn—not only torn but heartrending.

What remains for me to do in closing is to thank those who have made
the publication of this book possible in America: Jennifer Crewe and the
staff of Columbia University Press; Paul Berman, author of the foreword
to the present volume, with whom I began forging a friendship in 1981
while struggling together against the "assassins of memory"; and, finally,
David Curtis, who has shown himself (and not just for the first time) to
be an ideal translator, so that no author can dream of a better one.

January 23, 1995

The Jews

PART ONE

Origins and History

1

Forms of Political Activity in the Jewish World, Principally Around the First Century C.E.

This essay[1] originates in a sense of astonishment as well as in an effort to account for that by which I, following so many others, have been astonished. What is so astonishing? I quote a famous passage from the fifth book of Tacitus's *Histories*, where he describes the curious division among the besieged inhabitants of Jerusalem, right in the midst of Titus's siege of the city in 70 C.E.:

> There were three different leaders, and three armies. The long outer perimeter of the walls was held by Simon, the central part of the city by John who was also called Bargioras [an error on the part of Tacitus, who confused Simon son of Gioras with John of Gischala—PV-N], and the Temple by Eleazar. John and Simon could rely on numbers and equipment, Eleazar on his strategic position. But it was upon each other that they turned the weapons of battle, ambush and fire, and great stocks of corn went up in flames. Then John sent off a party of men, ostensibly to offer sacrifice but in reality to cut Eleazar and his followers to pieces, thus gaining possession of the Temple. Henceforward, therefore, Jerusalem was divided between two factions, until, on the approach of the Romans, fighting the foreigner healed the breach between them.[2]

Yet this version supposedly favors the theory of Jewish unity! I shall not speak here of the rabbinical sources, which delight in multiplying the number of factions. It should be pointed out, however, that Flavius Josephus's version is certainly much harsher than that of Tacitus. It is harsher, first because Josephus's version covers the entire duration of the war and second because, even if, as in Tacitus's account, Josephus's version ends with the division of Jerusalem into two opposing camps (John of Gischala associated with Eleazar and his Zealots, on the one hand, Simon son of Gioras, on the other), according to the Jewish historian no conclusive agreement ever was reached and, at the very best, only a tactical alliance was concluded: "For even the fact that the Romans were camping below their walls did not calm the sedition within the walls; the revolutionaries, after a brief return to some degree of common sense (βραχὺ δὲ . . . ἀνενόσουν) during their first sally, fell into a relapse, and, once again divided, they fought with each other, doing everything that their besiegers could have desired."[3] Actually, the understanding they came to on the occasion of a sally and, above all, when the first Roman assault occurred, was, according to Josephus, only temporary. At the time, Simon proclaimed by herald that the soldiers in the Temple could proceed in full safety to the ramparts—which was the least he could have done!—and John, though not feeling confident himself, gave them permission to do so.[4] The two chiefs did not surrender to the Romans together. John, dying of hunger underground, ultimately asked for Roman protection.[5] As for Simon, the chief of the upper city, he attempted a messianic appearance, emerging from the ruins of the Temple in a white tunic and a purple cloak. He had his throat cut in Rome during the Flavians' triumphant return home.

Of course, I am merely summarizing here a situation that, as I shall show later, was infinitely more complex. Of course, too, these divisions caused some surprise and occasioned much derision. One of the few historians not to express astonishment was Ernest Renan, whose reasoning was just the opposite of Josephus's: "Those who judge human affairs with bourgeois ideas believe that the revolution is lost when the revolutionaries 'begin to devour one another.' On the contrary, this is proof that the revolution has retained all its energy, that an impersonal ardor has taken over."[6] Why not—if one considers the Judean War to be a "revolution" comparable to the ones that began in 1789? The examples of 1793 or of 1936 (in Spain) show that foreign conflict is not in the least incompatible with civil war. Even so, I am not sure that the comparison made by Renan and picked up by many others—quite recently by David Rhoads[7]—is entirely valid. And if comparisons are to be made, why not mention, rather, the political clashes that took place in the Warsaw ghetto leading up to and even during the armed uprising of April 1943?

There is yet another way to solve the problem: say that it does not exist. This was the approach adopted by the Israeli historian, Yitzhak Baer.[8] In his view, this civil-war story is just a Roman invention. The Jews formed a unanimous front in defense of their way of life. As for Josephus, he borrowed his account of the civil war from the scene Thucydides sketched of the civil war in the Greek world, notably the description of the disturbances at Corcyra in the third book of *The Peloponnesian War*. It goes without saying that the influences Baer mentions are not merely imagined. But just because Aristophanes, Thucydides, or Plato might have inspired Josephus does not necessarily mean that the facts to which he refers are themselves imaginary. In a world dominated by rhetoric, the use of a rhetorical technique of presentation, one largely inspired by previous authors, is not at all surprising. Pausanias's narratives of the third-century B.C.E. Gallic invasion (tenth book of the *Description of Greece*) may have been modeled on accounts of the Persian wars,[9] but, if true, that would not allow us to strike this invasion from the history books.

Besides, why would Josephus and Tacitus have invented this civil war? In their minds, outbreaks of internal Jewish strife did not enhance in the least the prestige of the Roman world. The opposite, rather, would be the case. These divisions can be denied only in the terms of an ideology that excludes their very existence. Let us grant that, at most, Josephus's and Tacitus's histories force matters somewhat, as Baroque history does. What remains is the fact of division, and we must try to account for it.

The "fact," I said. But what mechanism actually allows us to interpret it? Practically all we have, to provide a response, is Josephus's narrative.

Let us therefore adopt an initial working hypothesis, that of class struggle: the opposing *groups* might have represented *class* antagonists. This is how the East German historian Heinz Kreissig reasons in his book on the "social connections of the Judean War."[10] After having analyzed minutely the position that each social group—from high clergy to prostitutes—occupied within the "relations of production," but without being quite sure where to place the rabbis, Kreissig finally broaches, on page 127 of his book, the problem of how to account for this war, which he terms "Judean," not "Jewish." It started with a threat of unemployment: eighteen thousand craftsmen, according to Josephus,[11] risked being thrown out of work following the completion of the Temple. Agrippa II, however, gave them work and settled the problem. I shall not go into the details of Kreissig's interpretation, which, moreover, is quite intriguing. According to him, we should distinguish a radical wing of the revolt—led first by the Sicarii of Menahem son (or grandson) of Judas the Galilaean, then by Simon son of Gioras, and supported by free peasants and slaves—and a clerical wing, which represented the revolutionary half of the group of the priests. Finally, it is supposed that there was a difficult-to-pigeon-hole group of people who had, as their leader, no less than John of Gischala, the Galilaean chief known for his "*unsoziales Machtgelüste*," his avidity for power devoid of any kind of social perspective.[12]

One of the difficulties with this explanatory hypothesis is that it cannot easily be reconciled either with the topography of the city or with the narrative of the events. From the very start of the insurrection, class oppositions certainly were flagrantly obvious. The Upper City was the city of the wealthy, and it is upon them that King Agrippa leaned for support against the Lower City and the Temple. Changes took place, however, after the fall of Galilee, and, even though Jerusalem then became a city of refuge, class oppositions continued to operate. With the support of conservative elements as well as the *dēmos* (which is not "the people"), the high priest Ananus opposed John of Gischala and his allies the Zealots led by Eleazar son of Simon. The latter called upon the Idumaeans to settle the conflict. A new actor then entered on the scene, Simon son of Gioras, a native of the Decapolis who kept in practice, from his base at Masada, by ravaging Idumaea. The part of Jerusalem he occupied was none other than the Upper City, the wealthy section. John and the Zealots split, but John of Gischala emerged as the winner of this confrontation.

We thus have the following situation: John and the priests (who constituted the Zealots' core) occupied the Lower City; Simon and the Idumaeans occupied the Upper City, where the *dēmos* was still to be found. This was the same dichotomy that prevailed at the start. I certainly have no doubts that many of the wealthy were killed. But were they all killed? And above all, the groups fighting among themselves in Jerusalem were not only social antagonists. A Galilaean party was opposed to the Idumaean party. The Idumaeans were a very special lot, known as a "turbulent and undisciplined people" (ἔθνος θορυβῶδες καὶ ἄτακτον).[13] They had an army of twenty thousand men (surely an exaggerated figure). Indeed, they are the object of the sole political debate found in the entire *Jewish War*, where opposing speeches are delivered by Jeshua, Ananus's assistant high priest, and by the Idumaeans' representative, Simon son of Cathla.[14] The text of Simon's speech is notable for the way he demands that the Idumaeans be allowed entry into Jerusalem, namely that their common city should be opened to the nation, τῷ ἔθνει . . . τὴν κοινὴν πόλιν.[15] The Idumaeans were, as regards other Jews, *homophyloi*,[16] members of the same tribe. They were described as being both relatives (*syngeneis*) of other Jews and by nature cruel murderers.[17] They maintained their individuality throughout the war, allying themselves first with the Zealots and then with Simon son of Gioras. At the end of the siege, however, they wished to surrender, which led to the execution of their leaders.[18]

With the rich and the poor, city people and country people, some oppositions were social and occupational in nature. With Galilaeans and Idumaeans, there were thus also regional oppositions. With Sicarii, disciples of Judas the Galilaean, and Zealots centered around the Temple, possibly also Essenes, ideological oppositions existed, too. But was that all? Among the Jerusalem combatants, there was still another category of Jews. The Diaspora? Nothing authorizes us to say that a distant Diaspora had attempted to reach Israel. For someone living in Alexandria, it would not have been a very easy trip. On the other hand, we do know that a curious category of Jews was present, the princes of Adiabene and their retinue. In the preface to *The Jewish War*, Josephus speaks of "our compatriots beyond the Euphrates, the Adiabenians" (τὸ ὑπὲρ Εὐφράτην ὁμό- φυλον ἡμῖν Ἀδιαβηνούς).[19] This passage refers to converts, recent converts (compared to the Idumaeans, who were early converts). Josephus recounts[20] the romantic story of the conversion of their queen, Helena, and of the benefits she would later shower upon Jerusalem. Located in the upper valley of the Tigris, Adiabene was a strategically important zone situated between the Parthian world and the Roman Empire. Ironically, Agrippa II asked the insurgent Jews[21] whether they thought their *homophyloi*, their brothers from Adiabene, would come to their aid. They did indeed come, as Josephus, the real author of the speech, knew very well they had done. He mentions by name, among the combatants, two relatives of the king of Adiabene: Monobazus and Cenedaeus, as well as a Babylonian. If it is true that the sons of King Izates surrendered to Titus,[22] no doubt it was because they had come to fight. These very recent converts had not yet had time, however, to become a part of the Jewish people—which offers me a good opportunity to underscore the paradox of a people whom one may join as a result of conversion and who are the sole people, with the exception of the Romans, who allow persons to become an integral part of their group from any point in the Empire.

None of this is simple, and the worst mistake would be to think that the various hierarchies intermingle. Naturally, there were overlaps. The Sadducees—about whom we are best informed, unfortunately, by what their adversaries said about them—were both a religious "sect" and a clerical aristocracy on good terms with the Romans. But classification according to ritual purity, the importance of which Professor Jeremias in particular has demonstrated,[23] is not to be confused with classification according to material wealth. In the famous example of the debate between Hellenists and Hebrews in the early Christian community,[24] the Hebrews furnish Apostles and the Hellenists Deacons, which again presumes a hierarchy— a rather mysterious one, to tell the truth—in which spoken language is one criterion.

In order to comprehend this situation, let us first back up a bit. How did one arrive at this *poikilon*, this diversity, that pertains to the political sphere in general [*le "politique"*], according to Philo of Alexandria,[25] and that also is Israel?

Under the Persian monarchy, at the beginning of the Macedonian conquest, and again in 200 B.C.E. when Antiochus III captured Jerusalem and Judea, if there ever existed a Jewish State, a Jewish political structure, it was that of a Temple-State, which was in fact similar to others known in the Seleucid world. Not that the Jerusalem Sanctuary possessed, in the strict sense of the term, a part of the land—this is the error of those who speak of an "Asiatic[26] mode of production"—but it was a financial, political, and religious center. "Now there is," writes Josephus, "no public money among us except that which is God's."[27] The Diaspora, as well as Judea, contributed to it, and the Diaspora began within Palestine itself.

It was under the familiar form of the Temple-State that the Seleucid King recognized the Jewish entity in the document known by the name of "Seleucid Charter of Jerusalem."[28] For the benefit of the Temple-State hierarchy, the *gerousia*, the priests, the scribes of the Temple, and the Temple cantors, the king established a system of fiscal exemptions. Beyond this hierarchy, there were only simple "inhabitants," some of whom, having become slaves, were freed by the king.

The tie between the Temple and the very existence of the Jews appears so strong that, outside Jerusalem, other temples were planned. During the Persian period, there was the Elephantine Temple in Egypt. The most famous of these temples, the Temple at Leontopolis in Egypt, was founded after the flight in 162, or fifteen years later, of Onias III, or IV, who claimed to be the interpreter of the prophet Isaiah.[29] One mentions wrongly in this connection the building at Qasr el-Abd in Transjordania, which in reality was a residence established at the end of the third century B.C.E. for the Tobiad Hyrcanus.[30] There was also Antioch, where the synagogue, described by Josephus as *hieron*, may have inherited some ornaments from the Jerusalem Temple that had been confiscated by Antiochus Epiphanes.[31] Finally, there was the rival sanctuary, that of the Samaritans, on Mount Gerizim, which was still functioning as a "holy place."

Yet from the Ptolemaic period, even from the Persian period, this hierarchy was beginning to lag behind events. A civic aristocracy had formed outside the religious aristocracy, as shown by the famous example of Hyrcanus son of Joseph the Tobiad, about whom Flavius Josephus has written a veritable novel of acculturation.[32]

The other important fact of note, to which Martin Hengel has drawn particular attention in his great synthetic study *Judaism and Hellenism*, is the development of the Jewish Wisdom Schools starting in the Ptolemaic period.[33] The Wisdom of Ben Sira (Ecclesiasticus), written in 180, presupposes the existence of schools that educate persons who, like Jeshua the son of Sirach himself, may feel a sense of admiration for the Temple without necessarily being a part of it.

What existed merely in outline form during Ptolemaic times took on considerable importance during the Seleucid period, with the revolt of the Maccabees. The idea that I would now like to develop is the following: the second and first centuries B.C.E., and again the first century C.E., were characterized by a process of creation of oppositions—of duplications, if I may so express myself—which operated on a whole series of levels. The revolt of the Maccabees was carried out in the name of zeal for the Law, the Torah, and W. R. Farmer is quite right to insist on the continuity that exists between the Maccabees and the insurrection of the year 66.[34] One central notion is common to these successive revolts: that of "zeal."[35] Zeal is directed, certainly, against the foreigner, but it is directed still more sharply against the Hellenized Jew. The revolt at Modin begins with an attack on a servile Jew: "A Jew came forward in the sight of all to sacrifice upon the altar in Modin in accordance with the king's command. And when Mattathias saw it, his zeal was kindled, and his heart quivered (with wrath); and his indignation burst forth for judgment, so that he ran and slew him on the altar."[36] The fate of a Seleucid functionary was decided next: "He [also] killed the king's officer who had come to enforce the sacrificing, [and] pulled down the altar."[37]

The fact that this murder occurred after the sacrifice, on the pagan altar, of an impure Jew, the son of Belial, is of capital importance. The political game did not consist of two players alone—Jews against Greeks—but three: "zealous" Jews, Jews partial to the Seleucids and to the "aggiornamento" of their religion, and Greeks from the king's entourage. There was even a fourth player, for we should not forget the two series of Hellenized cities that together ringed the land of Judea, from Akko (Ptolemais) to Gaza along the seashore and from Gerasa to Marisa inland. They also had their word to contribute to this debate.

Political action during the Maccabean period, as we may guess, thus entailed the purification of the Jewish land. The Maccabean army was a maquis of pure men who were purifiers: "And Mattathias and his friends went round about, and pulled down altars, and they circumcised by force the children that were uncircumcised, as many as they found within the borders of Israel. And they pursued the sons of pride, and the work prospered in their hand. And they rescued the Law out of the hand of the Gentiles, and out of the hand of the kings, neither suffered they the sinner to triumph."[38] The point at the horizon, then, was the image of a pure State, an ideological State that would apply and enforce the rules of Jewish law. The text I just cited is all the more striking in that, drawn from the first book of Maccabees, which was composed in honor of the Hasmonaean family, it was written at the end of the second century B.C.E.,[39] when the movement to Hellenize the Jewish State was already well under way. What had to happen happened. Like all ideological States, this Army-State organization created by Judas Maccabaeus collided with realities that obliged it to seek compromises.

The first and most renowned of these compromises was the one made at the start of the revolt over the principle of the Sabbath, the famous episode of the attack that had to be defended against on the Sabbath day: "Mattathias and his friends . . . said to one another, 'If we all do as our brethren have done, and do not fight against the Gentiles for our lives and our ordinances, they will soon destroy us from off the earth.'"[40] With an admirable sense of balance, the author of 1 Maccabees chooses precisely this point to place the alliance of the insurgent forces with the *Hasidaioi* (the Hasidim). We do not know whether the latter represented the future Pharisees, the future Essenes, or a sect of no importance with no future, but we do know that they were characterized by their absolute obedience to the Law: πᾶς ὁ ἑκουσιαζόμενος τῷ νόμῳ.[41] This is not just an accidental coincidence occurring in the narrative. Insistence on the alliance with the extremist legalists came at the very moment when compromises appeared necessary. This is a law of ideological movements. It would be easy to provide other examples. Following along the same line of thought, one could also condemn the Gentiles—without such condemnation hindering either the symbolic alliance with Sparta or the more practical alliance with Rome.

In the space of a few decades, the revolt gave birth to a large Jewish State—a "mini-Empire," to borrow an expression from Zeev Yavetz's unpublished lecture on "Jews and the Great Powers (During the Second Jewish Commonwealth)"—which extended far beyond the boundaries of ancient Judea, since it included the coast and the Hellenized Philistine cities, Samaria, which had been conquered in the time of John Hyrcanus, as well as a part of Idumaea (Edom). Aristobulus seized Ituraea, Alexander Jannaeus Gaza and some of the cities of Transjordania.

At that point, the same problems as the ones that had already characterized the insurrectional period reappeared, though now on an entirely different scale. What, one might ask, was the nature of the assemblage that had thus been constituted? Was it an ideological State? Yes, to the extent that the conquest aimed at "purifying" conquered territory, practicing, when need be, the massacre of its inhabitants according to the old principle of public anathema, the way Joshua is said to have applied it. This was the procedure followed at Caspin in the Golan at the time of Judas.[42] But, just as Mattathias circumcised children by force, mass conversion of vanquished populations now came to appear normal practice. The best-known example is that of Idumaea as recounted by Josephus: "Hyrcanus . . . , after subduing all the Idumaeans, permitted them to remain in their country so long as they had themselves circumcised and were willing to observe the laws of the Jews. And so, out of attachment to the land of their fathers, they submitted to circumcision and to making their manner of life conform in all other respects to that of the Jews. And from that time on they have continued to be Jews."[43] The alternative to conversion was, barring massacre, expulsion of the inhabitants: the taking of Joppa (Jaffa) by Simon was accompanied by the expulsion of the population.[44]

Another policy was set up in contrast with these various forms of Judaizing conquered territories. It consisted of enlarging the territory of the State without chasing out the inhabitants, all the while accepting a diversity of populations as a constitutive element of that State. In short, it consisted in the creation of a Seleucid State on a smaller scale while accepting what Édouard Will has called "the loose and motley structure of such a State."[45] Of course, these two policies did not follow one another the way Louis XIV succeeded Louis XIII. But roughly speaking, the era of John Hyrcanus already marks the progress of the second policy in overtaking the first. Adoption of the royal title by Aristobulus the Philhellenist, then by Alexander Jannaeus (103–76 B.C.E.), shows that a decisive move to the second form of State had taken place. The Jewish State was thenceforth a Hellenistic State, predominantly Jewish in composition.

However—and this fact is of capital importance—it is from this moment that, in the Judeo-Palestinian world, civil war supplanted foreign war as a structural element of political life. The last two centuries of the independent Jewish State were, in effect, two centuries of now overt, now covert civil warfare. The first features of domestic conflict were apparent as early as the break between Judas Maccabaeus and the Hasidim under Demetrius I. Sixty Hasidim were killed by joint action of the high priest Alcimus and General Bacchides.[46] John Hyrcanus fell out with the Pharisees.[47] Alexander Jannaeus fought against some people who may have been Pharisees, but whom Josephus calls quite simply Jews,[48] eight hundred of whom had their throats cut. The only respite took place during the reign of a woman, Alexandra Salome. With her sons, Hyrcanus II and Aristobulus II, civil warfare resumed without our being able to say which of the two kings was orthodox.

Everyone knows how this affair ended. The constitution of the three "sects"[49]—in the time of Hyrcanus I, according to Josephus—is the most classic testimony to division among the Jews. As for the time when Pompey came to Damascus and listened to the two kings (who, like Eteocles and Polynices—or, in more banal terms, like two Seleucid kings—were contending for power), Josephus's conclusion is that the Jewish *ethnos* was opposed to one as much as to the other and that the monarchy was doing little more than reducing the nation to slavery.[50] When the monarchy was reconstituted, with Herod proclaimed king at the Capitol under the protection of Octavian, it appeared, more than ever, as a foreign substance, an instrument of Hellenization.

Before the discoveries from Qumran, a clearly visible and well-known feature of Jewish political life was the Pharisees' opposition to the monarchy, accompanied by outpourings of otherwise repressed legalistic impulses each time State control began to slacken. Since the discovery and publication of the Qumran manuscripts, we know something more. This community rejected Israel as it existed at that time, as the Neture Karta reject modern Israel. Israel was themselves. The Temple was not the Temple of Herod. The "army of the end of time" described in the scroll of the *War Rule* was also themselves. On top of that, the corrupt Jerusalem of Herod and the Romans was, according to the Essenian *Commentary on Nahum*, Nineveh.[51]

Does it follow that what we have here is the classic schema of a people deeply faithful to its traditions but covered on top by a superficial Hellenized stratum? There were the Jews, and there was something else. What complicates things, however, is that this "something else" also was Jewish. Here, in fact, we enter into an endless series of duplications.

There were the Jews and there were the Greeks. There were the Jewish Jews and the Hellenized Jews: those of Caesarea, those of Galilee. Hellenism was present within the Essenian movement and there are Greek

documents to be found at Masada. Later, a part of Bar Kochba's correspondence would be written in Greek, too. All this is symbolized quite
well as early as the second century B.C.E. in the double name of Daniel:
Daniel, the symbol of revolt, and (Daniel)-Belteshazzar, a sobriquet for
any Greek king who is at the court of the "King of Babylon."[52]

Finally, there was the well-known break between Palestinian Judaism
and the Judaism of the Diaspora. Even so, we must reject the usual ways
in which this duplication is depicted. In the first century, the Diaspora
began at Caesarea, capital of the province of Judea, but, on the other hand,
while it did not necessarily shift about at the same pace as the Palestinian
community, the Diaspora could be subject to groundswells like the one
Suetonius speaks of in the Rome of Claudius's time: *impulsore Chresto*,
under the impulse of Christ.[53]

Everything takes place as though in a hall of mirrors. There is Diaspora-
like behavior at Jerusalem and, conversely, there is a Palestinian movement in the Diaspora (though, of course, there are dominant tendencies
in each case).

Let us now try to draw a spectrum of the different modes of political
action while also emphasizing the consequences of each one.

At one end we have the action of the notables. Such action existed in
Israel, though we know more about its role in the Diaspora. The communities of the Diaspora were governed by notables. These communities did
not constitute cities, *poleis*, but instead, at Alexandria and at Berenice,
politeumata, quasi-political groupings. At Cyrene, according to Strabo,[54]
the population was grouped into four categories: citizens, metics, *geōrgoi*
(farmers), and Jews. In a land like Egypt, where they were the third party,
Hellenized without being Greeks, political action was not always easy.
Between Ptolemy VIII Euergetes II and Cleopatra II, in 132 B.C.E. and the
following years, there was civil warfare. The Jews took the side of Cleopatra II against the Greeks of Alexandria. This is the classic behavior of the
minority's minority.[55]

In the first century C.E., under Roman rule, one well-known case is
that of the crisis of 35–40 at Alexandria, as documented in Philo's
embassy to Caligula and his denunciation of the prefect Flaccus. Philo is at
once a man of the book (and the book is, since the appearance of the Septuagint, one of the Jews' forms of political action), a theoretician, and a
practitioner of politics. In his *De Iosepho*, this very prominent notable pro-
pounded a theory of the political world as a world of the *poikilon*, of the
motley. His *Embassy* to Caligula was for him the equivalent of the Platonic
philosophers' return to the cave. This extraordinary account ends with a

famous meeting with Caligula, during which the Jewish delegation heard
the Emperor ask them one and only one question: "Why do you abstain
from eating pork?"[56] Diplomats and men of culture, the Jewish delegates
replied that Laws vary by peoples. Speaking of this behavior today, many
moderns would be tempted to speak of cowardice. They would be mistaken. When Caligula threatened to have a statue of himself erected at
Jerusalem, Philo and his friends rebelled. For them, it was not a matter of
defending their (dubious) right to speak as citizens of Alexandria. They
spoke of their rights "as citizens of a value that is more universal, that of
Jewish citizenship."[57]

The notable's behavior had its secret compensations. In his *De Congressu*, Philo treats in symbolic terms Abraham's union with Sarah the Jewess and the Egyptian woman Hagar (who nevertheless incorporates some
Greek features, too).[58] A two-columned list may be drawn up as follows:

HAGAR	SARAH
Classical teaching	Sophia
(ἐγκύκλιος παιδεία)	(philosophical teaching)
Paroikia (metic status)	citizen status

The education an average citizen normally received in a Greek city was
associated here with the condition of a metic. The higher education befit-
ting a *politēs* is reserved for the Jewish sage (who, at Alexandria, is not normally a citizen).

Finally and above all, the politics of the Diaspora had at its disposal the
crucial weapon of propaganda, the propaganda of the Diaspora directed
toward Palestine and propaganda directed toward the pagan world. The
weapons were books: a novel like *Joseph and Asenath*,[59] a narrative of the
conversion of an Egyptian woman and her wedding with a Jew; *Aristeas's
Epistle to Philocrates* (both sender as well as addressee were supposed to be
Greek), which sings the praises of the Septuagint translation;[60] and the
Sibylline Oracles, which integrated the God of the Jews into the schemata
of Hellenic culture.[61] We cannot gauge the effectiveness of this propaganda, but without it the spread of Christianity would be incomprehensible to us.

Is this a paradox? Whereas Agrippa II, in Josephus's account, used the
Diaspora as an argument *against* the revolt,[62] Agrippa I, in Philo's
account,[63] explained to Caligula that if he would abandon his plans he
would have friends everywhere, which also meant that if Caligula held to
them he would have enemies everywhere. It cannot be stated with certainty that this flexibility in the Diaspora remained without consequences.

It permitted the Jews to survive the Roman conquest; it permitted them to survive the catastrophe of 66–74; it permitted them, as early as the second century B.C.E., to penetrate into the capital of the Mediterranean world.[64]

But what about Palestine? Here I propose to set forth the facts—which are too numerous all to be laid out here together—by organizing them around two key ideas. The first idea is that the economic, social, and political conflicts were also conflicts of interpretation in which *scribes*—this category of the population that springs from the development of the Jewish School—played a central role. The Jews shared a common heritage, the Book, but no authority, not even the Sanhedrin, could claim a monopoly on interpretation. There were, of course, immediate reactions, such as the stoning of Saint Stephen (as recounted in the Acts of the Apostles), following Stephen's great speech in which he put the entirety of Jewish history into question,[65] giving it a meaning that ran contrary to the Temple. But there was no central authority. What did exist were donors of meaning, who were also inciters to action.

One of these persons appears in full light in an episode recounted by the author of the Acts of the Apostles.[66] When Philip climbed into the carriage of a eunuch, a highly placed official (*dynastēs*) in the service of the Queen of Ethiopia who was traveling from Jerusalem to Gaza, the official was in the process of reading the prophet Isaiah. Philip then asked him, "Do you understand what you are reading?" "How could I, if no one serves as my guide?" (Ἀρά γε γινώσκεις ἃ ἀναγινώσκεις; ὁ δὲ εἶπεν, Πῶς γὰρ ἂν δυναίμην ἐὰν μή τις ὁδηγήσει με;), came the reply. The text in question concerns "the servant of Yahweh," one of the very famous passages in what is called the Deutero-Isaiah.[67] The lamb to be slaughtered was no longer to be identified, thenceforth, with the entire people of Israel, but with the Messiah Jesus. That was how Philip interpreted the text: "Then Philip opened his mouth and, starting from this same scripture, announced to him the good news of Jesus" (ἀπὸ τῆς γραφῆς ταύτης εὐηγγελίσατο αὐτῷ τὸν Ἰησοῦν).

Here we have a marvelous example of what, in Essenian circles, is called a *pesher*, an explanatory commentary. Beyond time, as if time did not exist, a text is reread and updated.

What was to be chosen among all the things that were there to be interpreted? Here is where I wish to introduce my second theme: the Kingdom (in Hebrew *Malkhut*, in Greek *Basileia*). Why the Kingdom? Am I going to enter the labyrinth of scriptural interpretations of this term? Certainly not. It should nevertheless be noted that this word is situated at the point where the Greek tradition and the Jewish tradition join. The Kingdom is that toward which both Davidic messianism and Hellenistic monarchy were tending, a phenomenon that has been reflected upon throughout Hellenistic history. *Aristeas's Epistle to Philocrates*, for example, is a Jewish treatise on how to deal with a foreign monarchy, a treatise "On Royalty," but from the Jewish point of view.

The situation was quite different in Palestine. There, the Basileus was a "high priest" of Hasmonaean lineage, then an Idumaean who was not a high priest. The Hellenistic tradition entered into (a sometimes conflictual) competition with the Jewish tradition, where the King is the son of David, the one who will restore the Kingdom.

Today, through the Christian tradition, and notably by the traditional reading of the Gospel of John—"My kingdom is not of this world" (ἡ βασίλεια ἡ ἐμὴ οὐκ ἔστιν ἐκ τοῦ κόσμου τούτου)[68]—we are accustomed to divest the word *kingdom* of its political dimension. Things were not quite so simple at the time, however. There was constant play on every possible meaning of the term. Thus, at the moment of Christ's Ascension, the disciples ask him, Κύριε, εἰ ἐν τῷ χρόνῳ τούτῳ ἀποκαθιστάνεις τὴν βασιλείαν τῷ Ἰσραήλ;—which means both "Is this the moment you will restore the Kingdom in Israel?" and "Are you going to return to Israel monarchical sovereignty over the other nations?"[69]

Naturally, not all the political movements set loose in Israel during the first century were movements of literate people. Not a single one, however, was entirely unconnected with an updating of the text. This was true on all levels: on the level of the shepherd who became king and who learned somewhere about the idea of the Kingdom, and at the level of Flavius Josephus who, priding himself on his fame as an interpreter of dreams, decided that the ambiguous King announced in both texts and oracles was the Roman general Vespasian.[70] Elsewhere I have attempted to enumerate and to classify these now ephemeral, now enduring forms of Royalty—"hot" Royalties that sprang from an insurrection, like that of Menahem in 66 C.E., whose lineage might continue for generations, and "cold," nonmessianic royalties, that of Herod, those of the two Agrippas, and, to conclude, the only one that established itself for a long time, that of the Roman Vespasian and his successors.[71]

I do not want to enter today into the details. Much could be said, and our texts offer tremendous resources for a typology of messianic movements. Today, however, I would like to insist upon the consequences of a phenomenon I described earlier: the conflict of interpretations, the absence of any normative authority within both political and religious Judaism. This datum, in turn, hinges upon Jewish diversity, upon the fact that Galilee was not Idumaea, nor Idumaea Jerusalem, that those who spoke and wrote in Greek were not those who spoke and wrote in Aramaean or in Hebrew, that those who were Jews were not those who were Samaritans. And yet, God knows how the moderns have tried to reduce everything to a single unit: the Zealots, the Christians, the Essenes, the authors of the Apocalyptic writings. If only it could all be the same thing! We also have Christian Zealots, those of S. G. F. Brandon, for example,[72] Essenian Christians, who have been well developed since Renan, Pharisees at Qumran, and, as if it went without saying, Essenian Zealots, creations of G. Driver and C. Roth, concerning whom Geza Vermes recently wrote, cruelly but deservedly: "The most convincing testimony to the precariousness of the Zealot-Qumran hypothesis is perhaps that since the death of its two eminent but extravagant proponents it has been allowed to sink into obscurity."[73]

The idea that we must live with differences is not always one the exegete or the historian tolerates with ease. And what if difference were not accidental, but rather structural? What takes place in the case of an insurrection? Far from disappearing, differences deepen. In this case, each group held to an interpretation that was irreconcilable with neighboring interpretations. This was strikingly the case with the "Fourth Philosophy," that of the Sicarii, which was linked to the "dynasty" of Judas the Galilaean and which retained its individuality as a separate movement from the time of the Jerusalem insurrection to the fall of Masada. This was also clearly the case with the Essenes, even if they concluded makeshift agreements with others, as incontestably occurred. The supreme characteristic of these insurrections is that, not only did they concern and could they concern Jews and Jews alone, but in the long run each group had *its* interpretation of what it meant to be Jewish and tended to stick with it. The true Israel is what each group thinks itself to be.

The first fact—let us call it "insurrectional solitude"—is obvious. There was not—and for good reason—a single non-Jewish group in Palestine that made common cause with the Jews in this affair. There is no known tie between the Jewish insurrection and the various uprisings that shook the Roman Empire during this same period. To judge by Josephus's account, all the cities with mixed populations saw a part of their population expel or massacre the other part. All the *poikilon*, all this motley amalgam of Palestine, disappeared with one blow. In a single case, that of Scythopolis (Bet Shean), the Jews passed to the other camp—but to no avail,[74] since they still were massacred. In Josephus, Eleazar son of Jairus used the example of their fate to proclaim, at Masada, the end of the Jewish people.[75] A logic of separation was set into motion. This process of separation functioned not only between the Jews and the Goyim but within the Jewish world itself. The Zealots, according to a text of the Mishnah,[76] are those who separate mixed couples, a couple composed, for example, of a Jew and an Aramaean. Renan sensed this ideological logic quite well: "Principles create division, inspire the temptation to decimate, to expel, to kill one's enemies."[77] If, however, the laws of operation of ideologies hold within a relatively homogeneous ethnic group, how much more valid must they have been in the Jewish world of the first century C.E., which was, one might say, exploding in all directions.

We know what followed: the mutation proceeded in two opposite directions. One side cast off the moorings that had tied the universal God to a singular ethnic group: this is Saint Paul's road to Damascus, then to Rome. The other took over the conflict of interpretations and even gave to this conflict itself, in the Mishnah and then in the Talmud, institutional value, though to do that one had to renounce all attempts at immediate updating. In order for Judaism to triumph under its Christian form, the Kingdom had to become the Roman Empire. In the long run, it had to pass from the category of the Good to the category of Evil incarnate, from hope embodied in the son of David to the Beast of Revelations, only to return, with Constantine, to the category of the Good. Conversely, another Kingdom, that of God, had to lose for several centuries all possibility of identification with the powers of this world. In order for Judaism to become rabbinical Judaism, the wise men had to settle for repetition, not messianic incarnation. Mishnah in Greek is pronounced *deuterōsis*, that is, repetition.

There is another way of "telling the story" of this repetition. I shall borrow it from a Hasidic apologist cited by Gershom Scholem, after S. J. Agnon, at the end of his *Major Trends in Jewish Mysticism*:

> When the Baal Shem had a difficult task before him, he would go to a certain place in the woods, light a fire and meditate in prayer— and what he had set out to perform was done. When a generation later the "Maggid" of Meseritz was faced with the same task he would go [to] the same place in the woods and say: We can no longer light the fire, but we can still speak the prayers—and what he wanted done became reality. Again a generation later Rabbi Mose Leib of Sassov had to perform this task. And he too went into the

woods and said: We can no longer light a fire, nor do we know the secret meditations belonging to the prayer, but we do know the place in the woods to which it all belongs—and that must be sufficient; and sufficient it was. But when another generation had passed and Rabbi Israel of Rishin was called upon to perform the task, he sat down on his golden chair in his castle and said: We cannot light the fire, we cannot speak the prayers, we do not know the place, but we can tell the story of how it was done. And, the story-teller adds, the story which he told had the same effect as the actions of the other three.[78]

The factions that disputed among themselves how to interpret the Book are now long dead, although others have since come to replace them. Perhaps the only way to understand the virulence of their disputes and to restore a meaning to them is to "tell their story" historically.[79]

2

Flavius Josephus and Masada

Narrative and Archaeology

The recent *Atlas of Classical Archaeology*, edited by Moses I. Finley, informs us that "the impressive rock of Masada rises above the western shore of the Dead Sea south of En Gedi."[1] The author of the article on Masada adds immediately that the "flat and inaccessible top was well suited to withstand a siege." In addition, we are informed that the site was occupied originally by the Hasmonaeans and then, in 40 B.C.E., by "Herod, later 'the Great,' [who] took over Masada and, in the following decade, equipped it as a fortress." Finally, the author notes that "a band of Zealots" took possession of Masada; "their resistance to the Romans,[2] eloquently told by Josephus, has become legendary." The last lines of the text offer practical guidance for the use of the modern visitor.

As is quite natural, one glides immediately from a description of the site to its history and to the effect it has on us, men and women of the twentieth century. Indeed, it goes without saying that the "impressive" aspect of the site is not limited to the rock's steepness (there are others),[3] to the expansive view it affords over the Dead Sea and over what the Bible

"Flavius Josèphe et Masada" was originally published in the *Revue historique* 260, no. 1 (1978): 3–21, and then reprinted several times, notably in a more developed form as an appendix to Pierre Vidal-Naquet, *Il Buon Uso del tradimento* (Rome: Riuniti, 1980), pp. 161–83. These additions have been integrated into the present text, the first part of which was reproduced (with an introduction not reprinted here) in Alain Schnapp, ed., *L'Archéologie aujourd'hui* (Paris: Hachette, 1980), pp. 173–84. Reprinted in *JMP*, pp. 46–71.

calls the land of Moab (Transjordan), or to the difficulties encountered in climbing it, back when visitors had to take the "snake path" (which today has been replaced by a lift).

The Israeli archaeologist and politician Yigael Yadin has devoted to Masada a book whose subtitle—*Herod's Fortress and the Zealot's Last Stand*[4]—is indicative of its aim: broad popularization. Herod is the site's founder, but the siege is the episode around which the book is organized. Along with an abundance of archaeological documentation and photos of the dig, this book also contains numerous items of no scholarly merit, notably the photo of new Israeli tank-crew recruits taking their oath at Masada, the commemorative stamps, and the Masada medallion inscribed with the legend, in Hebrew and in English, "We shall remain free men, Masada shall not fall again."[5] He transparently plays upon words even in the chapter titles. The penultimate chapter is entitled "The Pioneers," and it is devoted to the voyagers and archaeologists who preceded Yadin to the site. The last one is called "The Volunteers," meaning the excavators. At the same time, these two words evoke other realities of modern-day Israel: the "pioneers" (*halutzim*) created the country and the "volunteers" were the core of its army. In other words, Masada belongs on the list of pilgrimage sites. Of course, many other such sites are to be found, in Palestine as well as elsewhere: there is the Holy Sepulcher and there is Troy; there is also the house in Shanghai where, in July 1921, the Chinese Communist Party was founded.

A pilgrimage site, as Maurice Halbwachs has shown,[6] is an encounter in people's minds and in their collective practices between a narrative and a space. When the space is not designated in precise fashion by the narrative (which in the last analysis is *always* the case), it can, if need be, be made up. Such fabrications may take many forms: that of the naive artisan (in the Holy Land, one is invited to visit the inn from the parable of the Good Samaritan); that, already more sophisticated, of ideological tourism (as at Shanghai);[7] and, at the height of this process of fabrication, the kind that feeds both the imagination and scholarly study, the literature on Homeric Troy furnishing us the most illustrious example.[8] The site of Masada offers no problems of identification: Masada was at Masada. The eight Roman camps, still not excavated, and the access ramp constructed by those conducting the siege are the physical proof of the siege's reality. Nevertheless, the fact that in this case the space happens to be real does not eliminate the problem.

Let us first note that Masada is a site for a *modern* pilgrimage.[9] Masada, writes Yadin, has been "elevated . . . to an undying symbol of desperate courage, a symbol which has stirred hearts throughout the last nineteen centuries."[10] An eloquent statement, but a false one, particularly if the "hearts" of which Yadin speaks are Jewish ones. This he tells us himself: the site was rediscovered only in 1838 by the American travelers Edward Robinson and E. Smith.[11] Masada was then one rock among others, which the Arabs called Qasr As-Sebbeh. Before Masada's name could be restored and before it could be endowed with the symbolic quality it has since acquired, the advent of Zionism and the formation of the modern State of Israel were required.

Yet we are not dealing here only with a site. A text would have sufficed to create a symbol and contain the seeds for a pilgrimage. The text in question, however, turns out to be that of Flavius Josephus.[12] This is rather peculiar, since a modern nationalistic myth is made to rely in this case on an author for whom the episode of Masada in no way parallels what, for example, the Crucifixion represents for believers in the Gospels. For Josephus, Masada represents neither martyrdom inflicted upon those fighting for the freedom of Israel nor the crowning moment of a glorious resistance movement but instead a penultimate episode in a revolt that was, in his view, a terrible mistake—heroic perhaps, but above all contrary to the will of God and to the will of the notables in Jewish society. Yadin is not unaware of this problem. After recalling that Josephus son of Matthias, once the general of the Jews in Galilee, later went over to the Romans, Yadin adds:

> Yet no one could have matched his gripping description of what took place on the summit of Masada on that fateful night in the spring of 73 A.D. Whatever the reasons, whether pangs of conscience or some other cause which we cannot know, the fact is that his account is so detailed and reads so faithfully, and his report of the words uttered by Eleazar ben Yair is so compelling, that it seems evident that he had been genuinely overwhelmed by the record of heroism on the part of the people he had forsaken.[13]

Clearly, this is the only interpretation that would allow one to base the Masada myth on a, so to speak, consenting Flavius Josephus. But is it justified?

Let us begin with a remark that is not a mere detail. Would we be correct to say (as Yadin does in the very title of his book, and as do innumerable authors whose names it would be pointless to cite here)[14] that Masada was the Zealots' ultimate refuge? The *Zēlōtēs*, those who burn with zeal, with jealousy for the God of Israel, certainly played a leading role in the war of 66–74, and the notion of zeal is central to an understanding of the political behavior of the Jews from the era of the Maccabees to that of the revolts against Rome.[15] For Josephus, the "Zealots" who struggled against the Romans had usurped the name: "For 'Zealots' they called themselves, as if these rascals were devoted to good works, not zealous for all that was vile—vile beyond belief."[16] More precisely, those called Zealots were not the whole of the Jews fighting against the Romans; they were the companions of Eleazar son of Simon who, shortly before the siege of Jerusalem, occupied the Temple and continued to do so until, defeated by the troops of John of Gischala, they were forced to rally to the latter.[17]

It would have been no calamity for Josephus if he had installed in the fortress at Masada those whom he called alleged Zealots and authentic "rascals." It turns out, however, that he does nothing of the sort. The occupiers of Masada, between 66 and 74, were not, for him, *Zealots*, but *Sicarii* who, if one excepts the brief episode during which they shared the place with Simon son of Gioras, controlled it throughout the war.

Now, despite a few incoherencies I shall not enlarge upon here,[18] the "Sicarii" comprise in Josephus's work a well-defined group endowed with some notable characteristics. They cannot be mistaken for mere "patriots." These representatives of the "Fourth Philosophy," as Josephus says, "agree in all other respects with the opinions of the Pharisees, except that they have a passion for liberty that is almost unconquerable, since they are convinced that God alone is their leader and master."[19] They were, if I may say so, Pharisees with the *sica* (a dagger) in their hand. Of all the Jewish groups revolting against Rome, they were the ones who were the most systematic practitioners of terrorist tactics. For them, everything that challenged the usurpatory State, its representatives, its accomplices, and its symbols was justified. The famous scene of "Render unto Caesar" was a polemic against the Sicarii.[20] In 66 Menahem was the representative of the lineage—one could almost say the dynasty—of Judas the Galilaean, the group's founder. It was he who then seized hold of Masada and returned to Jerusalem a "veritable king,"[21] which led to his assassination. It was his relative, Eleazar son of Jairus, who then escaped in the direction of Masada and held this fortress until the end, that is, until the collective suicide of the besieged.[22] It is entirely possible to contest Josephus's account, which places Masada apart from the principal currents of the great revolt. Good arguments can be put forward to this effect. For instance, in addition to such documents as the Hebraic text of the Wisdom of Ben Sira, which has no direct connections to the Sicarii, the excavations have brought to light a large number of coins struck at Jerusalem between 66 and 70.[23] The presence of these coins at the site show rather well that Masada was not cut off from the political center of the revolt. Yet one would still have to make an argument out of this fact, something Yadin fails to do.

Contemporary historiography has rightly denounced the positivist illusion that sources can be transparent. Through narratives—especially when, as here, one has only a *single* narrative—one must try to understand what happened or, barring that, understand the narrative itself.[24] How is the problem posed at Masada? We have the site and the digs, which have provided us with manufactured objects, coins, and manuscripts. Independent of them, we have Josephus's narrative account. This text is by no means univocal, however. Undoubtedly, it contains a certain amount of data that can be taken provisionally as factual, such as Herod's foundation of the fortress within the context of the erection of a network of fortifications designed to hold the Jewish people in check and the description of the palace overhanging the ravine. None of that is of concern to us here, and this is precisely what permits us to take the text to be factual. What remains are the pages of the seventh book of the *Jewish War*, which, as in Thucydides, are organized around a narrative account and a discursive speech. The *narrative* recounts to us how 960 Jews—men, women, and children who occupied the fortress—died. The *speech* is that of Eleazar son of Jairus, who had the responsibility for convincing the men to deal out death to the women and children and then receive it themselves. This is the classic opposition between *logos* and *ergon*. The discourse itself, however, is double. Eleazar did not actually convince everyone right away: "Eleazar's appeal . . . did not meet with the same response from all his hearers: some were eager to do as he said, and filled with something like rapture at the thought that death was so noble; others less heroic were moved by pity for their wives and families, and certainly too by the prospect of their own end; and as they exchanged glances the tears in their eyes betrayed the repugnance they felt."[25] A second speech was required to convince the besieged.

Josephus certainly took extraordinary precautions to unify all of this. Whereas the speeches studded throughout his work are slices of rhetoric comparable to those we may read in Livy or in Dionysius of Halicarnassus, with no effort being made to conceal their artificiality, here Josephus uses what Roland Barthes calls "the reality effect,"[26] a procedure designed to make us believe that a speech actually was delivered. For the speech to be known, survivors are needed. Josephus therefore specifies this fact at the required moment: "An old woman escaped, along with another who was related to Eleazar, in intelligence and education superior to most women, and five little children. They had hidden in the conduits that brought drinking-water underground while the rest were intent upon the suicide-pact."[27] What is required, indeed, is not only one survivor, but an exceptionally educated person with a companion and children to serve as that person's witnesses. Now, even if Josephus leaves the anonymous and educated female relative of Eleazar the time needed to listen to the speeches and the possibility of witnessing the first throat-cuttings before going underground, this suspect narrative tale can hardly be believed. But the fact that this narrative is there in order to make us believe that things happened as it says is beyond doubt. Everything takes place in coherent fashion. The Romans penetrate into the fortress. "Seeing no enemy, but dreadful solitude on every side, fire within, and silence, they were at a loss to guess what had happened. At last, as if giving the signal for a volley, they shouted, in the hope that some of those inside would show themselves. The noise came to the ears of the women, who emerged from the conduits and gave the Romans a detailed account of what had happened, the second of them providing a lucid report of Eleazar's speech and the action that had followed."[28] Josephus does not specify, but implies in a clear way, that the author of this "lucid report" was the "educat[ed]" woman.

Should we be shocked by this? Josephus has often been believed and no "progress in historiography"[29] has made his narrative disappear from modern historiographical rhetoric. Here are a few examples. Quite prudent, Renan is content to write that the Jews at Masada "killed each other . . . at Eleazar's instigation."[30] The Reverend Father Félix-Marie Abel is much less prudent: "But an inflamed harangue from Eleazar . . . induced [the group of Jews] to die rather than fall into the hands [of the enemy]. . . . The last one set fire to the palace and ran himself through with a sword." Nothing is lacking here, including the role of the two women: "The younger of these two persons, a relative of Eleazar, recounted the frightening drama."[31] In more summary fashion, the same tale appears in the new edition of Schürer's book: "When Eleazar saw that there was no longer any hope of resisting the assault, he addressed the garrison, asking them to kill their own families, and then one another. This was done."[32] No women are here, however, to recount the story, which thereby renders it incomprehensible. Finally, Yadin attains the very heights: "That night, at the top of Masada, Eleazar ben Yair reviewed the fateful position. The defensive wall was now consumed by fire. The Romans would overrun them on the morrow. There was no hope of relief, and none of escape."[33] Yet he, too, eliminates the lady witnesses.

In order to understand Masada, one must do something other than repeat Josephus. This is not an easy task, since, to borrow an image from Bismarck, one must juggle several balls at once, almost all of which are in the air. We have the connection of the text with the site and the connection of the speech-text with the narrative-text; and even within the speech, we have the connection between the first part and the second. Furthermore, while Josephus can serve as a basis for the study of Josephus, we must not simply remain at that point. How can one avoid a confrontation between the narrative and discursive features of this man who straddled two cultures, that of Greco-Roman historical literature (accounts of sieges and collective suicides are not rare: cf. Numantia, Saguntum)[34] as much as that of the Jewish literature of his age? Cannot Josephus's narrative be placed within the context of both these literary traditions? And, between Josephus's text and modern works, might there not be some intermediary? As a matter of fact, we happen by chance to have one—which testifies to what Claude Lefort has called the "labor" of the work.[35]

It seems that in southern Italy during the tenth century of the present era, under the name of the first leader of the government in Jerusalem in 66, Joseph Ben Gorion, a chronicle was written. Known under the name of the *Josippon*, the Hebrew translation of this book enjoyed, in various translations (in Ethiopian, in Arabic, in Armenian, later in English, in Latin, and so on), an immense success.[36] The *Josippon* is a Jewish history from Adam to Masada, adapted in large part from the *Jewish Antiquities* and the *Jewish War*, as known in their Latin versions. As the rabbinical tradition had already done in adapting under the name of Johanan Ben Zakkai the tales from Flavius Josephus that dramatized his life,[37] the author of the *Josippon* integrates into Jewish thought the historical work of the traitor who passed over to the Romans. A strange transformation, indeed. Let us glide over the fact that Masada (Metzada) becomes here Mezira.[38] The main point is that the speech is not delivered by Eleazar son of Jairus, leader of a dissident sect, but by an "Eleazar-priest" who had escaped from Jerusalem and who has plainly been made so much more orthodox that it is a case of pure fiction. The narrative, too, is thoroughly different. Of course, it is stated that, when they found themselves in a situation they no longer could resist and in order to spare their womenfolk and children from slavery, the men of the garrison killed their companions and their progeny. It is also specified, however, that summary but suitable funeral arrangements were provided for the victims. As for the men, there was no question of suicide—an act to which the Jewish tradition is hostile. They died fighting. After Eleazar's speech—which is therefore not a call to suicide—and the recital of the facts, "the priest Joseph" speaks again to utter a long lamentation that indicts the leaders of insurgent Jerusalem. In this way, the Jewish orthodoxy of the time rewrote the story and rewrote history.

Who can doubt that one should try to come as close as possible to the event as it genuinely occurred, *wie es eigentlich gewesen*, to use Ranke's formula? And who can contest that, to this end, one must set aside ideological readings, two fine examples of which are the *Josippon* text and Yadin's? But is the reference text, that of Josephus, itself a pure text? Ought we to set it aside, too, because of its impurity, by which I mean its ideological structure, once that structure has been defined and understood? But what would remain of Jesus if one "set aside" the Gospels? What would remain of the battle of Salamis if one "set aside" Herodotus and Aeschylus under the pretext that they are partisan authors? And will one think that it suffices to "neutralize" them in order to obtain the truth? The truth must be postulated, as Kant postulates the thing-in-itself, without hoping to attain it.[39] Our task for the moment, however, is more modest and practical: to bring the *logoi* into dialogue with the *erga*, maintaining an awareness of what each one is.

Should not one read the historical narrative as a text whose relationship to the event or to the excavation is not evident? Such was not, assuredly, the purpose of the Masada excavators: "It would be one of the tasks of our archaeological expedition to see what evidence we could find to support the Josephus record."[40] Josephus dominated the beginning of this investigation, and he greatly risked dominating the end, too, just like Homer at Troy. An act of narration, however, can hardly be "support[ed]" by "evidence." It is already a wonder that the bulk of Josephus's *description* should have been confirmed. Better still, indisputable traces of the Jewish garrison, and the Roman garrison that superseded it, have been found. Proof that the site was victim to a conflagration has been found—without, of course, one being able to establish that this fire was lit by the fortress's defenders. On more than one point (the discovery of "Qumranic" manuscripts, for example, or the discoveries of the synagogue and the "ritual bath"), the excavation brings us well beyond Josephus's testimony without ever formally contradicting it.

That said, as to the precise facts about the death of the last defenders we may ask what connections might exist between the text and the excavations. Let me first recall what Josephus says. The defenders began to cut the throats of the women and children, then "ten among them [were] chosen by lot to be the executioners of the rest," after which "every man flung himself down beside his wife and children where they lay, put his arms round them, and exposed his throat to those who must perform the painful office." With this task accomplished, the "ten" again drew a lot, "so that the one who drew the lot should kill the nine and last of all himself." The latter, finally, "set the palace blazing fiercely, and summoning all his strength drove his sword right through his body and fell dead by the side of his family." There were in all 960 victims.[41] It goes without saying that the corpses did not remain on the spot. The excavations have brought to light twenty-seven skeletons, including twenty-five in a cave. Of these last, six are women and four children.[42] As national funeral ceremonies have now been bestowed upon these remains by the Israeli authorities, Yadin denies having discovered bones of Roman soldiers or Byzantine monks.[43] Not having had access to the files of this excavation, I can only say that, on this specific point, Yadin is perhaps correct.

The same cannot be said of his statement that he found, near the southern gate, the one leading to the "water path," archaeological traces of the ten's lots. What, in fact, has he discovered? "Eleven, small, strange ostraca, different from any other which had come to light in Masada." Each one bears a name. "The names themselves were also odd, rather like nicknames, as for example 'Man of the valley' or *Yoav* ('Joab'). ('Joab' may seem perfectly ordinary, but it was extremely rare during the period of the Second Temple, and it was almost certainly applied to a man who was particularly brave)." We must cite at length what then follows:

> Had we indeed found the ostraca which had been used in the casting of the lots? We shall never know for certain. But the probability is strengthened by the fact that among these eleven inscribed pieces of pottery was one bearing the name "Ben Ya'ir." The inscription of plain "Ben Ya'ir" on Masada at that particular time could have referred to no other than Eleazar ben Ya'ir. And it also seems possible that this final group were his ten commanders who had been left to the last, after the decision had been wholly carried out, and who had then cast lots amongst themselves.[44]

A wonderful series of paralogisms, to be sure. Wishing with all his might to make the excavations coincide with the narrative, Yadin has been led to forget what the latter actually says. Josephus speaks of *two* drawings of lots. The first, conducted among all the men of the garrison, ended in the designation of *ten* (not eleven) people charged with cutting the throats of the other men. There is, of course, no reason for these ten persons to have had particularly remarkable names, and still less for the head of the garrison to have been among them. Also, without giving the reader any warning, Yadin drifts into a completely different hypothesis. The names are those of the top leader of the garrison and his ten lieutenants, something like the *polemarchos* and the ten *stratēgoi* at the battle of Marathon. What remains, then, of the first lot drawing and of Josephus's whole account? A number of ostraca have been found at Masada, some, the most numerous, with letters of the Hebrew alphabet, others with Greek characters, and still others with proper names inscribed on them. Yadin offers the reasonable hypothesis that some of these potsherds "had something to do with the rationing system of the Zealots during the siege."[45] Ten other no less likely hypotheses might also be offered.

Furthermore, one detail indicates the extent to which Yadin has become obsessed with finding "historical" characters, that is to say, ones known on the basis of a text. Among the ostraca discovered previous to those found at the southern gate, Yadin has found one that bears the perfectly normal name of Yehohanan, that is, John. Without hesitation, he comments: "One is greatly tempted to identify this name with Yehohanan ben Levi (John of Gischala), but as yet we have no proof of this."[46] It is time for us to stop: John of Gischala plays a key role in Josephus's account, but he never set foot in Masada. Let us therefore cease trying to shed light on Josephus's narrative of the death of the besieged garrison at Masada through an archaeology that has nothing to say here. Instead, let us now ask whether Josephus might serve as a reference for Josephus.

Discourse and Apocalypse

We have a narrative that ends in death and a discourse, that of Eleazar, that is a call to die. Does either one have any "precedents" in Josephus's account? In both cases, the answer is "Yes."

In the third book of his narrative, Josephus recounts what occurred at Jotapata (the city in Galilee in which he had established his military headquarters) after the place fell. With forty notables, he took refuge in a spacious and well-provisioned cave.[47] A woman intervened, however, not to recount the story to *us*—Josephus suffices—but to give away to the Romans the hiding place where she, too, had taken refuge.[48] One therefore had to decide whether to surrender or to die, since fighting was out of the question. Josephus decided to surrender in offering a "mental prayer" that contains the outline of a philosophy of Jewish history: "Inasmuch as it pleaseth Thee to visit Thy wrath on the Jewish people whom Thou didst create, and all prosperity hath passed to the Romans, and because Thou didst choose my spirit to make known the things to come, I yield myself willingly to the Romans that I may live, but I solemnly declare that I go, not as a traitor, but as Thy servant."[49] His companions, however, refused to surrender (despite a plea against suicide, to which I shall return) and gave Josephus the choice of death as a traitor or as a general.[50] Josephus then proposed a procedure similar to the one that was later going to be applied, according to his own narrative, at Masada: sortition. "Each man in turn offered his throat for the next man to cut."[51] We know the result: Josephus found himself alone and alive, with one companion left. They both decided, at the former's request, to give up the deadly plan. The episode ends, therefore, with the survival of both Josephus and his companion—as the Masada episode ends with the survival of the two women, the survivors being there in both cases to recount how the others died.

Life and death. At Jotapata, Josephus pleads in his own name against suicide, which guarantees at the very least that, *in his own view*, the Jewish tradition is hostile to suicide. At Masada, Eleazar, using arguments emanating from a very tangled Greek philosophy (that stretches from the Orphics to the Stoics), pleads in favor of suicide. The arguments answer one another. To commit suicide is to deliver the soul, it is to allow the soul to have with God that immediate commerce it lacks in life, except in sleep. "Why, pray, should we fear death if we love to repose in sleep."[52] Eleazar makes his own the old identification of *sōma* with *sēma* (the body is a tomb). At Jotapata, on the contrary, Josephus explains that the soul and the body are closely connected and even are related: they are *ta philtata*.[53] In both cases, it is of little importance that the vocabulary and the argumentation are really borrowed not from the Bible but from Greek philosophy. The important thing is that Josephus invokes Moses, "the wisest of lawgivers"[54]—which, of course, Eleazar does not do.

Nevertheless, Eleazar's speech in itself offers a few remarkable peculiarities to which our attention should be drawn.[55] In the first place, it is the only speech of any importance that is attributed to a "negative" character, an enemy of Josephus, and, as it happens, the leader of the Sicarii sect.[56] Second, it is a *two-part* speech, the second part of which leads to death. Last and most important, it is a speech that contains within itself an entire philosophy of Jewish history. This philosophy may be summarized as follows: God has abandoned forever the Jewish people; nothing remains to do but to die. It would be absurd to attribute such thinking to Josephus himself, whose entire work stands in protest to this theme. It is nonetheless easy to find the "positive" side of Eleazar's speech. We have already noted certain symmetrical elements in the narrative and prayer at

Jotapata. An even more enlightening parallel is perhaps to be found in the speech delivered before the walls of Jerusalem which Josephus attributes to himself in the fifth book of the *Jewish War*. It is interesting to note a parallelism that already exists on the formal level. Josephus's speech, too, is divided into two parts—and there is no other example of such a division in the work. Between the two parts are inserted a few formulaic examples of the sarcastic cries by which his compatriots succeeded in overwhelming him.[57] As opposed to Eleazar, however, Josephus convinces no one. Eleazar is a prophet of death and is heard; Josephus is a prophet of life who is heard only by himself and by the Romans, even though he proposes, at the end of his speech, to offer *his* life, if "[his] death would bring [his] compatriots back to their senses."[58] Like Eleazar's speech, Josephus's speech contains an entire philosophy of Jewish history, but one in which the accent is placed not on the war of men but rather on that of God: God alone was able to save Jerusalem and it is not for his people to resort to violence. Moreover, Josephus adds, one must distinguish absolutely between the political hegemony that is enjoyed by those with superior arms, by the empires that succeed one another in an order willed by God, and religious superiority which itself may be reconciled with nonviolence. The Jews can possess, and do possess, *this* kind of superiority: they cannot hope for the other kind. Also Josephus, in invoking Jeremiah, to whom he compares himself, proclaims that surrender is the way of life: "Jeremiah shouted from the rooftops that they were hated by God for their iniquities against Him, and would be taken into captivity unless they surrendered the City; yet neither king nor people put him to death. . . . But when I appeal to you to save yourselves you greet me with howls of execration and showers of stones, while I was exhorting you for your own good."[59] This is an astonishing transposition of a theme that actually was present in the Jewish consciousness of the first century C.E., "Render unto Caesar" being one example among others.

But it is now time to stop explaining Josephus solely by means of Josephus. This historian's texts belong, certainly, to a line of historical rhetoric that begins with Herodotus and Thucydides. It is, moreover, Thucydides who is being imitated from the very first lines of his book. A first path would therefore be to illuminate Josephus's *topoi* by means of the *topoi* of Greco-Roman historiography, and this is the path that has for the most part been followed. Is there not, however, another path? We offer the hypothesis that Josephus's texts can be illuminated with the aid of Jewish literature—specifically, apocalyptic literature.[60] What is this literature and how can it be useful for our purposes?[61]

   Apocalyptic literature is clearly situated in time: it appears at the start
of the Seleucid presence in Palestine, and the first great example of it is
the Book of Daniel (around 163 B.C.E.); it continues until shortly after the
second Jewish insurrection (135 C.E.). It is certainly possible to date its
inception earlier (one can speak of an apocalyptic mind-set in relation to
the prophet Ezekiel), and one could look for later continuations (in particular, in the case of late Christian reworkings), but this is a rather vain
effort, as are attempts to find the apocalypse everywhere, including in the
Mishnah and the Talmud.[62] This literature is therefore connected to foreign conquest and to resistance to this conquest, insofar as such resistance
seemed possible. It expresses, with all the force the phrase can muster, the
"vision of the vanquished." Under this heading, it has parallels in other
conquered societies (the best-known case being that of Egypt, with the
Oracle of the Potter).[63] One has often spoken, too, of the "messianism" of
Third World revolutionary movements. Nevertheless, one generally forgets to interpret as such the oldest and best known of these apocalyptic
messianisms, the Jewish messianism from the end of the Hellenistic
period and the beginning of the Roman era. And yet in this case as in the
others, what we witness is a dramatized expression of the conflicts provoked by the process of acculturation.
   On the other hand, it should be noted that this literature delves into
the past in order to act on the present and to foresee the future. While
prophecy may not uniquely be foresight, apocalypse can be said to be foresight of the immediate future. It defines the set of conditions, including
temporal conditions, for the restoration—for the instauration, rather—
of the Kingdom. Under this heading, it rereads and interprets the
prophets. When Jeremiah announces, "And this whole land shall be a des-
olation, and an astonishment; and these nations shall serve the king of
Babylon seventy years. And it shall come to pass, when seventy years are
accomplished, that I will punish the king of Babylon, and that nation,"[64]
Daniel interprets this to mean that the years are the weeks of years, sixty-
nine of which have already elapsed since the murder, in 171, of the high
priest Onias III, since the "Anointed" was "cut off"; we are in the second
half of the last week.[65]
   This backward-leaning literature is most often "pseudepigraphical" in
nature, the Revelation of John being an exception. It is placed under the
patronage and responsibility of the great ancestors, Abraham, Daniel, Elijah, Moses, Baruch, and quite a few others. This fact itself is common
enough in Greco-Roman literature.[66] What is less common is the association of pseudepigrapha with rereading. To tell the truth, pseudepigrapha

appears to be a particular case of rereading. The *Book of Jubilees* is a rereading and rewriting of Genesis, as Daniel is a rereading and rewriting of
Jeremiah. It may happen, however, that the work is placed not in the
mouth of a Jew but in that of a character from pagan mythology, as is
shown by the case of the *Sibylline Oracles*, which came from Alexandria and
were addressed, in part, to a non-Jewish public.[67]

Indeed, another aspect of this literature—and one of its most remarkable qualities—is that it has come down to us through numerous translations into the languages of peoples who have no particular reason to be
interested in the properly Jewish vision of the vanquished, even if they had
become, thanks to the process of Christianization, representatives of the
Verus Israel. In this way, specifically Jewish texts have been preserved for
us, not only in Greek, which is normal, but in Coptic, Ethiopian, Syriac,
and Slavic, whereas, for example, no Egyptian text has been preserved for
us in any foreign language other than that of the Greek occupiers, and this,
even though one could make some textual connections between the *Oracle of the Potter* and the third book of the *Sibylline Oracles*.[68]

A text like that of Daniel,[69] however, especially when it is translated, is
easily universalizable, if it is true that, to use Elias Joseph Bickerman's
phrase, "the Jews became the 'people of the Book' when this Book was
rendered into Greek."[70] This capacity for universalization was a long time
in preparation—since the Exile, in fact—and was expressed in themes
such as that of the "servant of Yahweh" in the Deutero-Isaiah.[71] A text that
can be dated with precision (shortly before 78 B.C.E.) and that exists only
in Greek offers an example of such universalizability: the prologue to
Esther,[72] where Mordecai becomes the vehicle for an unexpected transformation, since it is not the Jews who are threatened with death, or even
stricken with a temporary death, like that of Jesus, but rather an unfortu-
nate group of "righteous"[73] and humble (*tapeinoi*) people who are
promised the glory of "devouring the mighty" (*endoxoi*).

Finally, on the basis of this example and a few others, we must insist on
another fundamental characteristic of Jewish apocalyptic literature: such
literature makes use of a whole lot of odds and ends [*bric-à-brac*] borrowed
in large part from Hellenistic culture, that is, from the dominant culture,
and it is clearly obvious that the author of the prologue to Esther had read
the Greek tragedies. One could nevertheless offer many more examples
of these kinds of fix-up jobs [*bricolage*].[74]

Let us return to Flavius Josephus and to the speech of Eleazar son of
Jairus. The basic principle of an apocalyptic and messianic discourse is that
the Restoration, the Instauration, of the Kingdom is immediately possi-

ble,[75] it being understood that this Instauration must be preceded by tribulations, even death. When Josephus recounts the death by fire of a number of inhabitants of Jerusalem who had taken refuge at the gate to the Temple's outer court, he makes clear that "their destruction was due to a false prophet who that very day had declared to the people in the City that God commanded them to go up into the Temple to receive the signs of their deliverance."[76] "That very day" . . . while the Temple was already in flames. It is against just this apocalyptic mind-set that Josephus's entire narrative was written. It is because of his hostility to this mad hope that he states that he has diverted messianic aspirations onto the person of Vespasian.[77]

In this context, what does Eleazar's speech represent, what is the meaning of this "preaching of death,"[78] so surprising when coming from a Jewish mouth? The two parts of the speech share the theme of apocalypse, but an apocalypse that stops at the end of the first moment of Mordecai's dream. This theme is not that of the fall of Masada and of the ruination of the Jewish State but really that of the *end of the Jewish people*. The idea appears at the very beginning of the speech. The Sicarii are those who have sworn "to be slaves neither of the Romans nor of anyone else but God." Now, it should have been understood from the start of the war that "His once beloved Jewish race had been sentenced to extinction." This condemnation by God is total. There is no and there will be no "remnant of Israel": "We hoped, or so it would seem, that of all the Jewish race we alone would come through safely, still in possession of our freedom, as if we had committed no sin against God and taken part in no crime—we who had taught the others!"[79] Josephus thus places in the mouth of the leader of the Sicarii, of these men who were the "first to begin this lawlessness and this barbarity to kinsmen . . . , who left no word unspoken, no deed untried, to insult and destroy the objects of their foul plots,"[80] that is, in Eleazar's mouth an admission of guilt connected with a sermon of definitive death.

This theme is taken up again and developed in the second part of the speech, the part that, in Josephus's narrative, brings on death. Let us repeat it one last time: we are not challenging the existence of the event, even if it is attested to only in a single source. After all, even if it is Josephus's personal judgment that suicide is contrary to the Jewish tradition, the voluntary death of the defenders of Masada can still be inscribed within a series of facts that is hardly open to debate. For example, during Nicanor's war against Judas Maccabaeus (160 B.C.E.), at the point he was about to be captured, Razis, "a Jerusalemite elder," "fell upon his sword . . . he preferred to die a noble death rather than fall into the scoundrels' hands and suffer outrages unworthy of his noble character. Still alive, however, he got up in a fury of anger and ran, with blood pouring from him sore wounded as he was, right through the crowds; then, standing on a steep rock, his blood now drained from him, he tore out his bowels, taking both his hands to them, and flung them at the crowds. So he died, calling on Him who is Lord of life and spirit to restore them to him again."[81] This narrative, as we can see, is characteristic of an individual suicide "in the name of God" and is comparable to the collective suicide at Masada.

Whatever the case may be, in the second half of the speech Eleazar expands on the theme of the end of the Jewish people. Jerusalem has been taken, the Temple destroyed, but also destroyed is the Diaspora, that of Caesarea, that of Syria, that of Egypt. Even the Jewish population of Scythopolis has been destroyed, despite the fact that it took the side of the Greco-Roman enemy. Everything is dead for Eleazar, whereas for Josephus nothing is definitively dead. "Long ago, it seems, God issued this warning to the whole Jewish race together, that life would be taken from us if we misused it."[82] While the thematics of the first part remained fundamentally Jewish, the second introduces an entirely new argument. Not only is there a presentation of the Greek philosophy of the immortality of the soul, which fits rather well into the *bricolage* mentioned above, but also an example borrowed directly and overtly from the non-Jewish world, that of the wise men of India, of the "gymnosophists," as was said in the Greek world, "fakirs," as we say today. This example comes after those Eleazar borrows or claims to borrow from the Jewish tradition. Its position in the argument is decisive. The wise men of India "consign their bodies to the flames . . . by a pure desire for the state of immortality. . . . Are we not ashamed to show a poorer spirit than Indians, and by our want of courage to bring the Law of our fathers, the envy of all the world, into utter contempt?"[83] Foreign example and national tradition link up in this peculiar speech. No doubt the Indian example trailed about almost everywhere, including within the Jewish tradition, since Philo of Alexandria knew of the "gymnosophist" Calanus who, offering himself as a model at Alexandria, immolated himself.[84] One will nevertheless agree that his name makes a rather foreign sound in the mouth of a sectarian Jew.[85] If the city "that was believed to have God for her Founder"[86] is dead, if the entire Jewish people are, in Eleazar's view, bound for death, the apocalypse was leading not to the Kingdom but instead to destruction. In placing these words and these themes in Eleazar's mouth, Josephus says in his own way—which is sometimes tortuous—where, in his view, the danger and risk of death are to be found. It is precisely because, *for him, Masada was not the end of the Jewish people*—his narrative continues after Masada—and because, for him, the practitioners of the apocalypse were false prophets that he makes Eleazar's speech the unique example of apocalypse contained in his writings. This apocalypse, however, is closed; it is an apocalypse of death.[87]

3 | Flavius Josephus and the Prophets

For Claude Orrieux

Prophets Ancient and Modern, True and False

I am not an Orientalist and yet I am going to try, once again, to speak about Flavius Josephus.[1] A frustrating experience, no doubt, though also a banal one. I am doing nothing more than repeating the experience of those papyrologists who know in detail documents written in Greek but are unaware of the large mass of demotic texts. What we have here, quite simply, is the legacy of two great colonial eras—the ancient one, to which Josephus himself was a witness,[2] and the modern, the one whose end we have, in principle, lived. If Josephus wrote in Greek, if he is supposed to have been inspired by Sophocles and Thucydides, this is obviously because he was addressing himself to a Roman public that, even when its native tongue was Latin, read and wrote in Greek. And he tells us clearly (*Jewish War* 1.1.3) that he first wrote his *Jewish War* in his native tongue—that is to say, so far as we know, in Aramaean. But we do not possess a copy of this Aramaic text, the very existence of which some have come to doubt, and not the least trace of it remains, whereas the dominant culture, as a result of a historical accident, has preserved the Greek text, and indeed multiplied it.

Here, too, modern parallels are not lacking. Very soon after the end of

"Flavius Josèphe et les prophètes" combines the texts of two lectures given at the end of 1985 in Geneva under the auspices of the Ancient Near East Study Center. These lectures were drafted in preparation for the Cartigny Colloquium of 1986, whose theme was "History and Historical Consciousness in the Civilizations of the Ancient Near East." A volume was published with this title, *Histoire et conscience historique dans les civilisations du Proche-Orient ancien* (Louvain: Peeters, 1989), and my text appears there on pp. 11–31. Reprinted in *JMP*, pp. 197–227.

the Algerian War an anthology entitled "The Algerian People and the War" was published by a very politically active editor.[3] This anthology gave a platform to several hundred persons who, by the terms of the Evian Accords of March 18, 1962, were going to become Algerian citizens. Now, among this weighty assortment of documents, only one was written in Arabic (none in Kabyle), and still it did not figure in the anthology in question because the authors had put their hands on a translation that came from the police. It might be added that this singular document invoked the name of Allah and not the principles of 1789. Few people at the time were surprised that the professor who held the chair of Colonial History at the Sorbonne—the author, moreover, of several important works on colonial Algeria—did not know Arabic.

Treating Josephus and knowing neither Hebrew nor Aramaean, at least I will be conscious of my limitations. I am equally conscious of the enormity of the effort that must be undertaken if one wishes simply to become acquainted with the issues at stake. The latest bibliographical study on Josephus, that of Louis H. Feldman,[4] deals only with a rather brief period, and yet it contains no less than 3,539 items, many of which include double or triple entries. The last page notes the existence of a thesis[5] dealing with the Halakah in Josephus and in the tannaitic literature and adds that this dissertation "marks a good beginning towards a comprehensive study." A good beginning . . . but the battle has since continued[6] and is not threatening to let up.

Why this contemporary passion? Let us not be surprised. Even when they seek to eliminate—this is the least of their duties—ideological deformations and delusions, historians always write—whatever some cold fish might say—in the present. This is what Thucydides did, and he did so very consciously. In this long chain of present-oriented history, Josephus is a master link. If one takes his four preserved works (the *War*, written between 75 and 79; the *Antiquities*, an immense archaeology that rivals those of Manethon and Dionysius of Halicarnassus, with, as an appendix, a *Vita* [93–94]; and, finally, the *Contra Apionem*), one quickly grasps that they maintain highly complex relations among themselves and with their age. Flavius Josephus was successively one of the leaders of the Jewish resistance in Galilee and then an ally of Rome. He was witness to—and is our principle source for—the extraordinary diversity of the Jewish people at this time, this diversity being expressed both by the multiplication of sects and by the divisions among the besieged during the ordeal of the siege of Jerusalem.[7] Yet in his final work, the *Contra Apionem* (circa 100), he speaks of Judaism as if it were perfectly unified, as if it were endowed with a constitution, as if it represented a model *politeia*. Here we almost have an echo of the Pharisaic and rabbinical restoration that followed the great disaster. Josephus was, to the highest degree, a practitioner of ideological warfare. A general in Galilee in the *Jewish War*—I am speaking here of the book—in the *Vita*, when faced with the campaigns of Justus of Tiberias, he no longer is anything but an ever-ready friend of the forces of order and of the Romans who has taken all the necessary precautions to put back in their hands a country rid of its most dangerous characters, its most bellicose agitators.[8] Josephus is, one might say, the inventor of "the meaning of history," but it is a meaning that can vary at the slightest political stirring, as the successive editions of Stalin's *Short History of the Communist Party (Bolshevik) of the USSR* or, more modestly, Maurice Thorez's *Fils du peuple* have taught us.

Yet this practitioner has some fixed stars in his heavens. In the *Contra Apionem*—which is, let us point out, nearly contemporaneous with the "Council of Yabneh" and the sealing of the canon of the Jewish Bible—Josephus writes, "It therefore naturally, or rather necessarily, follows (seeing that with us it is not open to everybody to write the records, and that there is no discrepancy in what is written; seeing that, on the contrary, the prophets alone had this privilege, obtaining their knowledge of the most remote and ancient history through the inspiration which they owed to God, and committing to writing a clear account of the events of their own time just as they occurred)—it follows, I say, that we do not possess myriads of inconsistent books, conflicting with each other. Our books, those which are justly accredited, are but two and twenty, and contain the record of all time."[9]

All of a sudden I find myself, with the aid of this text and after my long introductory remarks, at the very heart of my topic. Is this a simple text that expresses a simplistic view of history? Perhaps not as much as might first appear. The reliability the Bible affords Josephus holds, in fact, only for an already distant past. Everything still proceeds without a hitch from the death of Moses to Artaxerxes, Xerxes's successor on the Persian throne: "The prophets subsequent to Moses wrote the history of the events of their own time in thirteen books."[10] But the historians' and the prophetic tradition (they cannot be distinguished from each other) is interrupted after Artaxerxes. After the fifth century B.C.E., there are still some writings, "but," adds Josephus, the history contained in these latter writings have "not been deemed worthy of equal credit with the earlier records, because of the failure of the exact succession of the prophets."[11]

There is, therefore, a *before* that would pertain to the realm of exactitude and reliability and an *after* that is much more problematic. This is an *after* in which, for example, drunks are permitted to write history, and, what is worse, it is a history that rivals Josephus's own.[12] Let us now complicate things a bit by introducing the prophecies and the prophets of yesterday and today.

I shall not seek here to see in Josephus, and particularly the Josephus of the *Antiquities*, testimony to what Israelite, and then Jewish, prophecy was. I know as well as another[13] that a prophet is not particularly he who announces, he who foresees the future, but he who sees and who speaks, beyond appearances, God's word to men. That, however, is not what one will find in Josephus. One would seek in vain in the *Antiquities* the slightest break in the historical discourse as occasioned by an explosion of prophetic speech. What, for example, was Abraham? "He was a man of ready intelligence on all matters, persuasive (πιθανός) with his hearers, and not mistaken when he conjectured about the future" (περί τέ ὧν εἰκάσειεν οὐ διαμαρτάνων).[14] One will naturally find in the Josephinian Archaeology more elaborate narratives than this one, although, as has been pointed out,[15] Josephus exhibits little interest, for example, in Isaiah.

Among those whom *we* call prophets, Josephus's model is clearly Jeremiah, the prophet of defeat and capitulation to whom certain moderns continue to compare him.[16] Already in his speech to the besieged in the *Jewish War*, Josephus himself makes this comparison. Jeremiah called upon the people and the king to surrender Jerusalem without a fight to the Assyrian enemy, though in vain, and neither does Josephus succeed in persuading his contemporaries to surrender the City to the Romans.[17] Prophetic speech therefore does not interrupt the course of history but rather confirms it in its majesty as being willed by God; such discourse creates no break, but simply reinforces the calm certitude of the historian. When it is a question of the distant past, moreover, everything is simple. Some dramatic events have succeeded other dramatic events, certainly, but historical discourse itself is one; following a model borrowed largely from the Greek historians, Josephus simply recounts what God has, very rationally, made of his people.

The present, this terrible present Josephus has lived and recounted— the social and political explosion, the messianic groundswell, the insurrection of 66, and the final defeat at Masada, this whole enormous movement that is the resultant of the great confrontation between two cultures, the Greek and the Jewish, since the second century B.C.E.[18]—also has a sort of logical simplicity to it. The present is the time of the pseudoprophets. Pseudoprophets? Both the word and the concept are Greek. The

Masoretic text does not recognize the existence of pseudoprophets; in Jeremiah, for example, good prophet or bad prophet, the whole world is *nabi*. The history of this word has been written.[19] It was constructed on the model of the Greek ψευδόμαντις, the false soothsayer.[20] It appears in the Septuagint, first as a verb—the pseudoprophet is he "who says false things," who announces peace, for example, when the country is under-going war and defeat[21]—then as a noun, the pseudoprophet becoming he who is, in his essence, a liar. The concept of pseudoprophet is in fact a product of the process of acculturation. It is through the denunciation of the practice of divination among the pagans that the meaning of this word was established in the Septuagint and in Philo.[22] In Josephus this develop-ment is taken to be an accomplished fact and is projected back onto the most distant past: the prophet who, in the time of Jeroboam, diverted a man of God from his duties at Bethel becomes a pseudoprophet.[23]

Quite obviously, the "pseudoprophets" play a key role in the narrative of the War of 66 and its prelude. Thus, under Nero, an anonymous (but, thanks to the Acts of the Apostles, a famous) man led to the Mount of Olives a crowd that was to help him set himself up as a tyrant.[24] And Jose-phus himself? He is not, properly speaking, a prophet, since their race has disappeared, but he is a dreamer and an interpreter of his own dreams. And we know by more than one rabbinical text that dreams, without delivering the whole truth, allow access to it all the same and demand to be interpreted: "An uninterpreted dream is like an unread letter."[25] To be an interpreter of dreams is to be today the closest kin to what yesterday was a prophet.[26] It is in this capacity[27] that Josephus, after having been captured at the end of the siege of Jotapata, intervenes before Vespasian. "The memory came to him of those dreams in the night by which God had forewarned him both of the calamities coming to the Jews and of the for-tunes of the Roman emperors. He was an interpreter of dreams and capa-ble of deciphering the ambiguous revelations of the Deity" (ἱκανός συμ-βαλεῖν τὰ ἀμφιβόλως ὑπὸ τοῦ θείου λεγόμενα). "He was familiar with the prophecies of the Holy Scripture, being a priest himself and descendant of priests." Inspired (ἔνθους γενόμενος) by this twofold book-learned and oneiric knowledge, Josephus addresses to God the silent prayer he has with great care preserved for us: "Inasmuch as it pleaseth Thee to visit Thy wrath on the Jewish people whom Thou didst create, and all prosperity hath passed to the Romans, and because Thou didst choose my spirit to make known the things to come, I yield myself willingly to the Romans that I may live, but I solemnly declare that I go, not as a traitor, but as Thy servant."[28]

Thus we have dreams, about which we can say nothing, except that the tradition of interpreting them dates very far back in written Judaism, and "revelations," "things said" ambiguously (ἀμφιβόλως), a word that appears here in its adverbial form, but that is to be found elsewhere, in its adjectival form, in a most famous passage: "But their [the Jerusalem revolutionaries'] chief inducement to go to war was an ambiguous oracle also found in their sacred writings, announcing that at that time a man from their country would become monarch of the whole world"—a passage that is all the more fundamental as it is confirmed on the factual level by Tacitus and Suetonius, without one being able to determine who had informed whom.[29]

Of course, no oracle is ambiguous in itself. It is proclaimed to be such afterward. An oracle that would proclaim itself to be ambiguous would lose all ambiguity. Ambiguity is a borrowing from the Greek tradition, that of classical tragedy and the oracles discussed in Herodotus.[30] This borrowing has a very specific function: to aid Josephus and those who speak through him to guard against the principal danger that, according to them, threatens the Jewish people (the eruption of messianism that has manifested itself in various candidates to a kind of kingship that was as much Jewish as universal; the apocalyptic idea according to which from the worst could come the best and from a Jerusalem in flames the establishment of the Kingdom). Against this capital danger, Josephus was the ally of a large section of the Jewish ruling classes, as well as an ally of the Roman conqueror. He initiated what F. Lucrezi has called "il capovolgimento del messianismo"[31] and what I have called the replacement of a hot kingdom by a cold one.[32] Josephus therefore presented himself before Vespasian and immediately announced to him that he—Vespasian—would be Caesar and *imperator*, and that the same would be the case for his son.[33] Such was, in the Orient, the only available form of monarchy.

Are we dealing here with a "historical fact"? It goes without saying that, even if Suetonius confirms it and if Appian, according to Zonaras, says as much,[34] we do not know what happened between the two men in this Orient buzzing with prophecies.[35]

Cynicism, realism, lies—Josephus was capable of using all these weapons, and even, ultimately, of inventing this episode of prophecy out of thin air *after* Vespasian, in the Year of the Four Emperors (68), was proclaimed *imperator* first by the troops of Caesarea,[36] then by the army of Alexandria.[37] The important thing is that here words are actions, and that this word would be repeated, much later, in the *Avot de-Rabbi Nathan* and other Midrashic texts, though it no longer will be attributed to the Hellenized Jew, to the court Jew who was Josephus, but to the rabbi who would go on, at Yabneh, to found Judaism as a religion separated from its State, Johanan Ben Zakkai; having escaped the besieged city of Jerusalem, Zakkai allegedly greeted Vespasian with the cry of "Vive Domine Imperator."[38] Here again, the question is not whether this event took place—it is quite evident that, at the moment the siege of Jerusalem, properly speaking, was taking place, Vespasian no longer was in Palestine—but how tradition has "retrodictively" turned it into a legitimating idea. This is all rather straightforward, and it is inscribed within a highly coherent process.

The real difficulty lies elsewhere. The question is twofold. At what moment, in Josephus's *text*, do things break down? In other words, when, still in Josephus's text, does one pass from transparent oracles to ambiguous ones? This first question is nevertheless tied to another, more basic line of interrogation which no longer concerns Josephus's text alone but also Jewish literature and the connection between this literature and the fact of historical diversity. What we must ask, then, is the following: When do the texts become ambiguous *in themselves*, by which I mean: When do they testify to the existence of a double identity, Jewish but also Greek?

As luck would have it, a single name, that of Daniel, provides an answer to both these questions. The text of Daniel, meant to be a prophetic announcement around 164 B.C.E., is a conglomerate of stories that are supposed to have occurred under the last kings of Babylon and under an imaginary Darius the Mede. Indeed, this text testifies to a major transformation of Jewish literature. Now, it turns out that Josephus's commentary on this text in the tenth book of his *Jewish Antiquities* marks, as a matter of fact, a fundamental break in his discourse.[39]

It is correct to read the text of Daniel as the first Jewish apocalypse, that is to say, as the first great manifestation of a literature of resistance that expresses the "vision of the vanquished" and the hope for revenge, for triumph on the part of the humiliated nation. But this general remark calls forth other ones that lead us into the details of the matter.

Let us begin with a striking fact, what is called "the bilingualism in the Book of Daniel,"[40] its Hebrew and Aramaean sources. Aramaean, which is described as the language of the royal court,[41] is used to express Israel's connections with the world, while Hebrew—a translated Hebrew—is used when Israel itself moves into the foreground. To this bilingualism corresponds a double name. Daniel is "Daniel, whose name is Belteshazzar" (that is, "Protects the life of the King") when the narrator speaks of him with respect to his connections with the court; he is simply "Belteshazzar" when the King summons him; and he is "Daniel" for the Jews and with the Jews. He is therefore not a hero of Judaean Judaism, but a Diasporic character and one symbol of the Jews' acculturation as well as of the limits thereof.[42]

Indeed, as Arnaldo Momigliano has shown, "Daniel" plays a fundamental role in Judaism's integration of the Greek theory of the succession of empires,[43] a theory that was for centuries one of the matrices of universal history. This theory appears both in the allegory of the Colossus with feet of clay, in chapter two, and in the succession of Beasts in chapter seven. The Colossus has a head of gold, breast and arms in silver, belly and thighs of bronze, legs of iron, and feet "part of iron and part of clay." This image expresses in spatial terms the races that, in Hesiod, have succeeded each other in time, and it is as a succession that the seer interprets it in announcing that, after the time of the Kingdoms, "the God of heaven [shall] set up a kingdom, which shall never be destroyed: and the kingdom shall not be left to other people, *but* it shall break in pieces and consume all these kingdoms, and it shall stand forever."[44]

This schema is fundamentally the same as the one in the vision of the "Four Great Beasts" that "came up from the sea."[45] From the lion with eagle wings to the bear to the winged four-headed leopard to the supreme beast with iron teeth and ten horns, they become more and more monstrous, as from the Babylonians to the Medes to the Persians to the Greeks of Alexander and his Seleucid successors. One ends with the famous vision of the "son of Man," whose reign will be eternal.

In this imperial collection, the Romans play only a limited role. They are *Chittim*, foreigners like the others, who intervene against the king of the north (the Seleucid) in his aggression against the king of the south (the Ptolemaic one),[46] a clear allusion to the "circle" Popillius Laenas drew around Antiochus IV in 168, just at the moment when he was promising to evacuate Egypt.

What does Flavius Josephus make of all this?[47] In the image of the Colossus, he limits the destruction to the gold, silver, and bronze. As for the iron, which is linked with Rome, it destroys the bronze and "will triumph forever" (καὶ κρατήσει δὲ εἰς ἅπαντα) because of the nature of iron, which is more resistant than that of gold, silver, and bronze.[48] As for the episode of the stone which, having been "cut out without hands," pulverizes the feet of the statue and itself becomes a mountain,[49] Josephus glides over it with astonishing elegance, making an exception in this case by separating history here from prophecy: "And Daniel also revealed to the king the meaning of the stone, but I have not thought it proper to relate this, since I am expected to write of what is past and done and not of what is to be; if, however, there is anyone who has so keen a desire for exact information that he will not stop short of inquiring more closely but wishes to learn about the hidden things that are to come, let him take the trouble to read the Book of Daniel, which he will find among the sacred writings."[50]

Will there be a day when Rome, too, will come undone?[51] Not only does Flavius Josephus, in conformity with the themes disseminated by the empire's ideologues, announce, or at the very least suggest, the existence of an eternal Rome, but he has Daniel predict Rome's victory over the Jews: "In the same manner Daniel also wrote about the empire of the Romans and that Jerusalem would be taken by them and the temple laid waste."[52] A text aimed at Antiochus IV, announcing his downfall, is thus turned around to suit other purposes—a rather normal procedure, since Judaism has never ceased nourishing itself upon successive readings and rereadings.

But Daniel who was "held in such great honor and such dazzling favor"[53] by the mythical Darius the Mede as Flavius Josephus was by the very real Titus, Daniel the "prophet of good tidings"[54] for this sovereign who accepted him into the aulic hierarchy when "Darius" conferred upon him the title of "first of his Friends,"[55] Daniel who "was not only wont to prophesy future things, as did the other prophets, but he also fixed the time at which these would come to pass,"[56] this Daniel might very well have been able to prophesy and to anticipate the fate of the court Jew Josephus at the hands of the Flavian emperors.

Masada, the Prophets, and the Historians

The second part of this study is devoted to Masada. It is not for me a pleasure—a rather dubious one at that—to retrace a path I had already opened in 1978.[57] But, I dare say, the landscape has changed since then. To begin with, the intellectual landscape: numerous new studies have been published, some of which have contributed something to the problem.[58] So, too, the archaeological landscape, a topic to which I shall return. Finally, the cultural landscape: in the country in which Masada is located, and which some call Eretz Israel and others Palestine, many changes have occurred which have to do with both politics and mythopoetics, to borrow H. Möhring's expression.[59] It is not totally vain to analyze these changes. They are of just as much concern to me as the various "landscapes" of which I have just spoken and in relation to which I do not claim to be entirely alien.

Let us begin by providing an illustration of the first half of our presentation. What took place on the rock of Masada, in 73 or in 74[60]—the mass suicide of the garrison's men and their families—constitutes a paroxysmal but in no way improbable example of those messianic-apocalyptic movements against which Flavius Josephus had entered into war. If one does not make the connection between this event and those movements, one is condemned to understand nothing of the event itself and will fail to realize that the way it is recounted is as important as what is recounted.

Indeed, on the level of historical methodology, no example is more evocative. This is so not only because all the techniques of which historical reason can make use, from archaeology to narrative analysis, are here summoned into action. It is also because, with an event like the fall of Masada, historians are obliged to place themselves between two dangerous extremes: first, that of the "pure fact," in which they cannot help but become stuck since the facts, even if they are archaeological, are in any event accessible only though discourse, and in this case only through the discourse of Josephus, our unique narrative source; and second, that of "pure discourse," which vanishes into abstraction if one forgets that on this rock people actually lived and, quite concretely, died.

"Masada," however, is not only a series of events more than nineteen centuries old, it is a myth of today and even, as has been said, a "complex" that is still evolving. It is not a matter of opposing, without further ado, the "real" to the "myth" and the "complex." Things are not so simple. Myth is not opposed to reality as the false to the true; myth accompanies the real and, if I dare say so, myth hems the real.

In his narrative of the Masada affair (which is situated, let us recall, not *at the end* of the war of the Jews but toward the end of this work),[61] Josephus recounts to us the following things: the siege conducted by the Romans, as commanded by L. Flavius Silva (it is on this point that archaeology has contributed information of capital importance); the two-part speech delivered by the Sicarii leader Eleazar son of Jairus, which incited his fellow soldiers to commit suicide; the collective suicide of the besieged, who were convinced by Eleazar's "performative" speech; the discovery by the Romans of what took place. The latter, who at first were struck by the silence that greeted them, learned from two women (one cultivated, the other old) what had taken place on the rock. It is this narrative, transmitted to the Roman authorities, that reached Josephus, who in turn transmitted it to us. Quite obviously, on this point Josephus wanted to be believed, even when what he was affirming did not pose any problem at all.

After others, and with others, in 1978[62] I questioned the pertinence of this narrative in relation to reality. It is only fair to point out that there still are qualified scholars who make this account their own without further ado. Here, for example, is what one can read in a very recent textbook: "The insurgents, seeing that the Romans were rushing to undertake the final assault, decided to put an end to their lives: when the fortress was taken on May 2, 73, two women and five children, out of the 960 persons who had dug in there, remained alive."[63] Even better, Louis H. Feldman, a noted scholar and the most knowledgeable expert on Josephus today, has attempted to establish the very details of this narrative. How were our two lady witnesses, the one who had the privilege of years and the one who held precedence by her higher level of education,[64] able to hear Eleazar's speech under favorable conditions? The answer is simple: "The acoustics in these underground sewers [where they took refuge] are excellent."[65] That statement was published in 1975, and Feldman has reprinted this version on his own initiative in 1984,[66] which goes to show that things change only very slowly.

Of course, one of the key questions concerning Josephus's credibility relates to the possible connections between his narrative and the excavations that were carried out at the site and then popularized by the man who directed these excavations, Yigael Yadin.[67] In my 1978 study I challenged Yadin's conclusions both as to their principles and in the details, maintaining, on the one hand, that a narrative bearing on a few days' time cannot, properly speaking, be corroborated by an excavation that by definition brings to light objects or monuments no one has ever seen together before,[68] and, on the other hand, that, in the case of the ostraca that supposedly served to determine by lot who would cut the others' throats, the texts used did not coincide with the objects found. I have been ignored,[69] condemned ex cathedra,[70] but never refuted, and sometimes even given approval in somewhat unexpected places.[71] Beyond the small change of various interpretations and anecdotes concerning the excavation,[72] I continue to think that narrative-archaeology, the novelistic archaeological writing of the sort "Eleazar left at five in the morning," is to be condemned in principle.

Once the hypothesis of a transparent narrative confirmed by a no less transparent excavation has been eliminated, it nonetheless remains the case that something has to be made of this narrative and of this excavation.

Should one be satisfied with simply *inverting* Josephus's narrative and the archaeological reading offered by Yadin? For Trude Weiss Rosmarin, Josephus's version is the version of the Roman military command. The

Masada combatants died as they should have, in heroic combat. The women and children were assassinated by the Romans who spread the suicide legend in order to cover up their own misdeeds.[73] Negative narrative transparency, however, has no more validity than a positive transparency.

Let us therefore grant once and for all that a text is not an immediate datum, that it is advisable to analyze the text, it being understood that the projector can be aimed either further away or less further. Narrative is a soft thing that hardens only when it is lined up in series so that it may be confronted with what conforms to it and what contradicts it.

Collective suicide is a *topos* of Greco-Roman literature.[74] This *topos* expresses principally the surprise of "civilized" historians when faced with a radical form of behavior that is more characteristic of barbarians than of Greeks.[75] What conclusion is one to draw from this? Certainly not that the existence of the *topos* makes the deeds untrue. Instances of human behavior can resemble one another, just as narratives can. How many historical episodes would disappear if one reasoned otherwise! It has been debated whether Xanthus truly had been destroyed by the Persians in 540.[76] No one is obliged to believe that at Astapa rivers of blood extinguished the flames.[77] No narrative bears within itself, down to its very last detail, the mark of truth or falsity.

Another way of proceeding would be to line up in series not narratives belonging to the same literature but to the same culture. Suicide will then be dealt with in the Jewish tradition as a "Sanctification of the Name" (*qiddush ha-Shem*) and included therein will be the suicide of Razis at the time of Judas Maccabaeus' war against Nicanor,[78] as well as the collective suicides that accompanied and followed the massacres of Jews in Rhenish and French villages at the end of the eleventh century during the First Crusade,[79] or, in 1943, during the Warsaw ghetto uprising. Of course, every narrative is a "trap,"[80] but it is not clear how one could dispense with narrative altogether.

To escape from this impasse, we must analyze Josephus's narrative on three distinct levels.

The first level has been defined both by myself in my 1978 study and, independently, by David J. Ladouceur.[81] Eleazar's speeches inciting suicide can appear as a reply, inside the work itself, to a speech arguing instead that suicide is a shameful act.[82] " 'It is a brave act to kill oneself,' [someone] will suggest. Not at all! It is a most craven act."[83] Now, the person who makes these arguments is none other than Josephus himself, when, at Jotapata, he pleads against the collective suicide from which he, individually, would then escape. The argumentation is certainly Greek in origin and it is inspired by the *Phaedo*.[84] The question, however, is not whether this discourse was inspired by an authentically Jewish tradition (and what, indeed, at the end of the first century C.E., was an "authentically Jewish tradition"?) but whether it expresses the line of argument Josephus wants to present as Jewish. And the answer to that question is undoubtedly in the affirmative.

One must therefore—and this is the second level—come to understand that the narrative of death, the narrative of the collective suicide of those besieged on Masada, is organically linked with the discourse on death. Eleazar's two-part speech is a reply to Josephus's two-part speech at Jotapata.

Indeed, all studies[85] of Eleazar's two-part speech have confirmed, with varying nuances, the astonishing character of these two oratorical moments. The first part of this speech delivered by the leader of the Sicarii—that is, by the leader of a sect Josephus condemns—is an admission of guilt. The Jewish people have been condemned by God: "We hoped, or so it would seem, that of all the Jewish race, we alone would come through safely, still in possession of our freedom, as if we had committed no sin against God and taken part in no crime—we who had taught the others!"[86] Undoubtedly Josephus himself, at Jotapata, had reckoned—at least, this is what he tells us—that Fortune had passed to the Roman camp[87] after God had decided to punish the Jewish nation. But the levels are not the same. Josephus explains elsewhere[88] that the Romans have succeeded the Assyrians, the Persians, and the Greeks, as the prophets had taught: they do not succeed the Jews, and the latter can survive. They cannot in the outlook being attributed to Eleazar.

The second speech made by the latter character is itself positive. It is a pagan encomium to suicide based on the Greek doctrine of the immortality of the soul. At no moment does it refer to specifically Jewish values and, in particular, to the Sanctification of the Name. It does confirm, however, that God, the only Jew in this sinister story, has decreed the annihilation of his own kind. "Long ago . . . God issued this warning to the whole Jewish race together, that life would be taken from us."[89] That this text is "dazzling" is beyond doubt, dazzling and effective. Indeed, in a frankly exceptional act for this intransigent and pitiless polemicist, Josephus underscores its efficacious beauty.[90] Nonetheless, the prophecy itself remains false. Listing other crimes committed by the Sicarii, Josephus continues his narrative beyond Masada, since the Jewish people continue to live and since for him Masada is not the end of Jewish history. It is the Christian, the Latin translators of Josephus, pseudo-Hegesippus, who interrupt his narrative at the end of the Masada episode. They do so because for them, theologically speaking, God has abandoned His people after the death of Christ. Such an outlook would be entirely foreign to Josephus.

Therefore, one must—and this is the third level—consider this narrative and this discourse as an expression of the very ideology of the practitioners of the apocalypse, of those who, quite particularly, made it their principle to accept no sovereign authority but that of God. That is to say, this speech is an expression of the ideology of the advocates of the "Fourth Philosophy," the sect that was founded by Judas the Galilaean, the presumed ancestor of Eleazar. Thus, it is the ideology of the Sicarii, that is, the men of the dagger.[91]

Were there only Sicarii in the historical Masada? There is no reason to think that this was necessarily so. The coins discovered there are those of the insurrection. The texts found at the site, such as the Wisdom of Ben Sira, have nothing of a separatist cast to them. But we are dealing here with Josephus and with his narrative. In it, the Masada episode plays an entirely specific role.

This narrative is, then, as I said not so long ago and as I repeat today, an apocalypse of death. This assertion has been granted neither by Arnaldo Momigliano[92] nor by Louis H. Feldman, who writes: "Vidal-Naquet concludes that it is against this spirit of apocalypse that the entire recital of Josephus was written. We may, however, remark that the language of the speeches is hardly distinctive of apocalyptic. Instead the speeches are a direct appeal to the defenders to commit suicide."[93] Yes, but to remain at this point is to forget that every apocalypse begins with death before issuing onto a time of resurrection and glory; it begins with the night before the transfiguration. The practitioners of the apocalypse, who waited for the world to topple, will not see it topple. At the worst moment of the siege of Jerusalem, when the Temple gate, burned by the Romans, collapses, annihilating the crowd of those who had taken refuge there, Josephus comments: "Their destruction was due to a false prophet who that very day had declared to the people in the City that God commanded them go up into the Temple to receive the signs of their deliverance."[94] With the narrative of Masada, with the two-part speech of Eleazar, Josephus seals the fate of the false prophets and registers their failure.

Was he the only one who did so? The Talmud will completely ignore the episode of Masada,[95] and this refusal is one aspect of the desperate apoliticism that was already characteristic of Johanan Ben Zakkai. Even later still, in the *Josippon*, a tenth-century Hebrew text inspired by Josephus via the Latin text of "Hegesippus," the episode is entirely transformed: no more suicide, a heroic death in combat, and a lamentation of ample length by the "priest" Joseph Ben Gorion.[96] Thus do narratives vanish before reappearing . . .

Masada: Politics and Memory

Of what type of politics did Masada provide the extreme and most radical example? It is to this third question that I would now like to respond by appealing to another historical technique, that of comparative history.

Our "false prophets," our Masada suicides, may indeed be inscribed within a vast concurrent totality, as well as within an even vaster whole extending over many centuries.

First, there is the concurrent whole, that of resistance to Hellenization, then to Romanization, which has been studied by such scholars as Samuel Kennedy Eddy and Ramsay MacMullen.[97] The Jews, in fact, were not the only ones who made use of apocalypse,[98] even if *their* apocalypses were destined to have a greater echo. Second, there is an even vaster totality, the conflicts we are still witnessing today, that is, those that oppose the order of the developed world to the rural or urban populations of the Third World.

When the dramatic events of Guyana unfolded in 1978, with the collective suicide of the members of a religious sect, some mentioned Masada.[99] The comparison was somewhat forced: the sect members were not under siege, nor were they combating rationalizing, authoritarian, modernist forces. Keeping everything in proper proportion, we can nevertheless say that this really is what we see at work in the Palestine of the first century C.E. as much as in the Protestant Cévennes region of France at the end of the seventeenth century, in nineteenth-century Brazil, and in the Mexico, Africa, or Madagascar of the twentieth century. And quite obviously, the fact that Christianity, which issued from Judaism, became a universal religion contributes to our understanding by adding a similarity of words and names to the similarity of situations.

Here I shall limit myself to two examples. My first example comes from E. Le Roy Ladurie and his description of the Protestant rebellions that began in 1688–89. A trait these rebellions share with our first-century insurrections is that both united peasants with clergy. Le Roy Ladurie summarizes the position of the famous pastor from the Refuge, Pierre Jurieu, as follows: "To hear it from Jurieu, the revolution on the rise was ordered along the lines of the old visions of the book of Daniel and fol-

lowed the periodization of the Apocalypse: first, a blood bath and the persecution of the righteous; then, with this trial passed, shall come God's
regeneration of humankind, the final fall of Babylon and of Rome, the pur-
ple-clothed debauchee; finally, the whole world will flourish again more
lovely than before."[100] This is but one example among many.

The book of Daniel? What a lovely history one could write of the theoretical and practical interpretations of this text in a nascent Christianity,
in the millenarianism of medieval Italy (which has been restored to our
memory by Umberto Eco's novel *The Name of the Rose*), among the English revolutionaries of the seventeenth century, and among so many others.[101] "The Memory of Daniel" would be a wonderful title for a book that
recounts the impression left by a fictitious character.

For my second example, which lies closer to Masada than the first, I
shall take a group that played a considerable role in Mexico during the
period from 1926 to 1929, the Cristeros group.[102] In this case, there was
an episode of secular and authoritarian rationalization in Mexico, that is
to say, an attempt to integrate into a modern State people who wanted
neither integration nor modernization.[103] In 1926, Catholic worship was
suspended. By the thousands, the Cristeros rose up and fought "against
King Herod" while proclaiming that "God is the supreme government in
all things."[104] This is almost exactly the definition of the sectarian advocates of the "Fourth Philosophy," who rejected the census, who refused to
use coins because they bore the likeness of Caesar, and whose adherents
died at Masada.

Analysis, however, can take us still further. During rabbinical times,
Masada was plunged into oblivion, as, moreover, was Josephus, who was
deliberately replaced in the exegetes' text of the first few centuries C.E.
by Johanan Ben Zakkai. The Cristeros experienced a similar fate. In 1929
dialogue between the bishops and the Mexican government was reestablished, worship was again authorized, and suddenly the ecclesiastical
bureaucracies, that of the Vatican as well as the local one in Mexico,
became literally bent upon making people forget their adventure in apocalypse. To reestablish a minimum of truth about this affair, the services of
a historian were required. This historian was Jean A. Meyer, who had to
employ all his cunning, to take roundabout approaches, and, especially, to
make systematic use of the techniques of oral history. His labor has
become an admirable example of what the relationship between Memory
and History should be.

In the case of the Cristeros, the tie with the past was not broken since
survivors were numerous, and even today they remain relatively numer-

ous. In the case of Masada, on the contrary, the mnemonic tie clearly was broken. Yadin wrote that Masada has been "elevated . . . to an undying symbol of desperate courage, a symbol which has stirred hearts throughout the last nineteen centuries."[105] This statement is as lovely as an antique, but it is a complete fake. For centuries Masada was only a text, and this text was read primarily by non-Jews who read in it what pseudo-Hegesippus had already read in it, one slightly delayed chastisement of the murderers of Christ. It is certainly in this spirit that it was read in Calvin's Geneva, where Flavius Josephus was placed on the list of approved Sunday readings. The site itself, which had become the Arab toponym Qasr As-Sebbeh, was finally identified as Josephus's Masada (the *Josippon* calls it Mezira) only in 1838 by the American travelers Robinson and Smith. It was much later still that the Zionist movement seized hold of it. The point of departure for the modern Masada myth is a six-verse poem in Hebrew by Isaac Lamdan, where Masada stands as the threatened symbol of Israel's hope. It is here that the famous formula "Masada shall not fall again" appears.[106]

Naturally, the tragedies of the Hitlerian era have contributed to this resurrection of the name Masada. But ironically, the man through whom we know all that could be known of this history before Yadin's excavations was frankly considered a traitor. Josephus was once judged and convicted of high treason in southwestern France, and his "trial," conducted under the terrible circumstances of the Vilna ghetto in Poland, was mounted on stage as a play.[107]

But clearly it is the creation—lived as a re-creation—of the State of Israel that was going to make of this rock, on which youthful tank-crew members, upon promotion, took their oaths of service, one of the mythical sites in the National Memory. In excavating the site in 1963–1965 and in calling the volunteers from around the world who came to assist him "pioneers," Yadin, a former chief of staff of Zahal, the Israeli Defense Forces, and a future vice prime minister, did no more than draw out the consequences that come with transforming into a national myth this old narrative of a historian suspected of treason. It can be stated as a general rule that one usually has much more respect and exhibits much more reserve toward what one does not know than toward what one does know. In the case of Masada, the excavation itself (with the sole exception of the manuscript documents discovered by the excavators) was not made the object of any scholarly publication. Masada therefore took on, until the Six Day War (which occurred two years after the completion of the excavations), even greater importance in the national consciousness.

That archaeology conducted in a country that is at once young and old—Theodor Herzl's *Alt-Neuland*—should be tainted by, nay, completely impregnated with nationalism is not exactly a big surprise. An example that fully parallels this one is that of Greece, the Greece of the *megali idea*, the Great Idea. The famous Greek numismatist J. N. Svoronos, for example, was asked by the Venizélos government to establish the Hellenic character of Macedonia—a disputed area if there ever was one—by means of the indisputably Hellenic character of the coinage of the ancient Greek cities located in this province.[108] The Albanians of today proceed in the same way with respect to the ancient Illyrians. In this way, one regresses even further from archaeology, whether nationalistic or not, into the realm of myth pure and simple. Whether it is a matter of establishing one's more or less direct descendance from Noah, of identifying with Plato's Atlanteans, or of mythifying the memory of the Bretons, the Goths, the Gauls, or the Francs, from the Middle Ages to Modern Times myth surrounds the birth of today's nations.[109]

One need only open one's eyes to notice analogous developments in our own world. I shall limit myself to two examples dating from 1985. First, it has been asked with great concern in Yugoslavia whether Homeric Troy should abandon the hill of Hissarlik to attain, between Split and Dubrovnik, the banks of the Neretva,[110] a notion that does not seem to have impressed the Albanians, the Greeks, or the Turks. Similarly, in Turkey, a book laying claims to serious scholarship has attempted to prove that the Etruscans were Turks, as an obvious etymology indicates—which thereby allows one to explain the birth of the Roman Republic, at the end of the fifth century B.C.E., as an anti-Turk coup d'état, inspired, of course, by the Greeks.[111]

And since the ancient Near East is at the center of this analysis, how can we avoid bringing up the exploit of an eminent professor of Beirut University who proves in an irrefutable manner that the true site at which the episodes of the Old Testament unfolded is situated not in Palestine but in Saudi Arabia?[112] After Jerusalem in Dalecarlia (Selma Lagerlöf's *Jerusalem: A Novel*, translated from the Swedish [Garden City, N.Y.: Doubleday, 1915]) and Jerusalem at Carpentras (Armand Lunel's *Jérusalem à Carpentras* [Paris: Gallimard, 1937]), we now have Jerusalem near Mecca. This theory is a late arrival, and the Saudi princes have had a narrow escape!

Masada has become a site of pilgrimage, that is to say, as Maurice Halbwachs had shown long ago, an encounter in the mind and in collective practice between a space and a narrative.[113]

But what of the situation today? A debate has recently been launched by G. W. Bowersock concerning the nationalistic tendencies of Israeli archaeology.[114] Israel's archaeologists are accused there of being interested, in the case of these ancient sites, only in the Israelite and Jewish strata while neglecting what is Canaanite, Roman, or Arab, and in general everything subsequent to the fall of Masada or Bar Kochba (135 C.E.). In like manner, Greek archaeologists neglect (to use language no stronger) Turkish documents, and no Turkish university has a chair expressly devoted to Byzantine history. Among the more specific criticisms Bowersock directs against Yadin, it is observed—somewhat excessively—that, whereas documents discovered in the 1960s concerning the (now contested) national hero Bar Kochba were published promptly, the same was not the case for thirty-five documents coming from a Jewish woman, Babatha, who had fled during the troubles of 132–135. These documents, Bowersock informs us, show that this woman entertained entirely normal and quotidian relations with her non-Jewish contemporaries. Her living example could thus serve as a scathing denial both of Jewish exclusiveness—a foundation stone of Israel—and of the theory behind the *Valley of Tears*.

As is the case when any debate is brought up to date, Bowersock's work was valid for a certain period of time, though perhaps it had already become partially outdated by the time it was published. Here I shall only venture to say (and I do so with extreme caution even though it results from my own observations)[115] that in Israel the national myths seem to have entered into a state of crisis[116] and that nationalist archaeology, as symbolized by Yadin until his death in 1984, without having in the least disappeared, is increasingly being contested and outstripped.[117]

I shall limit myself to one example. At the beginning of the fourth book of the *Jewish War*,[118] Flavius Josephus describes the site and the fate of the town of Gamala (Gamla) on the Golan Heights. It is a superb citadel site, perhaps even more impressive than Masada. Vespasian did not have an easy time besieging it. A first assault failed. Finally, however, the city fell and, as Josephus tells us, "Despairing of escape and hemmed in every way, they flung their wives and children and themselves too into the immensely deep ravine that yawned under the citadel. In fact, the fury of the victors seemed less destructive than the suicidal frenzy of the trapped men; 4,000 fell by Roman swords, but those who plunged to destruction proved to be over 5,000."[119] The only survivors, as at Masada, were two women (one of whom was a person of note) who had hidden themselves during the siege, but not one child, the Romans having been instructed to "sling" all the babies they had found.[120]

The site of this town was discovered by the Kibbutznik archaeologist Schmaryahu Guttmann (a veteran of Masada) after the Six Day War and excavated. Everything was set for it to become a new Masada.[121] To Josephus's text were added in this case local circumstances. The Golan Heights had been, before the 1967 war, a Syrian fortress with guns trained on Israeli Galilee. The area was conquered in a fierce battle against an army that had resisted, and it was attacked again in 1973. Today it is annexed. The site has been developed, though undoubtedly in a less luxurious fashion and a less comfortable way—there is no lift—than Masada, but it has been fitted out, all the same, in an evocative way. The visitor is accompanied to the very top of the citadel, the presumed site of the mass suicide, by texts written by Josephus that recount this sinister affair.

Nevertheless, a myth—especially a myth in crisis—is not so easily duplicated. Gamla is a site, it is not a mythical place. Might one henceforth—will one someday—be able to obey the celebrated commandment "Zakhor"[122] ("Remember") without succumbing to the grip of myth?[123]

4 | Apropos of *Zakhor*

A t the end of his lovely book, Yosef Yerushalmi, who teaches Jewish history at Columbia University, mentions a short story by Borges: "Funes the Memorious":

In fact, Funes remembered not only every leaf of every tree of every wood, but also every one of the times he had perceived or imagined it. He decided to reduce each of these past days to some seventy thousand memories, which would then be defined by means of ciphers. He was dissuaded from this by two considerations: his awareness that the task was interminable, his awareness that it was useless. He thought that by the hour of his death he would not even have finished classifying all the memories of his childhood.[1]

Baudelaire expressed this thought in another way: "I have more memories than if I were a thousand years old."

There are other ways one could summarize the weight of Jewish memory that hangs upon Jewish history, the fact that memory blocks history from exercising its rights. A novella by Aharon Megged, which is included in an anthology of Israeli prose edited by Mireille Hadas-Lebel,[2] offers a rather satisfying summary of the problem. It recounts the story of a young

"A propos de *Zakhor*," a book review of the French edition—*Zakhor: Histoire juive et mémoire juive*, trans. Eric Vigne (Paris: Découverte, 1984)—of Yosef Hayim Yerushalmi's *Zakhor: Jewish History and Jewish Memory* (Seattle: University of Washington Press, 1982), was published in *Libération*, October 29, 1984. Reprinted in *JMP*, pp. 228–32. [T/E: Quotations and page references cited in the present essay come from the English-language edition.]

Israeli couple. They are about to give birth to a child and they have a grandfather who is a refugee from Eastern Europe. What will the newborn child, a boy, be named? Menahem-Mendele is the grandfather's request. This is a Hebrew name and, at the same time, a name typical of the Diaspora. For this very reason the young couple reject it vehemently. They want to name their child Ehoud, a pure Hebrew name that would have no meaning in the Ukraine or in Poland. The old man is desperate:

> "You are ashamed to name your son Mendele, for fear that he might remind you that it must be wiped off the face of the earth, leaving no trace of a memory. . . . No perpetuation, no testimony, no stele, no name."

The stele and the name, the monument and the name . . . In Hebrew, this is pronounced *Yad Vashem*. And this is, following Isaiah 56.5, the name of the novella. It is also the name of the commemorative site of the Great Massacre situated on a hill in Jerusalem. In Hebrew, "Zakhor" signifies "Remember." In the Jewish tradition, remembering is a duty for those who are Jewish: "If I forget thee, O Jerusalem . . ." What exactly must be remembered? Aharon Megged's novella clearly shows that one can choose between two memories. To choose Mendele is to choose memory in a line of continuity. To choose Ehoud is to wager on a type of modernity that wears an archaistic mask. Such archaism, however, can itself be dangerous. After all, to take another example, Masada is not a memory resting on an ongoing tradition but instead a modern myth created by Zionism.

Zakhor consists of four short chapters. Each one broaches a fundamental question. At first, the Jewish people appear as "at once the most historically oriented of peoples and as possessing the longest and most tenacious of memories" (p. xiv). In reality, however, the relationship between the Jewish people and historical time has undergone extraordinary variations. True, ancient Israel invented a specific form of history and a specific form of man's relationship to history. The Greeks invented history as a work bearing on truth: something happened or did not happen. As for the Jews, they invented history as an existential dimension of man in time. High up in his palace, David catches a glimpse of Bathsheba. A sinful love ensues, along with the bitter reproaches of the prophet Nathan. David sends Bathsheba's husband to his death. Of this sinful love will nevertheless be born King Solomon and, later still, for the Christians, Christ. The meaning of history includes all this.[3]

After the destruction of the Temple in 70 C.E., however, all this will become congealed. At the Council of Yabneh and in the school founded by

Johanan Ben Zakkai, who had escaped a Jerusalem in flames and had received from the emperor the right to found a school, the rabbis established around 100 C.E. the accepted list of books of the Book par excellence, the Bible. From this list was eliminated everything that makes mention of the great drama of the confrontation with Hellenism, notably the books of the Maccabees. And yet, as Elias Joseph Bickerman wrote one day, "The Jews became the 'people of the Book' when this Book was rendered into Greek." From then on, the Jews prayed in their synagogues within the confines of a fixed history, a history that of course was endlessly commented on and repeated but that no longer was itself history because the future, barring some intervention by the messiah, was dead. At best, it would be only a repetition of the past. Flavius Josephus, it is true, was writing history during the same era, a history that issues onto the future but as Yerushalmi points out, "In retrospect we know that within Jewry the future belonged to the rabbis, not to Josephus. Not only did his works not survive among the Jews, it would be almost fifteen centuries before another Jew would actually call himself an historian" (p. 16). This other Jew was Joseph Ha-Kohen, who wrote *The Valley of Tears* after the Jews' expulsion from Spain.[4] No Jewish histories were written in the Middle Ages, not even a chronicle like the one written, for example, by Raoul Glaber around the year 1000. The only work that is slightly reminiscent of a book of history is the work known as the *Josippon*. This book, a clerical adaptation of Flavius Josephus, saw the light of day in tenth-century Byzantine Italy. After recounting the fall of Masada, the book ends with a great lament about the misfortunes of the Jewish people and the loss of Jerusalem. It is, however, during the Middle Ages that memorial books were born. These books have a parallel in our time. What are called "souvenir books" recall to mind communities that by now have disappeared.[5]

Judaism, therefore, has organized itself in history in order to survive in spite of history. In the West, the Renaissance had consequences that Yerushalmi has studied closely. Jewish erudition of a historiographical character reappeared at that time, notably in the sixteenth century with the *Me'or Einayim* (*Enlightenment to the Eyes*) by the Mantuan Azariah de' Rossi, the first Jew from the West to cite Flavius Josephus and to rely upon his work. While Yerushalmi can name a dozen works of this type, he also notes that it is not a Jewish historian who really was going to reestablish the foundations of Jewish history as a discipline. This reestablishment, which took place in the seventeenth century and was presented as a continuation of the work of Flavius Josephus, was performed by Jacques Basnage, a French Protestant who had taken religious refuge in Holland where he found freedom. Manasseh Ben Israel, a celebrated Jew who had been a friend of Rembrandt and who had negotiated with Cromwell the Jews' return to England, dreamt of writing, in Spanish, such a continuation, but this project was not brought to term. So much has History been lived as repetition that all of medieval—and even modern—Judaism has revolted against it. Does not the mourning of the Ninth of Ab commemorate the fall of the first temple as well as the second? To this double commemoration could easily have been added the Spanish catastrophe of 1492, even the massacres in Poland and the Ukraine in the seventeenth century.

When, after the great movement of emancipation got under way during the nineteenth century, Leopold Zunz founded the "science of Judaism," he set it on foundations that today we would label "positivist," that is to say, entirely separated from memory. Throughout that century and during a large portion of our own, memory and history have in some respects taken separate paths. History distrusts memory; it even builds itself up *against* memory. And to the extent that memory selects and eliminates when it makes its choices, it is understandable how this distinction may have appeared radical and fundamental.

But is this a permanent separation? I would be tempted to say, on the contrary, that, sixty years after Proust, it is high time that we began to integrate memory into history. This does not mean, of course, that we should give up trying to separate truth from falsehood; it means simply that man is not to be identified with the instant he is living and that it is as temporal being, a being endowed with memory, that man's integration into historical discourse should henceforth take place. *Zakhor*, Remember; the slogan again takes on contemporary relevance.

PART TWO

Emancipation and History

5 The Privilege of Liberty

In Memory of François Delpech, 1935–1982

On a field where ideologies and ideologues do battle, at last we have a book of history. And yet its author does not write from Sirius. Jacob Katz is a professor at the Hebrew University of Jerusalem. He was even its rector. The period and even the theme treated in this book have not always enjoyed good press in Israel. The period from 1770 to 1870 is said to be that of a liberal illusion, the illusion of the emancipatory and assimilationist West, an illusion from which one must one day detach oneself if one wants Jewish history, conceived of as that of an identity, to continue. Jacob Katz concludes his book on the following note: "It was inherent in the nature of Jewish existence that emancipation become a turning point in Jewish history, but by no means its termination." A turning point, certainly, but one with— it cannot be denied—some possibly disturbing dimensions. In 1870 Benjamin Disraeli was former prime minister of Great Britain, but he was a converted Jew. In 1870 Karl Marx, author of *Das Kapital* (vol. 1, 1867), was certainly socialism's greatest thinker, but he too, like Disraeli, had been a converted Jew since his childhood.

Jacob Katz nevertheless avoids the kind of retrospective pessimism (grippingly depicted at Tel Aviv's Museum of the Jewish Diaspora [Beth Hatefutsoth]) that would present the postemancipatory Jewish condition

"Le Privilège de la liberté" originally appeared as the preface to the French edition—*Hors du ghetto: L'émancipation des Juifs en Europe (1770–1870)*, trans. J.-F. Sené (Paris: Hachette, 1984), pp. i–xxvii—of Jacob Katz's *Out of the Ghetto: The Social Background of Jewish Emancipation, 1770–1870* (Cambridge: Harvard University Press, 1973). Reprinted in *JMP*, pp. 235–61.

as a gold-plated trap. Instead, he poses a great historical problem, and he does so with the breadth required.

To respond to the question at hand, to give it some meaning, one had to proceed like a painter working on several different pictures. It was not a matter of enumerating, once again, the symbolic milestones. Instead, one needed to study, to use another metaphor, both the microbe and the overall surrounding landscape[1]—the Jews, therefore their diversity, and also the society that sheltered them, received them, and accepted them or rejected them.

Not all of Europe was involved, and still less all the Jews. Included are the exemplary settings of bourgeois revolution: England, France, Belgium and Holland, Germany, Austria, Hungary (with certain reservations), and Italy. A priority, even, must be given to Germany, much more than to pre-revolutionary and revolutionary France—though it is understood that no genuine border existed between these two countries before the Revolution. Ideas and people circulated from one bank of the Rhine to the other. On the Jewish side, as well as on the Christian side, a city like Metz was a center of movement, of emancipation, communicating as much with the German principalities as with the heart of the kingdom.

I would be tempted to say that in this book, which provides both a social and an intellectual history, the central chapter, the pivot of the work, is chapter five: "The Image of the Future." There, Jacob Katz asks how the reformers, both Jewish and Gentile, depicted the reform to themselves, how they envisioned, in the near and distant future, the Jews' integration into modern society. It is indeed a central chapter, because this "action-image"[2] of a new society is in reality the result of a movement called Les Lumières in France, the Aufklärung in Germany, the Haskala in the Jewish world, and "the Enlightenment" in English-speaking countries, and because the confrontation between the program as conceived and its actual realization is the subject to which the rest of this book is devoted.

Intellectuals like Lessing, Prussian government officials like Christian Wilhelm von Dohm, lawyers like Pierre-Louis Lacretelle, even priests like the celebrated *curé* of Embermenil in Lorraine, Abbé Gregoire, and other such reformers had Jewish counterparts. Moses Mendelssohn, an intellectual as well as a silk merchant, influenced Lessing, Mirabeau, and Abbé Gregoire. Isaac Pinto, who hailed from Bordeaux, engaged in polemics with Voltaire. Not that there was a perfect symmetry between the two countries. Jacob Katz shows very clearly that in Germany the court Jews played a key role in the emancipation of the Jews, as the process was implemented in these lands. The Kingdom of France did have its own court Jew, Cerf-Berr (1726–1794), who followed very early on in the footsteps of his father by serving the German dynasts in Alsace but who also pleaded very effectively to the king of France and then to the Constituent Assembly for the emancipation of the Jews of Alsace within the confines of the French nation. Cerf-Berr was a court Jew, not a member of the bourgeoisie.[3] In contrast to him, the prominent Jews of Bordeaux, a Gradis or a Furtado, believed, like genuine members of the bourgeoisie, that the emancipation of the Jews would come about naturally. They saw the process of emancipation developing along the lines of their own integration into the world of business affairs in this large Atlantic port city.[4]

The reformers' program centered on three basic themes. However, each of these themes—civil society, the nation, and "regeneration," as one said back then, or "normalization" as we would say today—went beyond the Jewish question proper.

Judenreform in Germany aimed at the Jews' "civic betterment" (*Die Bürgerliche Verbesserung*), as in the title of one of Christian Wilhelm von Dohm's works (1781–1783). To envisage such betterment, it must already be granted that there exists a society that is at least "semineutral," as is said in the title to chapter four, a society in which the principal relationships between people would be regulated not in terms of religious status, one's hierarchal relationship to the sovereign, or the caste to which one belongs by birth or by election. Before 1789 a "semineutral" society was not yet conceived in the overall terms of civil society, but the fragments of such a society already existed—among Freemasons, for example. As it turns out, Jacob Katz has reflected and written extensively on the subject of Freemasonry.[5]

The nation is, if I dare say, the ideological expression of civil society; it is that which aids civil society to think itself as a whole. The reformers did not seek to emancipate the Jews, they were seeking to emancipate *their* Jews, and not everyone, even in their own country, had the right to be treated as such. Thus, the entire question in effect centers on the extent to which the Jews were recognized as having as their vocation no longer to be *a* nation, in the almost medieval sense of the term—there was a (Jewish) Portuguese nation at Bordeaux and another one at Bayonne—but to be part of *the* nation, which would soon come to be called the "Grande Nation," entering therein under the same heading (in France, for example) as the Protestants.

In people's lived experience at the end of the ancien régime and at the beginning of the Revolution in France, the responses varied from place to place. On the whole, the "Pope's Jews," who were by and large considered as citizens of the crown when they began trading in Provence and in Languedoc (their families retained for a long time originals or copies of patents granted them by Louis XVI), were favorably received, as was also the case, with various nuances, with the Jews of Bordeaux and with those living in the environs of Bayonne, where the only majority-Jewish town, Saint-Esprit, was located.[6] In 1789 the Jews of southwest France were even allowed to participate in electoral activities, and one of them—the Bordeaux shipowner David Gradis—almost was elected to the Estates-General as a representative of the Third Estate. To the extent that these Jews were still foreigners in the legal sense of the word, the "King's Procurator in the Chamber of Domains" in near-ritual fashion sought, by virtue of the right of windfall, to seize the goods of Jews who died in Paris. The Paris Parlement regularly dismissed his claims. The heirs of Jews from the region around Bordeaux or Avignon nevertheless won their cases more easily than the heirs of Jews from the East, whether Alsatian or German (both groups being called, moreover, "German"). It was in pleading a case for the heirs of a certain Abraham Vidal, a Jew from Bordeaux whose sister had married a man from Avignon, that, on January 14, 1784, the procurator (solicitor) Jaladon wrote the following words, which serve as a remarkable expression of the idea that the nation is the foundation of civil society: "In vain would one object that he [Abraham Vidal] was a Jew in order to conclude that he was not at all a Frenchman. In France, as elsewhere, it is not one's religion, but one's origins, one's birth, that makes one French or someone from any other nation; whether one is atheist or deist, Jew or Catholic, Protestant or Mohammedan, matters little: if one is [born] in France of a French mother and father, if one has in no way expatriated oneself, one is a natural Frenchman and enjoys all the rights of a citizen."[7]

While ideology is not to be confused here with reality, it remains true that, for the Jews of Avignon, Bordeaux, and Bayonne, the Revolution ratified as much as it transformed the existing state of things. The situation was quite different in Alsace, where the Jews appeared less as a religious community or a commercial bourgeoisie than a caste enjoying a monopoly on the practice of usury.

That said, it must be added that even in the best of cases proclamations of principle reflect only one aspect of reality. Even in France, the nation was a program. Cournot defined the society of the ancien régime as a "cascade of contempt." This cascade ran from Christians to Jews; it ran, too, of course, from the heights to the depths of the Jewish world. The oligarchies that controlled the Pope's Jews made one proclamation after another to warn against and to forbid residency by foreign Jews. Nevertheless, it was in this immigrant setting that significant numbers of domestic servants were recruited, an employment practice which proved to be an inexhaustible source of conflicts and contradictions.[8] Even between Avignon and Carpentras, each community had its limits. When the Jews of Carpentras recruited a rabbi from Avignon whose name (Ispir) betrayed a remote German ancestry, it was understood that if he should die before the expiration of his seven-year contract, his wife and his children would have fifteen days to vacate the premises. And between Avignon and Bordeaux, "outside" marriages were not looked upon very kindly.[9]

The Jews of Bayonne thought themselves as a race completely apart. "Their absolutely distinct origin dates back to the Babylonian captivity itself; all of them descended from ancient families from the tribe of Judah which, when the nation was allowed to rebuild its temple, took no advantage of the freedom thus granted them."[10] Among them could be counted, during the eighteenth century, just one Jew from Poland.[11]

The Jews themselves, and naturally their enemies, were aware of the fact that their integration into the nation raised difficult questions. The procurator who had defended the interests of the heirs of Abraham Vidal posed the problem quite well: "Considered as Jews, they are a part of this great people who endure despite its dispersion. Considered as persons who have been born or who have established themselves in France, they are subjects of the King . . . they are our fellow citizens."[12] This procurator-dialectician was capable of "filling out all the in-between spaces," as Pascal had said, but not everyone (though there were exceptions) fully shared these capacities. Both among the Jews and among some of their enemies, references to Palestine pertained more to the realm of symbolism than to that of reality. Nevertheless, it was from the real Palestine, for example, that the Jews of Metz imported the *etrogim* (citrons) they needed for the feast of Sukkoth, and the distribution of these fruits, moreover, brought into play the social hierarchies of their community.[13]

The main issue was the unity of the Jewish people in its dispersed state. Now, while the national principle opens up the boundaries within each nation, it closes those on the outside. This was symbolized, during the Revolution, by the famous inscription on the Kehl bridge: "Here begins the land of liberty." Modern anti-Semitism—or the new judeophobia,[14] if one prefers—as is symbolized rather well by a character like Grattenauer in Jacob Katz's book, begins here: the Jew is not to be granted the rights of the citizen because he is not the citizen of a single country.

In Germany and in France (though to different degrees), being in a ghetto had been a privilege when compared to the rule that closed off, in Germany, a number of towns to Jewish residency, and even, according to edicts that had never been revoked, France in its entirety. How could one pass from a cascade of privileges—which was one aspect of Cournot's "cascade of contempt" and which extended downward from the court Jew to the humblest inhabitant of the ghettos—to the new hierarchies of Liberal society? Between the requirements of liberty and those of equality, it was not easy to discover the solution at the two extremes of revolutionary tension.[15] Even after the proclamation of the decrees concerning emancipation and tolerance, even after the French Revolution, the court Jews still had some fine days ahead of them, including in France where, during the eighteenth century, their presence was nonetheless, as I had said, felt to a much lesser extent than in Germany.

"Regeneration" is the third theme in the program of emancipation. It began to take on a fundamental importance, as Jacob Katz shows, as early as the English Enlightenment, as symbolized, at the very beginning of the century, by John Toland and the group of Deists. In certain paragraphs of this chapter the aspirations of Jewish reformers and Gentiles are but one. Both groups hoped, as Zionist socialists like Borokhov had hoped at the end of the nineteenth century and the beginning of the twentieth, that the Jews would adopt the same range of occupations as their new compatriots. What they failed to appreciate was that the revolution then under way was, in fact, a bourgeois revolution and that the model being imposed upon the emancipated Jew or the Jew in the process of emancipation, who had been prevented for centuries from possessing or working land, was the bourgeois—in other words, the urban—model.

Without a doubt, the vast majority of reformers hoped to "normalize" the Jews, with the latter in the end either abandoning the "barbarous" aspects of their religion or converting to the Christian religion or to philosophy. Each of these options, moreover, was capable of serving as the mask for the others. Is there anything surprising about this? Should we think that there was a relentless effort aimed specifically at de-Judaizing the Jews? When, in 1787, the Academy of Metz conducted a competition around the now famous question, "Are there means by which the Jews may be rendered more useful and happy in France?," it was clearly raising the question of regeneration. This question, however, was also being posed on the scale of the entire nation. In 1790, for example, the Jews of Saint-Esprit (Bayonne) expressed their pride at participating in France's regeneration.[16] The disappearance of particularisms was, of course, what was being sought—though it was being sought under the same heading as the elimination of provincial dialects and regional languages, another of Abbé Gregoire's preoccupations.[17] In France, however, the Jews were an infinitesimal minority (barely forty thousand persons). An operation aimed at regeneration struck harder upon a minority than upon a majority better equipped to resist.

It remains the case that a number of Jews (and it is scarcely possible to provide a figure) accepted the challenge. A small number, the fringe group studied in chapter seven, envisaged conversion or a semiconversion in the style of David Friedländer. Conversions were certainly more numerous in Germany than in France. This remained the price one had to pay to enter into the army or into the upper reaches of the University.

A particular case is worth recalling here because of its symbolic value. Jacob Katz mentions briefly, again in his seventh chapter, a Freemason who was a Jew converted to Catholicism, Thomas von Schönfeld. He specifies that this person had been a disciple of Jacob Frank (1726–1791), who, himself a convert, had developed in Poland and in Austria a Western and modernistic version of the movement Sabbatai Sevi had launched in the Muslim Orient.[18] Conversion signified not Israel's disappearance but the fact that its exile had reached its conclusion and that Israel was now spreading enlightenment—that of a sect among the nations. Since Jacob Katz wrote his book, Thomas Schönfeld's history has been entirely rewritten by Gershom Scholem.[19] Born in 1753 at Brünn (Brno) in Moravia, Moses Dubruška, a cousin of Jacob Frank, received a dual education, both rabbinical and sectarian, and this duplication was repeated later, in 1775, by a conversion to Catholicism and a change of name—though without leading to a break with his sect, and rightly so. A new duplication took place when this secretly Jewish but publicly Catholic and naturalized German writer became, at Strasbourg and then at Paris, both a Frenchman and a Jacobin under the name of Junius Frey. Arrested on November 23, 1793, he was condemned to death as a conspirator and a spy on April 5, 1794, and guillotined the same day, at the same time as Danton. Did he remain to the very end a double man, a Jacobin and a Jew, who, in cursing Moses, wanted to establish enlightenment in this world? While this is Gershom Scholem's hypothesis, it is open to discussion.[20]

It was, in any case, a fine example of Jewish ambiguity. We also have, by way of symmetry, an example of ambiguity in emancipatory discourse. Lessing's *Nathan the Wise* (*Nathan der Weise*)[21] was, in 1779, one of the forerunners of the reform in the status of the Jews in German lands. The principal character, a rich Jewish merchant living in Jerusalem at the time of Saladin (the twelfth century), is inspired by the figure of Moses Mendelssohn, the philosopher-reformer. The play is indisputably a plea for mutual recognition among the "religions of the Book." There are three principal heroes: Nathan, a Jew; Recha (Rachel), his adopted daughter; and a young Knight Templar of German origin. At the end of the plot, it is revealed that the adopted daughter of Nathan is of good Christian stock and that the young Knight Templar was himself born a Muslim and even is a nephew of Saladin. How is one to read these permutations? Noting that the Jew alone has remained what he was at birth, should it be said that he functions as the pivot? Or should one observe that Islam and Christianity each obtains a new recruit and that the Jew remains without issue . . . ?

Seventeen-seventy to 1870: Jacob Katz has chosen these two dates in order to bring to light, within a long-term time frame, the mutations in the Jewish history he is studying. These are, of course, symbolic dates, and he does not restrict himself to respecting them exactly, which would in any case be meaningless, since the history he recounts begins much sooner in England than in Germany and even in France.

Let us nevertheless try to play this game and mark off the two end-points of this duration as one marks off a line in space. First, 1770: Moses Mendelssohn (1722–1788) was then the hero of the Berlin Haskala. He was also a German philosopher who published, in 1767, a treatise whose title is none other than *Phaedon: Or, On the Immortality of the Soul*. A German philosopher whom Kant cited appreciatively—can he really be a Jew and even a silk salesman, like Spinoza was a polisher of glass?[22] In dedicating a book to him, the Zurich illuminist and physiognomist Lavater (1741–1801) called upon Mendelssohn to convert. In 1770 Mendelssohn published his *Letter to Johann Caspar Lavater of Zurich*, a scathing reply. Recalling that the Jews were not seeking to convert anyone, he claimed the right to remain faithful to his tribe: "Our rabbis teach us unequivocally that the written and oral Law that constitutes our revealed religion is binding for our people alone. 'Moses commanded us a Law, an inheritance of the congregation of Jacob' [Deuteronomy 33.4]. All other nations on earth, we hold, were enjoined by God to adhere to the law of nature and the religion of the patriarchs."[23] All this was written in German, the language into which Mendelssohn—like Luther before him—had translated the Pentateuch. The commentaries with which he embellished these biblical texts, such as the *Qōhēleth* (Ecclesiastes), in 1770, were published in Hebrew, however, and once it became necessary to speak in Hebrew of the immortality of the soul, Socrates no longer was a valid interlocutor:

"What do we have to do, we the adepts of the true religion, with the son of Sophroniscus."[24]

Mendelssohn, too, is a superb example of the double man. Indeed, he follows a long line of others whom Judaism has produced since the time the author of the book of Daniel, during the second century B.C.E., insisted upon the fact that Daniel the Jew was called "Belteshazzar" at the court of Babylon. This dualism, which has so singularly enriched Jewish history, was to weigh heavily upon the Jews' relations with the Gentiles, many of whom found it difficult to bear the fact that their interlocutors were both similar and different and that the same man could hail from both Athens and Jerusalem.

Yet, we may ask, Is this a general characteristic of Jewish communities around 1770? Did Hebrew, for example, remain a common denominator of contrast between Jews and Gentiles? The registers kept by the heads of the urban oligarchies were written in Hebrew—a rather mediocre Hebrew, it would appear, at Carpentras.[25] The *institutional* history of a community like that of Metz, until 1789, was composed with the aid of documents written in Hebrew, and in particular the register (*pinkas*), which can be traced from 1749 to 1789 and in which was inscribed everything that marked the community as it reflected upon itself—but not, for example, Louis XV's 1768 visit to the town's synagogue.[26] This same community lived its social history in Judeo-Lorraine (a variety of Yiddish) and wrote it on the basis of texts that for the most part were French in origin.

Another way of looking at this symbolic date, 1770, is to ask oneself *who* was concerned, in the European Jewish world, by the problems Jacob Katz treats in his book. The Jews of western Europe who were truly concerned by the beginnings of the process of assimilation, "regeneration," and the eventual acquisition of citizenship constituted a small minority. One will see even in Holland—the land of tolerance par excellence—the Jews protest, as Jacob Katz points out, against their complete emancipation.

The debates surrounding Mendelssohn did not very often touch upon Poland. During the Berlin Aufklärung, the main phenomenon was not an impossible reflection on the possibility of becoming Russian or Polish but the explosion of a mystic form of pietism, Hasidism. Its founder, the Baal Shem Tov, had died in 1760, but his resurrection was being awaited—if the Redeemer did not come, in the next fifteen or fifty years—in the next sixteen or sixty years.[27] To the new national borders separating the Jews from each other at the end of the century was added the immense cultural boundary that opposed the Jews of one half of Europe to those of the other half. Would an insurrection (in the etymological sense of the term) like the one that swept through the entire Jewish world in the wake of Sabbatai Sevi's messianic proclamation (1655) still have been possible slightly more than a century later?

Let us now place ourselves in 1870, since this is the endpoint Jacob Katz has chosen. It now becomes all the easier, and all the more necessary, to indicate the relevant changes in contrast (whose stages Jacob Katz has taken such great care to enumerate for us) and to define correctly both the advances and the setbacks.[28]

In 1870 the French Jews, along with the English Jews, certainly were the most assimilated Jews in European Judaism. They were certainly also those who had best managed to benefit from the establishment of equal rights. Since the anti-assimilationist pressure that would later come from central Europe and from Yiddish culture had not yet made itself felt, one can speak, from this standpoint, of a golden age. Of course, in all of western and central Europe, Austria-Hungary included, equal rights had theoretically been achieved. But in this last country it was only at the moment of the Austro-Hungarian compromise of 1867, for example, that the Jews became, in principle, citizens like other citizens, able even to be admitted into the hereditary nobility. One additional reservation must even be made in the case of Austria-Hungary: it was not until 1895 that the Jewish religion came to enjoy the same rights as a recognized religion as the various forms of Christianity.

In France, by way of contrast, the rabbis, who had become, since Napoleon I, something approximating parish priests [curés] for Jews, were, since 1831, in the time of Louis-Philippe, civil servants paid under the same category as Catholic curés and Protestant pastors. This change was not achieved without engendering some protest. The last inequality, that of the oath more judaico imposed on Jewish parties in civil suits, was abolished in 1846, still under Louis-Philippe. By way of contrast, in April 1860 the Israelite "university" (community) of Nice campaigned for French annexation by pointing out that numerous exceptions to the rule of equality remained in the Kingdom of Piedmont. One complaint was that "the high schools and special schools in Sardinia do not allow our children any access."[29] Again by way of contrast, it was only on September 20, 1870, sixteen days after the fall of Napoleon III and after the Italian penetration into Rome (the last remaining tatter of the Papal States) that the last ghetto of western Europe was opened. And in England, it was only in 1858 that a Jew, a Rothschild, was finally able to sit in the Commons;

indeed, it was only in 1871 that Jews were allowed to be graduated from Oxford and Cambridge.

Nevertheless, the major contrast remained that between France and Germany. Certainly, one should not allow oneself to be carried away by what happened during the decades that followed. Certainly, too, propaganda offering a highly retrospective view of this whole history was developed in both countries.[30] The facts themselves, however, hardly leave any room for doubt. While legal inequality disappeared in 1871, at the time of unification, the mark of the ancien régime—what Arno J. Mayer calls the "persistence of the Old Regime"[31]—was infinitely more clear-cut in Germany than in any country of western Europe. German nationalism was constituted or reconstituted at the turn of the century with an anti-Semitic dimension to it, and this dimension was, at that point in time, absent from the French nationalism issuing from the Revolution. Wagnerian mythology provides us, in this regard, with an overpowering example.[32] It is not easy to account for this opposition—which, moreover, was not eternal.[33] The emancipation of the Jews that accompanied the French conquest surely played an important role, as did, to an even greater extent, the well-known and well-analyzed fact that the "bourgeois revolution" had, in Germany, come from above, and even, in the case of Bismarck, had been the work of the prince himself.[34] The career of military officer was, in fact if not in law, barred to Jews living in German lands. Under the Second Empire, if no Jews went beyond the rank of colonel—as they would do under the Third Republic—at least they were present, and their promotions, up to this rank, took place as a matter of course.[35]

For French Jews, the July Monarchy and the Second Empire tangibly were a period of tremendous upward social mobility. Undoubtedly, this rise in individuals' fortunes came at a cost: the dislocation of the traditional community. For example, it was during this period that the ghettos of the Pope's Jews were dissolved.[36] Ghetto communities hardly existed any more, except by virtue of the debts with which they were burdened, since their dispersed members were still obliged to pay them off. Alsatian Judaism alone survived as a villager Judaism.

In what political direction did the Jews then head? And how is one to explain the fact that, in no way persecuted by the powers that be, they became so numerous among the ranks of the republican opposition? As is true, within certain limits, of both Jews and Protestants, a minority has no other political choices but to enlist itself in the service of the prince (or of the ruling caste) or to struggle for ever more equality. In an overwhelmingly Catholic country like France, the Jews certainly played the first card—this was the great age of the Rothschilds—but most members of the two generations that followed the emancipation chose to present themselves as, and indeed to become, abstract citizens.

Allow me to choose a few concrete examples from my family's own tradition and archives. On May 7, 1843, the *Écho du Midi* published a letter from my great-great-grandfather, Moses (the Younger) Vidal-Naquet (1797–1874), a nephew of one of the delegates to the "assembly of notables" called by the emperor in 1806, a wine merchant from Montpellier where the Jews numbered, according to the 1841 census, only ninety-two persons, and a commissioner delegated by the consistory of Marseilles to the Department of Hérault. The occasion for his letter was that this Legitimist newspaper had taken a position against a Jewish candidate, the banker Bénédict Fould, for a by-election. On April 30, the newspaper had written: "Christians and Catholics, we cannot allow the children of Christ to choose a Jew for their representative and place under his care the task of legislating on the existence of the clergy and the Christian religion." Part of his response reads as follows: "At the temple or at church, one is a Jew or a Christian; in the acts of political life, one must above all be French. In fulfilling one's duty as a citizen, one can be at peace with one's conscience; the Jew who works for the good of a religion not his own is no more an apostate than the Christian who votes each year the maintenance costs of the Israelite religion."[37] Moses the Younger, it goes without saying, was religious; he sometimes studded his letters to his children with biblical passages written in Hebraic characters, but he could just as well, as in the letter I just cited, invoke the name of "the king of the French" while pleading his cause. In the next generation, the spirit of equality went much further. My great-grandfather, Jules Vidal-Naquet (1831–1889), son of Moses and of Numette Alphandéry, was openly republican. On December 3, 1851, he was arrested with his brother Gustave. Most of the Jews of Hérault had, moreover, shown themselves to be ardently republican. Rallying to the cause, Moses had run as an (unsuccessful) republican candidate in the municipal elections.[38] A republican under the Empire, a victim of the General Security law of 1858, Jules Vidal-Naquet, an often unlucky businessman, came into his own at the moment of the Empire's fall. His family became that of a republican notable. His brother-in-law, Eugène Lisbonne, who had been arrested with him on December 3, 1851, was named prefect for Hérault. He himself returned to Paris to serve his tour of duty in the National Guard.

On October 20, 1870, he wrote, via balloon, to his children who had stayed behind with their mother in Montpellier: "These events . . . show you, too, that I really was right to detest this race of kings and emperors who are the cause of all our misfortunes." He was a Freemason because that was the best way for him to express his ideal of the abstract citizen. None of his pre-1870 letters makes the slightest allusions to manifestations of anti-Semitism—which does not mean, of course, that judeophobia did not exist. It would be later, in the 1880s, that he engaged in polemics with those who were enemies of the Jews.[39]

Let us take a second example, very different from the first yet quite similar. The Reinach family—Paris-based but of German origin and, further back, Swiss—was destined for intellectual and republican glory in the period after 1870.[40] But let us get a grasp of Reinach family life before the Reinachs attained their glory. In the France of the Second Empire, there were few foreign Jews living in this country, and their requests for naturalization were generally greeted rather favorably. Some of these foreign Jews even became members of the French Academy of Inscriptions and Belles Lettres. James de Rothschild (1792–1868) himself felt no need to become naturalized. His sons were themselves to become French.[41]

Hermann-Joseph Reinach was born in Frankfurt in 1814 and moved to France in 1845, where he became a banker and railroad administrator. Along with the economist Frédéric Bastiat and the publicist Hippolyte Castille, he founded an inexpensive daily, *La République française*, whose title was taken up, after the fall of the Empire, by Gambetta. His fortune made, he retired from business in 1867. It is not in this capacity that he interests us here, but as patriot and educator. A passionate Francophile and a determined republican, he would not consent to make a request for naturalization until the fall of the Empire. An atheist, too, he was nonetheless possessed of a very strong sense of community. Neither he nor his sons contracted mixed marriages. Such marriages occurred only in the generation of his grandchildren. The three sons of Hermann-Joseph and of Julie Buding—Joseph (1856–1921), Salomon (1858–1932), and Théodore (1860–1928)—all went on to pursue exceptional careers, the first in journalism and politics, the two others in archaeology, the history of religions, and the study of Antiquity. The sons' behavior was, by the father's volition, an absolute model of scholarly excellence, as is often observed in minority groups who consider scholarly excellence to be a tool for social recognition. Hermann did not place his sons in high school. "He found its scholarly methods ineffective, since not enough time was left for relaxation and artistic initiative. Moreover, the university was under the Empire's command, and there would be no question of contaminating these young republican shoots with the evil imperialist weed."[42] When, finally, they entered Condorcet High School, starting in 1871, these young prodigies were called, after the initials of their first names, the *Je-Sais-Tout* [Know-It-All] brothers. The Republic opened wide their future. "The Reinach brothers proved that regenerated Jews could do as well as, and even better than, other French people. . . . Each success, like each failure, of a Jew had its effects on the entire community."[43]

But already in 1870, the French Jews found themselves faced with another question. Could they remain among their own kind? The era's horizons were liberal and imperial. How were these twin characteristics reflected beyond French borders, in the French Jews' relations with foreign Jews—those of neighboring countries, those of distant countries, and those who lived beyond the seas?

At the date we are now at in our discussion, the Jews of eastern Europe were not yet an issue. Certainly, the immense migratory movement that was their lot in the second half of the nineteenth and the beginning of the twentieth century was already under way, but it was affecting Vienna[44] and Berlin, not Paris, at that time. And while the German Jews were taking the path of emigration after the failure of 1848, it was toward America, where they constituted the great majority of Jewish immigrants, that they headed.[45]

It was in 1860 that the parents of Sigmund Freud, himself born in 1856, left Freiburg in Moravia for Vienna, bringing with them humiliating memories. The fate of these Jews—who were, and by far, the majority of the Jewish people living in Europe—did not yet have any significant repercussions on the fate of French Jews.

In this symbolic year of 1870, two events do indeed merit being taken as symbolic. On October 24, 1870, a decree of the governmental delegation at Tours, headed by Gambetta, imposed citizenship and French civil status upon forty thousand Algerian Jews,[46] not all of whom wanted it. The decree was made upon the initiative of Adolphe Crémieux, a former '48er, president since 1863 of the Universal Israelite Alliance, and a minister in the Government of National Defense. In reality, this question had already been debated for at least ten years and the Administration of the Second Empire had studied this possibility very closely.[47]

In the minds of several of its proponents, this act of naturalization was a first step, the second one being the naturalization of the entire Muslim group. The reality was and would be quite different. The Jews in Algeria were a humiliated minority who, in very great numbers, would choose to look to the colonial powers for support. Here we have a classic process, whether colonization be direct or indirect. The Christians in Lebanon, the

Armenians, the Greeks, and the Jews in the Ottoman Empire, and the Copts and the Jews in Egypt also all played, to different degrees and with varying levels of success, this profitable and dangerous game. The colonial power had every interest in leaning on such minorities for support and quite logically it did so.

It was on May 17, 1860, that the Universal Israelite Alliance was founded at the domicile of the Alsatian wholesale merchant Charles Netter. The Alliance brought together and was led by Liberals, among them a not very conformist rabbi, Élie-Aristide Astruc. The organizational committee included Alsatians, "Portuguese," and Jews from Avignon.[48] The founding manifesto, addressed to "Israelites" of all countries, was a manifesto of a universal France: "If you do indeed believe that the influence of the principles of 1789 is all-powerful in the world, that the resulting law is a law of justice, that it is to be desired that its spirit penetrate everywhere, that the example of the countries that enjoy absolute religious equality is a force; if you believe all these things, Israelites of the entire world, come, listen to our appeal, join, add your support!" Almost everywhere the Alliance founded French schools, some of which are still in operation. One of its most lasting creations, it turns out, was located in Palestine. Not that the Alliance was Zionist or pre-Zionist—one of the rare pre-Zionists in the West had been the German socialist and "Jewish patriot" Moses Hess—but it thought, like the emancipators of the end of the eighteenth century and the socialists of the twentieth, that a return to the land might "normalize" or "regenerate" the Jews. It was in this spirit that Charles Netter founded in 1870, near Jaffa, the farm-school of Mikve Israel (Hope of Israel) in order to reteach or teach agricultural work to local Jewish communities, an infinitesimal minority. Hebraized, the Mikve Israel farm was to become one of the most effective centers of Jewish colonization in Palestine.

As I have tried to show, the two dates that have served as endpoints for Jacob Katz's study were well chosen. The end of the eighteenth century and the beginning of the nineteenth (taking into account the Napoleonic reaction to revolutionary emancipation) definitely initiated a decisive "turning point,"[49] the one that gave birth to Franco-Judaism. When, toward the end of the Age of Enlightenment, a Jewish artisan dressed up, on a Hanukkah lamp, characters from the Maccabean epic as soldiers of the Revolution,[50] he was laying the foundations for an ideology that would continue throughout the nineteenth century and even beyond. The year 1870 opens another era: that of the exportation, outside Europe, of the revolutionary model for assimilating the Jews; that, too, of a return in force of anti-Semitism, with a particularly virulent outbreak occurring during the 1880s and 1890s—not only in France but still more in the rest of Europe, and even in Africa. The year 1870 represented, as I said, pretty much the high point of tranquil assimilation, of the "impassioned attempt to *normalize* the Jewish problem"[51] which was characteristic of France but which extended more or less to all of western Europe.

It is certainly not proper, when writing history, to foretell the future, but it is also not possible to think that, after 1870, there no longer was a Jewish question.

In a country like England, where ideological passions are less violent or at least different from those that express themselves in France or in Germany and where a unified synagogue was established in 1870, the course of assimilation from Cromwell down to our own times can be traced as if it were an almost mechanical process. The integration of assimilated communities was regularly thrown back into question by the arrival of new immigrants who had been driven there by successive waves of persecution on the Continent. These new immigrants at first expressed their indignation at the permissiveness of the local Jewry, but then they too became assimilated—sometimes to the point of converting, sometimes to the point of joining the House of Lords—until a new wave of immigrants arrived.[52]

That said, one must add that it is not possible, when thinking about these questions, to believe that simple automatic processes were involved. That would be unworthy of the subject Jacob Katz has treated and of the book he has written. There always comes a moment when the values of a historian show through the history he has written. Let us state things frankly: one will not write the same book if one judges, as a former prime minister of Israel said one day, that any Jew who contracts a mixed marriage adds one more unit to the six million victims of Nazism, or if one judges, on the contrary, that national or religious minorities are doomed to extinction and that only large groups have the right to exist.

It hardly needs to be said that I share neither one of these extreme opinions and that, while my own values are resolutely universalist and while I know that cultures are not eternal, as a historian and as a human being I cannot but rejoice at their external and internal diversity, their *poikilia*, as one says in Greek. Might I be permitted to add that, while I know that many crimes have been committed "in the name of liberty" and of other values dear to me, crimes committed in the name of national and religious exclusivism are also inscribed in the register of horrors?

Indeed, what is at stake in this historical debate is not the Jewish question alone, the Jewish Diaspora alone. A rather analogous problem is raised, for example, in the case of the Armenians. "The Armenians, whose inner psyche has been fashioned by the memorization of centuries of violence, threats, collective catastrophes, have buttressed themselves against this form of death that is proposed to them. Is not assimilation—called in Armenian 'dissolution'—the slow death of a body, the absorption of each of its molecules by molecules of another body?"[53] If it is granted that, for at least two centuries, the forward drives toward universalism have been followed by periods dominated by a pulling back and even a national narcissism, the present period, with its exaltation of more or less imaginary "roots"—some of which result from out-and-out frauds—and with its bouts of nationalistic fever, too rarely followed by healthy reflections on "national disenchantment,"[54] does not particularly lend itself to an understanding of why French Jews, at least, have in the end accepted rather easily the assimilation process that has been extended to them.

To understand the stakes involved in the debate as they are posed today, we must in reality reexamine two questions that themselves date back more than two centuries: the question of the Enlightenment and the question of the nation. "Do the figures of the Enlightenment drive one to crime?" The question has been posed in an ironic fashion with respect to the Marquis de Sade and to the relationship between his thought and that of Baron d'Holbach.[55] It has often been asked these past few years whether the figures of the Enlightenment, formerly sacralized in a naive way, have not been at the origin of racist anthropology and modern anti-Semitism.[56]

It seems to me that when one speaks of racism and anti-Semitism in the Age of Enlightenment, in reality several separate issues are being conflated. It is difficult, in the case of a discipline that had not yet become scientific, to speak of the "anthropology" of Enlightenment philosophers as a unified and coherent discourse. One can, of course, assemble a rather numerous set of texts that serve to justify, for example, the enslavement of blacks, but texts tending in the opposite direction also exist, and the latter have served and will continue to serve the opposite cause.[57] In any case, the racial hierarchy between "Aryans" and "Semites" is an invention not of the Age of Enlightenment but of the following era. One can build up a much more solid case for the "anti-Semitism" of the Enlightenment philosophers, for there are innumerable texts that call for the Jews to be held in contempt or that confirm the feelings of contempt they had already inspired.[58] These questions must nevertheless be arranged in series. The basic aim of the *philosophes* was not to strike at real Jews but to challenge, for purposes of "écraser l'infâme," a conception of history that made of Israel, of the Israel that preceded the Incarnation, the pivot of world history. In their view, this conception represented the weak point of Christian history and anthropology, the link that could most easily be broken. Also, they looked for and found all sorts of substitutes for the Jews in their role as vector of universal history: imaginary substitutes such as Plato's Atlantis, far-off substitutes such as India and China, contemporary substitutes like modern-day nations that were thenceforth assigned the dangerous role of "theophoric" people.[59]

Does it follow that such anti-Judaism, which is inseparable from the upheavals of the space and time characteristic of the Enlightenment philosophers, was also a form of anti-Semitism in the modern sense of the word? Did it lead to contempt for the Jews and to their proscription? Of course, there can be a coincidence, within one and the same philosopher, between a rejection of Judeocentrism and hatred of the Jews such as they were known in the philosopher's own time: this was patently the case with Voltaire.[60] Things become serious on the level of reality when philosophy claims to *separate* Israel from its Christian descendants instead of holding both in equal contempt. That a whole part of German philosophy at the turn of these two centuries, from Kant to Fichte and Hegel, gave in to this neo-Marcionite, or Gnostic, temptation hardly raises any doubts at all. Instead, it raises anew the problem of the rootedness of anti-Semitism in Germany.[61] Nevertheless, it remains the case that Kant's work opens up a universalism in moral law that could be turned against these premises.

The emancipation of the Jews in western Europe and, first of all, in France surely constituted a break. A break with the "sweet life"? With the warmth that comes from being among one's own kind? Let us not idealize the ghetto any more than the *shtetl*—the Jewish village of Poland. What we know of the Jewish quarter of Metz or of the "pit" in Carpentras shows us a stifling and stifled life under the reign of meddlesome and oppressive oligarchies. As soon as it became possible to leave the ghetto, a process that had more than just begun under Louis XVI, the Jews voted "with their feet," leaving the ghetto in massive numbers.

There remains the crucial, and still contemporary, question of the kind of national model being imposed upon them. One cannot ask more of an era than it can provide. The model of 1791 was addressed, it is true, to individuals, not to communities—or, as was said in Bordeaux and Bayonne, to the "nations." Jews were refused the possibility of a collective existence,[62] as the Le Chapelier law of June 14, 1791, prohibited both workers and bosses from forming "coalitions." As early as the Constitution of 1791, which was another legacy of the Enlightenment, the kingdom was said to be "one and indivisible." It nevertheless remains the case—in an example then without parallel on the planet—that revolutionary France recognized the French citizenship of all those who normally resided on its soil. A legacy of Rousseau[63] much more than of Voltaire, this model of a national contract was the broadest one hitherto proposed to men. During the same era, the "New Jerusalem" founded on the other side of the Atlantic excluded as well as included. The excluded were inhabitants of its soil, men born on its soil, Indians and blacks.[64] And yet—how can one hide it?—the sequels to this initial fanfare were less auspicious. As has rightly been observed, "It was the French Revolution that invented the two [extreme] responses to the Jewish question: the individual solution and the national solution. Naturally, it preferred the first, because revolutionary thinking could not imagine a better path to the 'regeneration' of the Jews than individual success within the model nation, namely, France. At the same time, however, the Revolution spawned the notion that the emancipation of the Jews—like that of any oppressed people—could assume a collective or national form."[65] When, however, the idea of the "Grande Nation" spread throughout Europe, it became, little by little, a complicated and degraded idea, with exclusions overtaking inclusions. The Jewish national movement itself was constituted only at the end of this process, in the worst of cultural and political environments, at the point where it was being called upon to disappear or be expatriated, with the consequences we can see today.

Of course, the fine tome of Jacob Katz, to whom I now yield, only recounts the beginning of this long history. May he give his readers, as he has given me, the chance to meditate on the Jewish laceration that lies at the heart of the history of Europe.

6 | Dreyfus in the Affair and in History

For Pierre Sorlin

ive Years of My Life is the account, published by Alfred Dreyfus in May 1901, of the years between Monday, October 15, 1894, the date of his arrest, and Wednesday, September 20, 1899, the date of his liberation. During these five years, he says, he was "cut off from the world of the living." In *The First Circle*, Solzhenitsyn describes the adventure of a Soviet diplomat, a privileged member of the regime who, in a few hours' time, crossed the world that separated his lovely apartment and his expensive clothes from the nudity of a cell and a prisoner. In a few weeks' time, Dreyfus, a wealthy officer of the French General Staff, found himself under arrest, interrogated by a commanding officer in the full bloom of delirium, locked up, judged blindly, degraded in front of the troops, shipped off—in the wake of a law made for him alone—to the islands off Guiana, and placed first in a prison with other convicts on the Île Royale, and then in a prison set aside just for him and his silent guards: Devil's Island.

The year is 1895. We are in the midst of the Liberal era, and of this Liberalism a few traces nevertheless remained. Dreyfus's property was not confiscated. Sometimes he received, though not always, some books, reviews, and mail, though, starting in March 1897, this mail was recopied

---

Preface to the republication of Alfred Dreyfus's *Cinq Années de ma vie (1894–1899)* (Paris: Maspero, 1982; rpt., Paris: Découverte, 1994). Reprinted in *JMP*, pp. 265–307. [T/E: An English translation of Dreyfus's book is still available—without, of course, Vidal-Naquet's preface—as *Five Years of My Life, 1894–1899* (New York: Peebles Press, 1977). The original translation, by James Mortimor, was published in New York in 1901 by McClure, Phillips.]

mail. The authorities lived in terror of a cryptographic system. Sometimes, with supreme ease, he was able to send telegrams. He knew nothing of the Affair until November 16, 1898. He was to discover it in earnest only during the trial at Rennes, in July 1899.

Suddenly, for almost two months running, beginning September 6, 1896, he was placed at night in irons. This was indeed torture, the torture of the "double shackles." It was a consequence of the Affair: his brother Mathieu, wanting to draw attention to Alfred, had launched the "canard," the false news, of his escape.

We learn from another source[1] the text of the letter he then addressed to the High Commandant of the Îles du Salut: "I have just been informed that I am to be placed at night in irons. I would be very grateful if you could tell me what infraction I have committed. Since I have been here, I believe I have strictly adhered to all regulations, all orders." An impeccable prisoner. No doubt about it.

And yet, when this model prisoner spoke of what he suffered, of what he alone suffered (let us recall that Cayenne then merited its name of "the dry guillotine" but also remember that Dreyfus was at the margin of this prison), it is little to say that his account is objective. Here, for example, is what top colonial inspector Picquié wrote on January 20, 1896, *before* the "double shackles": "The crime of this man is great. But its expiation is also great. How long will it last? It is likely that, after the tenacious hopes of the first few days, the isolation, the restiveness, the vain expectations, and the sense of emptiness surrounding him growing stronger day after day will win out over the resignation and perhaps also the health of the guilty party. The climate of Guiana will then find an easy victim."[2]

An objective account? Something more must be said. Dreyfus displayed more than just a bit of the mathematician and the rationalist. Julien Benda, a young "Byzantine" intellectual who was a Dreyfusard and who knew Dreyfus following his release from prison, recounts a visit he made in Switzerland to the author of *Five Years of My Life*. Two women were departing as Benda arrived, and Dreyfus remarked: "I don't mind that these ladies are leaving. They always talk to me about my case from a sentimental point of view. . . . From that point of view, once it has been said that I suffered a great deal and that I was brave to complain, everything has been said. . . . What I like to do is to talk about it from the scientific point of view, to seek the causes, etc."[3] And Benda adds, apropos, as a matter of fact, of this very book: "Faced with this—one might say, pathological—degree of objectivity, one cannot avoid thinking of the portraits certain thinkers sketch of the ideal objective man." As for the attitude of indignation his defenders wanted him to adopt at Rennes, "he said he was not capable of it, and declared that any effort on his part to do so would just make people laugh."[4] The remark is perfectly apt. When Dreyfus raised his voice, it became forced. He was indeed the "objective man," or, if you will, the abstract citizen.

This attitude was not, in his case, reserved exclusively for the public at large. I have before me some unpublished documents:[5] the notes Dreyfus took at Rennes, in July and August 1899, as commentary on the charges—those of 1894, which were being reused—and various hostile depositions that figured in the investigative records of the French Supreme Court. The response to Commandant Ormescheville's prosecutor's report is particularly striking. Like a Latin text with a facing line-by-line translation, Dreyfus notes at left the accusations, on the right the responses. One example: at left, "Captain Dreyfus underwent a long interrogation before an officer of the judicial police; his responses included a good number of contradictions, to say nothing more. Among them, some are particularly interesting to point out here, notably the one he made at the moment of his arrest, on October 15, last, when he was being searched; he said: 'Take my keys, open up everything you want at my home, you will find nothing.'"The response is not without its humor: "It is regrettable that the reporter did not point out all these alleged contradictions; he missed a good opportunity to tell us 'what more he had to say.' Captain Dreyfus, who had just been brutally searched, also threw his keys in the face of his accusers, saying to them: 'Go on, take my keys, too, open up everything you want at my home, I am innocent.' Now, that is what happened and nothing, indeed, was found. The reporter calls that a contradiction! Go figure."[6] "Objectivity" is also the choice whether to talk or to remain silent. Dreyfus tells us, very briefly, what he was reading, because Joseph Reinach had suggested to him that this "might interest the readers."[7]

At the time he was accused, he was reproached for keeping mistresses. Lieutenant Colonel Du Paty de Clam solemnly explained to Mathieu Dreyfus that a man who might be capable of cheating on his wife was also liable to deceive his country.[8] Dreyfus did not recopy Commandant Ormescheville's report on this delicate subject. He limited himself to inscribing in the left-hand column: "Private conduct, etc." and explained at right, with a few details, that he had broken off his "dubious" liaisons with women before his marriage.

His silence about women is consistent with bourgeois morality. More peculiar, given the context of the Affair, is Dreyfus's total silence about his belonging to or his refusal to belong to the Jewish tradition. Judaism is present in these pages as something neither positive nor negative. Anti-Semitism is itself absent therefrom. There is nothing out of the ordinary about this if we are talking about the 1894 trial: officially, Dreyfus was convicted of treason just as anyone, Jewish or not, who had turned over secret documents would have been. But Dreyfus then agreed to "play" the traitor and did not become indignant, for example, at the insults and blows that greeted him at La Rochelle. He did not want to be a Jewish vic-tim, and when he describes the scene of his military degradation, he does not mention the anti-Semitic insults reported by all witnesses. In his response to Ormescheville, one allusion and one detail were unavoidable: at the time of the final exam at the War College, General Bonnefond sys-tematically awarded bad grades to "the Israelite officers . . . on account of their religion." Dreyfus recalls "that he was led to protest, in the name of the Israelite officers, to General De Dionne, who acknowledged the fact."

On the other hand, neither in his book nor elsewhere does Dreyfus allude to what had nonetheless been one of the premonitory signs of the Affair: *La Libre Parole*'s 1892 press campaign against Jewish officers of the French army and the series of deadly duels that it had provoked.[9]

Is all this surprising? Dreyfus does not recount the Affair, as, for exam-ple, his brother did. He does not retrace its history, as Joseph Reinach did. He gives us, on Dreyfus, the (discreet) testimony of Dreyfus. His values are those of his milieu and his social class.

The Dreyfuses were recent members of the bourgeoisie. Alfred's grandfather "was a poor Jewish merchant from the village of Rixheim in Alsace."[10] The father became a rich industrialist from Mulhouse. French patriotism, an attachment to the Republic, and secularism were widely held values in this milieu. While in prison at the Cherche-Midi facility, Dreyfus, his grandson informs me, asked that the Grand Rabbi Zadoc Kahn be allowed to visit him. This request was denied.[11] He does not mention this fact at all. Did he believe "vaguely in the great clock-maker"?[12] In *Five Years* he limits himself to referring to his December 3, 1895, diary quotation of Schopenhauer: "If God created the world, I would not want to be God." He compares himself, on April 22, 1895, to the martyrs of Christianity.

Dreyfus shared these "secular" values, moreover, with the great major-ity of Dreyfusards. A number of them—Clemenceau and Labori for example—harbored a hostility to Judaism as a religious tradition or even as a "race," a hostility that bordered on anti-Semitism.[13] Sincere Christians and religious Jews campaigned for Dreyfus. They were not very numer-ous. Among the letters received at the time of the Rennes retrial (a selection of which were published by Pierre Dreyfus, Alfred's son),[14] only one, that of Raoul Allier, a professor on the Faculty of Protestant Theology in Paris, alludes to specifically Jewish values.[15]

One of the first readers of *Five Years*, Bernard Lazare, certainly had a right to address this issue since he had been one of the very first Dreyfusards and the first organizer of the campaign for revision. In fact, he could not help but react to this silence. Bernard Lazare had himself lived the Affair as a Jew. He wrote to Dreyfus May 17, 1901: "Never shall I forget what I suffered in my Jewish skin the day of your military degradation, when you represented my martyred and insulted race." We know that Theodor Herzl had the same reaction. Bernard Lazare tried to convince Dreyfus: "You are more a Jew than you may think, with your incoercible hope, your faith in the best, your almost fatalistic resignation. This indestructible fund comes to you from your people; it is your people who have sustained you."[16] A lovely passage, no doubt, one which Alfred Dreyfus and his family thought best to publish neither at the time nor decades after the Affair. Was the addressee convinced? Do we ourselves find this argument altogether convincing?

Before including, as an appendix to his book, a series of letters from civilian and military authorities that testify above all to his inalterable confidence in the rulers of the Republic, Alfred Dreyfus ended his account with a very brief mention of the Rennes trial and its aftermath: the renewed conviction, with recognition of extenuating circumstances; the pardon, which was preceded by withdrawal of the petition for revision; and his affirmation of an unshakable will for justice.

Nothing is more natural than his discretion on this score. The trial before the Court-Martial of Paris, which led on December 22, 1894, to Dreyfus's conviction on charges of treason, to his "deportation in perpetuity within a fortified enclosure," and to his "military degradation," was, by 1901, half-forgotten ancient history. That trial had taken place in closed session. The Rennes trial (August 7–September 9, 1899) was, for over a month, the object of headlines and editorials in all the press. While it included closed sessions, most of the facts were discussed publicly. Two armies of witnesses squared off against each other, and the ridiculous verdict, which may be explained by the hesitations of the military judges (ten years of detention and the "extenuating circumstances"), was still lodged in everyone's memory. Having been advised on June 3, 1899, that his conviction had been set aside by the Supreme Court, Dreyfus certainly was not expecting an affront and a verdict of this sort. It was at Rennes, and not on Devil's Island, that the values he had lived for began to collapse. It was after Rennes that he found it necessary to become a civilian.

When he published his book in May 1901, Dreyfus stated that his will for justice was not an empty phrase. He kept his word; he spared no occasion at the end of 1899 and in 1900 to demand justice, and he continued to pursue the recovery of his civil rights until the solemn decision—preceded by so many hesitations, so many small acts of cowardice—announced by the French Supreme Court on July 12, 1906.

"It should be remembered," wrote Péguy, "that between the Dreyfus Affair itself and the second Dreyfus Affair, there was a long period of steady calm, silence, total solitude. One had no idea at all, during that whole time, if the Affair would restart; ever."[17] In fact, and without there being any need to speak of "the degradation of the mystical into the political," the release of Dreyfus brought the Affair to a close. Well before the amnesty became law on December 27, 1900, a de facto amnesty was applied to the criminals as well as to the protesters, to General Mercier as well as to Lieutenant-Colonel Picquart, to the man who drew up the charges as well as to the man who crafted the revision. Amnesty, after all, is an age-old way of establishing "forgetfulness in the city," as was the case, for example, in 403 B.C.E. when the democratic victors at Athens instituted an amnesty after regaining the upper hand over their fellow citizens.[18]

So this is a time-tested technique for the "appeasement of spirits," by acts or by words, in the aftermath of a civil war. Antiquity furnishes us with the model. The revolutionary struggles and the crises at the end of the eighteenth century and throughout the nineteenth century offered countless occasions for the application of this procedure. Under the Third Republic, the amnesty of the Communards, which was applied in several stages and completed in July 1881, was simply a more recent example in the wake of many others.

In the case of the law of December 27, 1900, which was already being applied on a de facto basis as early as September 1899, what occurred was somewhat different. Of course, this instance of applying the procedure of amnesty really did involve an effort to "forget" civil strife. But the law established a shocking symmetry between Mercier and Picquart. And as a matter of fact, Picquart's name only appeared for the sake of symmetry. Above all, it was a matter of amnestying the generals who were guilty of abuses dating back to 1894, when they knowingly convicted an accused man on the basis of evidence that was not presented to him. They were equally guilty of having transformed the General Staff into a machine for the manufacture of forgeries. Their amnesty was a foregone conclusion. It undoubtedly would still have been proposed by the Waldeck-Rousseau government even if Dreyfus had been acquitted at Rennes.

In this respect, the amnesty offered something new. What was new was not the impunity of the generals. After all, those who massacred the Communards needed no amnesty. What was new was that one felt the need to ratify this impunity by way of legislation. Thus did vice render homage to virtue.

In this emergency situation, the amnesty of 1900 actually became a precedent. With my apologies for making the following parenthetical digression, I propose that we examine what occurred at the end of the Algerian War. As early as the signing of the Evian Accords (March 18, 1962) and the referendum ratifying them (April 8), the Government adopted a twofold series of amnesty measures. On March 22 and April 14, in conformity with the Accords, it amnestied, first in Algeria, then at home, acts committed "within the context of the Algerian insurrection." On these same days it amnestied infractions "committed within the context of the operations for the maintenance of order directed against the Algerian insurrection," in other words, acts of torture and assassination. Two of these acts were at the time the object of an investigation by a civilian judge: the assassination of Maurice Audin, an assistant professor at the Faculty of Sciences in Algiers, a communist who had "disappeared" June 21, 1957, and the tortures inflicted, in 1960 at Algiers, upon a young girl, Djamila Boupacha. Even before the second amnesty officially was proclaimed, the Minister of the Army wrote (on April 11) to his colleague, the Minister of Justice, to ask for assurance that the amnesty really did entail the dismissal of these cases. In the case of Djamila Boupacha, who was still alive, he specified: "In this last affair, it would seem opportune for a judicial decision [of dismissal of the complaint of brutal mistreatment] to coincide with the release of the plaintiff." A fine example of symmetry that recalls the situation in 1899 at more than sixty years' distance.[19] Nevertheless, the parallel is not absolute. While General Mercier did pursue a political career as a senator, he saw his military career cut short. And the same thing went for most of his accomplices. Quite the contrary in the cases of Algerian War French Generals Massu and Bigeard . . .

Upon his own request, Dreyfus alone was excluded from this amnesty, but, except for this one detail, his protests, like those of Picquart, Zola, Reinach, and Clemenceau, were of no avail. These protests, moreover, varied in their virulence.[20] Waldeck-Rousseau was able to declare to the Chamber on May 22, 1900: "There is no more Dreyfus Affair." Evidently, he was right. Yet this does not mean that this movement running through the depths of French society for almost two years, which furnishes historians with a geological cross-section of that society,[21] simply disappeared. Quite the contrary. The Affair generated or helped to generate a full blossoming of the workers' movement as well as a movement among intellectuals: unions, philosophical societies, popular universities. As Madeleine Rebérioux wrote: "Nineteen-hundred was to be the great year of Dreyfusism, whose crisis would soon begin."[22]

Waldeck-Rousseau's government of "Republican Defense," which included the socialist Millerand, facilitated, at least negatively, this evolution of events, if only because it put an end to the "nationalist" agitation that, as the counterpart of "Dreyfusism," had found in the Affair what it needed to feed its disturbing delusions.[23] By an accident that really is not one, the anti-Semitic agitator Jules Guérin's "Fort Chabrol" was liquidated on September 20, 1899, the very day Dreyfus left the military prison at Rennes.

Lurking beneath the last page of Alfred Dreyfus's book is something that was left unsaid: a violent conflict was splitting the Dreyfusist movement in two, and it led, notably, in December 1900—that is to say, during the very time the book was being written—to a complete break between, on the one hand, Mathieu and Alfred Dreyfus and, on the other, two of their principal defenders: Colonel Picquart and Attorney Labori.[24]

The person of Alfred Dreyfus, who for so long stood beyond challenge, was now being (sometimes discreetly, sometimes harshly) held responsible for what certain Dreyfusards saw to be the abortion of the Affair. To be brief, Dreyfus was accused of putting an end to the Dreyfus Affair himself because he had accepted a pardon under suspicious circumstances.

It is not easy being a symbol. Isolated on Devil's Island, but alive and writing, Dreyfus was a perfect symbol. Present at Rennes, but "a living ball of flesh" (to use Barrès's phrase), Dreyfus, the usually mute auditor of his own trial, had already begun to disappoint some people; he was reproached for being neither a great orator like Jaurès nor a great actor like Antoine, both of whom also were present at Rennes.

The question of the pardon and of the part Dreyfus played therein was quite another affair, and it merits being treated in some detail. On the two wings of Dreyfusism—among the most moderate of the Revisionists as well as among the most radical—one witnesses the very same theme being employed on various occasions for what obviously were two completely different songs.

I spoke of "radicals" and "moderates." Léon Blum, in his *Souvenirs sur*

l'Affaire,[25] speaks of "revolutionaries" and "politicians." One would nevertheless be wrong to interpret the debate solely in terms of Right and Left,
an opposition that, on the whole, did not have very much significance in
relation to the Affair, at least until the end of the summer of 1898.[26] Certainly, Clemenceau's newspaper, *L'Aurore*, was situated to the left of *Le
Temps* or *Le Petit Parisien*, but was *La Petite République*, which was socialist
but nonetheless supportive of the Government, to the right of *L'Aurore*?
Many factors entered into the equation, including, for example, the fact
that among some of the most determined Dreyfusards a certain profes-
sionalization of their activism had taken place; in September 1899, when
the Affair ended, it was with a certain sense of anxiety that these Dreyfusards witnessed the disappearance of that which had given them a reason to live. As we know, certain opponents of the Algerian War experienced a similar sense of loss at the end of the war.

During the Rennes trial, two different legal temperaments clashed
head on: Edgar Demange, on the one hand, Fernand Labori (the early
friend who also was the hero in the Zola trial), on the other. Demange was
unquestionably a moderate. In his plea, he pushed the spirit of "connivance"[27] to the point of invoking any "doubts" that might have remained
in the minds of the military judges. Labori led a strategy of "rupture" with
the system. An extraordinary debater who loved to rake the generals over
the coals, Labori was, in political matters, a very pale centrist.
Clemenceau the radical, moreover, argued that he should not even be sent
to Rennes.[28] He agreed not to plead the case under pressure from certain
"political" Dreyfusards tied to governmental circles, and from a man who
resembled a "politician" so little as Bernard Lazare, while Joseph Reinach,
a centrist and a disciple of Gambetta, was, on the contrary, in favor of letting him plead the case.[29]

For certain people, and among them there unquestionably was a certain number of Jews, the concern that justice be rendered to this particular man outweighed the fight for justice in general. Yet others, and notably
Clemenceau, harbored an attitude that was in some sort "aesthetic," nay
abstract, which made the very person of Dreyfus disappear to the benefit
of the *Idea*, as was said at the time. Still, it must be understood that the
reactions people had were complex. One witnessed Joseph Reinach, a
character on whom have been pinned some of the worst memories of the
strategy of opportunism, deliver, in the name of the then-young Human
Rights League, a report on the case of a few anarchists who had been
deported to Devil's Island, a report, moreover, that served to secure their
release.[30]

The debate over what is improperly called Dreyfus's acceptance of the pardon, a debate that took place within the revisionist camp, was launched by both wings of the coalition. While certain themes made their appearance immediately, most of them developed much later on, even later than the publication of *Five Years of My Life* in fact.

Le Petit Parisien—like its rival, *Le Petit Journal*, whose editorial writer was the fanatic anti-Dreyfusard Ernest Judet—was then a daily with a circulation of more than a million copies. *Le Petit Parisien* played a role for the most moderate at the tail end of the campaign for revision, but ultimately it rallied to the cause. Its weight came not only from its circulation numbers but from the fact that it was directed by Jean Dupuy, the Minister of Agriculture in the Government of Republican Defense. As early as Sunday, September 10 (the sentence came down the ninth), it came out with the headline: "Respect the Sentence," and its editorial stated: "Yesterday, on the eve of the sentence of the military judges at Rennes, we once again proclaimed in advance that we would bow to their decision. To make their decision, they looked at everything, examined everything. They were aware of evidence of which we remained ignorant. Henceforth, one should consider the Rennes sentence as the legal truth and the end of this sad affair."

It was *Le Petit Parisien* that became the first in the revisionist press to suggest (though much later, on October 1, 1900) that, in withdrawing his petition for revision, which he had signed the very day of his conviction, Dreyfus had basically agreed to put an end to the Affair: "There is talk of resuming, at the end of the Fair,[31] this sad affair that has done so much harm to France, and certain persons have begun to blow on its dead ashes in order to try to rekindle the flame. It is fitting for us to explain our position here clearly in this regard. We consider the Dreyfus trial irrevocably to be over. It would no doubt be too much to say that, in withdrawing his petition for revision, the former captain has recognized his guilt and granted the justice of his conviction, but it would be just as contrary to the truth to claim that this withdrawal, which occurred with a view toward obtaining the pardon that had been requested by his family, did not constitute Dreyfus's acquiescence to the definitive closure of this question."[32]

The radical wing of Dreyfusism also firmly latched onto this accusation, but at an even later date. In *La Grande Revue*, which he directed, Fernand Labori wrote:

As soon as the defense of Dreyfus ceased to be pursued on the high ground, as soon as it was viewed and conducted as a personal [*par-*

ticulière] defense, as soon as the physical person of he who until then embodied an immaterial principle became for his friends, I was going to say for his partisan supporters, the basic concern, the Dreyfus Affair ceased to be a human and universal affair.

The Rennes days and the acceptance of the pardon were terribly decisive in this respect. In accepting his pardon, Alfred Dreyfus in no way, by near or far, recognized his guilt. For reasons that are not at all for me to judge, he preferred his immediate liberty to the heroic, uninterrupted continuation of the effort to obtain judicial rehabilitation. . . . He thereby behaved, however, as an independent and isolated being, not as a man enamored of humanity and conscious of the beauty of social duty: he acted as a pure individual, not as a member of the human collectivity in solidarity with all his kind. At the same stroke, whatever might have been the grandeur of the role he played, he no longer represents anything.[33]

One of those who had, in September 1899, shared the responsibility for the decision that had been made, Jaurès, responded to Labori.[34] After recalling his own hesitations, he added: "As great and impersonal as was the cause to which we had given ourselves, a human individual was involved who had suffered enough in all the fibers of his being, in his heart and in his flesh, so that his very life should not have become the immediate stakes in a new battle. He himself could accept this sort of truce without any loss. . . . History proceeds like nature, sometimes by a dazzling explosion of forces, sometimes by the silent and slow maturation of seeds. They are mistaken, those who believe this process of growth to be inert and sterile when it does not manifest its latent energies in the suddenness of thunder and the violence of lightning. May Labori be reassured. His brilliant and blazing action continues, in the secrecy of the covered furrow, to ripen the seeds of full justice."

Later still, in the weekly he was then editing, *Le Bloc*, on February 2, 1902, Clemenceau took his turn to go on the offensive, evoking the days of September 1899: "It was then that Messrs. Waldeck-Rousseau and Millerand, Dreyfusards-come-lately, appeared; they succeeded where Méline had failed and were able to stop the course of justice with the aid of the condemned party himself, along with that band of perjurers and forgers whom the house of Jesuits claimed to be above the law."[35]

Thus were the parameters of the debate defined. This debate cannot be settled as one might settle a debate over conscience. To understand better the course of events in September 1899, we must return to the days following the verdict, situating ourselves successively on three different levels. First, let us ask how the debate over the pardon—if, indeed, there really was a debate—was framed in the revisionist press.[36] Next, let us take a look at the negotiations that took place between the Dreyfusard leaders and Mathieu Dreyfus on the one hand and the Government on the other, examining, quite particularly, how the Government *presented* its policy to the Dreyfusards. Finally, let us endeavor to find out how those in power explained to themselves their own policy. It is on this last level that perhaps there is a bit of something new to be gleaned. Each one of these levels nonetheless represents a dimension of the truth.

In *Le Petit Parisien*, which we have already mentioned, the first pardon that might have been up for discussion was the proposal to dispense with the military degradation to which Dreyfus had once again been condemned. On the twelfth, the newspaper featured a reprint of a Havas dispatch from the previous day which noted that the judges themselves were making this request via the general commanding the Rennes military district. On September 14, the newspaper took the opportune occasion to feature an article on the glory of the army. That same day, it said that a "pardon would be the easiest way to close the matter and to provide a solution to all the judicial affairs that have been grafted onto the Dreyfus Affair." It announced, on September 21, at the same time and without much commentary, Dreyfus's pardon as well as his withdrawal of the petition for revision.

The idea of the pardon was launched elsewhere. In *Le Siècle*, a Liberal organ, the newspaper of Yves Guyot and Joseph Reinach, the latter headlined page one on the eleventh: "The Honor of France Must Be Redeemed." The pardon was *one* of the solutions proposed. Others were envisioned: a governmental petition to the Supreme Court, a trial aimed at "the really guilty parties, the false witnesses," which would entail a new revision. As for the pardon, it should be immediate: "Is it, furthermore, necessary to add that the pardon, dictated by sentiments of the most elementary humanity . . . will be accepted, by the martyr himself as well as by the friends of justice, only as a transitional measure."[37] On September 22, after the pardon was granted, Reinach entitled his article: "Verdict Torn Up," noting, " 'We are breathing more easily,' Labori writes me."

Without mentioning *Le Siècle*'s suggestion, *Le Temps* made the pardon idea its own. Its reaction to the verdict in the issue dated September 12 (which was published on the eleventh) came in the form of caricature: "What characterizes this decision is the fact that it is eminently nuanced." Had Dreyfus not received a "considerable amelioration of his physical fate and his moral position"? Hébrard's daily then went on to strike a serious note by recalling that the right to grant a pardon is absolute: "If, therefore, the president of the Republic thinks it his duty to sign a pardon for Drey-fus, no one would have any basis to criticize this sovereign decision. . . . This denouement would be achieved without any new agitation." It is really the Affair itself that one was talking about closing out. On Septem-ber 18, the newspaper could announce in the same breath the upcoming pardon and the opening of the proceedings of the High Court responsible for judging Déroulède along with a few civilian nationalists. The pardon signed, this newspaper could write (issue dated September 21): "The par-don was implicit throughout the Rennes decision. General Mercier gave us an inkling the other day of the same solution and he did not seem to see anything inconvenient about it."

"Cowardly Sentence" was the title of *La Petite République* of September 11, which appeared on the tenth. "Let speak the thunderbolt," wrote Jau-rès, the thunderbolt being Labori. The day before, in an article written at a time when he harbored no illusions concerning what the verdict would be, Jaurès had proclaimed at once the coming of the revolution and his support for the Government: "The moral and social consequences of a guilty verdict would be incalculable. They would create a state of revolu-tionary awareness that would not long hesitate before exploding in actual events. But a parry will have to be made in response to the most pressing matters. . . . Whatever might have been the weaknesses of the Govern-ment of Republican Defense, deceived and ill-served by several of its agents, all republicans, all socialists, all revolutionaries, even those whom it has so carelessly and so despicably struck out against, will have to rally round it." The same mixture was served up again the next day: "This time, I very much hope that the advice of the timid is going to be set aside. At this decisive hour, it would be a crime on our part to weaken, by the least reproach, the republican government. Its sole error was its failure to sus-pect the depths to which the wickedness of militarism would go. It would be unpardonable now if it failed to respond vigorously to the monstrous challenge that, through the Rennes judgment, the reactionary forces have launched against it."

But how was one to respond? On September 12, Gérault-Richard, commenting on the gesture of the judges who had asked that Dreyfus receive a pardon concerning his military degradation, wrote: "The execu-tioners are demanding a pardon," and he went still further: "One is ascrib-ing to the judges of the Court-Martial the intention to sign a petition for pardon in favor of their victim. What Dreyfus needs, however, is not a par-

don but 'reparations.'" He also commented severely upon the attitude of
Le Petit Parisien. On the fourteenth, for reasons I shall soon explain, an
about-face occurred. Gérault-Richard spoke of "pacification." Dreyfus's
pardon would constitute, certainly, a deal, but it also would be an act of
justice: "Monsieur Loubet will not stand for an innocent man being tor-
tured. He will give him back his freedom."[38]

On September 17, Jaurès offered a lyrical rendition of the impending
pardon: "You miserable and stammering jailers, ashamed of your work,
the gates will open in spite of you and captive justice will escape from
your hands." On September 20, the newspaper wrote that if the pardon
were signed, "we would without reservations congratulate the Government." The headline on the twenty-first, after Dreyfus's liberation, read:
"Justice Will Be Done." The same day, Galliffet launched his famous "General Order": "The incident is closed." "The incident remains open,"
responded Gérault-Richard on the twenty-third. This, obviously, was only
an affirmation of principle.

"Toward Victory" was the bold headline of *L'Aurore* on September 10.
"Do you know," wrote Clemenceau, "that with one more vote an acquittal would have been declared?" For a few days, the political line of *L'Aurore*
was clear: the Affair continues. "That's the denouement? Sorry, folks"
(September 11). At that time, Dreyfusards were still counting on the
Supreme Court. Émile Zola entitled "The Fifth Act" an article of September 12 in which he explained that what had just occurred was only the
fourth act.

Clemenceau was therefore planning to lead an extraordinarily brilliant
campaign—but without proposing any alternative to the Government of
Republican Defense and without directly reproaching in the least Dreyfus
and his family. At bottom, Clemenceau's article of September 13 said
nothing other than what Jaurès had already said, even if Clemenceau
expressed himself in scathing terms: "The present cabinet has been
accused of being the Government of acquittal. It has been preoccupied,
above all, with not meriting this title and it has succeeded without too
much difficulty. . . . This is not the time for recriminations. . . . Even if its
actions have principally been failures, this cabinet will at least have saved
us from a government of bandits." It is, he proclaims, undoubtedly "the
duty of the accused and of those who speak in his name" to exhaust all the
resources of the legal machinery. But what can one expect from a military
court of review? "An imbecilic law leaves it to military men to judge faults
committed by military men. It would be just as wise to ask the judges to
pronounce their opinion on the military strategy conducted at Metz or

Sedan in 1870. On the Metz and Sedan of Rennes, it is a general who will pronounce a decision,[39] thanks to the evidently imbecilic axiom that a general must be better versed in law than a colonel." There remained, it is true, the Supreme Court, "which will be obliged to say whether it suffices to put feathers on one's head and to disguise oneself as a Chinese general in order to have the right to destroy in man everything that justifies him." Yet, Clemenceau proposed no angle for approaching the Supreme Court.

In his furor, Clemenceau's sense of the aesthetic played a role. Evoking in the *Aurore* of September 14 the (averted) possibility of a second military degradation, Clemenceau set himself to imagining: "Well, if I could forget about the martyr for a minute, I would regret not having the lovely lesson afforded by a second parade. . . . It goes without saying, doesn't it, that one would go fetch Esterhazy for this festive occasion? It is he, after all, who, in the name of the French army, having sworn *on his honor* that Dreyfus wrote the uhlan letter and financed a procuress, tore off the buttons and broke the sword of this 'unworthy' officer. That would be a pretty sight. . . . And . . . Lauth on a pedestal, wearing the dazzling decoration of Galliffet, shining like the sun, would sharpen his teeth on Picquart's skull."[40] In the same article, Clemenceau denounced "the Pharisees of *Le Temps*" but had nothing else to propose. The *Aurore* of the seventeenth launched a new "petition for Dreyfus," underscoring the flagrant inadequacies of the pardon, which it nevertheless described as "entirely desirable."

On the eighteenth, Clemenceau launched a campaign against the amnesty, which he (rightly) judged would be the complement to the pardon: "They are thorough. Now they need the amnesty. Amnesty for them, of course. The innocent man himself will be contented with a dishonorable pardon." On the twentieth, it was Francis de Pressensé who spoke of the need to go further than the pardon ("The Pardon: And Afterward?"). The next day, on a full front page, *L'Aurore* announced the "Declaration of Captain Dreyfus"[41]—his rank ostensibly being restored to him; and on the twenty-second, Zola wrote publicly to Lucie Dreyfus: "And yet, this day is still a great day of victory and celebration." Finally, on September 24 Clemenceau had some harsh words to say. They enable us to reconstruct a summary of his thinking: "Dreyfus takes care of Dreyfus, which is good." He also provided some commentary on Galliffet's "General Order" ("The incident is closed"): "Galliffet bows before the pardon he proposed. He bows before himself. I really believe that he will be the only one to honor His Excellency with this mark of respect."

What happened in the meantime? I will not contrast here "appearances" to "reality"—the newspaper articles and the secret meetings pertain as much to one as to the other—but simply what was said and what was not said, which, moreover, we can never know in full. What materials do we have at our disposal? One handwritten account jotted down by Joseph Reinach in the heat of the moment, on September 13, when the pardon had still been decided upon only in principle;[42] the reminiscences of Mathieu Dreyfus, which were written down several years afterward, sometime previous to 1908;[43] finally, the historical presentation published by Reinach in 1905,[44] a more "dressed up" text than the narrative written in September 1899. It was through Reinach's book that the public at large learned in detail of the negotiations between the Dreyfusard leaders and the Waldeck-Rousseau government.[45]

How can we summarize these events, which consist of conversations among the Dreyfusards with the participation of Mathieu Dreyfus, discussions with Waldeck-Rousseau and Millerand, voyages, and decisions?

According to those who witnessed these events, originally the pardon was Reinach's idea. The latter wanted it to be immediate: "A pardon a month from now contains nothing but pity. Tomorrow, it is a resounding repudiation of the judgment." It was the job of Galliffet, as Minister of War, to take the initiative: "The military judgment, hardly yet handed down and before the ink has dried, will be torn up by the head of the army." Even Dreyfusards little inclined toward extremism, like Yves Guyot, were more than reticent. On the tenth at 5:00 P.M., in the offices of the *Radical*, there was an explosion: "Thunder from Jaurès, howls from Clemenceau, who cried: 'It is the end of the campaign, of the struggle, of the battle, the pardon will satisfy sensitive souls: we will lose all our troops.'" Reinach was immediately suspected of having "become the General Staff's man,"[46] an accusation that can very easily be explained in terms of the logic of ideological movements. Bernard Lazare and Victor Simond, director of *Le Radical*, supported Reinach.

On the morning of the eleventh, Mathieu Dreyfus arrived from Rennes and demanded that Reinach insist upon the matter with Waldeck-Rousseau. The physical and emotional state of Dreyfus required his immediate release. Waldeck-Rousseau received the Dreyfusard leader. As soon as the first word was spoken, he said "Yes." "For twenty-four hours, the same thought had obsessed him. Nevertheless, there were difficulties. . . . What will the army say? . . . 'It clearly is the Government smashing the Rennes sentence to pieces,' said the president of the Council of Ministers. 'Can't we wait a few weeks?'" Waldeck finally allowed himself to be convinced. He planned to go see Loubet and Millerand. He would hasten the convening of a court of review. Until the latter had given its confirmation, the sentence would not be definitive and pardon would not be possible.[47] "The measure would have finally been adopted without great trouble, except for the fact that Millerand's keen legal eye had revealed a difficulty that for a moment appeared insurmountable."[48] The Rennes judges had committed a legal error, for they had neglected to rule on the type of surveillance to which the convict should be subject after his punishment. The petition would therefore be admissible, but the judgment would be reversed, by a third Court-Martial, only on this one point—which would be disastrous. To this legal argument, Millerand added the following: "And the World's Fair? Isn't the Fair in danger?"[49] As Minister of Commerce, the Fair fell within Millerand's sphere of responsibilities.

These narrative accounts therefore present as *purely fortuitous* the need for Dreyfus to desist from pursuing his petition for appeal. The very principle of desistance (which gives the appearance of approval of the sentence) nevertheless created a scandal among the Dreyfusards: Jaurès, Clemenceau, Sigismond Lacroix, who met at 5:00 P.M. at *Le Radical*. Mathieu himself said, " 'No. Too bad. He will die in prison.' 'Oh, look who's talking,' cried Clemenceau."[50] Millerand then brought Mathieu and Reinach, who played the devil's advocates, to the ministry, where they were to be joined by Jaurès, Clemenceau, and Gérault-Richard. There, Clemenceau was extraordinarily violent in his words: "I could not care less about Dreyfus, let him be cut to bits, let him be devoured!"[51] Gérault-Richard concluded by saying: "The people will find that things have played out very well. They couldn't give a damn about a petition for appeal before the top brass."[52] Everyone ended up yielding, even Clemenceau, though with very ill will.[53] Millerand then gave his word that Dreyfus would be pardoned the following day, September 12, during the morning meeting of the Council of Ministers. Mathieu reached Rennes that night and saw his brother at 6:00 A.M. In turn, Alfred Dreyfus, too, yielded. Mathieu telephoned Millerand that the petition had been withdrawn. At the Council of Ministers, however, Loubet, still fearful of the army, refused to grant an immediate pardon. A medical excuse had to be provided. Mathieu released Millerand from his promise for the meantime. Professor Delbet was sent to Rennes. Everything having been taken care of, the pardon was signed following Galliffet's report to the council meeting on the nineteenth. The pardon was both medical and political. It was not a complete destruction of the Rennes sentence. For a moment, Reinach felt "suffocated" in the presence of Loubet's prudence: "What a pity not to understand the role of poetry in politics."[54]

Several ministers, notably Delcassé in Foreign Affairs, were thinking along the same lines as Loubet. A phrase from Picquart to Reinach summarizes rather well the sentiments of those who were most committed to an immediate pardon: "One should never count on the success of that which is conceived in beauty."[55] On the eighteenth, the High Court met to begin the trial of Déroulède and some of the other nationalist militants.

This, then, is what the "narrative" of the pardon teaches us. Yet it is now possible to go further—not in order to attain some impossible "total truth" but at least in order to perceive how Waldeck-Rousseau and Galliffet, the main officials responsible for preparing the pardon, prepared their decision and justified it to themselves.

For this purpose, our sources will be the papers of Waldeck-Rousseau, basically the letters he received from Galliffet, not all of which have remained unpublished (these documents are essential because it was with Galliffet that he dealt concerning the pardon question), along with his personal notes and a few official documents he has preserved.[56] Galliffet was to say later, in 1904, "I do not believe any Frenchman knows less about the Dreyfus Affair than do I."[57] And he claimed at that time that he was not sure if Dreyfus had solicited his pardon or not.[58] Back in 1899, after his entry into the Waldeck-Rousseau government, his behavior was cynical,[59] sometimes surprising, but, when all is said and done, coherent. His entry into the ministry had a precise signification: "It remains the case, of course," he wrote to the president of the council, "that we love, protect, and defend the army, while maintaining it strictly within its sphere of duties."[60]

The governmental participation of Galliffet, the gunman of the anti-Communard repression, was balanced by that of Millerand. The neutrality of the working class was assured by the latter minister, the neutrality of the army by the former. The army's neutrality nevertheless had its price: there would be no prosecutions against military men who had been compromised by the Affair, and the Minister himself was to remain totally neutral during the Rennes retrial. That is to say, he would give a free hand to the Government's commissioner in the case, and even more so to General Mercier. At this price, Galliffet hoped the military judges would acquit Dreyfus.

This Cabinet, which had passed for a Cabinet in favor of acquittal, nevertheless counted among its numbers only one sincere Dreyfusard, Millerand, and he was a last-minute or second-to-last-minute Dreyfusard. Its leader, however, would soon become convinced of Dreyfus's innocence.[61]

As the Rennes trial unfolded (August 8–September 9), these calculations fell apart. On September 7, Galliffet became aware of the situation and predicted conviction: "Attorney Labori might have ruined everything." Galliffet went on to conclude: "We must coolly place ourselves on the level of strict legality, imposing absolute subordination to the sentence."[62] The next day came his famous and often published[63] letter. Contrary to Waldeck-Rousseau, who had seriously envisaged annulling the Rennes sentence in case of a conviction, Galliffet intended to respect the sentence, failing which the Government would be in the following posture: "On one side, the entire army, the majority of the French (I am not speaking of deputies and senators), and all the agitators; on the other, the Cabinet, the Dreyfusards, and the foreigner."

Once the verdict was handed down, Galliffet increased his epistolary output, going so far, on this occasion, as to write several times a day to the president of the council, though we are not always able to determine the exact order of these letters. Three letters were addressed on September 11. They show that the kind of pardon he had in mind was simply a pardon concerning Dreyfus's military degradation. And yet, even this sort of limited pardon already implied that Dreyfus's petition would have had to be withdrawn. Attorney Demange played a key role in this affair: "The report and the decree have been prepared as concerns the pardon for the second military degradation, but this decree cannot be signed so long as Dreyfus does not withdraw his petition. This procedure, as presented by Attorney Demange, seems to me propitious, politic, and pacificatory, beyond all description; I beg[64] you, therefore, to obtain from Attorney Demange Dreyfus's consent to withdraw the petition at the earliest possible occasion and to inform us immediately when it has been done." And once again, at 11:15 A.M. the same day: "General Lucas writes me to ask that there not be a second execution. He did so only in response to the impressions he gathered from the military men at Rennes. One more reason for Attorney Demange to obtain from Dreyfus the key to pacification, the sooner the better."

Still on the same day, the situation evolved even further. Waldeck-Rousseau received Reinach. And speaking this time of a real pardon, Galliffet wrote to Waldeck-Rousseau: "May the heavens aid you so that your talent will provide you with the words that displease neither your friends nor the army. The latter is, I have told you, somewhat meticulous—and any phrase written by the Government that would leave Dreyfus a glimpse, *even in the future*, of anything other than a pardon, a pardon motivated by pity, would stir up tempests more dangerous than the one you are wishing to calm."

On the next day, Tuesday, in a letter written at 2:30 A.M., Galliffet seemed to be completely ignorant of the Millerand negotiations, the legal findings of the Minister of Commerce, and even of the decision made in principle by Dreyfus to withdraw his petition: "The court of review will not annul the judgment, be sure of it. It will render a complete judgment in one sitting. Therefore, without worrying any more about the withdrawal of the petition, the Government will have on Tuesday [the nineteenth?] its hands free to offer or propose a solution, after having taken the pulse of Lady public opinion."[65] On several more occasions, and until September 19, the date when the petition actually was withdrawn, Galliffet returned to the question without knowing whether or not the court of review would meet, but also *without ever posing* the problem raised by Millerand. Thus, on the thirteenth: "It is not possible to advance or postpone the court of review. Here is what my feeble common sense tells me. With a pardon coming after a (more than likely) rejection from the court of review, it will appear that we have wanted to await the action of this final military jurisdiction without seeking to shield Dreyfus from it. This thought is stupid in itself and consequently within the grasp of the greatest number of our citizens."

On the fifteenth, there was a change in discourse: he gave his approval for a doctor to go to Rennes, but he still did not know whether the pardon would be granted after the withdrawal of the petition or after the meeting of the court of review. On the nineteenth, after the council meeting, he agonized over the idea that the pardon might be signed before the withdrawal of the petition: "It would be original, to say the least. They are going to heap on us, and especially on me, a shower of abuse. I could not care less."[66]

All of that is not greatly coherent from a legal standpoint and it does not corroborate Reinach's narrative account. The levels do not overlap. In contrast, Galliffet was quite consistent on the political level. On Wednesday evening [September 13], he expressed his desire to take upon himself the responsibility for the pardon order. But it was for Waldeck to draft it and to write the report: "I ask you to include therein all the seasonings of the circumstances. I am speaking of those seasonings of a military character, such as respect for the judgments of military tribunals, etc. I firmly believe that in the view of the army—it is the army that most preoccupies us at the moment—this would make things much better. I think that the same goes for the bourgeoisie."

In a long letter of the seventeenth devoted to opinion within the army, he lays down the terms of the choice. The pardon must be inspired by a sense of pity. One must choose between the Dreyfusards and the army. The military men "are outraged by Reinach's articles in *Le Siècle* and those from *L'Aurore*. The latter [the Dreyfusards] will not be satisfied in any way and their support would not strengthen us. Better to have that of the army, around which the majority of the country would certainly rally." Before these same military men Galliffet had given his word that there would be an amnesty: "I told them very clearly that among the resolutions made by the Government there was the one that the sponge should be thrown in the ring concerning the entire past history of this affair."[67]

There was the army; there were also the Catholics. He writes on the morning of the sixteenth: "If Monsieur Delcassé said two words to the nuncio, the Catholics of France would be asked *by the pope* to line up on the side of those wishing for there to be a pardon. The nationalists would find that a bad joke indeed."[68]

All this served as preparation for the "General Order" of September 21, which was read to all regiments: "The incident is closed." Galliffet sent it to the president of the council—too late, however, for its publication to be blocked: "This order is inspired solely by the presidential decree and the report that preceded it. *Alea jacta est*. It will hand the army over to us. Be assured of it. It will give us, perhaps despite themselves, all the moderate Republicans. It will alienate from us those who have already decided to fight us." In picturesque terms, Galliffet offers his resignation: "One cartridge is left and I am a good target. Let you and your colleagues fire upon me. If interests higher than those of the army render it necessary. We are in a bloody mess, you and I."

And Waldeck-Rousseau? We do not know how he responded to Galliffet. Nevertheless, we do have one document of capital importance bearing on his political calculations: the notes he took, clearly intended for the speech he was to give September 12, 1899, to the Council of Ministers, where the principle of pardoning Dreyfus was going to be decided.[69]

The presentation is perfectly clear and articulate. One can "let nature run its course," that is to say, one could intervene on the legal level, so that the Rennes judgment would be overturned by the court of review, or the Government could file a petition of appeal, or it could appeal (to the Council of State?) by filing a request for remedy since the court had exceeded its powers. This implied the holding of other trials, that of Henry's widow against Reinach, the one brought against Zola, the one pending against Picquart, not to mention, naturally, the inevitable appearance of General Mercier before the High Court. And that would mean "six months of polemics and insults" and "as many Dreyfus trials"; even if the

Government refused to pursue the case, it would still be called upon to do so, by the Dreyfusards, that is.

The conclusion was clear: "Dreyfus alone can end the Dreyfus Affair, *by accepting the verdict*.[70] A pardon then [is] possible—and at the same time it *heralds the amnesty*." The two measures therefore are interconnected in a fundamental way. "The pardon," Waldeck says again, "comes only *after withdrawal*." It is a "declaration born of the verdict." The verdict, indeed, was divided. The pardon is a "new declaration," a "way of satisfying justice." Yet these formulas are equivocal. What is not equivocal is what then follows: "It is a remission of the penalty that settles [a] controversial question."

"Who will criticize it?," asks the president of the council. Not the Anti-Dreyfusards: "It is, for the most compromised, a pledge of amnesty." "And the others? Public opinion will not follow them if they criticize what the interested party and his family will themselves have accepted." Clemenceau and his friends are therefore beaten in advance. There certainly are abroad, in Milan, Rome, Brussels, Darmstadt, and Pest, protests against the verdict. The English press is particularly virulent. All these things will calm down if there is a withdrawal of the petition. Déroulède is in prison? If one wants "public opinion to turn toward defense" (of the Republic), "the revisionist agitation must cease."

All that is quite limpid. Millerand could sincerely ask Dreyfus to desist on account of a judicial error; Waldeck-Rousseau—just like Galliffet—made light of this small problem. What really was at issue, as Clemenceau had suspected, was to oblige Dreyfus, in desisting, to put an end to the Affair himself. What we have here is an almost perfect example of Machiavellian political practice.

Do we need any additional proof? In his letters to the president of the council, Galliffet had insisted that one take special care in drafting the pardon decree. On the morning of the nineteenth, he transmitted a text to the Guardian of the Seals for an opinion. "I believe that this copy is correct, but I cannot state so positively. The one that will be sent tomorrow evening to the *Journal Officiel* will be copied and reviewed with care by myself." On the thirteenth, he had explained to Waldeck-Rousseau that it was for the latter to draft, if not sign, the text. It was then that he spoke of the "seasonings of the circumstances." The text he sent to Waldeck-Rousseau,[71] which was paradoxically of a more liberal cast since it spoke purely and simply of "remission of the penalty" and "of the military degradation that is its consequence," was not retained. That text would seem to indicate, moreover, that the general was incapable of transforming into legal terminology the intentions he had revealed in his correspondence.

The president of the council also saved a corrected copy of the definitive text, the one that was sent to the *Journal Officiel*. It is a revealing document, because it expresses a conflict between two different conceptions of the pardon, the one for which Reinach and the Dreyfusards leaders had tried to win acceptance—an annulment, by the Government of the Republic, of the sentence—and the one that prevailed, at least if we are to judge by what is contained in the official language.[72]

Whereas the original text—which is different, moreover, from the one Galliffet had drafted—has: "Dreyfus (Alfred) is granted a total remission of his penalty of ten years' detention which was pronounced against him by judgment of the Court-Martial of Rennes," the definitive text, corrected in another hand, writes that Dreyfus was granted a "remission of the rest of the penalty." Undoubtedly, some of the changes that were made testify to a concern for legal exactitude.[73] Even so, it is difficult to mistake the signification of the correction I just mentioned. The five years at Devil's Island had been erased by the annulment of the 1894 adjudication. To remit "the rest of the penalty" is now to keep in the Rennes sentence the years at Devil's Island. While Dreyfus continued to be dispensed with the penalty of military degradation, the "legal incapacities" from which the draft of the decree relieved him remain implicit in the final text. It was not a question, therefore, of an erasure of his penalty, but, as the president of the council noted, of a "remission of the penalty."

Could Dreyfus and his family have refused to play the game? De jure, yes. De facto, it is not very clear how any resistance would have been possible. At most, Dreyfus might have held out for a few weeks, the time for the court of review, and then a new court-martial, to meet and settle the question anew. After that, as Reinach said to Mathieu Dreyfus at the Ministry of Commerce, "If your brother lives until January first, he will be pardoned anyway, in the same heap as three- or four-hundred common-law convicts."[74]

To be fair to Clemenceau, it must be said that, in his ferocious opposition to the pardon, he saw rather clearly what was coming: "The pardon was inevitable; the Government had to erase, by means of the immediate pardon, the effects of an iniquitous conviction. . . . It did so and I congratulate it for that. It did it badly, and I complain about that" (*L'Aurore*, September 24). Done badly? It was with horrendous cunning that the prisoner Dreyfus was manipulated into becoming himself the instrument for the termination of the Affair. Much later, a man with a perversely lucid mind came to understand this game rather well; here is what Georges Sorel wrote, in 1909, in *La Révolution dreyfusienne*: "Waldeck-Rousseau judged that the Dreyfusard agitation had to be brought to a close by pardoning Dreyfus, yet one still had to find a solution that spared the pride of the Revisionists and that did not seem too humiliating for the Court-Martial which had just handed down its conviction. It was decided that Dreyfus would not ask for the pardon but that he would nevertheless make an act of submission by withdrawing his petition before the court of review."[75] Indeed.

On the first page of his *Souvenirs sur l'Affaire*, Léon Blum describes a drawing by Félix Vallotton that had been published in *Le Cri de Paris* on October 1, 1899, a few days after the pardon.[76] Dreyfus, in civilian clothes, looking dark and serious, is seated; he holds near his right leg a young boy, his son Pierre, and on his left knee a young girl, his daughter Jeanne. The caption reads simply: "Father, a story [*une histoire*]!" Léon Blum comments: "A story? Captain Dreyfus was then incapable of telling his own." This phrase does him a little injustice. *Five Years of My Life* really is Captain Dreyfus's story, as he lived it, as it swept down upon him. It obviously is not *the* story, the *history* [*l'histoire*] of the Dreyfus Affair, the one its penultimate and remarkable historian called, cruelly, "The Affair Without Dreyfus."[77]

In French, the word *histoire* is wonderfully equivocal. It can designate everything from the nursery-rhyme story all the way to the most scholarly historical study, from the true tale to erudite or novelistic fiction. Thus was it then as it is in our time. Two "Epinal" or cartoonlike images clashed during the Affair: "Story of a Traitor" and "Story of an Innocent Man." The second is hardly less fictive than the first. One learns, for example, in the second that, unmasked, the "uhlan" Esterhazy quite naturally took refuge in Germany.[78] Actually, it was in England that he settled. The Affair had hardly ended when historians started to reflect on its import. Ernest Lavisse, the national historian[79] who entered the fray rather late and somewhat discreetly, reflected on the "two Frances lying within the same borders"—one the inheritor of the ancien régime, the other of the Revolution—whose clash, being a component of the national temperament, should be allowed to take place, while preventing it, however, from spilling over into civil war. All this is revealed by the Affair, for "The Affair is to the trial as the sea is to the ship: the former extends infinitely beyond the latter."[80]

A short time later, in May 1900, in the midst of municipal elections (which in Paris were to lead to a victory on the part of the nationalists), Gabriel Monod, director of the *Revue historique* and one of the very first Dreyfusards, gave a lecture on the "lessons of history":[81] "Have we not better understood the past in the light of the present, understood the Wars of Religion, the [Catholic] League, the Revolution, understood how, blinded by prejudice, peaceful crowds can become hateful and murderous, how noble passions, such as love for one's country, can, under the influence of false ideas, be perverted and led astray to the point of committing crimes? Have we not learned how one's milieu, one's education, one's political or religious affiliation can make minds that are, I would not say equally enlightened, but equally sincere see the same facts under different lights?"

Can one, however, separate the history from the historians? The Dreyfus Affair was indisputably a major turning point in French historiography.[82] Great works were published, others were planned: Charles Victor Langlois and Charles Seignobos's *Introduction aux études historiques* [Introduction to historical studies], a misunderstood breviary of positivism, was published in 1898. It was in the course of this same year that Jaurès, beaten in the elections, set to work on his *Histoire socialiste*, the first volume of which, *La Constituante*, appeared in 1901. Madeleine Rebérioux has spoken, apropos of the Affair, of a "historical magisterium."[83] What strikes historians of today is not only their forerunners' engagement in the battle, it is also the latter's break with their specializations—which were less rigid, it is true, than today—in the name of the universality of "method." Jaurès, author of the *Preuves*, was a professor of philosophy. All three Reinach brothers, for example, were to become involved in the struggle. Théodore was a Hellenist and a historian of Antiquity, Salomon an archaeologist and a historian of religions. Both would publish books and brochures. Joseph, in contrast, was the statesman in the family, but it was he who published the monumental *Histoire de l'Affaire Dreyfus*, which, despite its obvious weaknesses, remains today the major historical source-book on the Affair. Academic historians still refuse to recognize him as one of their "colleagues."[84] Also involved were medievalists: Arthur Giry and Gaston Paris, for example, played key roles. Their involvement may be explained in particular by the role expertise in handwriting played in the Affair, as this was a domain in which former students of the École des Chartes excelled. Yet the Affair was not simply a matter of handwriting, of attributing the famous memorandum to Dreyfus or to Esterhazy: "On August 30 [1898], Arthur Giry succeeded in the enormous scoop of exposing, on the basis of the best tested procedures of textual criticism, the 'Henry forgery,' on the very day the Colonel confessed."[85]

Yes, there were historians involved, but what kind of history did they write? Without any doubt, it was of the most traditional kind, yet one whose virtues we regularly rediscover, since it consists in establishing facts in the series, the concatenation in which they took place. The masterpiece in this domain is a short book by Jean Jaurès entitled *Les Preuves*, which began as a series of articles in *La Petite République*.[86] There are few proofs as convincing, for example, as Jaurès's dismantling of Dreyfus's alleged "confession"; this effort was an authentic work of an investigating magistrate, not only a demonstration of the forgery that was involved but a philological analysis of the way in which it made its appearance. He also proved to be more than a match for Henry's confessions, entitling one of his articles in *La Petite République*: "An Evident Fake." And yet, the same Jean Jaurès also was the initiator of the *Histoire socialiste*, an entirely different sort of history, which was as concerned with precision and exactitude as any other but which was capable, too, under the banner of Marx, Michelet, and Plutarch, of stirring up "long-range hopes and vast ideas."

Julien Benda, who stated that the Dreyfus Affair was for him "a sort of mold [in which he] poured all the great moral conflicts to which [he was] since then the witness"[87]—though that did not prevent him from swallowing the Rajk show trial[88]—recounts that, while meeting with Zola one day, it came to him "to say that the Affair set against each other men attracted to colors, parades, and uniforms and men attracted to the idea, artists and intellectuals." Zola replied, "as if crushed, 'Well, it's true, it is a conflict of temperaments that is at the bottom of this affair!' He had not yet caught sight of this fact. I left convinced that the true values of Dreyfusism were to be found elsewhere than in this brave man, who seemed to me good only for self-sacrifice."[89] Leaving aside what, in these formulas, belongs to the level of provocation or pertains to error pure and simple—the symbolists, for example, were Dreyfusards[90]—it remains the case that they allow us to pose a true problem. The Dreyfusards fought in the name of reason [*raison*]—"We will prevail because we are right [*Nous aurons raison parce que nous avons raison*]," said Anatole France—but the passage from the potential present to the real future presupposed nonrational actions: Zola's *J'accuse*, for example, was a brilliant punch in the face that did not always land squarely. Reason could not do without some troops and activists—and on this terrain, Jaurès's intuitions proved fertile.

But that is not all. Even during the crisis itself, the two adversaries related to each other through mimicry. At the 1894 trial, scarcely any effort was made to prove Dreyfus guilty. Henry's antics are typical in this regard. When Dreyfus demanded that Henry bring before him the man who had accused him [Dreyfus] of being a spy, "with a theatrical pose, and beating his breast, [Henry] added: 'When an officer has a secret in his head, he does not confide it even to his cap.' Then, turning toward me, he exclaimed: 'And there's the traitor.' " Handing over secret evidence to the judges in a deliberative chamber is quite the contrary of an attempt to establish proof.

Things proceeded in an entirely different manner at Rennes. There, the prosecuting generals, Mercier and Roget, tried to *demonstrate* guilt through the use of rational discourse. The expert Bertillon came to their aid with his paranoidal demonstration that Dreyfus's handwriting was like a secret fortress. And yet such paranoia was not visible to everyone, and the mimicry of reason proved more dangerous than delirium.

The same rule applies in the genre of history. I have noted elsewhere the extraordinary work of two Action Française activists who signed themselves "Henri Dutrait-Crozon." In a rational demonstration that lying is truth, they integrated into their mendacious discourses the greatest possible amount of true discourse.[91]

There was not, however, just mimicry. Occultism, spiritualism, spy mania, and myths of a huge plot existed in both camps. Mathieu Dreyfus, for example, consulted a clairvoyant from whom, he informs us, he learned many things. This took place, it is true, at the beginning of the Affair, in a climate of overwhelming isolation.[92] But beyond these zones of obscurity, there was above all the dazzling eruption of the press. No one has better described its role than Jean-Pierre Peter:

> Under these circumstances, where the authorities displayed such concern for secrecy and shadowy dealings, the press served as an open valve. Gossip, yarns, corroborated as well as baseless revelations, all these helped relieve one's desire to know, to know at any price, whatever it might be. With greater or lesser skill, with cunning or carelessness, given to fabulation but exciting people's passions in the best interests of those it was serving on both sides, the press ultimately assured on everyone's part a certain amount of participation in a debate that, behind closed doors, some were trying to avoid. But what deceptions were contained in this effervescence![93]

This statement itself shows that a modern history of people's mentalities, fabrications, and imaginaries would find in the Affair ample amounts of material.

Need we provide an example? One of the strangest episodes in the Affair is the story of what has been called the Imperial forgery, a docu-

ment "written" by Emperor Wilhelm II that, one way or another, is supposed to have implicated Dreyfus.[94] From 1894 until 1899 and for a short
time thereafter, this was a key piece of evidence in the Anti-Dreyfusard
arsenal of arguments. Jaurès, for example, devoted the last chapter of his
Preuves to what he calls "the ultrasecret file," this mysterious correspondence between the Jewish officer and the German emperor. Quite obviously, he had no difficulty demonstrating the palpable absurdity of this
version of Dreyfus's guilt. But even as the pardon was being granted, *La
Croix* was still explaining (September 21) that if the Dreyfusards were
accepting a pardon instead of acquittal without looking too sour about it,
this was because they now knew that there existed against their hero an
overpowering piece of evidence, a letter from Wilhelm II: "Send me as
soon as possible the aforementioned documents, make this scoundrel
Dreyfus hurry, signed Wilhem [*sic*]."

For some time to come, similar rumors continued to circulate,
although the leaders of the Anti-Dreyfusard party never publicly accepted
responsibility for them. Then, in this camp—or what was left of it—this
piece of "evidence" was abandoned. "Dutrait-Crozon," for example,
speaks of it as a legend.[95] In contrast, the revisionists, by which I mean the
artisans of the second revision, worked hard at hunting down this forgery
which, they suspected, might have been presented surreptitiously to the
Rennes judges. A good part of Dreyfus's *Souvenirs* [*The Dreyfus Case*] is
devoted to this investigation. Jaurès made it the central theme of his
speech of April 7 and 8, 1903, which marked, to use Péguy's phrase, a certain "parliamentary political resumption" of the Affair.

At the same moment, in another attempt to write, with the methods
of historical criticism, a history of this forgery, Raoul Allier, a professor
at the Faculty of Protestant Theology, published (first in *Le Siècle*, then in
book form) a study on "the annotated memorandum."[96] Allier's method
was the same as the one Jaurès had employed in the *Preuves*: "It was indispensable for one to place oneself before the Dreyfus Affair as before a
historical problem, no doubt a serious one, but similar to all other historical problems." And Allier made reference there to a famous forgery
that had fooled even such an expert as Salomon Reinach: The "tiara of
Saitaphernes."[97]

The question we should be posing, however, is the following: Did the
"Imperial forgery" actually exist? The question is not whether this document is a fake: the tales that have been concocted on this subject are really
of a burlesque quality. The question is whether the Imperial forgery ever
existed, like the Henry forgery or the Saitaphernes tiara did.[98]

To prove that this document, whose effects are undeniable, never existed is difficult and, in the end, impossible.[99] Its very existence is nevertheless suspect for all sorts of reasons. No one claims to have seen it, though many assert they had seen a man who had seen it. "The man who saw a man who saw the bear," however, is not a completely reliable witness. That it should have been mentioned with more or less discretion is one thing; that it existed at all is another. Nothing allows us, for example, to maintain that it was manufactured by Henry.

In reality, two forms of the legend of the Imperial forgery exist. According to the first, Wilhelm II was supposed to have exchanged letters directly with Dreyfus or letters with the prince of Münster, the ambassador to Paris, letters in which Dreyfus was named. According to the second, the memorandum—written, it was said, on onion-skin paper—was supposed to be the carbon copy of a memorandum on heavier paper, annotated by Wilhelm II himself.

The astonishing thing is that some strange symmetries exist between these two versions. For example, according to the already cited September 21, 1899, issue of La Croix, there existed, in addition to the original of the document, seven photographic reproductions. According to L'Intransigeant of December 13, 1897, the letters exchanged between Wilhelm II and Dreyfus, with Münster as intermediary, were eight in number, seven of which came from Dreyfus. The documents "had been photographed, and it is the photographs that were placed before the judges of the Court-Martial." Raoul Allier himself "wondered if the eight letters ever existed in the state of actual physical forgeries."[100]

The Imperial forgery is incontestably tied to another legend, that of the "historic night." The date of this phantom event has varied between December 12, 1894, and January 6, 1895. That "night," war almost broke out between France and Germany. General Mercier, Minister of War, stood ready to mobilize as he waited to find out whether or not the German ambassador, who had demanded to be received by Casimir-Perier, the president of the Republic, was going to ask for his passports. What could he have wanted to "reclaim" if not precisely the restitution of the annotated memorandum or letters from his master the emperor? But full justice has already been done to this legend.[101]

Of course, a document that is supposed to have been written and a "historic" night during which one awaited the outbreak of war do not exactly lie on the same level. The force of the annotated memorandum, the Imperial forgery, is that material existence has been attributed to it. Where, however, are we but in the realm of *telling*, a telling that has manifested its power and that thus gives to the Affair its full dimension?

What now remains for me to do is to explain in a few words why I have written this long preface. Some of the reasons why I have written it may appear evident to the reader. Other are less clear, so permit me to render them explicit.

The last person to preface Alfred Dreyfus's book was François Mauriac. He had entitled his text "The Dreyfus Affair as Seen by a Child,"[102] a child who had been "weighed down by the chains" of the anti-Semitic environment in which he grew up, though he later was to abandon its legacy. My own heritage clearly is different: no legend of the "Judeo-masonic syndicate," but on the contrary a *histoire*, in all the senses of the term, that was recounted to me during the Second World War, the *histoire* of a crime, of blindness, but also of victory and rehabilitation. It also happens that I have before me some "proof" of this long Dreyfusard tradition, a copy of *Cinq Années de ma vie* [*Five Years of My Life*] dedicated in 1901 to my great-uncle Emmanuel Vidal-Naquet (1859–1930), who at the time was the director the *Cote de la Bourse et de la banque* [Stock market and bank quotations], the *Cote Vidal*, a financial daily that had played a role in the struggles surrounding the Affair.

The Dreyfusard publisher at the time—the one, for example, who published in 1898 the *Lettres d'un innocent*, that is, Dreyfus's letters to his wife—was the bookseller P.-V. Stock. In 1938 Stock published his reminiscences of his activities, providing therein the following portrait of Emmanuel Vidal-Naquet: "He was an extraordinary Dreyfusard, to the point that his health really was gravely affected and that he had come down with an alarming case of nerves; he arrived at my house each evening after dinner, and, even with the store closed, he nevertheless remained there, keeping me up past midnight!"[103]

The same book reprints a letter from Emmanuel Vidal-Naquet, which evidently dates from May 1901:

> Dreyfus has sent me his book and—between you and me—I felt a pain in my heart not to see your name on the cover; no doubt, there are reasons for this . . . at least one must believe so. But it did something to me, all the same. I remember the period, still not so far off, when, in the disarray of my brain, I almost had to drag myself to your place, looking for the latest pamphlet on the Affair. And this I did every night.[104]

Dreyfus's book had indeed been published by another publisher, Fasquelle. Fasquelle was also Zola's publisher, as well as the publisher, after the Affair, of Reinach's *Histoire*. He had been a Dreyfusard but had not played a large role in the campaign for revision.

Cinq Années de ma vie is being published, today, by François Maspero, a publisher and bookseller at whose bookstore many of us went to find "the latest pamphlet" on this or that "affair" lying close to our hearts. It may be thought that this book has thus returned to its natural place.[105]

7 | Jewish Prism, Marxist Prism

I first became aware of Enzo Traverso and his work in early 1989, when Michael Löwy asked me to participate on the academic committee that was going to examine this Italian researcher's thesis on *The Marxists and the Jewish Question*. I accepted his invitation without any a priori enthusiasm, despite my esteem for Löwy (notably on account of his studies on libertarian Judaism).[1] I also accepted to sit on the thesis committee in spite of the fact that I am not truly a specialist either on Marxism or on the Jewish question. I have, however, for the past third of a century intervened so often outside my official field of studies—ancient Greece—that it would not have been very serious for me to have advanced this reservation as a pretext for declining the offer.

Reflecting back upon my acceptance, I can tell myself today that one of the reasons for accepting—though probably an unconscious one—resided in the fact that the title read not "Marxism" in general, but "the Marxists." This plural was not an innocent addition. Marxism is a doctrine that certainly has claimed to be one and indivisible, though it was not, and this unacknowledged lack of unity has entailed either the covering-up of internal disagreements or the excommunication of dissidents. The Marxists themselves are men and women who have adhered to this doctrine

"Prisme juif et prisme marxiste" was originally published as the preface to Enzo Traverso's *Les Marxistes et la question juive* (Paris: La Brèche—PEC, 1990). Reprinted in *JMP*, pp. 339–54. [T/E: An English translation of Traverso's book was recently published (without Vidal-Naquet's preface) as *The Marxists and the Jewish Question: The History of a Debate (1843–1943)*, trans. Bernard Gibbons (Atlantic Highlands, N.J.: Humanities Press, 1994).]

and to this ideology, but they have done so on the basis of motivations and interpretations so varied that they have often clashed with each other, sometimes even more than with their political adversaries.

I thus set to reading Enzo Traverso's work. When the thesis came to be defended, as we say in our academic patois, on May 5, 1989, I immediately expressed my desire to see it become a book, as is now the case, thanks to a dynamic publisher.

The first virtue of this book—there are many others, but this is, in some sort, the fundamental one—is that it is a secular book in all senses of the term.

Some people act as if Jewish history belonged solely to members of the (real or imaginary) Jewish community. They think that this history can be limited to a retracing, on the level of reality as well as on the level of the imaginary, of this community's destiny. No one, obviously, should try to remove the Jews from their own history, but no one has the right to turn this history into one's own private domain. That one cannot recount the destiny of a human group without feeling a minimum of sympathy—nay, without giving oneself the means to achieve a certain level of identification with that group—is an indubitable fact. Enzo Traverso has given himself these means, for example by learning to read Yiddish. He thus possesses the feelings of sympathy as well as the sense of distance necessary to undertake a work in the field of history. Any other requirement would amount to saying that only a Greek of today is capable of writing the history of ancient Greece—which would be as absurd as wanting to write this history without knowing Greek.

Eighteen forty-three to 1943: What do these two dates, which frame Enzo Traverso's presentation, signify? They are at once *ideological*, in the most refined sense of this word, and *concrete*, by which I mean social, political, even military.

Eighteen forty-three is the date of publication, in the *Deutsch-Französische Jarhbücher*, of the young Marx's essay *Zur Judenfrage* (*On the Jewish Question*), which we are to understand as: "On Bruno Bauer's Essay *Die Judenfrage*" (*The Jewish Question*). Today, this obscure quarrel among Left Hegelians would be totally forgotten, and would merit to be so, had not one of the disputants emerged from obscurity to become Karl Marx, "maestro di color che sanno," at least in the eyes of those for whom everything that bears his signature possesses a parcel of authority. Is Marx's text anti-Semitic? If a text is to be judged by the usage that has been made of it and by the impression that it leaves on us today, one would no doubt have to respond in the affirmative. Has not the latest reprinting in French of this bit of juvenilia been undertaken by the tiny abject band that is endeavoring to expunge from the Second World War the reality of the great massacre?[2] Situating this text in its 1843 context, it appears above all to be almost exclusively ideological in character. Written in the "wooden language" of sectarian groups, it is wonderfully ignorant of the reality, and notably the very existence, of the *Yiddishland* of eastern Europe. This point being said and recalled—Enzo Traverso himself does not fail to do so—it is fitting to add that, against Bruno Bauer,[3] this text proclaims as self-evident the Jews' right to political emancipation, even if this emancipation is seen by the young Marx as radically inadequate in comparison with his program for the total emancipation of society.

Nineteen forty-three: a young Belgian Trotskyist, a former Zionist who wrote under the name Abraham Léon and who died in 1944 at Auschwitz, had just completed an essay entitled *The Jewish Question: A Marxist Interpretation*. This book was the final attempt, before the disappearance of the *Yiddishland* and of *yiddishkeit*, to understand in Marxist terms the following strange situation: the survival, through history and not against history, of the "Jewish people." As one knows, what occurred in 1942 and 1943 does not pertain to the realm of ideology alone. Historical irony, as one says, has it that the war being waged in the East, which was then in high gear (Léon's text is nearly contemporary with the battle of Stalingrad), was being conducted by Hitlerites who were indissolubly against both the Jews and the Marxists, these two groups being considered by them to be one and the same entity. While rather problematic in itself, the phrase "Judeo-Marxist" was sufficiently pregnant with meaning to provide a basis for their largely successful attempt to annihilate the Jews, first in the East, then in the West.[4] Nineteen forty-three was, in addition, the year of the Warsaw ghetto uprising (April–June), in which Marxist militants, Left Zionists, and anti-Zionists from the Bund[5] played a capital role. It was also the year of the revolt at the Treblinka camp (August), which was launched with a slogan—"Revolution in Berlin!"—that appeared, even to those involved in the revolt, to be a mockery of Marxism.

Eighteen forty-three is certainly not just the date of Marx's essay. In the West, and specifically in France, the July Monarchy completed, with regard to the Jews, the emancipatory program that had been defined in 1791 by the Constituent Assembly but that was then delayed by Napoleon. It is under the reign of Louis-Philippe that rabbis began to receive, like Catholic parish priests and Protestant pastors, a state salary. After being Doctors of the Law, they thus became parish priests for Jews.

It is under this same bourgeois king that the last inequality disappeared, viz., the rule that Israelites subject to the law and all Israelite witnesses be required to make before the court a special oath *more judaico*.[6]

This was also an important time in the history of modern anti-Semitism, which was shifting from hatred toward the murderers of Christ to hatred directed against "financial feudalism," as symbolized, according to Fourier's disciple Alphonse Toussenel,[7] by the Rothschilds, but also by the Protestant bankers of Geneva. Despite these lively polemics, nothing was able to hinder in a serious way the forward march of the French model for the emancipation of the Jews, which consisted in their emancipation within the boundaries of the nation. In neighboring Italy, which was still only a "geographical expression," the Jews made themselves Italians under the same heading as the Piedmontese, the Lombards, or the Tuscans. They were not to "receive" emancipation; they emancipated themselves as Italians.[8]

Nevertheless, an entirely different world also existed. In 1843 a very serious threat weighed upon the Jews of Russia, that is to say, mainly those of Poland. An edict by Czar Nicholas I ordered them to be expelled from a large thirty-mile-wide zone along the western border of the Russian Empire. The protests against this order began in the Prussian, therefore German, Jewish community of Königsberg, which had benefited, like all the communities of Germany, from the repercussions of the French Revolution. From Königsberg, the protests spread throughout western Europe. In Frankfurt, Vienna, London, and Paris, the Rothschild family made this protest its own and tried to press governments to take a stand. In the end, the edict was not put into effect, without one being able to say exactly what motivations lay behind the Czar's change of mind.[9] It is impossible to understand anything about Judaism, anti-Semitism, and Marxism in relation to the Jewish question if one fails to take into account the following twofold, contradictory fact: an abyss separated the "assimilated" Jews of France, Italy, and Great Britain from the Jews of *Yiddishland*, a linguistic, cultural, and national abyss; and yet something also unified them, so that the Dreyfus Affair resounded from Paris to Moscow and the Beilis Affair[10] from Kiev to London.

Something, yes; but what? Religion? Throughout that secular century many Jews detached themselves from the religion of their ancestors. On the level of principle, moreover, no obstacle prevented a Jew from Bordeaux or from Paris from becoming an "Israelite" Frenchman or Frenchwoman. Jewish nationalism? In western Europe it was practically nonexistent. Either under its Zionist form or in and through the organizations connected with the Bund or else in "territorialist" movements,[11] it developed in a serious way only in the Russian Empire and, to some extent, in the Austro-Hungarian Empire, notably in Galicia. This development of various nationalisms should have, at least theoretically, radically separated the Jews of the East from the Jews of the West.

My sense is that, against the models issuing from the French Revolution, two key factors served to maintain, and even to develop, a common feeling of belonging. The first is, quite simply, anti-Semitism, the "Judeophobia" that took on new forms in the nineteenth century and that experienced, under Hitler, its most radical forms. It mattered little to the German dictator whether the Jews were believers or not, just as their devotion to this or that nation or to their own brand of nationalism also made little impression on him. For them, however, his hatred served to bring them together.

The second of these two factors (which is connected, moreover, with the first) is that these diverse communities did not remain isolated, each remaining in its own place and little by little coming to be impregnated with the local national values. They all communicated with the others and, above all, there was the process of emigration. Some Jews emigrated toward America, of course, where they adapted to a multicommunitarian society. A small minority of others headed in the direction of Palestine and built there a "national homeland" (whose consequences we are well aware of today). But perhaps still more of them emigrated within Europe and even within empires. In the nineteenth century, Vienna became populated with Jews who came from Moravia, like Sigmund Freud's father, or from Lembert (today Lvov, in the Ukraine, former capital of Hapsburg Galicia). Relations were far from idyllic between old communities and new immigrants, and one can cite numerous instances of new immigrants protesting against the contempt "Israelite Frenchmen" or "Germans of the Mosaic faith" displayed toward them. This migratory movement nevertheless encouraged the circulation of ideas and, on occasion, the spread of the kind of revolts on which Marxism nourished itself.

In a novel written by a compatriot of Enzo Traverso, the Italian writer Primo Levi, a Soviet Jew wonders "if there were Jews in Italy. If so, they must be strange Jews: how can you imagine a Jew in a gondola or at the top of Vesuvius?"[12] The action of the novel, which begins in 1943 in the occupied USSR, consists, as a matter of fact, in the establishment of contacts that were apparently inconceivable; some of its heroes will end up in Italy, whereas, heading in the opposite direction, Primo Levi himself traveled the road to Auschwitz. From an Italian Jew to a Jew from Russia, the

contrasts pass through all the hues of the prism. I shall return to this point
later.

I said that Enzo Traverso's book is a "secular" one, and it is time to comment upon this adjective. There are, in effect, two contrasting versions,
both of them religious, that depict the mutual relations between Judaism
and Marxism. In one version, there exists a sort of revolutionary essence
of Judaism, which may be seen in either a positive or a negative light. This
is how Ernest Renan reasoned throughout his works, making the Prophets
the ancestors of socialism: "One was rabidly enthusiastic [*enragé*] about
justice in Jerusalem when, at Athens and at Sparta, no protests were raised
against slavery."[13] The same argument appeared in 1894 in Bernard
Lazare's book *L'Antisémitisme, son histoire et ses causes*, which would serve as
a breviary for several generations of anti-Semites and for many other
modern prophets who came to identify messianic redemptionism with
libertarian socialist utopia.[14] Walter Benjamin, who is studied in the
eighth chapter of Traverso's book, was one of these men, among the greatest, and his dialogue with Gershom Scholem, who himself had chosen the
national path, still today sounds a doleful note.[15]

Although proceeding in the opposite direction, this was also the reasoning of European nationalists of every stripe. From Maurras to Hitler,
and with every possible nuance, these nationalists saw in Judaism and the
Jews elements that were corrosive and destructive of traditional society.

It goes without saying that this essentialism, like all forms of essentialism, is a lie. It is one thing to remark that a persecuted minority, placed
under the skewed historical conditions of the societies in which they live,
produce thinkers and ideologues who identify emancipation with social
upheaval. It is another thing to affirm that this same minority, whether it
rises against Babylon or against Rome, is at all times pregnant with revolutionary aspirations. And even if the Exodus has furnished an intellectual
model for many liberation movements, it does not follow that the Exodus
itself was, from the very outset, a movement comparable to those that
have been inspired by it.[16] One need only open one's eyes to see that the
teachings of the Prophets ill resist the logic of actual historical situations
and that the oppressed can very well become in turn oppressors. The Jews
invented neither capitalism (as Werner Sombart thought) nor revolution.

It is not true to say—and Enzo Traverso makes easy work of stamping
out this other myth—that anti-Semitism is a fundamental character trait
of Marx and the socialist movement itself. Since conservative forces took
the upper hand in contemporary Judaism, that is to say, since a nationalis-

tic form of Judaism asserted itself and triumphed (consciousness catching up with the event only after the fact), this legend has been asserted in even more spirited fashion than its contrary. To be convinced of this, one need only open a review such as *Commentary*.[17] This legend nevertheless neglects some key facts. While it is true that an anti-Semitic (and most often non-Marxist) form of socialism has existed from time to time, the workers' movement as a whole has weighed in much more often on the side of emancipation than on the side of persecution. It has been the classes representing the ancien régime, both politically and socially speaking, that have held out the longest against the simple idea of equal rights. The anti-Semitic French writer Édouard Drumont had some socialist admirers; he himself was, with some tragicomical features, a conservative terror-stricken by modernity. The Russian Revolution began with such a radical emancipation of the Jews of the Russian Empire that it was seen, by its adversaries and by some of its partisans, as a Jewish revolution.

If we have found it necessary to trample upon both of these nearly symmetrical mythologies, we do not do so in order to proclaim that between the Marxists and the Jews everything has proceeded as in the best of all possible utopias. Historical reality is rarely painted in such brilliant colors.

Enzo Traverso's book goes far toward untangling the history of a century of misunderstandings. Marx and Engels and most of their disciples did not succeed in grasping the singularity of nineteenth- and twentieth-century Jewish history in Europe, nor did their disciples comprehend, starting in 1933, the rise of the perils that culminated in the Hitlerian genocide. One is tempted to say that, in the Marxist lineage of thinkers, only one person escaped this basic tendency to miss the point: the Bund leader and theoretician, Vladimir Medem. There is something tragic, it is true, to these misunderstandings, and in no way have Jewish Marxists been spared. Of all the schools of Marxism that date from the first half of the twentieth century, the most subtle was the Frankfurt School, which moved to New York after Hitler took power. The great majority of the sociologists, anthropologists, and philosophers belonging to this school were Jews. Until the war, they always considered the anti-Semitic dimension of Hitlerism to be secondary. In 1942 one of them, Franz Neumann, published the first edition of his *Behemoth*.[18] The book took its name from the Jewish apocalypse (Behemoth is the monster that reigns over the land as Leviathan reigns over the sea) but the analysis of Hitlerian anti-Semitism is cursory and superficial, and it is not placed at the center of the book. And yet it was a student of Franz Neumann, Raul Hilberg, who finally comprehended, on a factual level, the breadth of exterminatory racism.[19]

In December 1942, a Trotskyist, Abraham Léon, completed his book, *The Jewish Question: A Marxist Interpretation.* (Of all the great Marxist leaders of the twentieth century, Trotsky is probably the one who came closest, though only at the end of his life, to a lucid vision of the Jewish question and the Hitlerian menace.) Léon certainly had sized up the grandeur of this drama, but he reasoned in the same terms as those apocalyptic Jewish movements that had arisen as early as the second century B.C.E. and through the first two centuries C.E.: "The very paroxysm, however, that the Jewish problem has reached today, also provides the key to its solution. The plight of the Jews has never been so tragic, but never has it been so close to ceasing to be that."[20] For a century, the revolution, as distant goal or immediate revelation, was the horizon of the "Jewish question" for the majority of Marxists. Enzo Traverso is right to say that the Marxists have no better grasped the fact of Jewishness than they have understood the nature of women's oppression, nor have they reflected any more successfully on this problem than they have on the problems raised by the existence of sexual minorities.

To understand the reasons behind these misunderstandings, one must reflect—as Enzo Traverso does—both on the place the Jews occupied in nineteenth- and twentieth-century European nations and on the nature and evolution of Marxism, properly speaking. I spoke before of a "prism." Indeed, it does not suffice simply to take cognizance of the evidence and note the fact that while the French Jews were a very highly assimilated community, the Jews of the Russian Empire, like the Armenians, the Poles, and the Uzbeks, were an oppressed nationality, but with a few notable peculiarities, viz., their concentration in the cities of the western and central parts of the empire, their specialization in certain trades (as financial intermediaries, and as craftsmen more than as an industrial proletariat), not to mention the existence of church- and state-sponsored anti-Semitism.

It is not enough to note this extreme. On the contrary, the essential thing to see is the capital importance of intermediary spaces in the particular cases of the pre-1918 German and Austro-Hungarian empires. There, law was of the Western-European type, but in social practice things proceeded quite differently. While Berlin, Frankfurt, and Vienna were metropolises that transformed Jews into Germans or Austrians, at the end of the process one found not the French professor or the British lord but, to take up the terminology Enzo Traverso borrows from Hannah Arendt and Max Weber, the "parvenu," with his successes in the economic sphere, and the "pariah," that is to say, specifically the intellectual who cannot in fact become a university professor (need we recall Freud's fate?) or find a post in the upper levels of administration.

To this situation must be added the fact that ideas, and not just people, travel. The narrative of assimilation migrated eastward, which explains how Lenin, for example, who was inspired by Kautsky when it came to examining the agrarian question in Russia (even though the problem markedly differed there from the problem as it was posed in the Central European empires) was inspired by Alfred Naquet when it came to commending the process of Jewish assimilation.[21]

Highly varied as it was, the Marxist prism was not a mere transposition of the prism of the Jewish condition. Who, however, could seriously doubt that the former received inspiration from the latter? Who even can doubt that Marxism is itself only one particular instance of the transposition of reality, which has its parallels in other ideologies? Enzo Traverso himself emphasizes this point: between the thought of Vladimir Medem and that of a bourgeois theoretician of Jewish national autonomy such as Simon Dubnow,[22] more than one comparison can be made. The French, Italian, and British Jews had a great deal of difficulty understanding the Jews of the Russian Empire and the varieties of their nationalism. Conversely, however, in the view of a number of "Russian" Jews who had been won over to a secular form of the idea of nationhood, the French Jews were fooling themselves in thinking that they were Frenchmen and Frenchwomen like other Frenchmen and Frenchwomen. They were Jews by birth, nay by "race," who could acquire French "citizenship" but not French "nationality."

In Marxism, as Enzo Traverso shows, the dominant tendency was assimilationist. Assimilation was thought of—and, by and large, lived—as a legacy of the Age of Enlightenment which Marxism, in a wholly natural way, had adopted as its own.

Places have their importance. Marxist thinkers are not found everywhere, nor is the Jewish question posed everywhere. The Dreyfus Affair enabled French socialists to rid themselves for a long time of the residual anticapitalist anti-Semitism that still was straggling along here and there, but it did not lead any "Marxist" to reflect seriously on the Jewish question. This question scarcely was posed, save among the anti-Semites and a few prophetic souls such as Bernard Lazare, and it was not posed by any Marxist except Georges Sorel, whose absence from the pages of Traverso's book is undoubtedly regrettable.[23] Antonio Gramsci is the only Western Marxist thinker who figures in this book, though he is not discussed with great originality. He is nevertheless presented in such a way that one can grasp his intelligent perception of the nature of anti-Semitism.

Quite naturally, this essay focuses on Germany, the Austro-Hungarian Empire, and the Russian Empire. It does so within the (already extensive) limits of the author's linguistic competence.[24] A number of these Central and Eastern European Marxist theoreticians were Jews. Even among them, certain ones, such as Franz Mehring or Wilhelm Liebknecht, deliberately made themselves outsiders with respect to their fellow Jews and exhibited a certain complacency toward a particular kind of anti-Semitism that came in the juvenile form of a populist anticapitalism. For the Austrian Marxist of Jewish origin Victor Adler, the Jewish question was simply a quarrel among members of the bourgeoisie. That is exactly what Guesde thought at the time of the Dreyfus Affair.

Assimilation was conceivable within the context of a nation, preferably a great nation. It also could be imagined as assimilation into a victorious proletariat in the case of "non-Jewish Jews" (Isaac Deutscher), those "rootless cosmopolitans" who so nobly played their part in the Russian Revolution and the German Revolution.[25] Aspirations toward assimilation also could be inverted into an appeal to form elsewhere, and without looking too carefully where one's feet would land, a normal society in which class struggle would be allowed to play itself out. This is the meaning the "Judeo-Marxists" who rallied to Zionism gave to their actions, Ber Borokhov being their most characteristic representative. As Enzo Traverso shows quite well, they shared the same conception of nationhood as Karl Kautsky, Otto Bauer, or Joseph Stalin.

Was there any "Jewish self-hatred" among the "Jewish Marxists" (in the sense in which Enzo Traverso employs this term), whose basically Christian estimation was that Judaism would fulfill itself through its disappearance? *Jüdische Selbsthass*[26] is a notion that has served for much—too much. It is an argument advanced in our time against any Jews who allow themselves to adopt, with regard to the Jewish establishment, dissident positions. Nonetheless, this phenomenon actually did exist, and not only in the extreme form it manifested itself in the case of an Otto Weininger, a Viennese Jew who hated both Jews and women.[27] When, in 1923, in the very midst of the nationalist crisis, Ruth Fischer proposed making the hanging of Jewish German capitalists a "priority," she clearly was laying it on rather thick.[28]

It does not require much explanation, in psychological terms, to

understand why the members of a minority who were more or less persecuted, more or less victimized (an abyss lies between the situation of
German Jews emancipated by law in 1848 and that of the Jews of Warsaw
or Kiev), and who placed their confidence in the German or Russian proletariat, worked to erase the differences that separated them from overall
society. In fact, they did so to the point of forgetting that specific threats
existed. In this way, they played into the hands of their enemies. The theoreticians of the Bund were perfectly well aware of this problem, but they
did not dispose of the means that would have allowed them to make real
their reflections on the issue of national autonomy.

Beyond individual and national variations and beyond the infinite variety of times and places, it is clear that the question raised by Enzo Traverso
in his book is that of Marxism's ability to resolve these types of problems,
of which the Jewish question is only one particularly acute example.

In keeping with the spirit of this book, let us now in turn ourselves pose
a few questions.

Marxism never presented itself as a theory and a practice of the liberation of oppressed minorities, even if, in actuality, it has been led to
recruit extensively among the members of such minority groups. Marxism took itself to be a theory and a practice for the liberation of the working class and, through the latter, of all society. Nevertheless, and contrary
to what Marx had foreseen, the nineteenth century was the century during which nationalism exploded onto the world stage, and the twentieth
century has imitated the nineteenth on this score. The movements that
continued through the struggles for decolonization pertain to the class
struggle only on the planetary level. To propose, as certain people had
been tempted to do during the Algerian War, an alliance of the French and
Algerian proletariats against their respective bourgeoisies was the purest
sort of utopianism. European Judaism did not constitute itself everywhere as a national minority. Where it actually was so constituted, the
class struggle did not easily correspond with the schemata worked out by
Marxist theoreticians. And these theoreticians most often preferred to
forget that this lack of correspondence actually posed a problem.

Throughout these years, Marxist thought took a "progressive" form. It
advocated the kind of "progress" that proceeds in a straight line. Apart
from a few exceptions such as Rosa Luxemburg, Trotsky at the end of his
life, and, especially, Walter Benjamin, it did not think regression, notably
modern technological barbarism. In anti-Semitism it saw most often an
archaic leftover, not understanding that anti-Semitism could ally itself

with modernity and could even color the latter entirely. Even the Frankfurt School, which did not share this "vulgar Marxist progressivism,"
remained blind on this question. It is with some amazement that one dis-
covers what Horkheimer wrote in 1939 on the subject, when he reduced
anti-Semitism to a purely economic contradiction of capitalist development.[29]

A still more grave fact, perhaps, is that Marxism claimed to be "scientific." And it was on the basis of its "scientificness" that it earned the support of so many intellectuals. At the same time, however, this claim to scientificness involved a negation of the scientific outlook, in that it gave pri-
macy to authority. Even at the time of the Second International,
Marxism's structures were authoritarian, Kautsky or Mehring posing
then as the guardians of orthodoxy. That did not prevent certain people
from straining at the bit, wanting to go in one direction or another
(Edouard Bernstein, Rosa Luxemburg). In the name of science, the
guardians of the temple nevertheless kept their vigil. It turns out that, on
the questions of concern to us here, their thinking was most often horri-
bly impoverished. One will be convinced of this by reading, for example,
the quotations Enzo Traverso has chosen from Kautsky's work.

The establishment of the Soviet Union aggravated this situation to the
extent that it engendered a state-sponsored Marxism, therefore a state-
sponsored "science," even though the latter did not gain the upper hand in
a day. In many people's minds, Leninism remains an object of worship, and
Lenin's thoughts on the Jews, which went back and forth, continue to be
viewed as arguments delivered by an authority on the matter.[30]

Certainly, forms of dissidence also existed among the Marxists who
remained faithful to the Second International. Equally characteristic is the
fact that Trotsky in exile was much more lucid on this question than Trotsky in power.[31] In any case, nothing worse could have happened to a critical and dialectical type of thought than to become the ideology of one,
and then of several States. The death of *this* Marxism, of this normalizing
Marxism, is the necessary condition for its hypothetical rebirth. Let us
therefore thank Enzo Traverso for having cleared the ground and marked
out the terrain.

PART THREE

Destruction, Memory, and the Present

8 | The Hero, the Historian, and Choice

For Arnaldo Momigliano

"One imagines Plato and Aristotle never wearing anything but the flowing robes of pedants. They were
honest people and, like others, they laughed with
their friends." People "like others." Despite this addition, the "honest" persons to which Pascal is alluding here evidently constituted only a minuscule elite, the elite he had known, frequented, and read during his
"worldly" period. One of the consequences of democracy is that the circle from which we recruit our saints and heroes has widened immeasur-
ably. The "flowing robes of pedants" have disappeared. Nonetheless, we
still refuse to see in our heroes "people like others," marked like us all by
the grayness, the "nearly so" of everyday life. And yet heroes have experienced all that: before heroism, always; during their most exalted acts,
almost always. But because for one day, for one hour, they have tran-
scended the norms, heroes have to be born heroes, grow up heroes, live
heroically. This is true for collectivities. (How many of us, today, cannot
stand having had martyrs close by.) They would, as I said one day,[1] prefer
martyrs who wear plumed helmets and white gloves, martyrs for military
parades and press releases.

What is true for collectivities is even truer for individuals. How can it
be denied that two men, more than all others, have come to symbolize
Jewish heroism in the Warsaw ghetto? Historian and tireless archivist of

"Le Héros, l'historien et le choix," which was published in *L'Écrit du temps* 10
(Fall 1985), is a revised and expanded version of my preface to Marek Edelman and
Hanna Krall's *Mémoires du ghetto de Varsovie: Un dirigeant de l'insurrection raconte*
(Paris: Scribe, 1983). Reprinted in *JMP*, pp. 387–98.

the ghetto, Emmanuel Ringelblum was the intellectual hero. It is mainly on the basis of documents gathered by him and hidden by his friends that today the history of this period can be written. A historian to his finger-tips, he took care not to note only heroic deeds. Mordecai Anielewicz had the more traditionally heroic role of the military hero of the insurrection. Representing Ha-Shomer ha-Za'ir, he was the leader of the Jewish Fighting Organization. In a renewal of the gesture of the besieged at Masada, he committed suicide on May 8, 1943, along with a number of his comrades and after he had killed his girlfriend. Anielewicz's statue, an imitation of Michelangelo's *David*, now watches at the edge of the Negev over the Yad Mordecai kibbutz. A street named after him in Warsaw lies at the heart of the new quarter that has been built upon the site of the old ghetto.

Poland's Jewish Historical Institute, which "pokes sorrowfully over the cold ashes"[2] of a great history, has recently published a new volume from the Ringelblum archives.[3] One of the documents reproduced in this vol-ume is an admission ticket, dated August 26, 1938, to the municipal casino of Venice (*Casino municipale di Venezia*), a ticket delivered to one Emmanuel Ringelblum of Poland. A heroic historian should not frequent casinos; he should stick to museums and archives. With complete naïveté—for the original document is reproduced—the editor has also provided a "translation": *Municipal Museum of Venice*.[4]

The principal author of these "Memoirs From the Warsaw Ghetto," Marek Edelman was one of the five directing members[5] of the Jewish Fighting Organization, which had endeavored to lead the insurrection. In it he represented the Bund, a Jewish Socialist party founded in Vilna in 1897 that favored both the autonomy of Jewish culture in Eastern Europe and its being maintained in place. The sole survivor of the five, Edelman knew Mordecai Anielewicz, the military leader of the insurrection, very well: "He was a gifted boy, an avid reader, and very active. Before the war, he lived on Solec. His mother was a fishmonger. When he worked at the stand, she sent him to buy red dye in order to color the gills of the fish so that they would appear fresh." Delivered on various occasions,[6] this bit of testimony has been the cause of scandal. Can a hero have had a miserable childhood, nay, even a somewhat marginal one as concerns the laws that govern honest trading practices? This actually became a topic of discussion. Some were willing to grant that Mordecai's mother engaged in such practices, but her son? Do I really dare say that this portrait of a starving young man who "hid his plate with his hand for fear that someone would take it from him," of this young man of twenty-one who wanted so much to be a hero, gives us a sense, precisely, of what a profoundly human brand of heroism is?

The Warsaw ghetto uprising: few periods of contemporary history have seen so many spotlights bear down upon it. Documents, testimony of all sorts from both victims and executioners, and novelistic recreations, it seems that everything has been said about the fighting itself as well as about the great lock-up, deportation, and massive extermination at Treblinka that preceded it.[7] What can we learn from Edelman's book that we do not know already? Do we really need any new documents about the vitality of the intellectual and political life of the ghetto's inhabitants or about the tremendous misery that reigned there? Must one reopen the files of the Jewish police in order to reflect once again on the ambiguous role of the Jewish Council, on its temporary privileges, and on the fate its members ultimately shared with the rest of the ghetto's inhabitants? Should one seek to know even more about the prison within the prison, the walls that were duplicated and reduplicated, the progressive contraction of space? One will, of course, rediscover here all these themes, provided to us with a particular personal accent, but is this really essential?

This work—and here we have the first element of a response to these questions—is made up of two very different texts, and their juxtaposition creates a sort of electrical flow of current.[8] The first text is a report, published in 1945, that was addressed by Marek Edelman, then aged twenty-four years, to his party, the Bund. He describes Poland's Jewish society in its atomized state in 1939. He depicts therein the role of political parties, and quite particularly, of course, the role of his own party in reestablishing control and building resistance. He also shows there the extermination effort at work. To those who ask: "What did one know and how did one know it?," this report furnishes some elements of a response, based on the testimony of a Polish railway employee: "Every day, a freight train filled with people coming from Warsaw took this branch [the one that led to Treblinka] and returned empty. No food convoy passed by here, and the Treblinka railroad station was off limits to the civilian population. Tangible proof that the people being taken there were executed." No doubt, this information will set off a round of laughter from the tiny abject band that has found its identity and its reason for living in the denial of the great massacre . . . [9] But this text, written after the liberation and dedicated to the memory of the clandestine leader of the Bund, Abrasza Blum, should also be read as a military report, a nobly partisan document. What Saint Augustine called, in the tenth book of the *Confessions*, "the immense palace of memory" has not yet opened all its galleries.

The second text, the main part of the book, is an interview with the Polish journalist Hanna Krall that dates from 1977. The man who speaks, and whom Hanna Krall has been able to draw out by speaking on her own, is no longer a soldier who is victorious amidst the most frightful defeat. He is a cardiologist, a doctor working in a large hospital in Lodz who is in daily contact with another kind of misery—not comparable, certainly, to the kind he witnessed in 1942, but a misery that ends, all the same, in death. He is a man who has lived, thought, and reflected, a man who has remembered, a man who will yet live and who is living still. A member of Solidarity and a delegate to its congress, he was interned after the December 13, 1981, coup. In April 1983, he refused to play the role assigned to him by the Polish authorities during the commemoration of the ghetto uprising. On account of this refusal, he received an order not to leave the town of Lodz for several days.

Might the cinema also be able to say here what writing tells us? Creating in his own way a new type of historical film, Marcel Ophuls has, in *The Sorrow and the Pity* and then in *Memory of Justice*, contrasted what men say today, before the camera, with what they proclaimed in 1943. But can the camera grasp the slow advance that makes a man relive 1943 today in another way than he lived it then, so as to make us sense that truth is perceived in depth through the order of time? This is what Proust was able to teach us. Is it because he, Edelman, survived that Edelman can present himself—opposite Anielewicz, the man of the instant—as the man of duration? Anielewicz did not live, says Edelman today, something that perhaps was worse: being present, day after day, on the Umschlagplatz, the "transshipment point," being present before those who left for Treblinka.

This is not—not only, at least—a matter of the "hindsight" afforded by time, of an objectivity that might finally be established. In 1977, as in 1945, blind spots remain for the narrator. Did the red-and-white Polish flag and the blue-and-white Jewish flag fly together over the ghetto during its insurrection? Numerous witnesses say so, beginning with SS General J. Stroop.[10] Edelman never saw it in 1945. There is no reason for him to remember it in 1977, which is all the better since other witnesses dangerously embellish their memories. More disturbing to note is that—on account of organizational patriotism?—he mentions only one group of combatants, those of the Jewish Fighting Organization. Nevertheless, another group also existed, the Jewish Military Organization, which was directed by "revisionists" and career officers. It played a key role in the fighting at Muranowska Square.[11]

All this is rather banal. What is less so is the witness's ability to question himself today about what yesterday was an everyday experience, to dredge up the kind of details that ordinarily interest the novelist, not the historian. Does not the interview with Hanna Krall begin in this way? " 'You wore that day[12] a soft red wool pullover. A beautiful pullover, of angora wool, you added.' 'It came from a very rich Jew.' 'Over it, leather suspenders crossing in the front, with a lamp in the middle.' 'If you had seen me!' 'That's what you told me when I asked you about April 19!' "

A novelist's vision, I said: the equivalent, in short, of the famous formula Paul Valéry refused to write: "The Marquess left at five o'clock." But the time of narrative is a part of history, too. A novelist, a man of memory, Adolf Rudnicki, recounts for us the following detail which he gathered in 1942, at the moment of the first great massacres. A little girl was in tears: "Never had he seen so much despair on the face of a child, even where he had come from. Someone had opened the window and the little girl's beloved canary escaped as swiftly as it could. This was the reason for her despair. And then Jozef saw that it was possible to suffer just as much because of a canary as from the death of entire families, of thousands of people."[13]

Remarkable is the fact that, as obvious as it may be, the connection between history and memory is far from always expressed. Herodotus writes "in order to prevent what men do from fading with time" (1.1), but of his own memory, as the mark of temporal distance, he tells us nothing; he speaks to us only of what he has seen and of what he has heard. Before him, it was the poets who invoked the goddess Memory. Thucydides speaks to us of his own memory only in order to tell us that he could not trust it to report the speeches he had heard (1.22). The historians of today are practically ashamed of memory. They work to erase it qua memory. And while they may have read Chateaubriand or Proust, rare are those who have learned to reflect on memory, to make something of the transformations it contributes to the representation of the past throughout a human life, and even along the path of several generations.[14] Work after work has been published during the past thirty years, all of them trying to tell us what, according to the memories of the young and the old preserved on audiotape, happened *that day*. Yet these works do not represent the kind of reflection on memory I am speaking about, but precisely the opposite. In such books, indeed, it is not a matter of making explicit our relationship to the past, but of suppressing the distance that separates us from it, of acting as if the representation of it rendered it actually present.

It is in the cinema that an awareness of this problem has arisen. Let us contrast here two different models. The films of Marcel Ophuls, *The Sorrow and the Pity* and *The Memory of Justice*, play on memory by setting up a confrontation between what people said yesterday and what they say today. This confrontation forces them to look for themselves at their frozen past. Claude Lanzmann's film, *Shoah*,[15] presents us with memory in its pure state: people who lived the extermination process from 1942 to 1945 are shown, but no image that is not of today is presented. The trains are those of today, the scale models are those visible today. Not a single document of the period that is only of that period has been used. The Jewish child who sang at Chelmno when the camp was called Kulmhof is today an old man singing beside a river that has not ceased to flow, in accordance with Heraclitus's inexhaustible maxim. This memory-history, an investigative work as well as a work of art, is given to us in its pure state. I do not think that a written text could have expressed the same thing.

In Edelman the 1945 account was still impregnated with military values. But what do these values represent today? Did the few hundred men (220, says Edelman) who took to arms in April 1943 save the honor of the Jews by showing, as is sometimes said, that Jews were capable of fighting? Have they, as has sometimes been written with good intentions, "rehabilitated" the Jewish people by anticipating the "military exploits" of Israel? The Warsaw ghetto insurgents fought because the values of war had been imposed upon them in an unavoidable way. And of course, who among us is not, still today, proud of their fight? But were these the only values? When an adolescent girl, as Edelman tells us, boards a train wagon so as not to leave her mother to travel alone to Treblinka, is that not heroism, too? And the "graceless" deaths of those "ghastly swarthy types" who lacked all elegance, those deaths, too, are inscribed in the great register.

Military values . . . One must see what they imply, what they entail. In an anecdote we encounter again here in his book, Marek Edelman recounted in *L'Express* magazine how a young female combatant chose "to kill herself at the moment the uprising gave out. Her name was Ruth. She shot herself seven times before she was successful. A beautiful tall girl with peach-soft skin. But she wasted six of our bullets." If one must shoot, one must not waste bullets, even if it is to prevent "peach-soft skin" from being handed over to the pleasure of the enemy.

And certainly there is the fundamental question of dignity. "One day, I saw a riot on Zelazna Street. People were crowding round a wooden cart on which stood a small aged Jewish man. He wore a beard. At his sides stood two German officers—two large handsome men next to this small, bent-over Jew—wielding large tailor's scissors. Convulsed with laughter, they cut his long beard in locks. . . . It was then that I understood that the most important thing was not to let yourself be put up on a cart, never and by no one." It is around moments such as these that reflections like those of Frantz Fanon are born. But are warriors the only persons capable of attaining their dignity?

There is also the flow of time and what it brings, sometimes things of a fraternal character. For example, a bouquet of yellow flowers is sent anonymously each year to Marek Edelman on the anniversary of the uprising—though with a single interruption, in 1968. There is the ridiculous, too, often so. For example, a soldier of the Wehrmacht wrote one day to the author of the book, who has now become a *Sehr geehrter Herr Doktor* (the "very honorable Mr. Doctor"): "I saw dead bodies in the street, many corpses covered with papers, I remember it, it was horrible, we are both victims of this terrible war. Might you write me a few words?" The ridiculous, but also a renewed sense of the tragic: "It always was a matter of dying, never of living. I even ask myself whether this can be called drama. Drama implies a choice, something must depend on you. There, however, everything was settled in advance. Today, at the hospital, life remains an option, and I must each time make a decision."

Decisions nevertheless had to be made in 1943, too. Yet it is only today that they appear tragic. With a sense of cruelty, for himself and for us who read him, Edelman tells us the story of some prostitutes, and even one pimp, who were staying in Anielewicz's shelter during the uprising. These prostitutes were good girls who fed the insurgents. After the suicide of the leader of the uprising and of most of his companions, Edelman and the survivors regrouped in a cellar where they again found the young women. "The next day, we descended into the sewers. We all went down, I last, and one of the young women asked me if they could pass over with us to the Aryan side. I answered 'No' to her. You see. Above all, don't ask me why." This book, which states that in 1943 there was no room for choice, is throughout a reflection on choice, choices of today and choices of yesterday. The choice of the sick man who chose whether to live or to be left to die; the choice of the doctor who selects those whom he will try to save, who wagers for life; the choice of the nurses in the ghetto who broke the leg of an old man so that he would not be deported; the choice of the first president of the Jewish Council, Adam Czerniakow, who decided to die alone, without alerting his brothers to what was happening, in the month of July 1942. The choice of whether to be victim or executioner, even though one may later become a victim.

Among all the choices with which we have become familiar by reading concentration camp literature, permit me, since Marek Edelman and Hanna Krall explicitly and emphatically challenge both history and historians on this score, to put an end to one choice they have posed to the historian. "We are not in the process of writing history. We are speaking of memory," says Hanna Krall to Edelman. And elsewhere, Marek Edelman to Hanna Krall: "The order of history is but the order of the dead. History took place beyond the Wall [that separated Jewish Warsaw from Aryan Warsaw], there where the reports were drafted, the radio messages sent, the appeals for help launched. Today, every specialist in the field knows the texts of the dispatches that were sent and the notes that were written by the governments involved. But who knows the fate of the boy who had to be buried alive because smoke was filling the cellar? Who knows it?"

And it is true: history prefers order to disorder and the historian who writes it is not always going to look any further. It is equally true to say that history is lazy and that historians are too often loathe to update their list of heroes.

Those of whom we are speaking were privileged persons, and this was true, in the most material sense of the term, of the men and women of the Warsaw ghetto uprising. Those who had remained alive until that time were in large part the privileged, rich people who had been able to have a bunker built, those who had been allotted (temporarily) the "life tickets" the Germans were distributing via the Jewish Council to those, notably workers or policemen, whose survival, it was judged, might be momentarily useful. One also had to be privileged in order to be armed and to fight—with or without a red pullover—a fact Marek Edelman makes us feel on a visceral level. One even had to be privileged in order to kill oneself, as Mordecai Anielewicz and his friends did. All this has been handed down to us as if through "golden windows on the black night," to use the beautiful image of Adolf Rudnicki.[16]

Even more than that must be said. Thanks to the extraordinary undertaking of the historian Emmanuel Ringelblum, we can come to know life in the ghetto in historical terms, situating ourselves almost on the same level as that adopted by the novelist or filmmaker, that of the individual lives of the great and small. For, contrary to what is often thought, it does not suffice to replace the history of individuals with a history of anonymous persons, with a history laid out sequentially. The overall groups that must be defined and distinguished, these groups, too, we must recall, were made up of individuals. We must try to bring the traces of them together, combine them when we find them; and we should bring their memories into mutual dialogue when they still exist.

But how far can the historian go? Historians can reconstitute the life of the ghetto. Can they comprehend its death?

Here we must return to Bergson and to his classic critique of the idea of nothingness. An intelligent fish, he said, might be able to conceive of the nonhumid, not dryness.[17] One can and one should try to discern the unknowable. A rationalistic and Marxist (i.e., optimistic) historian, Isaac Deutscher, nevertheless admitted failure when it came to understanding the *why* of the Nazi's decision. Here is how he concludes: "Perhaps a modern Aeschylus and Sophocles could cope with this theme: but they would do so on a level different from that of historical interpretation and explanation."[18]

It was at Treblinka that the vast majority of Warsaw's Jews were annihilated. Who can provide testimony as to what Treblinka was? An infinitesimal number survived, again privileged persons, those who were used by the Nazis to operate their machinery of death. A few executioners, too, whose memories have been explored, cross-checked. We can see both groups speak today in *Shoah* and their itineraries have carefully been traced as far back as is humanly possible.[19] At the point of departure for this itinerary of death, at the ghetto's now disappeared border crossing stood Warsaw's Umschlagplatz. Marek Edelman was present there each day.

But what can the keenest speech, that of the eyewitness turned historian, do here? It can perhaps border on, but it cannot penetrate, this immense gulf of silence that swallowed up the city.

9 | The Historian and the Test of Murder

For many years now we have awaited not "this kind of book," as one ordinarily says, but this book, the French translation of Raul Hilberg's *The Destruction of the European Jews*.[1] It is truly the work of a lifetime. Begun in 1948 by a very young specialist in political science who was a student of Franz Neumann's (author of *Behemoth*,[2] the magisterial analysis of the Nazi phenomenon) at Columbia University, Hilberg's book was first published by the University of Chicago Press in 1961. Despite the quarrels that arose around it, and whatever might have been the pioneering value of the attempts of Gerald Reitlinger (or, in France, of Léon Poliakov), *The Destruction of the European Jews* compelled immediate recognition as the major work on the subject. It was the main factual source, in 1963, for Hannah Arendt's famous "report on the banality of evil," *Eichmann in Jerusalem*.[3] A few of us implored more than one publisher to translate this great book, but for a long time our pleas were in vain. May the Fayard publishing house be thanked. It has done better than simply translate the 1961 edition. The edition now offered to us in an excellent translation—and the undertaking was not an easy one—is the revised edition of 1985, which has subsequently been supplemented even more. Nearly 1,100 pages in length, the task perhaps seemed a daunting one. But it was well worth the effort. One leaves this volume feeling a bit disoriented, almost dumbfounded, and yet educated almost beyond what one imagined was possible. Let us not say

"L'Historien à l'épreuve du meurtre" was originally published, in an abridged version, in the newspaper *La Croix* on May 28, 1988, and then reprinted in full in *L'Écrit du temps* 19 (Fall 1988): 147–52. Reprinted again in *JMP*, pp. 399–406.

that this is a definitive work—none such exist—but, instead, the most complete and informative one that exists on this terrible subject.

Raul Hilberg asked himself *how* a group of at least five million Jews (the majority of whom lived in Eastern Europe and in the Soviet Union, though there also were many in France, in Italy, in what today is called the Benelux area, and extending all the way to Greece) was killed. By posing the question of *how* they were killed he treats after his own fashion the question of *why* they were killed. Three principal actors were involved: Hitlerian Germany and its satellite regimes, the Jewish communities themselves, and the outside world, the last of which remained quite silent and, to say the least, ineffectual. Hilberg entitles a brief inaugural chapter "Precedents." One would be tempted to say that this chapter, like the chapter on poetic licenses in Théodore de Banville's *Petit Traité de poésie française*, should have included but a single line: "There are none." Even the Armenians, in 1915, experienced only an archaic form of massacre—radical in its scope, certainly, but not industrially organized. Hilberg himself, when he turns to a study of the murder sites, writes: "The most striking fact about the killing-center operations is that, unlike the earlier phases of the destruction process, they were unprecedented. Never before in history had people been killed on an assembly-line basis" (p. 863). The Jewish communities were led by notables who believed that they could adapt to persecution through the use of nonviolence, playing the game of the adversary, sacrificing if need be the members in order to preserve the head, and proclaiming the principle that "one can live under any laws." This was how the *Judenräte*, the Jewish Councils,[4] reasoned, as did, in France, the leaders of the Union Générale des Israélites de France (General Union of Israelites of France), the UGIF.

The Jews who were going to be killed first had to be *defined* legally. They then had to be *expropriated*, *concentrated* in ghettos or in what took the place of ghettos, and thus separated from the majority communities where they had more or less become integrated (rather well, for example, in Hungary and in France, quite badly in Poland and in Romania). The mass killings had already begun in the Soviet Union with the exploits of the Einsatzgruppen, but it was the process of *deportation* that led them to the *killing centers*, to the gas chambers, where one witnessed the triumph of the anonymity of the murder process, which was complemented by the almost ritual cleanliness of the murder technique. All this was the work of a quadruple apparatus (an apparatus, moreover, that was riddled with tensions and conflicts): (1) the ministerial bureaucracies and the State administration, in particular that of the railroads; (2) the army; (3) industry and finance, which recovered all that could be recovered; and, finally, (4) the

Party, which maintained control over the SS and the Gestapo. Thus does one draw up an organizational chart of the killing process. This description holds for the central apparatus. It holds, too, for the local apparatuses: those of Antonescu's Romania, for example, or the one that operated in France, for, as Hilberg writes, "To the French bureaucracy fell the burden of performing a large part of the destructive work, and the roster of Frenchmen in controlling positions of the machinery of destruction is impressively long" (p. 609).

The various resistance movements, as we know, offered only a feeble response to this killing enterprise, at least until the tide of war began to turn with Stalingrad and the Allies' landing in North Africa. It was then that some in the satellite States, in France, in Romania, and in Bulgaria, began to wake up and take notice, though it was in 1944 that the tragedy of the Hungarian Jews was played out. All this is coolly laid before us, with, at most, the addition of some icy black humor. Hilberg never fails to note, for example, the importance of national rivalries: the Romanians accepted this or that measure only if it had also been imposed upon the Hungarians, and vice versa. As we also know, the resistance of the spiritual forces in all these countries also was weak: for every Father Bernhard Lichtenberg, pastor of Saint Hedwige's Cathedral in Berlin, who was deported and who died because he had prayed in public for the Jews, whether they were baptized or not, how many total conformists there were!

This is a great book, no doubt about it. A book is great, however, only to the extent that, in addition to inspiring admiration for such a gigantic effort, it also gives rise to reflection, even criticism. I shall certainly not start insulting a historian of this caliber by pointing out here or there this or that imprecision in the details, or some unexpected silence on one topic or another. I have, of course, noticed some problems, as will others as a function of their learning and of their area of expertise. Such problems are the inevitable ransom one pays for the vastness of the subject. At the very most, I shall remark that, in the section on Vichy France, the "statutes" of October 1940 and June 1941 could have and should have been studied more closely.

But it is not here that lies the essential point, or even an important one. Hilberg's narrative account is presented as an analysis of an infernal machine that was set in motion in 1933, or even somewhat earlier, since it was in December 1931, therefore under the Weimar regime, that a "tax on fleeing" aimed at those leaving Germany was established. This machine certainly had its fits and starts, its grindings and creakings. In questions of "racial impurities," for example, the Führer did not want to go after women. They were pursued anyway, though under different pretexts— failure to report a criminal, for example. Everything began in earnest as soon as the Jews were separated from their fellow citizens by *defining* them, which was a prelude to *marking* them. Toward the end of his book Hilberg writes, "When in the early days of 1933 the first civil servant wrote the first definition of the 'non-Aryan' into a civil service ordinance, the fate of European Jewry was sealed" (p. 1044).

It is precisely this claim that I cannot accept, and for two reasons. First, I find this analysis unacceptable because the process *could have been stopped*. In September 1939, Hitler decided to exterminate the incurably ill and the mentally handicapped. A murder machine was then set up to operate at Treblinka. The protests that followed, led by the Bishop of Münster, the Count Clement von Galen, at the very least, singularly slowed this assassination march. An analogous protest might also have slowed the murder of the Jews and the Gypsies. Indeed, the latter murder operation was carried out only under cover of a radical ideological war, the one unleashed June 22, 1941, against the Soviet Union. This time, Count von Galen silenced his protests. Indeed, he even howled with the wolves. The Jews and the Gypsies were killed along with the Bolshevik "commissars." All three groups were defined as the enemy to be targeted and struck down, and from the East the murder machinery then turned round toward the West.[5] Second, I find Hilberg's analysis flawed also because there is a difference—not of degree, but of kind—between legislation, as ignoble as it might be, and assassination. Hilberg makes this point himself when he quotes the following letter from Himmler, dated July 28, 1942: "I request urgently that no ordinance be issued about the concept of 'Jew.' With all these foolish definitions we are only tying our hands" (p. 368). South African apartheid, as abject as the apartheid instituted under the laws of Nuremberg, has not yet led to mass murder, and the same goes for its modest imitation, Israeli apartheid.

If Lanzmann's superb film, *Shoah*, in which Hilberg himself participated, shows anything of historical merit, it shows that the decision to kill, to kill mechanically, first with trucks and then with gas chambers, the decision to kill at Chelmno, Belzec, Treblinka, Majdanek, Sobibór, and Auschwitz, represents not a change of degree but a change in kind.

This reality can be attained only partially through the use of administrative documents (which constitute the underlying skeleton of Hilberg's work), through the reading of an *amtsprache* (administrative language) that has to be decoded. As Hannah Arendt has shown in her deep reflections upon it, this was the only language Eichmann spoke. One can touch upon the reality of the Shoah by approaching it through the longtime living memory, today on its way to extinction, of actual witnesses. And of course, Hilberg has used such testimony, all kinds of testimony. It is by using an eyewitness account concerning Treblinka, as noted by a German magistrate, that he recovered the story of a dog named Barry: "Barry was a very large Saint Bernard who appeared first in Sobibór and then in Treblinka. He had been trained to maul inmates upon the command, 'Man, grab that dog! [*Mensch, fasst den Hund!*]'" (p. 898). History is made of memory, too, so there can be no question of opposing memory to history. Nor is it a matter simply of integrating "oral sources," or what were oral sources, into the mass of contemporary documents by placing them as citations in footnotes—which is in fact what has been done by Hilberg, who, moreover, devotes only a few lines in his appendix, "Notations on Sources," to "oral history." It is a matter, rather, of setting memory in motion, of doing, in short, for history what Proust did for the novel. This is no easy task, but *Shoah* has shown that it is not an impossible one—provided that the rest of us historians can recall, as the historian Henri I. Marrou taught us long ago, that writing history is also a work of art. Of course, this task presupposes, in addition, that one make use of the tools of historical criticism, for, like administrative language, memory, too, must be decoded, though in a different way.[6]

In two other books that appeared at the same time as the French translation of Hilberg's book, we are reminded, though to very different degrees, of the foundational power of memory. Margaret Buber-Neumann's "Deported to Ravensbrück" is the second part of her "Prisoner of Stalin and Hitler," the first part of which, "Deported to Siberia," was translated into French from German in 1949 and republished in 1986.[7] Companion of the German Communist leader Heinz Neumann who was assassinated in the USSR in 1937, the author of this book was handed over, along with other "dissidents," to Hitler in early 1940 by his then-accomplice, Stalin. For my part, I have never forgotten the shock her testimony elicited in Paris during the suit Kravchenko brought against *Lettres Françaises* in 1949. The poet René Char was literally bowled over at the time, as I myself can testify. This incident provides a wonderful occasion to reflect upon what humanity, in all senses of the word, is capable of doing. It is also a good occasion to meditate on the diversity of the forms of oppression, on their resemblances and their differences. Arriving from Karaganda via Moscow and Brest-Litovsk, Margaret Buber-Neumann was at first dazzled by the order that reigned at Ravensbrück. She was soon to sing a different tune as she passed through all the different strata of concentration camp society (who can forget her evocation of the Jehovah's Witnesses or her portrait of Milena, Franz Kafka's lover?), came close to being exterminated by gas (a practice that did not exist in the Soviet Union), and, in 1945, traversed a Germany in the grips of madness, finally to return to Bavaria.

Germaine Tillion's *Ravensbrück*[8] offers us an entirely different kind of book. In reality, it is the third version of a text originally written in 1945 for an anthology of writings about Ravensbrück by a group of French deportees and published in 1946 by Albert Béguin in the *Cahiers du Rhône*. At the time, it was entitled *À la recherche de la vérité* (In search of the truth). Germaine Tillion (who was friends at Ravensbrück with Margaret Buber-Neumann and her French translator, Anise Postel-Vinay) contributed, she tells us today, "what was possible, that is to say, disjointed information, still drenched in the flow of reality, but scrupulous and stripped of what to me seemed merely personal." To read it properly today, it must be read in light of and along with the two other versions. In this way one will see that as early as 1945 Germaine Tillion was obsessed with historical truth. As early as the time she spent in the camp, in fact, she knew that the truth was both attainable and fragile. The years have passed, the archives have been opened, and it now has become possible to lay out sequentially the testimony of eyewitnesses for purposes of historical investigation. This third book is more scholarly than the previous two. It establishes, notably, that extermination by gas really did occur in a camp that was not, properly speaking, an extermination camp in the sense Treblinka had been such a camp, a reality that certain not very serious-minded persons (I am not thinking here of that tiny abject band of "negationists") had, in good faith, called into question. Yet it is also more personal, since Germaine Tillion publishes here texts, poems, and sketches of a poignant humor, though also statistical notes she had jotted down while still in the camp, writing at that time being a synonym for living. For those who have known, as I have known, Germaine Tillion, in her capacity as a scholar but also in the struggle to bring to light another truth—that of torture in Algeria, which is mentioned in the second *Ravensbrück*, the one published in 1973—her book is itself a great lesson. May it be so for everyone.

10 The Shoah's Challenge to History

It is not easy for a historian to grasp the Shoah. It is less easy still, when one is not a specialist on these issues, to judge the work of others, of those who, on all levels, have tried to inform us about the immense event that tears through the heart of our century: the genocide of the Jews and the Gypsies.

I will try to do so nonetheless, while remaining very conscious of my limitations. But perhaps these limitations themselves will prove, under the circumstances, to be an advantage.

As I have already done on another occasion,[1] I shall start with a page from Thucydides, this time taken from the third book of *The Peloponnesian War*.[2] The Athenian historian recounts what happened in 427 B.C.E. during the civil war between oligarchs and democrats at Corcyra. This is certainly a minor episode in comparison with the European civil war of 1914 to 1945, which both the poet Paul Claudel and the historian Arno J. Mayer have rightly called the thirty year war, but it nevertheless is an episode that would forever impress this defeated general, this statesman who, with

"Le Défi de la Shoah à l'histoire" was originally published in *Les Temps Modernes* 507 (October 1988), then reprinted in François Bédarida, ed., *La Politique nazie d'extermination* (Paris: Albin Michel, 1989) under the title "L'Épreuve de l'historien: Réflexions d'un généraliste" and in the anthology edited by Bernard Cuau et al., *Au Sujet du "Shoah": Le film de Claude Lanzmann*, introduction by Michel Deguy (Paris: Belin, 1990). Reprinted in *JMP*, pp. 407–18. An earlier translation of this essay appeared as "The Holocaust's Challenge to History" trans. Roger Butler-Borruat, in *Auschwitz and After: Race, Culture, and the Jewish Question in France*, ed. Lawrence D. Kritzman (London and New York: Routledge, 1995), pp. 25–34.

lucid reflection, wrote the history of his own time. "There was death in every shape and form," wrote Thucydides. "And, as usually happens in such situations, people went to every extreme and beyond it. There were fathers who killed their sons; men were dragged from the temples or butchered on the very altars; some were actually walled up in the temple of Dionysus and died there."[3]

All this occurred at Corcyra. But, Thucydides adds, this commotion, this rupture of consensus, this *stasis*, as is said in Greek,[4] soon overtook the entire Hellenic world and resulted in a war that was at once international and civil in character. He also adds the following: "To fit in with the change of events, words, too, had to change their usual meanings. What used to be described as a thoughtless act of aggression was now regarded as the courage one would expect to find in a party member; to think of the future and wait was merely another way of saying one was a coward, any idea of moderation was just an attempt to disguise one's unmanly character; ability to understand a question from all sides meant that one was totally unfitted for action."

Thucydides' description concerns only what he calls the level of "justifications" (*diakaiōseis*). Today, we would perhaps say "ideological pretexts." But it goes without saying that this same remark also holds when it comes to narrating actions. Thucydides himself recounts[5] how, perhaps in 424,[6] the Spartans "brought about the disappearance" of two thousand helots. These helots' only wrong was that, in addition to having served the Spartans well, they were sufficiently courageous that they were deemed likely to rebel at some point in the future. Echoing some coded language gathered at Lacedaemon, Thucydides tells us: "They [the Spartans] made them disappear without anyone knowing how each had disappeared."

Today, we are far from Thucydides. Obscure victims of a war among what Voltairean history labeled a few "cantons" in a country of slight significance when weighed on the scale of empires, these two thousand helots are small in number when compared to the millions of persons, Jews especially but also Gypsies and Soviet citizens, who perished in Hitler's workshops of death. As a historian of ancient Greece, I do not think, as Thucydides himself thought, that the paroxysmal "calamities" he describes (which he compares, moreover, to a volcanic eruption or an earthquake)[7] "happen and always will happen while human nature is what it is." In other words, I believe more in the variations than in the permanence of human nature. But Thucydides moderates his own statement by adding immediately, "though there may be different degrees of savagery . . . as different circumstances arise."[8]

Yet it is not, or not only, this sort of lesson, like some sort of general rule, that I wish to draw today from Thucydides. It seems to me that his teaching here is threefold. First, he reminds us that it is possible to write a history of the present. But, and this is my second point, every history, including a history of the present, obviously presupposes the taking of some distance with respect to one's material. Finally, and here is perhaps the essential point, all history is comparative history, even when one does not think so. To constitute the two thousand helots as a historical whole [*ensemble*] when each helot had his own life and his own death, one obviously must construct the set [*ensemble*] "helots."[9] To us, this would seem to go without saying; it would seem to be, as one says, "obvious," but in reality it is not so, any more or any less than the set "Jews" or the set "National-Socialist Germany."

One need only know how to read in order to discover that historiographical issues have now become paramount. One such historiographical debate is the quarrel between "functionalists" and "intentionalists." The first group runs the risk of dissolving the unity of the facts—or, better, the *whole*—in a dust cloud of details. The second group, which rightly places the emphasis on a murderous ideology, runs the risk of writing a discourse that, like mythical speech, remains self-enclosed and unable to take the time factor into account. It is obviously useless to contrast here "facts" with "interpretations." The chronicle most stripped of commentaries is itself an interpretation.

As for the great quarrel among our German colleagues, the now-famous Historikerstreit, what it shows, precisely, is that the main issues laid before a public of citizens are historiographical issues. If one were to take stock of this quarrel today by comparing it to the acts of a colloquium organized in 1982 at the École des Hautes Études en Sciences Sociales in Paris,[10] one would notice that herein lies the essential difference between yesterday—a not yet very distant yesterday—and today. There were nought but three of us, Saul Friedlander, Amos Funkenstein, and myself, back then who were preoccupied, directly or indirectly, with these sorts of questions. Subsequently, the debate has switched abruptly from focusing on direct history to reflection upon the succession of interpretations.[11] If that is indeed the case, it is quite naturally because the historiographical literature is already so impressive.

It is impressive on a world scale, certainly. But I must add immediately, and with all due respect to the pioneering role played by Léon Poliakov and to the activities of the French Center for Contemporary Jewish Documentation or the French Institute for the History of the Present Time (which originated the present volume [*La Politique nazie d'extermination*]),

the contribution of France and of the French historical school in this historiography has been rather slight. Although, long ago, a French state university thesis was written on "The Nazi Concentration Camp System"[12]
(and it did not concern the process of extermination properly speaking)
and although other studies are now being prepared, it is not unfair to say
that the extermination of the Jews, the Gypsies, and the mentally ill by the
Third Reich is a subject that has been rather neglected in French academic
historiography. Whence the role, in this ongoing historiographical effort,
of a trained jurist like Léon Poliakov, a biochemist like Georges Wellers, or,
quite belatedly, a specialist in ancient history like the author of these lines.
No doubt, this has sometimes been the case in other lands, too: the author
of the major book on *The Destruction of the European Jews* (which has finally
been translated into French)[13] is not a historian by training but a political
scientist—a fact that ought to comfort those who deem the history of the
Second World War to be too serious a matter to be left to historians alone.

Without an excessive sense of patriotism for the craft of historian, one
may nevertheless legitimately think it better to know Byzantium or Louis
XIV, *too*, than to travel only along the *Roads to Extinction*, to borrow the
title of Philip Friedman's posthumous book.[14] Arno J. Mayer has just
demonstrated this point brilliantly: to understand Operation Barbarossa,
the offensive directed against the USSR that, like a new crusade, was to
provide a time and a place for the implementation of the Hitlerian genocide, it is not completely useless to know what the Crusades were and
what the myth of Frederick Barbarossa had become.[15] Too often, in
France, one finds, in place of any sort of analytical or synthetic history, the
kind of "sensational debasement of the tragic" that our American colleague
Cynthia Haft has criticized.[16] Paradoxically, and at the risk of reprimand-
ing myself and of being caught in a contradiction, I would say that the sole
great French historical work on the great massacre, the one that is guar-
anteed to endure through time, is not a book but a film, Claude Lanzmann's *Shoah*. I shall return to it below. But, we may ask right now, why
this long period of drought in French historiography? Why this lack,
which only now we are beginning to fill? I see three main reasons, each
very different from the others.

The first reason is political. It is encapsulated in what Henry Rousso
has called *The Vichy Syndrome*.[17] Every work on the extermination of the
Jews poses the question of France's collaboration with this policy. That is
to say, each work poses the question of the continuity of French history
through the years of the Vichy regime, which was not just a government
declared illegal in 1944 but also an administrative apparatus, a police

force, and a system of justice. In this regard, the questions posed are not fundamentally different from those that were raised in Germany during the "historians' quarrel"—with, however, this one dissimilarity: the German break of 1945 was perhaps more violent than the French break of 1944. In any case, we should not be surprised to see that, in the case of France, the role of non-French historians like Marrus and Paxton, or non-specialists like the jurist Serge Klarsfeld, has been major.[18]

The second reason is also political but concerns, rather, academic politics. French universities have long adopted a timorous attitude toward the most contemporary of historical topics. Resistances are only now beginning to give way, as the growing number of theses on the Algerian War that recently have been defended or that soon are going to be defended is beginning to show. Let me recall, simply, that in 1935 the historian Jules Isaac was not allowed to obtain from the Sorbonne the right to register his state university thesis on Poincaré's ministry (January 1912–January 1913) because the subject inevitably raised the question of Raymond Poincaré's personal responsibility in originating the war.[19] When I was a student, a third of a century ago, the following adage was, rightly or wrongly, attributed to Aimé Perpillou, one of our geography professors at the Sorbonne: "Until 1918, there is history, from 1918 until 1939, geography,[20] afterward, it's all politics."

The third and final reason is epistemological. Breaking in part with the original inspirations of the review that was founded in 1929 in the midst of economic crisis and in part as a response to this crisis, the historical school known as the "Annales" has for the most part opted for the "long term" over the event, the latter often being considered a mere wrinkle in time, or even just "the foam on top."[21] The Hitlerian crime belongs, however, within a short-term time frame, even if the long term can be used to set things in perspective.

Should the issue of historical revisionism be excluded from debates surrounding the great massacre?[22] It seems to me both legitimate and regrettable to set aside the work of these revisionists. It is legitimate to do so in that "revisionism" represents no historical school, no type of historical discourse, but is instead the pure and simple suppression of the historical object under study. Someone has spoken of "revisionist" writings as "intellectual excrement."[23] I accept this expression, but are there not laboratories in which excrement, too, may be taken to be analyzed? Since when did lies, forgeries, myths, and the world of the imaginary cease to be objects of historical study? Contemporary historiography has grown to the point that a celebrated series, the "Bibliothèque des histoires" directed by Pierre Nora, repeats again and again the following formula: "We are experiencing an explosion of history." And yet it is claimed that we are incapable of integrating into our historical analyses the analysis of contemporary "revisionism"!

In what way can the study of such revisionist writings be fruitful, even enriching? Let us pass over the few corrections of detail one might have to make. It was not the revisionists who taught historians that there were no gas chambers at Buchenwald. And in current debates over the number of victims of the "final solution," their contribution is, properly speaking, nonexistent. "Revisionist" discourse took no interest in setting facts in sequence or placing them in perspective. It is, rather, the discourse of a sect. And as we have long known, the discourse of this sect has a totalitarian calling to the extent that it claims to be a true discourse that is faced with a reigning lie. This was what the Bolshevik party claimed in 1917, and we find the same attitude in Maurrasianism and in the discourse of Action Française. As it turns out, a few works that were written at the beginning of the century with a pretense to being legitimate history (notably, *Précis de l'affaire Dreyfus* by "Dutrait-Crozon,"[24] the pseudonym for two officers of Action Française) are, it seems to me, the clearest forerunners of present-day revisionism. An ideological expression of French nationalism, the work of "Dutrait-Crozon" takes care, even in its actual physical appearance, to imitate the look of a German *Lehrbuch*.[25] The *Précis* is an ultrascholarly work, replete with references that for the most part are accurate and with corrections of details that sometimes are useful. And yet it lacks one "detail" of particular importance: Dreyfus's total innocence of the charge of treason. In other words, it is missing the "truth" that, as Zola proclaimed in *L'Aurore* on January 13, 1898, was on the march and that would have to be fought for if it was to triumph.

Certainly, no historian who has reflected on the theory and practice of the historian's craft shares the "prejudice that the historian's language can be made entirely transparent, to the point of allowing the things themselves [*les faits*] to speak; as if it sufficed to eliminated the *ornaments of prose* to be done with the *figures of poetry*."[26] While it is true that the labor of history requires "unending rectification," fiction, especially when it is deliberate, and genuine history constitute, no less, two extremes that never shall meet. Revisionist discourse pertains not to an analysis of historical language but to a theoretical reflection upon the lie, a reflection that has been going on ever since Plato.

Historical sociology, of course, also has its word to offer in this affair. I have written that this negationist discourse is the discourse of a sect, but it happens sometimes that sects become State organizations, for example in times of great social upheaval. This is what occurred in Russia in October 1917, and it culminated, along paths that perhaps could have been resisted, in a Stalinist type of historical discourse. Stalin's *Short History of the Communist Party (Bolshevik) of the USSR* furnishes us with the perfected model.

As far removed from the State as these minuscule revisionist sects now engaged in their shady practices in France, in Germany, in Italy, and in the United States may now appear, they do no more than prolong and make their own, on the level of the ridiculous, the Nazis' authentic attempt to cover up their crime throughout the time this crime was being committed. The Nazis used, for example, the coded language of "special treatment." More specifically, under pressure of defeat, first in the East and then in the West, starting in 1943 they burned the corpses and systematically destroyed, first in the slaughterhouses of Poland and then at Auschwitz, the actual weapons of their crime. State-sponsored crime and state-sponsored lies went hand in hand at the very heart of the SS apparatus. This apparatus was responsible for the murder and for the forgetting of the murder. In fact, it was responsible for both at the same time.

The National-Socialist State is dead. Nothing more remains of it but fraudulent ghosts of its former self. Nevertheless, whenever the question of the great massacre of Armenians in 1915 is raised, the example of contemporary Turkish historiography is there to show us that those who deny the crime can become established in power. Those who do so believe that they can thereby uphold the fiction of a pure and unified national history.

But let us return now to our sect and to the connection we have postulated between crime and denial. The "revisionists" have undertaken to deny the Nazi genocide in its totality, but—whether their names be Arthur Butz, Wilhelm Stäglich, Robert Faurisson, or Henri Roques— they have placed their emphasis, quite particularly, on denying that the gas chambers were a tool of extermination. Many people have not understood the importance of this question. In what way do the gas chambers have a specificity, not only in relation to the Gulag (which is obvious) or in relation to other methods of state-sponsored terror, but also in relation to the Nazi concentration camp system as a whole, and even in relation to the collective murders carried out by the Einsatzgruppen in the USSR? Between death by gas and death by bullets, or even death by exhaustion or by the action of exanthematous typhoid, is there a difference in degree or a difference in kind?[27] My personal response is that there is a difference in kind. What, in the context of the SS State, do the gas chambers actually *represent?* Not only, or not essentially, do they represent the industrialization of death—by which I mean the employment of industrial techniques for purposes of killing and not for production (which was still being carried out, moreover, just beside the slaughterhouses). While the "crematory ovens" of Auschwitz were highly refined tools, the techniques used to operate the gas chambers were of a very low level. The essential issue does not lie there. The key point is the *negation of the crime within the crime itself.* The problem has been posed very well by a German lawyer, Attorney Hans Laternser, during the course of the Auschwitz trial (1963–1965).[28] Starting from the moment the order to kill was given, those who *selected,* not—as is often said and as I myself once happened to say—in order to separate those fit for work from those unfit but in order to separate those who would be sent to replace the disappeared work force from those who would be killed right away, were in reality not killers of Jews but saviors of Jews. This lawyer was expressing in his own way something real: the reality of the diffusion of responsibility, the reality of the near-disappearance of responsibility. Who, then, was the killer at Auschwitz? Was it the person who put the Zyklon B tablets under the lid that led into the gas chambers? All the operations from the directing of victims as they left the trains to the undressing and cleaning of bodies to their placement inside the crematoria were basically under SS control, of course. But all this was done through the intermediary of members of the *Sonderkommandos* who, in the end, were the only ones placed in direct contact with death. The crime can be denied today only because it was anonymous.

It is time now to conclude. I said that the only great French historical work on the theme of the Hitlerian genocide is Claude Lanzmann's film *Shoah.* In what way does this film question the historian? As Lanzmann himself has remarked, his presentation breaks with historiographical tradition. It starts at Chelmno, in December 1941, with the use of gas trucks. If extermination by gas does indeed have the symbolic importance I give to it, Lanzmann is right to begin in this way.[29] Yet historians find themselves faced with a challenge here because historical discourse, whatever kind it may be, cannot easily escape what Spinoza called the *concatenatio,* the chain of causes and effects. How, indeed, can one avoid tracing things back from the gas chambers to the Einsatzgruppen and then back, step by step, to the exclusionary laws, to German anti-Semitism, to what separates and distinguishes Hitler's anti-Semitism from the anti-Semitism of Wilhelm II, and so on and so forth, all the way back to infinity? This is how Raul Hilberg has proceeded in his admirable book. Historical discourse is capable of all kinds of ruses, however, including the major ruse

that consists in concealing the fact that something new occurred at
Chelmno. The Nuremburg laws were still laws. So were the Vichy statutes.
The members of the Einsatzgruppen saw, in that awful face-to-face
encounter between executioner and victim, those whom they killed. But
the majority of the Germans living at Auschwitz did not see the Jews and
the Gypsies die in the gas chambers.

The second question Lanzmann's film poses to historians is perhaps
even more fundamental. His attempt has a mad side to it: he has made a
historical work where memory alone, a memory of today, is called upon
to bear witness. As Michel Deguy has said, "The actors stand in relation to
themselves as if they were their own sons, each one is engendered by he
who he was in the agony of his youth."[30]

One day, before *Shoah*,[31] it occurred to me to write that one of the
problems present-day historians are faced with is the problem of introducing into History the "teaching," if I may so express myself, of Marcel
Proust, that is, the search for time lost as at once time lost and time rediscovered.[32] This is what Lanzmann has achieved in this film, where but a
single document is presented to us and where everything rests on the
questions he poses today to his witnesses and on the answers they provide
him. And, as I am well aware, behind each of these questions lies the entire
historiography of the Shoah, which Lanzmann knows as well as a professional historian.

Between time lost and time rediscovered lies the work of art. The challenge to which *Shoah* subjects historians lies in the obligation it places on
them to be at once scholars and artists. If they do not face up to this challenge, historians will lose, irremediably, a portion of the truth they are
pursuing.

11

On an Interpretation of the Great Massacre: Arno Mayer and the "Final Solution"

The historian is a free man. Since this proposition is perhaps not as "basic" as it might appear, I would like to convince the reader of the French translation of Arno J. Mayer's book, *Why Did the Heavens Not Darken? The "Final Solution" in History*, of its truth. In the traditional image one has of the historian, such freedom does not, to say the least, play a leading role. The historian is commonly viewed, rather, as a slave, a slave to facts, as one says, a slave to the documents on which he bases his work. Who will deny that this sort of servitude exists? Who will contest the idea that it is the elementary duty of the historian to read many—one never reads all—of the primary and secondary sources? The true work, however, and with it one's freedom, begins afterward, later, when the last document has been read, the last index card filed, for then begins the labor of interpretation.

This is a free labor, then, one that presupposes freedom for he who reads as well as for he who writes. No history is possible where a State, a Church, a community, be they even respectable ones, impose any kind of orthodoxy. Yet, on the other hand, no book—however new, however rich in sensational documentary material or profound insights—can be considered a "definitive" work. We encounter this adjective too often in

"Sur une interprétation du grand massacre: Arno Mayer et la 'Solution finale' " originally appeared as the preface to Arno J. Mayer's *La "Solution finale" dans l'histoire*, trans. Marie-Gabrielle and Jeannie Carlier (Paris: Découverte, 1990). Reprinted in *JMP*, pp. 437–52. [T/E: The quotations and page references from Mayer's book come from the 1990 Pantheon (New York) English-language paperback edition: *Why Did the Heavens Not Darken? The "Final Solution" in History*. The first American hardcover edition dates from 1988.]

reviews of history books: "Here we have a *definitive* study on . . ." There is
no such thing as a definitive study. History is always to be revised, always
to be redone.

It is to be revised, to be redone, I said. I did not say: to be destroyed, to
be undone. By its very nature, the subject of Arno Mayer's book—the murder, by Hitler's followers, of several million European Jews, the "Judeocide" as he calls it—attracts perverse souls. The event was denied even as
it was occurring, and it has been denied since then for self-serving or ideological reasons. Yet, while denied by some, it has also been sacralized by
others to the point of making it the object of rites, of celebrations, of an
entire orchestrated set of religious activities. The historian knows how to
recognize the sacred—as an object of study; he cannot participate in it
himself without becoming an imposter. Every self-enclosed form of discourse belongs to the realm of myth, not to history. Speaking of a number
of his "dogmatic" or "skeptical" critics, Arno Mayer, in a statement I heartily
endorse as reflecting my own attitude, writes as follows: "They only see
absolute truth and falsehood, unqualified certainty and uncertainty. This
stance is at variance with the historian's task, which is to conceptualize and
portray reality in its disconcerting diversity and complexity, particularly
when facing extreme and incomprehensible events" (p. 453).

It is now time to say it: this book by Arno Mayer arrives to us from
America with a scent of scandal. A certain Jewish establishment has
unleashed against it a campaign of criticisms, nay calumnies, comparable
to those directed so tirelessly, a quarter century ago, against Hannah
Arendt's *Eichmann in Jerusalem*.[1] Some have even dared to compare the
theses defended in this history book to those developed by the so-called
revisionists,[2] as if an author who devotes the entire twelfth chapter of his
book to a study of the actual extermination sites could be suspected of
sowing doubt as to the existence of the gas chambers. Let it be said once
and for all: these accusations bring only ridicule, nay dishonor, upon those
who proffer them.

That does not mean that this great book brings us the truth as it is
henceforth to be taught. History does not operate like the media, where
the latest bit of news chases off "page one" the bit that had appeared there
the day before. Mayer's book adds itself to many others presently available, to Claude Lanzmann's masterpiece *Shoah*, to Raul Hilberg's classic
book, *The Destruction of the European Jews*, to the highly varied colloquia
devoted to this unfathomable subject (including one at the Paris École des
Hautes Études en Sciences Sociales in 1982 and a quite recent one organized by François Bédarida)[3], and to an entire collection of German,

American, Israeli, and—more rarely—French historiography. In no way
is the goal of Arno Mayer's book the replacement of this huge library.
Rather, it aims to give us a different—nay, as is the author's bent, a somewhat provocative—interpretation.

What sort of interpretation? Arno Mayer explains his intentions very
clearly in his "Personal Preface" and his "Prologue" (chapter one), as well
as in his "Afterword," where he replies to his critics. Perhaps those pages
render my own presentation "useless and dubious," like Descartes in the
eyes of Pascal. I shall nonetheless try to offer here a few words. I do so first
because I have been a friend of Arno Mayer ever since one fine day in May
1968—though this friendship has never proceeded without its disagreements, and even some extremely lively clashes, including on the subject
of this book. Next, because this is a great book on this great subject; it is
coherent, superbly developed, and I defy anyone to put it down once he
or she has picked it up. Finally, I have agreed to say a few words about this
book because, on the whole, it offers an interpretation that is rich in
meaning and significance, even though, as is inevitable, it also elicits discussion, even objections.[4]

From the first pages of his book, Arno Mayer lays down a principle: we
must learn how to exit from the Cold War. The Hitlerian genocide was
perpetrated while the Soviet Union and the Western democracies were,
by the force of circumstances, allied against the Nazi will for total conquest. In their hopes and sometimes through their actual fighting, the
Jews found themselves in this same coalition, even though their sufferings, their resistance, and their deaths were largely ignored by the coalition forces. Salvation could come to them only through a shared victory.

The history of this genocide was itself written, in the main, only after
this coalition was dissolved and while a portion of the Jews, with the solidarity of many others, launched into a high-risk adventure in the Middle
East that led them into head-on confrontation with the Soviet Union and
its allies.

In the last analysis, the key concept in the writing of this history has
been taken not from history but from political science. It is the concept of
totalitarianism. Hitler and Stalin suddenly became almost twin brothers.
Between Auschwitz and the Gulag, there was no difference in kind.

In no way do I wish to deny the operative character of this concept of
totalitarianism as it has been applied by Hannah Arendt, Claude Lefort,
and so many others. It remains the case, however, that at the center of this
approach was the idea that communism, unless destroyed through war,
would establish indestructible dictatorships.[5] Now, this idea has proved to

be false. Everywhere (except in China, Albania, Vietnam, and Cuba) the "totalitarian" powers have collapsed, and the Cold War has disappeared, even if it has been replaced by other conflicts. On this point, Arno Mayer has gotten the jump on his century.

We are touching here on a very difficult question, one that lies at the very heart of this book. To understand the genesis and the development of the Hitlerian genocide is, first, in some way to restore the lived experience of the crime. That is to say, it is to follow the progress of Hitlerian *ideology* until the moment this ideology began to be *acted out*, from the fall of 1941 until the final spring, that of 1945. In other words, the work of a historian such as Mayer aims at the restitution of a *present*, indeed, a very short-term present. The Hitlerian ideology was what it was; it was "syncretic," as is said. It was born of an ancient, even warmed over, hatred of modernity.[6] And some Jews actually were the carriers of the seeds of this modernity, though this sometimes engendered conflicts within their own communities.[7] As murderous as the Hitlerian ideology was, its mere existence nevertheless is not enough to account for its actually being acted out. Paul de Lagarde, one of the ideologues who unquestionably paved the way in the nineteenth century for the rise of Adolf Hitler, wrote: "One doesn't negotiate with trichinae and bacilli, nor are trichinae and bacilli educable; one exterminates them as quickly and completely as possible." The historian Fritz Stern, who cites this text, comments as follows: "Few men prophesied Hitler's work with such accuracy—and approval."[8] What Stern says is true, but these words, which the Nazis both knew and made explicit, did not kill immediately. For one to reach the point of direct murder, duration and simultaneity had to be combined in a unique blend. Forgive me, if you will, this use of a Bergsonian vocabulary.

Arno Mayer begins, or almost begins, his book with a polemic against Fernand Braudel and the apologists for the "long-term" view of history. In the long-term view, Mayer says, there is no room for the Judeocide, a relatively rapid episode. Arno Mayer's challenge to the "long-term" view in some respects rings true, but in his own view the history of the Judeocide actually unfolds over a long-term, a medium-term, and a very short-term period.

The long term begins with the First Crusade (1095–1099), the Emperor Frederick Barbarossa (1152–1190), and the first Thirty Year War (1618–1648). These references to olden times serve as paradigms for extreme violence, for mass murder, and, especially during the Crusade, for the murder of Jews. At the same time, they also are models that have had real effects. The period of the first Thirty Year War witnessed a confrontation between the Machiavellian policies of various modern States, but it also saw the birth of modern rationalism. Hitler gave the name Barbarossa to his grand offensive operation against the Soviet Union (which had been prepared as early as 1940) because Barbarossa, who had disappeared in the midst of a crusade, was the archetype for those "hidden kings," destined to reappear gloriously, who played a significant role at the beginning of the modern era.[9] This choice was not the result of chance. Hitler took himself to be the leader of an ideological crusade against "Judeo-Bolshevism," and the SS, all due allowances being made for similarities and differences, really were the new Knights, the new soldiers of the Nazi Church. The fact that he takes completely seriously this vocabulary which his predecessors have neglected is one of the magisterial contributions Arno Mayer has made.

The medium term concerns the major shock Arno Mayer calls the second Thirty Year War (1914–1945), a shock that upset Europe and put it on the road toward decline. For the Jews, this age was at first the era of the final fulfillment of the emancipation process that had begun during the Age of Enlightenment. This "golden age" came to an end in Germany in 1933, but it includes the work of the Russian Revolutions which, despite all else, in this area at least can be described as emancipatory. Let us pause here a moment, for the pages Arno Mayer has written on this topic are among those that have given rise to polemical responses. One may judge, as for my part I do, that in Arno Mayer's vision of Bolshevism, and more particularly of Stalinism, some illusory elements have entered into the equation. Not everyone will accept, and for my part I do not accept, the image of Stalin that arises from these pages: a despot, certainly, and comparable to Hitler with respect to the kind of regime he imposed on "his" peoples, but also a rational leader in war who knew that, sooner or later, he would have to confront Hitler. The liquidation of Red Army officers during the 1930s and the 1941 surprise alliance do not coincide with this image, but the essential question does not lie there. Still less is the question whether or not some sort of "Judeo-Bolshevism" actually existed. For Mayer to be in the main correct, it is necessary and sufficient that a Hitlerian fanaticism existed and that, in the view of the leader of the Third Reich, Judaism, Marxism, and Bolshevism were all one and the same thing, the diabolic incarnation of which being the Soviet Union. Now, on this point proofs abound, and Mayer's demonstration, it seems to me, is not easily subject to refutation. Nor is it simply a matter of Hitler and his kind. It was not just a band of declassed hoodlums who took power in January 1933. At least until the July 20, 1944, plot against his life, Hitler relied upon traditional elites, among which the nobility was able to hold its own. Nothing is more gripping than to read, in the fifth chapter of this book, the account of the ceremony at Potsdam (March 21, 1933) where, standing next to old Marshal Hindenburg and the young chancellor, the *Kronprinz*, son of Wilhelm II, played a central role. Of course, Hitler did not borrow only from the old Germany of the Hohenzollerns, and even of the Hohenstaufens. He knew, too, how to make use of the symbolic capital of the workers' movement. Arno Mayer could have painted a lovely diptych by combining the "day of national resurgence" at Potsdam with the 1933 May Day celebrations in Berlin, but the latter appropriation is infinitely better known, and Mayer feels comfortable recalling it in just a single line.

The short term is the time of the war itself and, more precisely, the time of the Russia campaign, Operation Barbarossa, and, more precisely still, that of the obstacles this campaign encountered in the fall of 1941. The first gassings of Jews took place at Chelmno in December 1941, after the definitive failure of the attack against Moscow (Operation Typhoon). Here we have Mayer's central hypothesis: the massacres *of the Jews* (and not the massacre *of Jews* or of Soviet Jews alone) stems from a decision made in the fall of 1941, a decision made not in the exaltation of victory, of the crusade's triumphal success, but in the bitterness of a first setback: the Soviets did not collapse, Kiev was taken later than planned, neither Moscow nor Leningrad had fallen.

One will read, further on, Arno Mayer's argument for this hypothesis. On one key point, his correctness must be recognized. The final decision really was made in the fall of 1941, most likely in September. Philippe Burrin arrived at an analogous date in a book centered around this same problem, and he did so by taking an entirely independent path.[10] In any case, the decision had already been made, and at the highest levels of State, when, on November 6, 1941, Heydrich, the top official responsible for Jewish affairs, wrote to *Gauleiter* Wagner that "at the highest level (*von höchster Stelle*) Jewry has been designated with the greatest vigor as the responsible incendiary in Europe, which, in Europe, must definitely disappear (*der endgültig in Europa verschwinden muss*)."[11]

This point should now be considered to be settled. As for the rest, the solutions proposed by Arno Mayer will not convince everyone, first of all me. Should it be granted, for example, that the Einsatzgruppen offered cover for and incited the local pogroms more than they themselves killed directly during the first weeks of the invasion? There is no doubt that, in the Baltic countries and in the Ukraine, this invasion actually did set off reactions that were all the more violent as the Jews might have appeared to be props for the existing regime. Equally established is the fact that the German military wanted to protect themselves by hiding behind local initiatives. Nevertheless, as Arno Mayer himself notes in the eighth chapter of his book, as early as June 27 a Wehrmacht unit and a "special commando group" (Einsatzgruppe) indulged in a massacre of two thousand Jews at Bialystok. Using documents with which I am familiar, I can say that the responsibility of similar units is perfectly well established in the case of the massacres that began in July in the Baltic countries.[12]

The other sticking point is to be found in the very notion of *failure*, a notion shared, moreover, by both Mayer and Burrin. Once again, discussion and objections are called for concerning chapter eight, notably with regard to the following formula: "Indeed, the decision to exterminate the Jews marked the incipient debacle of the Nazi Behemoth, not its imminent triumph" (p. 235). But when did the debacle begin? It is on this point that, inevitably, Mayer is less clear: Was it during the last days of July? In August? September 19, the day Kiev was finally taken at such a high cost? December 1, with the resignation of von Runstedt? Or even December 8, with the suspension of offensive operations? Failure can be established by the historian, and Arno Mayer is perfectly well entitled to judge that the fall of 1941, not the fall and winter of 1942 (Stalingrad and the Allied landing in North Africa), constitute the turning point in the war. Nevertheless, he would still have to prove—and neither he nor Burrin does so—that in September or, at the latest, in October, Hitler and his crusaders were conscious of their failure. My sense is that things should be taken in another way.[13] The "archaic" idea animating Hitler, which comes across in the above-cited letter from Heydrich, is that blood calls for blood. Eminently responsible for the Judeo-Bolshevik conspiracy which supposedly lay at the origin of Germany's misfortunes and of the war itself and being, in addition (unlike the leaders of the Soviet Union) available, the Jews had to pay. Hitler says this out loud on January 30, 1942, at the Palace of Sports in Berlin. Mayer quotes him in part; a fuller quotation reads as follows: "For the first time, it will not only be others who will be bloodied [*werden verbluten*], but this time and for the first time, the ancient Jewish maxim will be put in practice: 'an eye for an eye, a tooth for a tooth" (see Mayer, pp. 307–8). Everything is there, including the secret substitution of the German people for the Jewish people as the chosen people.

Such is then, boiled down to its essential points, the thesis Arno Mayer defends in this book. Total war demands not only material and human resources, it also demands the definition of an ultimate enemy, preferably one that might be available to be killed. Conceived of as the incarnation of all the poisons from which Germany was suffering, the Jews occupied this role, first in the East, then in the West. As for the historical truth of the matter, it has nothing to do with any kind of dogma or with what would be furnished by some sort of *ultimate document*, the kind historians dream of discovering. Between the theory expressed in so many public and private bloodthirsty declarations and the methodical practice of murder, there always remains some dissonance. And it is perhaps in this dissonance that this long sought-after truth is stirring.

I spoke at the beginning of this preface of the freedom of the historian. It is time for me now to return to this point. For, in my mind, it is not solely a matter of a freedom to interpret, nay, even of the freedom to be mistaken, but also of the still more fundamental freedom to choose one's subject, to define it, to compose it as one composes a work of art— though in this case the work of art always remains unfinished, it calls forth others, like the *Phares* (guiding lights) in Baudelaire's famous poem. Let us offer a few examples of the possible positions one might adopt.

Arno Mayer has devoted a few pages to the Hitlerian gas chambers, which have become the object of so much sarcasm among those enamored of detail. He does so in chapter eleven on Auschwitz and in chapter twelve on the "extermination sites" properly speaking: Chelmno, Belzec, Sobibór, Treblinka (which, logically speaking, actually could have preceded the earlier chapter). The subject does not truly have the same importance for him that it does for others: "Indeed, the killing by asphyxiation may be said to have intensified the torment of the camp's Jews in degree, not in kind" (p. 362). It is also a question about which he expresses some critical doubts—not about the fact itself, but about the exact physical character of the chambers (dimensions, capacity, etc.) and about their precise function in the selection process that awaited the new arrivals: Were all those who were not, according to the SS's logic, deemed fit for work eliminated immediately or did some among them die a "natural death" (which, it goes without saying, was perfectly criminal) without the direct intervention of the asphyxiant gases? Did this last category not represent, at Auschwitz, the majority of victims? Gathered here in condensed form, we have almost all the types of problems a historian of these times and of these questions necessarily encounters, but the examples I just gave have, I believe, a still more general import.

Let us take up these three questions again in succession.

The first, that of the import and historical signification of the gas chambers, is, in my view, contained within the larger problem of how to compose a work of monumental proportions. What, for example, was the choice Claude Lanzmann made in *Shoah*?[14] This film is not centered directly on the event itself but on the memory the surviving actors have retained of it forty years later. *Shoah* begins not with the Nuremberg laws or the first SA parade before a victorious Hitler but with the tale of the truck gassings at Chelmno in December 1941. This date marks a break— in the history of the Judeocide, that is—for these were not the first deaths induced by asphyxiant gases. Such gases, Mayer recalls, had been used against invalids and the mentally ill as early as 1939. As early as September 3, 1941, moreover, Soviet prisoners of war were exterminated at Auschwitz with the aid of Zyklon B. What the gases introduce is not additional sufferings inflicted upon the victims; it is extremely likely that the actions of the Einsatzgruppen or simply life in the overpopulated and famished ghettos caused much more suffering than this death masked as a shower. What the gassings introduced and what is, in my view, of capital importance is not the use of industrial techniques to deal out death, for in themselves these techniques were of a rather low level. What the gassings offered that was new is the anonymity of the executioners opposite the anonymity of the victims and, in the last analysis, their innocence. For, in the gassing system, no one did any direct killing. Even if his mode of composition is totally different from that of *Shoah*, this change, I feel, should be of concern to Arno Mayer since it is directly related to Nazi policy. That is to say, it lies at the very heart of the subject he has undertaken to examine.

The second problem, that of the gas chambers at Auschwitz, is of a different order. It pertains less to a historical analysis, in the sense that Mayer practices such analysis, than to a form of research that is, properly speaking, technical in character, even archaeological in the full sense of the word.

A technical expert of this (somewhat sinister) kind of archaeology exists. His name is Jean-Claude Pressac, and his major work was published in New York a little more than a year after Mayer's book first appeared.[15] Arno Mayer and Jean-Claude Pressac: here we have a diptych one would not even dare dream of depicting. On the one hand, we have a professional historian of the old European school, a Jew who stands very far to the Left but who teaches at the ultraelite Princeton University. On the other, we have a pharmacist with a practical knowledge of chemistry from a poor outlying district of the Paris suburbs who stands even further to the Right than Mayer stands to the Left and who, to tell all, not long ago was a "negationist," but one who, having a taste for research and technical questions, spent months upon months at the Auschwitz museum, at the scene of the crime, thumbing through papers rediscovered and catalogued by the Poles and systematically comparing various testimonies, writings, designs, blueprints, and still-standing ruins. For Jean-Claude Pressac, the questions that lie at the heart of Arno Mayer's investigation—Nazi ideology, its causes, and the date this ideology began to be acted out—are, properly speaking, devoid of all interest. The "cause" of the Auschwitz gassings is "human folly," and nothing more. Similarly, while the questions Pressac has raised were examined by Mayer with a critical eye, he was assuredly not in a position to resolve them.

Was such an archaeological effort really necessary? Certainly not in light of the blinding evidence of 1945. But the answer is "certainly yes" today, in the face of the campaign of the negators. But no less is the answer "certainly yes," I would say, on the properly historical level, because on this level everything must be subjected to measurement and calculation, because someone's capacity for murder is not to be evaluated on a subjective basis alone, because the written or graphic evidence—which is of an excellent quality—has to be judged in the light of the German archival records, even if the words we read on the blueprint sheets do not always correspond to the actual usages, even if the "morgue" (*Leichenkeller*) was in reality used as a gas chamber. It is a scholarly success that today we are able to say that such important evidence is to be assigned a divisor coefficient of four, and we would be greatly wrong to go around sulking about it. The Nazis' crime is not lessened if we renounce some cooked figures. The question of the *exact* number of victims is not the essential issue. Arno Mayer says this explicitly more than once, and on this point I can only agree with him. In any case, no one will now (after Pressac's book, I mean) be able to speak, apropos of the Auschwitz gas chambers, of "rare and unreliable" sources, as Mayer has done (p. 362). Historical research does not progress in linear fashion, but it manages, all the same, to make some progress.

Was there both "natural" death and death by direct assassination at Auschwitz? This third question merits a few words, if only because of this: two equally honest historians who have no substantial differences between them can still diverge to a profound extent on an important point. Arno Mayer does not consider it established that *all* those who were not registered in the Auschwitz camp were *directly* assassinated. He thinks—and on this point he is correct—that a certain number of them (the aged, young children) died en route and that the fact that they were being transported already by itself constitutes murder. The debate, however, does not bear on these persons. It bears on those who actually arrived at Auschwitz. On this point, it seems to me, Arno Mayer's position is destined to become a classic case of overly critical historical analysis. True, he provides a few words of explanation in his afterword, where he limits himself to stating that if the thesis he is defending is not demonstrable, neither is the opposite thesis. But this explanation remains unconvincing.

I can understand the reasoning behind this faux pas. Auschwitz does not offer us a very good example of extermination pure and simple. That symbol is to be sought, rather, at Belzec or at Treblinka, in the collective assassination centers Arno Mayer studies in the twelfth chapter of his book. And about these murder installations, let it be said in passing, we have infinitely less information than we do about Auschwitz.[16] Auschwitz was a complex camp with very different levels of imposed suffering and exploitation, from the factories of Auschwitz III so remarkably evoked by Primo Levi to the "family camp" or the Gypsy camp, where a visitor not knowing what was really going on could have believed life there was almost normal. Even within Auschwitz, a certain number of detainees (like Arno Mayer's grandmother at Theresienstadt) might know only the outer circles of hell, Limbo, if you will. What is said here about Auschwitz can also be said, on a lesser scale, of Majdanek.

It nevertheless remains the case that, everywhere the Nazis had control (for example, in the convoys that started arriving from France and from Holland in 1942), those who arrived at Auschwitz-Birkenau on the famous "Jewish ramp" but who were not enrolled in the camp simply disappeared. On this point, the proofs are both negative and positive: no one, to my knowledge, returned from Auschwitz who had arrived on one of the convoys in question but who had not been enrolled. All the testimony, which inevitably comes either from the personnel in charge of surveillance and assassination or from enrolled detainees, some of whom approached very close to the death machinery, leads one to the same conclusion. Typhus and other causes of "natural" death certainly killed many at Auschwitz, as they killed many at Bergen-Belsen, where there were no gas chambers, and at Ravensbrück, where there was one chamber whose function was the elimination of "marginal" people rather than mass extermination.[17] I do not think that typhus and other causes of "natural" death killed those "countless" (Mayer's expression) unenrolled persons, at least when they survived the voyage and the initial shock of arrival.

On this point, therefore, I resolutely part company from my friend Arno Mayer. That does not prevent me from no less resolutely recommending that everyone read his book. While drawing up what Paul Veyne calls an "inventory of differences" (which is one of the main tasks of the historian), I still hold Mayer's book to be a great one because he has placed the Judeocide as a whole (as well as its near-most crime, the murder of the Gypsies) within the context of another whole, the Nazi concentration camp system. Divided between the logic of murder and the logic of production, this system experienced insoluble contradictions. It was itself the product of an ideology of conquest and murder, and anti-Semitism was *one* of its aspects—a capital one, certainly, but not the only one.

In a letter written to me a year ago (August 15, 1989) concerning Ravensbrück, Germaine Tillion makes the following point, which summarizes rather well what I have just attempted to express here: "Ravensbrück was only the spoke of a wheel, the immense revolving wheel of the concentration camp system. At its center lay the flame of the Jewish genocide, visible everywhere, known everywhere, bursting out toward the edges. . . . That of which we had a presentiment has proved to be true: the same personnel circulated day to day from one camp to another, they operated both the killing machine and, a few meters away, an industrial complex—all this was calculated, to the point of issuing meticulous, senseless orders. . . . For this reason, there were, until the very last day, a thousand camps in each camp—except, probably, in those camps about which we know almost nothing: Chelmno, Belzec, Sobibór."

Let us now read, in Marie-Gabrielle and Jeannie Carlier's excellent translation, Arno Mayer's book, his fine effort to grasp this revolving wheel in its entirety, his exceptional attempt to account in a critical way for what, in the end, remains unthinkable. *Why Did the Heavens Not Darken?* asks the English title to this book, a question borrowed from a Jewish chronicle of the massacres that took place in the Rhineland during the First Crusade. Why, indeed? Let us leave it to a historian to try and pose this question. It is not one for theologians to lay hold of.

12 | And by the Power of a Word . . .

This message, or, if one prefers, this testimony (I do not belong to the species of judges) is that of a historian who has always, as my friends Anahide and Levon Ter Minassian and Gérard Chaliand know very well, been fascinated by the Armenian example. It is also that of a Jew who cannot help but raise in his mind the question of the resemblances[1] and differences between the fates of these two strange human groupings. Both groups have been victims of a major historical crime, both are split between a (real or fictive) center and a dispersed periphery, both have had to grapple with the maddest ideologues, who sometimes are their own ideologues, both find themselves torn between memories still weighing on them and a history that does not always succeed in setting them free, and both must grapple with the Great Denial . . .

Indeed, the analogies are particularly striking. In the western world, both Diasporas have chosen the model of bourgeois life and commerce, sometimes finance. A peasant people in the two zones they occupied (the northwestern part of the Ottoman Empire—historical Armenia—and Cilicia), in towns the Armenians became, like the Lebanese, merchants and shopkeepers. In exile, they had their own Rothschilds who were

Invited to participate in the sessions of the Russell Tribunal that were held April 13–16, 1984, I was unable to free myself to attend. The text reprinted here ["Et par le pouvoir d'un mot . . ."] develops a message read publicly during this session. It was used as the preface to a book edited by Gérard Chaliand, Claire Mouradian, and Alice Aslanian-Samuelian for the Tribunal Permanent des Peuples (Russell Tribunal), Le Crime de silence (Paris: Flammarion, 1984). Reprinted in JMP, pp. 453–62.

named the Gulbenkians; they even had, in the Soviet Union, a Mikoyan who could be defined, opposite Stalin, as a "court Armenian." In the Armenian consciousness of today, the Armenian Republic of the USSR, ever so removed from the Western model, nevertheless functions as the site of the nation's physical embodiment: "The Armenians have their *Israel*: it is Soviet Armenia. All authorized speeches present Soviet Armenia as the motherland of all Armenians. All observers note that it plays this role for the Armenians of the Diaspora only for the length of a tourist visit."[2] This split is more often spoken about than actually lived, but are not things the same with the Jews of the West and Israel . . . ?

Armenians and Jews have their ideologues who fight against assimilation, "dissolution," the abandonment of cultural and national values. Of course, Soviet Armenia is not a land for colonization, let alone a site of return. A few attempts were made in this direction after the Second World War, but they were quite ill received. Nevertheless, a sort of abstract Zionism (abstract, because stripped of the least chance of realization, for lack of a protective empire) still develops among some young people who are drawn toward historical Armenia, this other Palestine.

If resemblances do exist, dissimilarities and even a radical opposition also exist, to the point that, just as legitimately as one compares their fate to that of the Jews, one might also compare the fate of the Armenians to that of the Palestinians—though in the latter case, of course, with no genocide thrown into the bargain at the outset, but rather an expulsion, a pushing back. Concentrated in the "Russian" part of historical Armenia, the Armenians of the Soviet Union, their eyes fixed upon the "bluish snow" of Mount Ararat—"a gigantic pyramid or Mayan temple rising from the flat plain into our sky"[3]—consist in large part of refugees from Turkey and, now, their descendants. These Armenians define themselves in relation to the lands that once were theirs beyond the bluish line, just as the Palestinians say that they are from Jaffa or from Akko, from Haifa or from Ramle.

In other words, as concerns a goodly portion of this Soviet population, the analogy that forces itself upon us is the analogy with the Palestinians of Jordan, who also have swarmed into the Arab Near East and beyond without losing their identity.

Should one then be surprised, under these circumstances, by the constant support the PLO gives to the Armenian Delegation (which is striving to prolong the existence of an ephemeral republic that disappeared in December 1920, when it found itself caught between the Soviets and the Turks)?

Armenian political life, therefore, also appears dispersed, torn between a slow but sure adaptation to the bourgeois models of the countries welcoming them and a desperate sense of marginalization. Though once does not make a habit, the countries that have welcomed them really have been welcoming in this case. Of all the foreign communities that have established themselves in France, for example, since the beginning of the century, none has been better greeted, better integrated than the Armenian community. A rare fact: the social mobility of this community and the successes of a number of its members have not created any genuinely hostile reaction. And conversely, a myth of the Christian West as Savior still exists among a number of Armenians, which thereby gives them something in common with, for example, the Maronites.

The Palestinian dimension may also be seen to be present, however, in the existence of terrorist organizations—which, moreover, are divided among themselves. One would be tempted to use generational differences as a summary form of classification. The first generation, the one that survived the great massacre, led a hard life adapting to its new situation. Today, that generation has disappeared almost completely. The second generation benefited from the efforts and the money accumulated by the first. This second generation has provided a good number of the members of the assimilated population. The third generation, as is classic, is in search of its roots, and it is so precisely because to a large extent it has lost them. It is principally this latest generation that has furnished the Armenian community with its abstract "Zionists" and terrorists. Immediately after the First World War, terrorism was sporadic and it struck at individuals; when it reappeared in 1975, that is to say, two generations after the massacre,[4] it struck less at individuals than at offices. That it also reemerged at the beginning of an economic crisis is obviously not just happenstance.

As the Hitlerian genocide helped to rigidify, nay, to freeze Jewish identity, the genocide of 1915, which was decided and perpetrated by the government in Constantinople and the Ittihad (Union and Progress) movement, has contributed in a decisive way to the rigidification, even the freezing of Armenian identity. These two events are even more closely connected to each other, however, than might appear at first sight. The first reason for the close connection, of course, is that the massacre of the Armenians was able to serve as a model,[5] though this phenomenon is of secondary importance. What really matters, what is of capital importance is that the intentional murder of the Jews (and of the Gypsies) has, as an aftereffect, served to illuminate and define in its very meaning the massacre of the Armenians as *state-sponsored massacre*, the inaugural moment in the already long series of state-sponsored massacres. Here we notice the properly totalitarian dimension of the phenomenon common to both these instances of genocide, that of the Armenians as well as that of the Jews. Nevertheless, it must be stated and repeated for all to hear: no light is shed on either the one or the other by speaking of a "Holocaust." A holocaust presupposes the presence of priests. Neither in 1915 nor in 1942 were there any priests on the scene, but instead the servants of the totalitarian order of the two nation-States, employing varying technologies.[6] This remains true, whatever the clutchings and contortions in the thinking of some members of both groups. Need we recall the following truth: having suffered an attempt at genocide gives one a "right to remember,"[7] not a right to be decorated with a medal?

It was during the four years following the collapse of the Central European empires and of their Bulgarian and Turkish allies—i.e., between the end of 1918 and the month of August 1923 (the date the Lausanne Treaty was signed)—that the Turks established their discourse of denial. What we are saying is that this discourse was constituted as one by-product of the creation, by Mustapha Kemal, of a unitary and centralized Turkish State.

The Sultan's government immediately recognized the crimes committed by the officials of the Union and Progress group, the Ittihad of Talaat and Enver. It condemned them to death in absentia before the military tribunal in Constantinople. At the time, the facts appeared to be well established, and the coded telegrams that established the responsibility of the central government were translated and read in public.[8] Even better, a Kurdish general, Mustapha Kemal,[9] offered the following deposition to the military tribunal in January 1919:

> Our people perpetrated these unheard-of atrocities and led the country to ruin in their own self-interests. They doused little children with petrol and burned them alive. They violated little girls and young women before the eyes of their bound-up parents. They stole all their belongings and their estates and deported them to places as far distant as Mosul. They gathered the innocent folk, led them aboard freighters and dumped them into the sea. They ordered the preaching of sermons in the mosques urging all loyal non-Muslims to accept Islam, and they were responsible for many forced conversions. They forced old and hungry men to walk for months and perform the labor of slaves. They imprisoned young women in

houses and forced them into humiliating acts unheard of in the history of any nation.

Yet, as early as 1919, a first riposte also began to be prepared: the deportation was legitimate, but not the massacre. Soon, only the deportation would be mentioned.

After Kemal Ataturk came to power, the discourse changed radically. Real or imaginary, the unity of the Turkish country had to be achieved. The Armenian problem was resolved by massacre and expulsion. The defeated Greeks, who had embarked on a mad military adventure, became the object of a population exchange that allowed them to remain (temporarily) only in Istanbul, which had its status as the capital removed. The Kurds became no more than "mountain Turks" (which did not prevent them from revolting in 1925). At Lausanne, Ismet Inonu, Kemal Ataturk's deputy, could calmly declare: "The responsibility for all the calamities endured by the Armenian people in the Ottoman Empire thus falls upon its own doings, while the Turkish government and people resorted, in every case and without exception, to measures of repression or retaliations, and only after exhausting all their patience." This boils down to saying that, in a country where different cultures clash, the majority culture is always right, the minority always wrong. The Turks certainly are not the only ones who have reasoned in this way. What came to pass later, starting in 1923 and continuing until the present day, pertains to minor variations in a discourse that had already been fully constituted, each section thereof itself being replaceable without effecting the least change in the basic overall argument.

This, in turn, amounts to saying that the nonexistence of the great massacre of the Armenians (which, after the Second World War, would come to be called the genocide of the Armenians) was going to become state-sponsored truth in Turkey. Or better: it has become a national truth with a totalitarian dimension to it, responsibility for which everyone—government officials, diplomats, academics, and even professional historians—has taken a share in assuming. The law that governs this kind of discourse is expressed perfectly in the *witz* (witticism) of the cauldron, which Nadine Fresco has opportunely recalled apropos of the genocide of the Jews[10] and which might be transposed as follows: "There was no genocide of the Armenians; this genocide was entirely justified; the Armenians massacred themselves; they were the ones who massacred the Turks."[11]

The gravest thing is that the very people who wish to challenge the established social order in Turkey adopt this nationalist argument as their

own, repainting it in "progressive" colors. And of course, as in all massacres, there are in such reasonings some shreds of truth that have been
transformed by madness. To the military arguments advanced by some—
in April 1915, the Turks were threatened both by the Russians in the north
and by the Franco-British forces who, without knowing it, had almost
broken through the Dardanelles—are added some considerations about
imperialism. The Armenians, unlike the Kurds a Christian minority, actually were being used in part, like the Copts and the Maronites, by the
Western imperialist powers—including, moreover, on this occasion,
German imperialism—and they might have welcomed the Russians as
their liberators. This had not prevented the Armenians, so far as one
knows, from answering the Turk mobilization order.[12] Nor is it clear how
this potential sympathy for the enemy could justify the skewering and
roasting of Armenian babies. Were these babies the accomplices of imperialist powers? But there are, as one knows, instances of genocide that,
while being denied, also proceed, it is nevertheless quite discreetly suggested, in the general direction of History.[13] Perhaps the gravest thing of
all, however, is that this state-sponsored truth has taken on international
dimensions, whether it be Paragraph 30 of the United Nations' report on
genocide, which was devoted to the case of the Armenians but which was
removed in 1978 for having committed the crime of offending Turkey; the
U.S. State Department's November 1981 denial of the very existence of
this instance of genocide; Israel's yielding to Turkish pressure on the occasion of a conference on genocides in history; or, finally, the Russell Tribunal itself, which, in 1967, condemned under the abusive name of "genocide"[14] the American crimes in Vietnam, but which—in order to satisfy
the wishes of the Turkish judge (who was supported, in the name of Islam,
by the Pakistani judge)—removed the murder of the Armenians from the
list of genocides that have taken place in history.[15]

I am not one to be suspected of underestimating the importance of historical "revisionism" in the matter of the extermination of the Jews.
When, on the day after the electoral success of Jean-Marie Le Pen's far-
right French National Front in the European Community elections of
June 17, 1984, a journalist mentions, among the causes for this success, a
"loss of memory" and historical "revisionism" concerning the Jewish genocide,[16] I am tempted to say that the journalist has hit the mark. Everything
is happening, indeed, as if a taboo has been lifted. That said, and whatever
the abundance of revisionist publications, especially in Germany and in
the United States, the revisionist international is still nothing but a tiny
abject band that poses no serious threat in the Western world to historical

awareness of the Jews. In certain Arab countries, there certainly exists a form of state-sponsored revisionism that stems in large part from the "war racism" Maxime Rodinson has analyzed,[17] but no country, even for reasons relating to oil matters, has agreed to adopt a similar vision of history. As for Germany, it has acknowledged its crime.

Let us try and imagine, then, what the Armenian minorities might feel. Let us imagine a negationist Robert Faurisson as a governmental minister, a Faurisson president of the Republic, a Faurisson general, a Faurisson ambassador, a Faurisson president of the Turkish Historical Commission and member of the Senate of the University of Istanbul,[18] a Faurisson member of the United Nations, a Faurisson responding in the press each time the question of the genocide of the Jews is raised.[19] In brief, a state-sponsored Faurisson paired with an international Faurisson and, along with all that, a Talaat-Himmler blessed, since 1943, with an official mausoleum in the country's capital.

That the State in which the murder was committed denies the very existence of the murder and succeeds in convincing many others to share in this denial—sometimes in the name of self-interested diplomacy and sometimes in the name of the respect due to all peoples—poses, after all, a few problems for the victims' heirs.

That a fixation on genocide, an obsession with genocide that fails to perform the "labor of mourning," also involves a danger is quite self-evident. The identity of a people cannot be limited to the disasters it has suffered. Just as one must protest against the "lachrymatory" conception of Jewish history, against its transformation into a permanent *Valley of Tears*,[20] so the most conscious Armenians know that their culture does not totally consist of terrible memories and that a culture that nourishes itself on genocide alone will quickly become a dead culture.

In this particular case, however, the key does not lie in their hands.

Between the Armenians and the Turks reigns a strange, a sinister dialectic. The Armenians can, through terrorism, disturb the functioning of the Turkish State by striking at its diplomats and ministers. It serves nothing to point out, as governments favorable to the Armenians often do, that the present Turkish government is not responsible for the atrocities committed by the Committee of Union and Progress. The present Turkish government is responsible inasmuch as the Turkish present acquits the Turkish past. That a Turkish head of government may one day imitate the famous and oft-recalled gesture of Chancellor Brandt in Warsaw is not, however, something that depends on the Armenians themselves. The real question that is posed—and this is why things are so difficult—is the very identity of the State founded by Mustapha Kemal as the unitary (nay, Jacobin) successor State to the Ottomans' hierarchal, multinational empire. Paradoxically, the fate of the Armenian cause lies perhaps in the hands of the Kurds, the Kurds who once killed so many Armenians.

The right gesture or the right word may yet come some day, and everything will then become possible, including reconciliation.

"And by the power of a word, I recommence my life . . ."[21]

13 A Wonderful School . . .

"Y ou know, if you get out of here, it's a wonderful school . . ." These words, which provide the title to Nadine Heftler's book, were the last ones she heard from her father, Gaston Heftler, on the train ramp at Birkenau, just as the SS were making a twofold selection: between men and women, on the one hand (during the voyage, families still were allowed to remain together) and, on the other, between those who would be enrolled in the camp and would thus be given a reprieve and those aged persons, children, and men and women of all ages who were to be condemned to immediate destruction in the gas chambers of the Birkenau *krematorium*.

The Hitlerian genocide certainly should be measured in numbers: the number of victims, the number of those deported, from the plains of Russia all the way to France and from Italy or Greece all the way to Norway, along with, of course, as the epicenter of the massacres, Poland. This was the Poland of the ghettos, the Poland of the killing centers, and also the Poland of the two camps in which murder pure and simple coexisted with murder deferred: Auschwitz and Majdanek. In these two camps some survived, thanks to the German defeat and to the incoherencies of the SS bureaucracy. Nadine Heftler's life was saved, as also was Primo Levi's, though under extremely different circumstances. Stricken with scarlet fever, the Italian chemist was abandoned by his executioners and liberated by the Russians. Nadine Heftler left the Silesian camp on January 18, 1945. Through a series of dramatic episodes, which she recounts for us—

"Une Bien Belle École . . ." originally appeared as the preface to Nadine Heftler's *Si tu t'en sors . . . Auschwitz, 1944–1945* (Paris: Découverte, 1992), pp. i–ix.

death march, the train that led her to Ravensbrück—she finally ended up in Malchow, a far-off camp annex which was the woman's camp par excellence. It was there that she was liberated by a wave of American tanks on May 2, 1945, two days after Hitler's suicide and six days before the unconditional surrender of the Hitlerian Reich.

Nadine Heftler's itinerary was an individual one. Naturally, some shared this or that stage of it—but no one shared with her all the stages. This is a good point to remember: whether they were rounded up on the streets of Warsaw, arrested in Paris by the Vichy police on July 16, 1942, concentrated in this or that ghetto before being shot or deported en masse, or even apprehended in their home by two courteous and "proper" gentlemen during a simple identity check, the victims of the genocide were individuals—"the art personal, the souls singular," as we read in Paul Valéry's poem La Cimetière marin (The sailor's cemetery)—millions of individuals, each by definition irreplaceable.

Among these individuals, we need not go to any lengths to honor the obscure. For one's own kith and kin, a departed one is always illustrious. Arrested in Lyon on May 13, 1944, by the Germans and not by the Vichy regime, Gaston Heftler (born January 25, 1891), his wife, Hélène (born July 6, 1900), and Nadine, the author of this narrative (born, like her parents, in Paris, July 22, 1928), lived in Montluc near the famous historian Marc Bloch, without ever knowing him. Bloch had been arrested under the name Maurice Blanchard on March 8, 1944, and from there was taken out to be shot at Saint-Didier-de-Formans, near Lyon, along with a number of other members of the Resistance, on June 14—whereas Nadine and her mother were already at Auschwitz by then and her father, as far as we know, had already been gassed. Resistance member Marc Bloch was Jewish, but he was not a victim of the genocide.

In convoy no. 75, which left Drancy for Auschwitz on May 30, 1944, there were, according to the register compiled by Serge Klarsfeld,[1] 534 men, 470 women, and 104 children less than eighteen years of age, including Nadine Heftler, or 1,108 individuals. A few have, as one says, made a name for themselves. This was the case with Marc Klein, a professor of medical biology at the Faculty of Medicine of Strasbourg. He lived to testify.[2] It was the case, too, with the poet and essayist—to whom we owe Baudelaire et l'expérience du gouffre (Paris: Seghers, 1948)—Benjamin Fondane, who was deported under his original name, Benjamin Vecsler. He did not survive. It was also the case with those whom the German lists called Lucien and Marguerite Vidal (born respectively in Paris on February 27, 1899, and at Marseilles on May 20, 1907), who were deported under the abridged name they had rejected throughout the war and years of persecution, deeming that it would lack dignity to abridge their family name. Lucien Vidal-Naquet was my father. Marguerite Vidal-Naquet (maiden name Valabrègue) was my mother. Neither one returned. Meeting Nadine Heftler a few months ago, I met for the first time a person who had made with them what Jorge Seprun called "The Grand Voyage." Perhaps they even had been in the same train wagon? Nadine Heftler thinks she remembers—but is there not a little kindness in this testimony?—that my mother helped hers calm the children in the wagon by encouraging them to sing. She does not think that my mother went inside the camp, and I believe that what she says is true. As for my father, a survivor told me in 1945 that he may have come into contact with him as late as November 1944, but I know nothing for certain and, at this late date, I undoubtedly never will know anything.

Books, as is said, have their destiny. When, thanks to François Gèze, this manuscript fell into my hands, I could not help but be struck by this coincidence of fate. Nadine Heftler is only two years from being my contemporary, and she is closer still to being the contemporary of Anne Frank, who died at Bergen-Belsen. After Anne Frank suffered this fate, her work, the *Diary*, and her person have suffered the foulest of calumnies at the hands of the tiny international orchestra of the assassins of memory whose French musicians are named Robert X, Pierre Y, and Serge Z. Anne Frank, too, before becoming a symbol, was an individual. But above and beyond this now ineffaceable connection between the fate of the Heftler family and my own, I deem it necessary, indispensable even, to publish this book. I should now like to say why.

This narrative was written in 1946. It is published today as it was written by a young girl, not yet eighteen, soon after her return to France. She wrote it as a sort of dialogue with her parents—with her father, from whom she was separated immediately, and with her mother, who, exhausted, was, according to what Nadine was told on the spot, gassed on October 14, 1944. She wrote it as one drafts, for those whom one loves, the text of a burial stone; it is a *writing* for those who have no tomb.

François Gèze immediately understood—and I thank him for it—that this text had to be published as is, with simply a few minor corrections of spelling and syntax.[3] Notes that would add precision to or, when need be, rectify this or that secondary or major point were found to be indispensable. These notes have been prepared by Anise Postel-Vinay, a former Ravensbrück deportee who, alongside Germaine Tillion, has become an authentic specialist of the history of the deportation, and by Annette

Wieviorka, a professional historian and author of a key work on the "reception" of the deportation and the genocide in the immediate postwar period.[4] In the name of the author and the publisher, and in my own name, I thank them for having rendered, discreetly, this very great service to Nadine Heftler's book.

The book is thus a book of that era, written in the language of the forties. A myriad of details will strike the reader. Does one still know, for example, to take one minuscule example, that a haircut "à la garçonne" was called that because of Victor Margueritte's famous novel La Garçonne, which created a scandal soon after the First World War? Did Nadine Heftler know it herself when she employed this then-current expression? Another detail of a different level of importance: in 1946 the Germans were still called by the unflattering term "les Boches." Some of the publishers to whom Nadine Heftler offered her manuscript proposed to replace the word Boches with "Germans" or "Nazis." This correction might have been opportune, had the book been published in 1950, for example. In 1992 it would have made absolutely no sense. Nadine Heftler's book must be considered first as a document, a fossil that has reemerged after several decades buried in the ground. It is initially under this heading that it can and it should attract the reader's interest and, indeed, fire the reader's passion, today.

Interest in what, and why? A former Auschwitz deportee/member of the Resistance, General Rogerie, had the felicitous idea a few years ago of reprinting some of the eyewitness accounts that had been written as early as 1945 but that have in most cases been forgotten in the meantime.[5] These immediate eyewitness accounts offer passionate reading today. Not that they necessarily say things more truly than later testimony. Are they not, on the contrary, often "caught in the flow of reality," as Germaine Tillion would say? Rather, they offer to the historian of today the irreplaceable flavor of the truth of a bygone era, transmitted in the language of that era and struck with the stamp of evident fact. Nadine Heftler has nothing particular or new to tell us about the gas chambers (which some have shamelessly attempted to strike from history); she simply saw, like so many others, the flames shooting from the krematorium and knew, early on the twenty-second of October, 1944, that her mother was their victim. A few weeks later, she noticed that the gassings had been discontinued, and she owes her life to this November 1944 interruption and to the destruction of these murderous installations. On this point, her testimony, which was written in isolation—it is perfectly clear that she had not read at the time what we now call "concentration camp literature"—adds to that of many others, fully corroborating them. The same may be said for many other pages of this simultaneously old and new book. What did one know of Auschwitz at Drancy? On the then-reigning illusions concerning the Germans, who remained "very well-behaved," and on Auschwitz, which was perhaps "a sort of ghetto where a certain amount of liberty reigned," Nadine Heftler fully confirms what we already knew. The lie was necessary for everyone concerned—for the Nazis, for those who helped them maintain order, for the victims themselves who could in this way bear the unbearable and even, ultimately, for certain survivors, who owed their salvation only to this halo of illusions with which they had armed themselves till the very end.

Concerning the world of the concentration camp, too, Nadine Heftler adds her stone to the edifice of our knowledge. She saw and perceived the various hierarchies in the concentration camps. She saw them and perceived them after her own fashion, which is sometimes candid and in no way conceals her own prejudices. On one point of capital importance, she even contributes something new and important. The "children's block," where Mengele conducted his famous twins experiments, was, for the last weeks of 1944, so ill known that certain people took it to be merely legendary. This site of privilege, whose extraordinarily exceptional character at Auschwitz Nadine Heftler restores to us in a direct and sincere way, is thus delivered to history. We knew that in each camp there were a thousand camps, each one distinct and not always communicating with the others. Beside Birkenau, Auschwitz I even appeared "magnificent." There were a thousand camps and a thousand ways of seeing and sometimes of not seeing. Nadine Heftler saw: she traversed Auschwitz, Ravensbrück, and Malchow, taking in their diversity, their social and temporal thickness. She saw and she helps us to understand. She knows, for example, that the striped pajamas, that symbol of 1945, was in reality a sign of privilege.

Let us try to go a little further. In the years immediately following the liberation of the camps and the return of the deportees, two sorts of books rose above the level of banalities. There were two sorts of great books. There were the works of minds capable of synthetic thought, capable of apprehending not this or that camp but the concentration camp phenomenon as system, as social symbol. Thus we have Eugen Kogon's *Der SS-Staat* (Munich: Heyne, 1948), David Rousset's *L'Univers concentrationnaire* (*The Other Kingdom*, trans. Ramon Guthrie [New York: Reynal and Hitchcock, 1947] and *A World Apart*, trans. Yvonne Moyse and Robert Senhouse [London: Secker and Warburg, 1951]) and his *Les Jours de notre mort* (Paris: Parvois, 1947). Marxism, and the theory of class struggle, inspired many of these authors, including some people like Germaine Tillion who

thought of themselves as deeply removed from Marxism but who nevertheless inhaled it as part of the ambient atmosphere of the time.[6] In these
synthetic reconstructions, the "flame of the Jewish genocide," to borrow
Germaine Tillion's phrase, had some difficulty illuminating the system as
a whole, whereas in truth that system is incomprehensible without its
radicalism.

Meanwhile, other books were being written following an entirely different method. On the basis of an individual experience, an experience
situated in space and time, and starting from a meditation on memory,
these other works have been elevated to the level of universality which
alone establishes them as works of art. This was the case with Primo Levi's
If this is a man (translated from the Italian by Stuart Woolf [New York:
Orion, 1959]), as well as with Robert Antelme's *The Human Race* (translated from the French by Jeffrey Haight and Annie Mahler [Marlboro, Vt.:
Marlboro Press, 1991]). The latter book has remained without sequel, but
Primo Levi did not cease, from one book to another and until his death,
to deepen our understanding of the experience that had made him both a
slave and a dead man on reprieve. Many years later, Raul Hilberg's *The
Destruction of the European Jews* resumed and brought to a conclusion the
study of the systematic dimensions of the event, while, as a great artist of
Hell, Claude Lanzmann intercut the memories of actors and witnesses
in *Shoah*.

Nadine Heftler is neither a David Rousset nor a Primo Levi. And yet,
beyond the level of mere historical incident, she offers us something
essential and new. What? Herself. Who is she? A child, a French *bourgeoise*
of fifteen. The Nazis took her to be a Jewess because the majority of her
ancestors practiced this religion with which she was no more familiar
than I was at her age. Her father had even been baptized, and the disappearance of a baptism certificate plays a small role in this sinister story.
Let us not speak here of "assimilation." She is French, period. Her father
participated in the Great War as a fighter pilot. When they came to arrest
the family, she was in the process of studying a poem by Lamartine, and
at Auschwitz she loved to have people recite Racine to her. She does not
speak of Vichy. This was not 1942. In 1944, whatever infamous deeds the
militia might still have been committing, most deportations were undertaken directly by the Nazis. This was the case with her parents as well as
with mine. The Nazis' relentlessness was such that on August 22, 1944,
while France was in the midst of being liberated, a convoy that left Cler-
mont-Ferrand that day reached Auschwitz, apparently without encoun-
tering many obstacles.[7]

For Nadine, France serves as a standard for grace and beauty. When she suddenly came upon a beautiful landscape in Upper Silesia it was for her a French landscape.

This is a French *bourgeoise* whose criteria are the bourgeois criteria of what may be considered "distinguished" and what may not. Many of her companions are not "distinguished." She asks herself: "Why should someone try to gain respect when one has the misfortune of belonging to such a vulgar sort of people?" She is not the only person who has ever reasoned in this way. One of her young companions had what was then called an "adventure," from which resulted a baby who was born and who died at Auschwitz. What would her parents say upon her return?

Nevertheless, as the months passed Nadine discovered more and more about the universe of incarceration and then the concentration camp universe. Nudity might serve as a fitting symbol for this progressive discovery. At Montluc, Nadine notes, "It was there that I saw for the first time so many nude backs." At the time of her arrival at Auschwitz, she records, "It really was a frightful spectacle to contemplate all these nude women, some with their bellies tumbling out in four or five folds, others bearing the scars of a cesarean section, and certain ones, indeed, having a chest that goes down to their belly." But there is something worse, the ultimate stage in the revelation of genuine nudity, that of corpses: "A dozen female cadavers laid out, one next to the other, completely nude, some of them with their eyes still open." Nadine Heftler has become an adult.

There can be no doubt that what took place was a sort of "initiation" in the sense anthropologists give to this word, an initiation into a world where she wanted, desperately, to survive. Indeed, there was an initiation in a twofold sense: adaptation to a new universe and a change in age class, that is to say, her entry into adulthood. Rites of separation, rites of marginalization, rites of acceptance, all of these rites—which, in 1909, Arnold Van Gennep had labeled "rites of passage" (*Rites de passage* [Paris, The Hague, and New York: Johnson Reprint Corporation, 1969])—find their counterparts in the difficult test through which Nadine passed, and from which she emerged victorious. Without knowing it, she employs the language of ethnologists: "I had to be born under the most difficult of conditions possible." This is exactly what the ethnologist calls a ritual death followed by a new birth.

The central episode, the one that provides the key to the meaning of the whole book, is obviously Nadine's separation from her mother, followed by the latter's death. "Until then, I really did not exist, I had no personality, no force within me. With Mama gone, I had the feeling that I was suddenly being brought to life. From the zero that I was, and this word is not too strong here, I had to become in a few minutes a unity of my own." The extraordinary fact is that appearances were going to play against this evident reality. Nadine was saved during the initial selection process because, though a child, she appeared to be an adult. Having become a woman who had decided to live, it was at this point that she went on to play the child and to enjoy the privileges of the inmates in the "children's block." It was then, too, that other adult women began to exist for her. Before the disappearance of her mother, Nadine mentions no names, first or last. Afterward, Hélène Bruner, Estelle, and a few other names appear. Having decided to live, Nadine played the rules of this terrible and sinister game. And if, in order to survive, it was necessary to steal—to "organize," as one said in camp lingo—"organize" she did. With the luck she had—the luck that permitted her, at each turning point, to choose the path that led to safety, to do, in short, the opposite of what the heroes of Greek tragedy do—how heavy must have been the weight of this abominable initiation into the universe of Auschwitz, this game of hopscotch in which Heaven constantly lay next to Hell?

14 | The Harmonics of Szymon Laks

In his first published narrative account of his time at Auschwitz, the Italian chemist Primo Levi, who arrived in the camp at the end of January 1944 and was able to survive until the Russians' arrival because he was recruited as a chemist by the rubber engineers at Auschwitz III, explains in the following terms what it took to survive:

> At Auschwitz, in 1944, of the old Jewish prisoners (we will not speak of the others here, as their condition was different), *"kleine Nummer,"* low numbers less than 150,000, only a few hundred had survived; not one was an ordinary *Häftling* [detainee] vegetating in the ordinary *Kommandos* [detachments], and subsisting on the normal ration. There remained only the doctors, tailors, shoemakers, *musicians,* cooks, young attractive homosexuals, friends or compatriots of some authority in the camp; or they were particularly pitiless, vigorous and inhuman individuals, installed (following an

"Les Harmoniques de Simon Laks" was originally published as the preface to Simon Laks, *Mélodies d'Auschwitz*, trans. from the Polish by Laurence Dyèvre (Paris: Cerf, 1991), pp. 9–18. [T/E: An English-language version of Szymon Laks's book previously appeared as *Music of Another World* (Evanston, Ill.: Northwestern University Press, 1989). The page numbers and quotations cited in the present essay are those of the 1989 American edition. In one case, however, despite the generous and diligent efforts of Heather Kenny at Northwestern University Press, I have found it necessary to translate on my own a quotation (concerning music as a "consumer object") from the French, as the English in this now out-of-print volume could not be found. See also n. 9 of the present essay.]

investiture by the SS command, which showed itself in such choices
to possess satanic knowledge of human beings) in the posts of
Kapos, *Blockältester*, etc.[1]

Se questo è un uomo (*If this is a man*) is an eyewitness account written in
1946. What makes it exceptional is that it did not remain mired in the
immediate, that it was inseparably narrative account and analysis, testimony and reflection.

It would not be true to say that, upon their return, the deportees kept
quiet.[2] Many tried to speak up, even if they did not always know how to
express themselves and even if people did not always want to listen to
them. It would nevertheless be true to say that, in the immediate postwar
era, it was not easy to have at one's disposal both lived experience and a
capacity for reflection.

Primo Levi and a few others (Robert Antelme, Eugen Kogon, David
Rousset, Germaine Tillion) did have this twin ability. But in Primo Levi's
specific case, what was in his first book a simple theme proved capable of
continuing development for over forty years (the writer took his own life
on April 11, 1987) and in an infinite variety of ways. The chapter from
which I drew these few lines is entitled in Italian "I sommersi e i salvati,"
or, word for word, "the submerged and the saved." Forty years after
Auschwitz, this chapter became a book, *The Drowned and the Saved*.[3] Primo
Levi describes there what he calls the "gray zone," the zone that harbored
the great majority of those who in the future were going to be saved from
what was, for them, only the Limbo next to Hell: "The privileged prisoners formed a minority . . . those who survived." This was much truer still
at Auschwitz than at Ravensbrück or Buchenwald. At Birkenau (Auschwitz
II), the first privilege of all, for those who reached the "Jewish ramp," consisted in not being exterminated immediately. Such a privilege was, so to
speak, nonexistent at the four killing centers, Belzec, Chelmno, Sobibór,
and Treblinka. Next came the opportunity to be clothed and fed under
close to "normal" conditions. As one traveled up the scale of the camps'
hierarchy, *power* became the practical condition for survival: "Like
Rumkowski, we too are so dazzled by power and prestige as to forget our
essential fragility. Willingly or not we come to terms with power, forgetting that we are all in the ghetto, that the ghetto is walled in, that outside
the ghetto reigns the lord of death, and that close by the train is waiting."[4]

In *The Drowned and the Saved* Primo Levi examines Auschwitz in light of
all that his culture has given him, from the reading of Shakespeare to the
reading of the historians of the world of concentration camps. Between his

first narrative and this almost final analysis he had discovered a third mode of expression that was at once analytical and autobiographical. It is as a chemist that he wrote and published in 1975 *Il sistema periodico* (*The Periodic Table*, trans. Raymond Rosenthal [New York: Schocken, 1986]), a description of a life in twenty-one elements, from argon to carbon passing by way of zinc, tin, and uranium, each new element being inserted, one after the other, into this first-person narrative. Thus were professional life and intellectual life reunited in Primo Levi's work, the writer here making use of the arms and the language of the chemist.

If it is thus with an evocation of this now deceased witness that I have introduced the few pages my friend André Laks has asked me to write at the threshold to his father Szymon's book, I have done so because, as soon as I first read it, the name and the work of the Italian writer came to me both as a reference point and as an analogy. I did not know at first how right I was.

I never knew Szymon Laks and I hardly know anything about him today except what his son has told me directly or through documents he has communicated to me.[5]

Szymon Laks was born in Warsaw on November 1, 1901, and died in Paris on December 11, 1983. He belonged to a family of largely Polishized Jews who practiced very little the religion of their ancestors. He did not know Hebrew and did not speak Yiddish. He began his musical studies at the Warsaw Conservatory but left Poland in 1926, as his two brothers had done before him, to go to Vienna and then, tempted by its attractions, to Paris. More concretely, he left as much to flee anti-Semitism as to finish his musical education. Szymon Laks became a polyglot who, in addition to Russian and Polish, spoke French, German, and English, yet never broke his fundamental tie with Polish musical and literary culture. Throughout his life, including, as one shall see, at its most dramatic moments, he was, in the strongest sense of the term, an intermediary, a cultural mediator and interpreter. As a musician, he was both a pianist and a violinist, a composer connected with the Association for Young Polish Musicians in Paris, and an orchestra conductor. Like so many others, he wrote light music and music for films under various pseudonyms, and, before the Great War, he accompanied silent films on his violin. After the war, he became, in addition to his profession as a musician, a writer who published Polish books in London and a translator into French of books written in Polish. Later, in 1974, he translated an important Polish samizdat, *L'OEil de Dayan*, three novellas written by "Korab"[6] which evoke, in a very vivid way, the aftermath of the 1968 anti-Semitic crisis.

Sensitive to Polish anti-Semitism and in favor of Israel (which was "at war for peace," as he said), Szymon Laks nonetheless never gave in to the sort of primitive anti-Polish sentiments that too often characterize those whom I shall call "professional Jews." Jewish themes certainly appear in his music, for the most part after the war and notably in his "Eight Popular Jewish Songs" (1947) which set Yiddish poems to music. He was also the musician who turned the poems of Julian Tuwim into songs. I shall say nothing about his music. Indeed, when I listen to the aforementioned "Popular Songs" or to his "Elegy for Jewish Villages," I find it difficult to know how to separate the emotion the themes he deals with inspires in me from a sense of musical judgment which, in my case, is more rudimentary than informed, anyway.

After all, the book the reader holds in his hands [*Mélodies d'Auschwitz / Music from Another World*] is not a book of music, not even a book about music, but a book about the place occupied by music and, even more, by musicians, these bards of Hell, in this very special place that existed as a concentration and extermination camp between July 1942 and October 1944. A Jewish alien in Paris, therefore a predesignated victim, Szymon Laks was arrested in 1941 during the first major roundups, interned at Beaune-la-Rolande and then at Drancy, and deported to Auschwitz, where he remained until the evacuation of the Birkenau camp in October 1944. From there he went to Kaufering, a subterranean factory which was a *Kommando* of Dachau. It was after the evacuation of this latter camp, at the end of April 1945, that he was liberated by the Americans on the third of May. On the eighteenth, he was back in Paris again.

As for Primo Levi, he was not evacuated. Sick with scarlet fever, he had remained behind at the camp, and from there he was liberated by the Soviet army and repatriated under conditions he recounts in *La Tregua* (*Moments of Reprieve* [New York: Viking/Penguin, 1987]).

Szymon Laks's first narrative account was written in two voices, his own and that of his friend René Coudy. Both had been members of the Birkenau orchestra, one as violinist, the other as saxophone player. Szymon Laks had even become conductor of this orchestra. It is René Coudy who says "I" in this eyewitness account which was published in French in 1948 as *Musiques d'un autre monde*.[7] As for Szymon Laks, he appears under the name André, the name he would later give to his son. With a bit of artifice, musical language subtends this book as the language of chemistry provides the chapter titles for *The Periodic Table* or as music, once again, allowed Claude Lévi-Strauss to express themes and variations in the first volume of his *Mythologiques*.[8] "Alla tedesca," "Presto con fuoco,"

"Decrescendo," and "Dominant Seventh" are some of the titles of the twenty-two chapters of *Musiques d'un autre monde*, which ends on a "Final Chord." We have here, perhaps, an excess of musicality, but in the flood of survivors' narratives, the musical code lent some originality to this book. The date of publication, let us not forget, was 1948, when one had not yet fully gauged the depth and breadth of Auschwitz and of the genocide it symbolizes *today*. In 1948 the concentration camp par excellence was still Buchenwald, because it was from this camp that survivors had returned in greatest numbers.

In comparison with the 1948 text, *Music from Another World*, which was written in 1978,[9] is as if clarified and purified. Certainly, it too is divided into chapters with musical titles: an overture, melodies, and a coda, three in all instead of twenty-two. The book is full of reflections, and sometimes polemics. Was the act of harmonizing polonaises at Auschwitz a form of resistance? Was music at Auschwitz the highest expression of Polish patriotism? To these questions Szymon Laks offers precise answers that sometimes have the effect of a cold shower. It is not, however, only on this level that I would like to invite the reader to read this book, for the true, the serious question it poses is that of the place of an art, music, at this site of death. And *this* question is inseparable from another, one that I, after Primo Levi, posed at the beginning of this preface, and, as we shall see, it is one that Szymon Laks poses, too, after his own fashion, at the beginning of his book: How and at what price did the survivors survive? No one is better situated than Szymon Laks to raise these questions and to attempt to respond to them. A slave among other slaves at the beginning of his deportation, he was suddenly removed from the mass by a voice that cried in Polish: "Is there someone here who speaks Polish and knows how to play bridge?" Bridge led to the orchestra, since Szymon Laks also knew how to play the violin. At first, he was a member of the orchestra while also participating in the works of this *Kommando*. Next, he was engaged as a music copyist, a *Notenschreiber*, that is, a permanent member of the orchestra. Finally, he became the orchestra's conductor, named to this post by J. Schwarzhuber, the camp leader later named head of the Ravensbrück camp, where he was to practice on a smaller scale the extermination methods he had learned at Birkenau.[10] Without resorting to violence, Szymon Laks was able to traverse all the different layers of the "gray zone" and to retain a personal identity, whereas he had thought that he, like Jean Valjean in *Les Misérables* (to whom he compares himself), had lost it completely in becoming no. 49543.

His first reflex was to describe everything in black-and-white terms.

"White became black and black white, values were turned around 180 degrees" (p. 18). Szymon Laks rediscovers here almost exactly the same terms as those used in a famous passage from Thucydides,[11] where the latter describes how values were turned upside down during the civil war on the island of Corcyra. "Feelings of dignity and humanity," Laks says, "were regarded as an offense; logical reasoning, as a sign of madness; compassion, as a sign of pathological psychical and moral weakness. On the other hand, the basest human instincts, previously tempered by education and culture, changed into genuine camp virtues, becoming one of the necessary—but not sufficient—conditions for survival."[12] The judgment seems pitiless. But precisely because Szymon Laks is capable of formulating it and because he was, it seems, capable of formulating it even while in the camp, he was by and large able to escape the rule as he had defined it. The world he describes on a black-and-white background is not a world in black and white. It is not even uniformly gray. For Hell to function properly, it befits the circumstances that Hell be an inegalitarian place. Under the circumstances we are speaking about here, the secret of the entire affair is that the artists with whom Szymon Laks was living were not poets or painters but *musicians* and that (German culture being what it was) these musicians had a zealous audience. Menuhin could have survived at Auschwitz, but not Picasso.

What purpose did the Birkenau orchestra serve? Szymon Laks destroys any romantic legends. No, the orchestra did not play before the gallows or before the gas chambers, though the pervasive odors on members of the *Sonderkommando* who were in direct contact with the corpses sometimes stole into the room where the orchestra was rehearsing.

The musicians' official task was to accompany the departure of the *Kommandos* of workers and to greet them upon their return. They approached death close up—they even happened to benefit from it, as when they inherited music stands from the "family camp" that served as a relay station, a staging point, between the model ghetto of Theresienstadt in Czechoslovakia and the gas chambers of Birkenau—but they did not accompany death. Once, at Christmastime, they played a famous German carol, "Stille Nacht, heilige Nacht," to the sick in the hospital. The reaction was brutal: "Enough of this! Begone! Clear out! Let us croak in peace!" "I did not know," Szymon Laks comments, "that a carol could give so much pain" (p. 99).

Besides, this was not the social function of the musicians of Auschwitz. Szymon Laks explains matters brutally: "Music is the consumer article par excellence and, as such, it is subject to the art of 'organization.'[13] . . . At the time [in 1944], with the uninterrupted surge in 'gassed meat' and the prosperity it brought to the privileged classes of Auschwitz society, this industry took on the dimensions of a hitherto unknown luxury."The role music thus played may be explained by the existence of a "horizon of expectation." For the camp's aristocracy, the SS and the *Prominente* (the upper stratum of detainees), music occupied the top rung on the list of symbolic goods. For those who performed it, it represented a sort of survival-capital. This might mean survival for a few weeks, as in "Sängerin,"[14] the upsetting narrative (or novella?) of a Polish writer, Zofia Posmysz, which recounts the final weeks in the life of a Polish singer of Jewish ancestry who gained a bit of respite by teaching one of her codetainees to sing Schubert in German.[15]

For the members of the orchestra, music, much more than a simple matter of respite, was a matter of survival itself. One suddenly comes to the realization that the "private" function of the musicians, in the service of the *Prominenten*, was infinitely more important than their public function. Szymon Laks describes this private function with a terrible and sinister sense of humor, for example in the case of birthday concerts, which were closely regulated by ritual. Each had to be given what that person expected: Jewish music for one, some German folk song for another who couldn't stand listening to anything else. The upper SS aristocracy—a J. Schwarzhuber, or a P. Broad, who in other connections are known to historians through the testimony they gave at one or another of the great postwar trials—might be surprised while getting out of bed and thus rediscover, through the escape provided by music, a fleeting moment of humanity, as if the only possible dialogue between the SS and the detainees at Auschwitz passed, upon a background of murder, through the medium of music. Let us remain, for the space of one more phrase, in the language of music. A book is beautiful when it awakens in us, by that mysterious phenomenon known as resonance, some sense of harmonics, musical harmonics, poetic harmonics. And since we are, in Szymon Laks's book, among the bards of Hell, let us recall a verse of Ulysses from the *Divine Comedy*, which Primo Levi recited at Auschwitz to a Frenchman:

> *infin che'l mar fu sovra noi richiuso*
> ("Until the sea was closed over us.")[16]

15 Presentation of a Document: The Journal of Attorney Lucien Vidal-Naquet

The text I wish to present to you, the *Journal* kept by my father, Lucien Vidal-Naquet, between September 15, 1942, and February 29, 1944, is not completely new to the reading public. Large excerpts from it were reproduced in a Jewish monthly publication in 1960. These excerpts were accompanied, however, by commentaries so insulting (no community is without its fundamentalists) that I felt obliged at the time to protest.[1] Ten years later, a collaborator of this same review dared to write in *Combat* (April 8, 1970), the better to insult me, that this "gentle lawyer," this "mild Frenchman," this "meek Jew," went to end his life at Auschwitz, in the gas chamber, "as one takes one's retirement." The reader will understand that, under these conditions, I have for the past thirty years felt some reticence about speaking once again of this testimony.

When he began writing his journal, Lucien Vidal-Naquet intended at first to continue, by jotting it down on paper, an "internal monologue" then "gnawing" at his mind. He also was thinking of his loved ones who would perhaps read it later. Beyond this modest, family-oriented ambition, he wanted to be able one day to confront history as he would write it with his memories and even "try to express oneself with frankness on the events afflicting the universe today." An overall vision, therefore, a

Originally published in *Annales: Economies, Sociétés, Civilisations* 3 (May–June 1993): 501–12, "Presentation d'un document: Le Journal de Me Lucien Vidal-Naquet" served as the introduction to Lucien Vidal-Naquet's diary, which was published in the same issue, pp. 513–43, as "Journal (15 septembre 1942–29 février 1944)," with annotations by Pierre Vidal-Naquet.

planetary one. The tone does not lack in eloquence—a judicial eloquence, for the author of this journal was a lawyer—or in classical solemnity. At its point of departure is a reflection upon the decisive turning point in the war, the invasion of the Soviet Union; people knew by then that, despite some German victories, the *Blitzkrieg* had failed in the East. There is no point of arrival. Lucien Vidal-Naquet simply mentions, on February 29, 1944, the decision my mother and he had jointly made: "I write these lines in Marseilles, where we are holding on, despite threats of evacuation, despite the threat weighing upon us that this area, too, like the northern zone, will be 'occupied,' despite so many perils I do not even wish to mention now, as if remaining silent about them would somehow help ward off fate. This is where we have decided to wait. Will we be able to carry out our plan?" The answer to this question was given on the afternoon of May 15, 1944. That day, the Gestapo led Lucien and Margot Vidal-Naquet away on a one-way trip to Les Baumettes, Drancy, and then Auschwitz. As early as his internment in Marseilles, the author of this journal also underwent torture. The four children (three boys, one girl) were saved—the last one temporarily—because their father had always told them not to try to rejoin their parents if something went wrong and because their mother was able to save directly or aid in the escape of two of them, thanks to a chain of solidarity in which a domestic servant, teachers, and friends barred for us the road to death.

Every person who provides testimony should be presented to the public. In his disrupted relationship with a country that seemed to be rejecting him, Lucien Vidal-Naquet did not fail to present himself: "I am no longer but a second-class citizen on the very soil where I was born and where my loved ones sleep." This country to which he devoted a cult of worship, a cult that was closer perhaps to that of Péguy than to that of Barrès, was rejecting him.

Everyone who testifies and, a fortiori, everyone who testifies in a private journal, expresses an individual point of view. But—may the reader permit me this trivial remark—an individual is not just an individual. The *Carnets* of Pastor Boegner and the *Journal* of Charles Rist[2] are the work of two Protestant members of the bourgeoisie. One of them certainly has a more acute and critical mind than the other, but they both react in fundamentally similar ways to events and respect the same moral principles. Lucien Vidal-Naquet's *Journal* is assuredly quite different from that of another Jewish *bourgeois*, Raymond-Raoul Lambert, the leader of the UGIF (General Union of Israelites of France), who was engaged in a daily struggle to save what could be saved of "works" and men, but who, in trying to counsel Xavier Vallat (sometimes described by him as "charming"), took the enormous moral risk that is symbolized in the notion of "cutting one's losses."[3]

When I read *L'Étrange défaite* of Marc Bloch (1886–1944),[4] and each time I reread this book and its accompanying texts, I was struck by the resemblance between it and what my father wrote, even though the jurist was thirteen years the junior of the historian. I am also in a position to know, after having read Marc Bloch's letters to his son Étienne during the "phony war" of 1939–40,[5] that the system these two men used to educate their children was the same: the same authoritarianism, the same concern for scholarly excellence, the same fondness for intellectual and moral rigor.

Both Marc Bloch and Lucien Vidal-Naquet belonged to a very precise social category, that of de-Judaized bourgeois Jews (as Lucien Vidal-Naquet's boyhood companion and friend Raymond Aron expressed it),[6] that of those men whom Pierre Birnbaum called "madly in love with the Republic."[7] The de facto break with their religion, the adoption of first names that were Christian or that were likely to be interpreted as such, and adherence to the religion of republicanism were old traits in his family on the paternal side, since they date back to his grandfather Jules Vidal-Naquet (1831–1889), who himself never used his first name Aaron.

Lucien Vidal-Naquet was born in Paris on February 27, 1899, therefore in the midst of the Dreyfus Affair. His father and his uncle were ardent participants in this affair. His father was a lawyer who had been admitted to the bar in 1892. While he belonged, on his father's side, to an "old family" from Avignon and Bordeaux (and it was someone from the former region, Marguerite Valabrègue, whom he married at Marseilles in June 1929), his mother, one of five daughters of a wealthy glass-manufacturing industrialist, was born in Odessa in 1873. My great-grandfather had emigrated to Brussels in the mid-1880s and the international dimension of Judaism was highly present on my father's maternal side since one of my great aunts had married a Belgian and another a Russian who had left Russia only in 1914. The French women by marriage nevertheless made up the majority: three of five. If I provide these details, it is in order to recall that the overly famous opposition between Jews said to be "of old French stock" and foreign Jews, an opposition that contains some shreds of truth, does not overlap *completely* with reality. And if I speak of an "old family," it is only by convention. All families are old. A passionate interest in genealogy began in my family late in the nineteenth century. I have hundreds of items of evidence. It appeared again at the time of Vichy and the Occupation, not that any of us had to prove that we were established in France for five generations, as the parents of Claude Mossé had to do (I mention her because she, too, like me, teaches ancient history and because she, too, like me, belongs to a family from the Avignon region) in order to be admitted to university, but simply because my father wished to prove to himself his centuries-old roots in French soil. For obvious reasons, he did not pursue a similar investigation on his matrilineal side. And as genealogical research oftentimes is accompanied by surprises, he discovered that the maternal grandmother of his paternal grandmother, born in 1796, was the daughter of the Catholic servant girl of his ancestor Nathan Astruc. This discovery greatly amused him. We even had some "Aryan" blood in the family!

He did not enter the 1914 war for the obvious reason that he was still going on twenty at the time of the November 11, 1918, armistice. He nevertheless recalls in his *Journal* his pride at having, as a French soldier, taken the route to Strasbourg in 1919. To judge by his correspondence, his participation in the occupation of the left bank of the Rhine was accompanied neither by feelings of reservation nor by a sense of hatred. He was certainly in favor of a strict application of the Treaty of Versailles. But when Clemenceau failed on January 17, 1920, in his candidacy to the presidency of the Republic, he wrote to his parents three days later: "I am overjoyed to see ourselves rid of the Tiger . . . but pained, on the other hand, to cause grief to a man of his age, after all the services he has rendered."[8]

He thought of preparing for the Council of State, and this was one of the career models he proposed to me for my future, should there be one. He eventually took his oath as a lawyer on November 15, 1922, after attending the Department of Political Sciences in Paris, and immediately became the colleague of René Viviani. (Viviani, the president of the council in 1914, was, as one said at the time, an "Algerian," that is to say, a "pied noir" or Algerian colonist of European descent who, to keep his voice in shape, learned by heart each year a tragedy of Racine). He was also the colleague of Attorney Rosenmark. Secretary of the Conference of Lawyers in 1926 in a class that was to give two presidents to the Paris bar (Maurice Alléhaut and Paul Arrighi), he entered the offices of Alexandre Millerand. It was there, especially, that he received his legal training.[9] He was faithful to Millerand until the death of the former president of the Republic, and it was in order to pay his last respects to him that he made his final trip to Paris as a free man.

Politically, he was certainly the total opposite of a revolutionary. Was he an "old reactionary," as his best friend, Jacques Millerand, told me after the war? He is quoted as saying, "The situation will remain grave so long as Poincaré is dead," a phrase that offers a rather good example of his characteristically caustic humor.

Certainly, it was Poincaré the intransigent nationalist opposed to Germany who had won his approval. He was nonetheless tied by friendship to César Campinchi (as whose ghostwriter he sometimes served), the radical architect of a navy that unfortunately did not have the opportunity to serve any other purpose than to keep the ministries of the Vichy government filled, Vichy being "the society for the protection of admirals."[10] And a good number of his friends (André Boissarie and Raymond Lindon being two of them), were, after the war, supporters of the Radical Socialist Pierre Mendès France. He told me in 1943 that "one must be of the Left, believe me," but when I asked him which politician best represented his ideas, he named Paul Reynaud, undoubtedly because this man of the Right was also an antifascist, an advocate of the modernization of the army, and a supporter of France's alliance with Russia. He was intransigent on the question of the Republic and, conversely, on that of dictatorship. One might hear, in my home as well as elsewhere, some kind words about good dictators—not Hitler, of course, but sometimes Mussolini and, especially, Salazar. His cutting response: there are no good dictators. In other words, after the rise of Hitler he found himself on the side of those who, whatever their political affiliation, wanted to put up some resistance. He was ardently opposed to the Munich pact and his wartime letters show that he considered completely aberrant the policy that consisted of keeping a vigil, arms at order, along the Maginot Line.

He was a man of great classical learning: Latin and Greek, of course. He found mathematics discouraging, however, and he suffered greatly when, as a noncommissioned artillery officer, he had to work on trigonometry, aided by a carpentry worker who was more gifted then he[11] and with whom he became friends at the same time he became friends with the Jesuit Father Yves de Montcheuil, who was later shot at Grenoble.

He liked not only Chateaubriand and Corneille but appreciated the modern poets, as well. During the war, he gained sustenance from Aragon, Éluard, and Pierre Emmanuel, and not just because they were poets of the Resistance. When he spoke in his *Journal* (September 15, 1942) of the "silence of abjection," he was making an implicit reference to Chateaubriand and to his *Mercure* article (July 4, 1807), but the context reminds us once again of Marc Bloch. Let us compare the two formulas: "In the silence of abjection, might we hear the call to arms resound!" and

"My only hope . . . is that when the moment comes we shall have enough blood to shed, even though it be the blood of those who are dear to us."[12] Just as characteristic is his allusion to *On the Crown* (208): "The cry of Demosthenes resounds forever down through the ages, like that of a truth that refuses to die. I swear by Marathon and by Salamis . . . Germany's victory does not dishonor us. What dishonors us is our consent, our having reneged" (October 10, 1942). My boyhood pal and friend Robert Bonnaud, who was himself of working-class stock and who now teaches the history of history at the University of Paris–VII, knew my father in 1942. He had been struck at the time by the latter's diction, which, he said, was that of an actor of the French theater. My father did not think he spoke very well, for, what *la Berma* (Sarah Bernhardt) had been for Proust, the great Racine actress Julia Bartert, *la Divine*, was for my father. He often visited her during her retirement, heard her recite *Bérénice* twenty times, corresponded with her, and was advised, upon her death during the Occupation, that he had been mentioned in her will.[13]

Did he feel Jewish? The question is inevitable and the answer is not easy. He did not have a true Jewish cultural education, at the very most a certain familiarity with the Bible. He did not speak Yiddish, which he considered slang, nor, moreover, Provençal or the Judeo-Provençal of his paternal ancestors. During the war, in order to come to terms with the defeat, he translated a book written in German by the Swedish author Viktor Vinde, *Eine Grosse Macht Fällt*, and he began to study Russian seriously. He nevertheless enthusiastically mentioned a Yiddish theatrical production he had seen before the war. He was an atheist, he did not practice religion, of course, and he was not a member of the Consistory. At the time of his marriage to Margot Valabrègue at Marseilles June 17, 1929, he did no more than tolerate the presence of a rabbi. Against Vichy and the Nazis, he evoked not Ezekiel but Victor Hugo's 1853 anti-Napoleonic book *Les Châtiments*. Not a single biblical reference is to be found in his *Journal*, where he mentions Valéry, Michelet, Péguy, La Fontaine, and Beethoven. Like every educated man of his era, he was shot through with Christian references. On June 10, 1944, while passing before the Chartres cathedral, he repeated to himself Edgar Quinet's cry: "O France, Christ of Nations," which has greatly shocked certain Jewish commentators.[14] In speaking of the Jews at the beginning of his *Journal*, and after having formulated the maxim, "I feel as a Frenchman the insult that has been addressed to me as a Jew," he writes, "Today, I very strongly believe— since the distinction has been made between us and France—that France was us, and it is with a terrible wrenching feeling that I separate myself from her, if, as the sneering masters of the present hour affirm, it is in them and not in us that France is incarnated" (September 15, 1942). In reading these lines, I wondered whether there was not here a very distant echo of the "remnant of Israel" that alone is Israel (Isa. 10.4 and passim). But de Gaulle did not think otherwise, except that the latter experienced no doubts.[15]

There is hardly any point in mentioning that Zionism was entirely alien to his way of thinking, though this says nothing about what his attitude might have been in 1948 or 1967. When, in 1946, I read Sartre's famous *Anti-Semite and Jew*, I thought without hesitation that Sartre would have described my father, too, like Benda or Bergson, as an inauthentic Jew, because he had wagered on universality. I felt the same thing about myself.

During the war, he took the risk of not wearing the yellow star when he was in Paris, the star his brother wore. He rejected the UGIF on principle for exactly the same reasons Marc Bloch did.[16] He was nevertheless in no way ashamed of being a Jew. I recall a violent discussion between him and my mother when he refused to go see his sister at Saint-Agrève under the name of Vidal alone. He knew that even before the war he was surrounded at the Palace of Justice by a discreet form of anti-Semitism, but he never sought to hide his origins either by conversion or by any other means. In this domain, he pushed imprudence very far.

No doubt it has been necessary to provide these details, but it is incumbent upon us today to ask a certain number of questions about this text that extend from the most general—How did Lucien Vidal-Naquet view the evolution of events in the world, in France, and concerning the threat weighing upon the Jews?—to the most specific—What were the terms in which he posed the choice of his own destiny?

Like the majority of Frenchmen, he was interested only in the European war. No allusions to Japan are to be found in these pages. At the start of the *Journal*, the main event was the resistance being put up by the Russians: "Hitler will have found in the Russia campaign his Waterloo where, without any possible doubt, he will succumb." Quite wrongly, as we now know, he adds, "Hitler has not conducted an ideological war against Russia" (like de Gaulle, he says "the Russians"), "he has thrown himself upon Russia as a man confined breaks a window pane; he needed raw materials not obtainable by political means; he therefore has had recourse to arms." The truth is rather the reverse; it was Stalin who was obliged by Hitler to make an appeal to antifascist ideology as a way of defending himself and of mobilizing, in addition, all sorts of other ideologies. From the start, Hitler led a radically ideological war, a crusade.

Naturally, this view evolved as the war went on. He notes, with both hope and illusion, on October 11, 1942, what André Boissarie had told him: an alliance was possible between the prisoners of Europe and the German Communists. Contacts had already been made. Like the Communists, but for other reasons, he worries about the delay of the allied offensive in the West, and he denounces what he calls "Anglo-Saxon torpor" (December 27, 1943). Quite quickly, the Italian campaign appeared to him a failure. He notes the same day, "It is toward the Russia of the Soviets that the faces of oppressed peoples turn." So also the Yugoslavs, the Greeks, and even, according to him, the Committee of Algiers. He speaks, as well, of the "useless massacres committed in occupied territory by the Anglo-American raids" and of the "destitute" state in which the French army in North Africa seemed to have been left.

As concerns France, his rejection of Vichy—of the "group of gangsters presently in power in France" (December 17, 1942)—was absolute and this rejection began with a rejection of the armistice, "this crime against which I have never ceased to protest" (September 15, 1942), which was true. He violently rejected all hypotheses that Vichy might be playing both sides—even when Vichy strove to give such hypotheses credence, as at the end of December 1943 in the episode of the speech Pétain was unable to deliver—speaking of the "legend of playing both sides" (December 27, 1943). In November 1942 he feared lest Pétain grant himself easy victory by passing over to the right side. When Admiral François Darlan was killed, he wrote on December 25, 1942: "I will simply say that justice has been done." He did not have words harsh enough to characterize the men of Vichy and their accomplices still in power in Algiers. Let us give an example of the tone he used:

> In order to protest against the imprisonment of the magistrates who had handed down a decision that ran contrary to the will of the occupying authorities, the entire magistracy went on strike. A magnificent gesture, which shows what judicial independence is in a country where the judiciary truly is a third power. But do you think that it is the French magistracy that has adopted this wonderful attitude? What an error you have made! It is the Belgian magistracy that is offering ours this—for us—damning example!

The anti-Hitlerian writer who affected him the most during the final period of the Occupation was undoubtedly Bernanos.[17]

Can one situate Lucien Vidal-Naquet on the political spectrum of 1942–43? For "fear of being or seeming cowardly," he wrote to Léon

Blum, who answered him on September 27, 1942, in order to salute this "elegant and courageous" gesture.[18] He read and reread (November 4, 1942) with admiration Blum's declarations at Riom where Blum and others were being tried for their conduct during the 1939–40 war, and he adopted almost as his own Blum's famous opening line: "And if the Republic is today in the dock, we will be its witnesses and its defenders."[19] His commentary on Léon Blum at Riom can be summarized as follows: France's defeat has two fundamental causes, "extraordinary military incompetence" and the treason of key industries that were neither willing nor able to carry out programs "democratic governments, breaking with the constant inertia of their predecessors, had had the courage to conceive and adopt." This is a retrospective—and perhaps, even, insufficiently critical (incompetent generals had been maintained in their posts at the head of the General Staff)—rallying to the Popular Front of 1936. Lucien Vidal-Naquet adds:

> Léon Blum's crime is the crime committed by all those who *dream* of bettering—not those who *want* to better—the human condition, not by pity but by a spirit of justice. It is impossible to read these pages without being overtaken by a sense of respect for this nobility, this loftiness of thought, which makes the author a prince beyond comparison with his judges.

Lucien Vidal-Naquet reproaches Léon Blum not for the policies of the 1936 government but for his confidence in republican Germany. It is obviously the old admirer of Poincaré and the disciple of Millerand who is speaking here.

At bottom, Lucien Vidal-Naquet was a Gaullist who summarized his political program as follows (December 27, 1943): "Put the Germans out and the traitors in." A Resistance member, he joined the Musée de l'Homme network in October 1940 and then, through his sister-in-law and General Bloch, the National Front's network. He obviously did not speak in his *Journal* of these activities, but he does note on October 10, 1942, after passage of the work-force requisition law, "an obscure awakening of national consciousness; resistance is beginning to take shape." It was his brother who, in 1942, introduced Fernand Grenier to General Bloch.[20] In *Le Palais Libre* and *La Marseillaise*, Lucien Vidal-Naquet wrote, I have been told, under the pseudonym Ronsard. Nonetheless, the clandestine newspapers most often seen around the house were *Combat* and *Les Cahiers du Témoignage Chrétien*.

That said, Lucien Vidal-Naquet was a bourgeois patriot, which is exactly what he claimed to be. This is the meaning he gave to his Gaullism. Liberty-Equality-Fraternity, yes; democracy, yes; but a government of elites: "General de Gaulle's gesture, which permitted 'bourgeois' patriots to associate themselves with him and to fight under the banner of the Cross of Lorraine, will have had the virtue of providing the bourgeoisie with the opportunity to play its part in the trial we are now undergoing, so that, having suffered the hardships, it too will be able to share in the honor." Of course, he adds, "everything remains to be done in the social field," and freedom of any sort is better than the order of slavery and strongboxes. It is not an indifferent point "that at the hour when the party of the executed and of the victims of Hitlerism take power and guide France toward its new destiny . . . the bourgeoisie, too, will be able to enumerate its sacrifices and its injuries and say: 'And I, too, have suffered for freedom'" (October 10, 1942). It was only quite recently, and even after I drafted this presentation, that I came across his final political text, a note to be sent to London via the Gallia network on May 16, 1944, that is, the day after his arrest. It was a very sharp-minded analysis of the crisis of the Vichy regime, which Lucien Vidal-Naquet himself summarizes as follows: "In one way after another, the Vichy government is revealing its organic impotence and showing the clinical signs of its irremediable and inevitable decomposition. The cadaver sputters; as Barrès would have said: *Iam foetet* (already, it stinks)."

What did he know of what we call the Shoah? He spoke of it most often by omission. For example, he asked himself on January 9, 1943, whether he might have been better off as a prisoner of war—as were most of those who, in June 1940, shared his military adventure—"rather than . . ." On January 25, 1943, he speaks of "forced labor in Poland and Russia." No camp is named in the *Journal*, and I have no recollection of any being mentioned in the house. No allusions to the gas chambers. In early 1944 the name "Auschwitz" appeared for the first time at our house in a poem by François la Colère (whom Lucien Vidal-Naquet immediately identified as Aragon) which was entitled *Le Musée Grévin*: "Auschwitz, Auschwitz, O such bloody syllables." But there was no suggestion, in this text, that the Jews were being exterminated.

Apropos of my uncle Germain Lang-Verte, who was arrested near Perpignan in early 1943, and of his brother Frédo, one spoke at the house of the "salt mines of Silesia." On July 17, 1943, however, the decisive word finally was uttered. He had just read the memoirs of Henry Morgenthau about his mission to Constantinople,[21] a work in which he recounts "the frightful massacres of Armenians which were organized methodically under the eyes and with the complicity of the Germans, who were the masters of the Turkish government." This is, it should be added, a somewhat excessively stated appreciation of the matter. The Germans were not "masters of the Turkish government," and while they tolerated and covered up the massacres, they were not active accomplices. Lucien Vidal-Naquet adds, however: "Why should one be surprised, after reading this, that these same Germans, with the same methodicalness, have organized the annihilation of the Jews in all the parts of Europe that bend beneath their rule?" Did he fully understand, that day, the import of the words he was using? Frankly, I do not know.

What is certain is that arrests—whether or not they were followed by deportations—began to strike those close to him very early on. Paul Godchaux, his first cousin by marriage, and Pierre Masse, his colleague and friend whom he had reproached for having voted in favor of delegating full powers to Pétain on July 10, 1940, were arrested during the summer of 1941. The first was freed from Drancy in a state of near-death in March 1942; the second, who was deported in December, never returned.

The episode that affected him the most, however, was the suicide, on January 17, 1942, of his friend and classmate Jacques Frank,[22] whose funeral he attended. Jacques Frank, a veteran officer of the Great War, was arrested on August 21, 1941: "You are the Jew Jacques Frank. Follow me!" That is how an officer of the peace spoke to him. He left Drancy November 2, on grounds of poor health, an excuse that was still being granted at the time. Husband of a woman who was called, in those times, an "Aryan," he could not bear the idea that he risked bringing any misfortune upon his loved ones.

At Marseilles the circle narrowed even further. The roundups of January 1943 made him understand the meaning of the word *terror*.[23] Next, it was the billeting in our house, in February, of Germans from the Todt Organization, the very ones who would later turn him in to the authorities in May 1944. Then it was, on March 16, 1943, the arrival of the Gestapo at the home of his mother, who fortunately was confined to bed and therefore could not be transported on account of a fractured leg. At this point, his mother, his sister, and his nephews decided to take refuge in the town of Dieulefit. Aware of the dangerous situation he found himself in, he wrote on October 22, 1943, to the oldest of his nephews, Gérard Brunschwig:

We are in an unstable situation here. Certain incidents that occurred at the end of August, which concern us personally, have shown us

the dreadful precariousness of our situation. At any instant, and perhaps even before I finish this sentence, some event may occur that
would oblige us to change climes.[24]

One thing was absolutely clear: Lucien Vidal-Naquet refused to enter
into the Vichy government's game. That is to say, he refused to play the
French Jew willing to sacrifice the foreign Jews or close his eyes to their
living tragedy. And this really was Vichy's policy, as we know today. Naturally, the Nazis could not have cared less about this distinction, which they
nevertheless feigned to take into account, the better to "serialize," in
Sartre's sense, both the Jews and Vichy.

For all sorts of obvious reasons, this game was not one to enter into.
On this point, Lucien Vidal-Naquet's lucidity and solidarity were
absolute. Although he speaks on December 17, 1942, of the deportation
of Pierre Hirsch, François Montel, and Pierre Masse, who "undoubtedly
paid with their lives for the crime of being French Jews," he writes on September 15, 1942: "We have just handed over to the beasts the foreign
Jews, who had found asylum among us," the "we" indicating here that he
was separating himself neither from France nor from the Jews. On October 14, 1942, he comments on a meeting between Pierre Laval and Raymond Lachal, director-general of the French Legion of Veterans. After a
protest lodged by some of France's bishops, Laval justified handing over
to Germany "stateless Jews," who were deemed to be sowers of the black
market. Lucien Vidal-Naquet comments:

> The game is over. There was only one turn, so, leaving aside the
> question of the veterans, all Jews can expect the same treatment as
> soon as all non-Jews are placed on the same footing. . . . Laval, who
> wants people to think that he saved veterans while handing over the
> Jews he labels "stateless," knows very well that, among the "stateless"
> are a good number of men who enlisted in the service of a country,
> France, that has now betrayed them. The trick is really too
> grotesque.

And again, on January 25, 1943, after the Marseilles roundup, there is this
note, aimed probably at certain French Jews:

> Some, who push prudence to the point where it can be labeled cow-
> ardice, nevertheless persist, against the most blinding evidence, in
> declaring that these are just "normal" measures affecting only aliens.
> This is false, substantively false, it is the most flagrant sort of false-
> hood. Let me add that, were it true, the crime would still be just as

glaring. I have felt these past few days the most frightful pangs that ever can wound the heart of a man.

What Lucien Vidal-Naquet also refused to accept was privilege. He certainly was pleased to learn that the Council of the Order of the Paris Bar,[25] followed on February 13, 1942, by the Paris Court of Appeal (with the aid of some archival documents sent to me by Marc Knobel I have been able to add to the *Journal* on this point) proposed to inscribe his name, along with that of thirteen other lawyers, on the list of those who, by reason of their eminence, were to be allowed, outside the *numerus clausus*, to remain at the bar. He did not know that on April 4, 1942, Xavier Vallat struck his name and that of eight other lawyers from the list of exempted persons and announced the opening of a Secret Societies Service inquiry into the matter. Did not the very fact that someone had been proposed for an exemption suggest that the person might be a Freemason?

On November 12 he learned that "by a general and negative decision by the Guardian of the Seals," Vichy had rejected the proposal of the Council of the Order. The next day, he writes, "It is difficult to imagine the calm with which I greeted this news. It is rather of indifference, if not of relief, that I ought to speak." He was opposed to President Millerand intervening in his favor: "It was my judgment that I had a right and I spurned all favors. . . . What remained was Vichy; I told myself that it would be a breach of my conception of honor to accept something from this regime, to the point that I, supported in this decision by my wife, very seriously envisioned refusing any waiver it might consent to grant." His attitude was identical to that of the Hellenist Pierre Guastalla, who wrote in October 1941 to Jérôme Carcopino that he would not request any remedy for the loss of rights to which he had been subjected as a result of a statute whose lawfulness he did not recognize.[26]

On May 12, 1942, the day his disbarment took effect, he wrote to Charpentier, the president of the bar:

> Faithful to my oath at the very moment the law releases me from its obligations, I fail to appreciate a measure that excludes from the bar a lawyer who has never eluded any of his duties, be they professional, familial, or national, and I limit myself here to recalling Bar President Liouville's[27] words in praise of freedom: Love it, for it is the lifeblood of peoples. When it beats no more in their veins, they die.[28]

There remains the ultimate question: What was to be done? Paris and clandestine resistance, London, or Algiers and open combat? On several occasions, Lucien Vidal-Naquet mentioned each of these three possibilities and the obstacles that stood in the way: What would an officer of military justice do in Algiers? He does not mention, however, one other possibility: Dieulefit, the village in the Drôme region where his mother, his sister, and his nephews—one of whom, Gérard Brunschwig, had in January 1944 joined the maquis. A house awaited our family there. In 1940, as he worried his colleagues with his audacity, he banteringly responded: "It is my temerity that will save me,"[29] and in November he thwarted a first house search.

He speaks in his *Journal* of his absolute inability to conceive of departing "for America or other climes" (October 10, 1942) and he speaks also—and this is a persistent theme—of his pride "in not slowing his pace to feel that he is being pursued." Though he also spoke that day of preparing his return to Paris, which his sister-in-law Hermine Lang-Verte had done in order to participate in the Resistance, he did not act on this plan. Perhaps the secret to this attitude, which culminated in the drama of May 15, 1944, should be sought in words already spoken by Jacques Frank in 1942, words that Lucien Vidal-Naquet, according to the testimony of Maurice Alléhaut, adopted as his own in March 1944: "I do not want to be the wandering Jew."[30]

PART FOUR

History, Memory, and the Present

16 | Reflections at the Margins of a Tragedy

E
ven though the modern Zionist movement[1] was born in Paris in the aftermath of the Dreyfus Affair, in reality its main roots lie in Eastern European communities that today either have disappeared altogether or are now in the process of disappearing. In that region there still were, on the eve of the Second World War, some eight million persons who spoke the same language, Yiddish, who shared the same culture, and who possessed all the attributes of nationality except a homogeneous territory. It matters little here how this community preserved, or rather transformed, itself through history. Personally, the theory of the "people-class," as formulated by Abraham Léon[2] in a book that seems to be taking on the virtues of a dogma, has always seemed to me dangerously inadequate. A notorious fact is that large groups of Jews were able to preserve themselves in a significant way only where religious belief systems stemming from Judaism continued to reign and where Judaism was both maintained and rejected as a witness, that is to say, in Christianity and among the ranks of Islam. In India there were, and there still are, "Jews," but the latter are hardly anything but an insignificant religious sect that has been integrated into the caste system. Anti-Semitism never made its appearance either in India or in China, where there also were groups of Jews. Everything follows from this, including the commercial role played by certain groups of Jews, who remained indispensable, but marginal, with respect to society as a whole.

When nationalist movements triumphed in the nineteenth century

"Réflexions en marge d'une tragédie" originally appeared in *Partisans* 52 (March–April 1970): 193–99. Reprinted in *JMP*, pp. 149–60.

upon the ruins of Christian Europe, that is to say, when the terrain on which modern class struggle develops came into existence, what options were available to the Jewish communities on that continent? In the West, where Jews constituted only an infinitesimal, loosely structured minority, the path chosen by a majority of them was that of *assimilation*, which most often meant assimilation into the liberal bourgeoisie. This sort of assimilation, as we know, did not proceed without difficulties and Western-style anti-Semitism is in part a reaction *against* assimilation. The Jews of Eastern Europe were much too numerous, much too homogeneous, and they had much too great a cultural advance over the surrounding populations for things to proceed in a similar way. Modern forms of nationalism do not define themselves only in terms of what they *include* but also in terms of what they *exclude*. To be Romanian is to define oneself also as non-Greek, non-Bulgarian, non-Magyar, non-Russian. For all nationalist movements, the exclusion of the Jews was something that went without saying. (The same thing occurred, one will note, in a large portion of the Arab East, for example when the Baath party was formed; the latter extended its appeal to Christians but completely ignored the Jews.) Despite this fact, a portion of the Jewish bourgeoisie tried to make themselves Polish, Romanian, or Russian. In great numbers, the intellectuals chose the revolutionary path in the hope that the socialist revolution would accomplish what the bourgeois revolution had not been able to do. The Judaism of Eastern Europe really did serve as the blood bank of proletarian revolutionary movements. The Jewish popular masses often showed themselves to be concerned with preserving their cultural autonomy while remaining at the same time where they were. This explains the great success of a socialist party like the Bund in the former Russian Empire, a party that continued to enjoy majority support among the Jews of Poland as late as 1939.[3] We see, therefore, that, while in the West Judaism more or less chose or accepted to be defined as a religion and sought assimilation within the dominant society, the problem was much more complex in Eastern Europe. Here in the West, an "atheist Jew" appears, or at least long appeared, to be a contradiction in terms. Nothing was more natural in Warsaw or in Kiev. Both the attempts at assimilation and the struggle for revolution or cultural autonomy were to fail in the end. The Hitlerian massacre—recollection of which would seem to bore some of our comrades—was to annihilate both efforts. After having made extensive use of their Jewish cadres, the "socialist" revolutions later rejected these same people as "cosmopolitans." Poland has just provided, once again, a remarkable demonstration of this process.[4] It helps little to explain to those affected that this revolution is not the right one, that it has been "disfigured" or "betrayed." They have the deep-seated feeling that they can wait no longer, and they know that at the hour trains were heading toward Auschwitz neither "liberal" America nor the "socialist" USSR (which in 1941 had at least preserved a great number of Jews) placed the Jews' safety on the top rung of their concerns.

It is on this terrain (I am summarizing here, of course, a long-term evolution) that the idea of the "Jewish State" and the Zionist movement triumphed. From the outset, this movement was predicated on the view that assimilation was impossible, revolution vain, and anti-Semitism perennial. From its origin, the goal was to "normalize" the situation of the Jews by transforming the "people-class" into a complete society. In its own way it, too, is an assimilationist movement. The choice of national language, Hebrew, allowed a more complete rallying of the Jewish community, since it brought together more than just Yiddish-speaking people and enabled Jewish people to find points of support in a more or less mythically reconstituted past (somewhat similar to the way the Arab national movement, with its ideology of "Renaissance," also reconstitutes the past of the Abbasid or the Omayyid caliphate). The Zionist movement's objective, Palestine, lay under Turkish sovereignty, certainly, and it contained an Arab population. But in a world dominated by the conquering bourgeoisies of the West, this did not appear any more disturbing to the Zionists than the presence of Indians did to American pioneers during their march westward. From its beginnings, therefore, the Zionist movement looked to Western imperialism for support. Of course, all the other recently formed national movements acted the same way and, as is often recalled, the Arab League was at its beginning a mere creation of the Foreign Office. In the case of Zionism, however, the mortgage appears more difficult to pay off, in that foreign protection was needed not only for the development but also for the very installation of the Hebrew nation on Palestinian soil.

Should, then, the Zionist settlement and colonization movement, and later the creation of the State of Israel, be presented as the result of an imperialist "plot" hatched against the Arab peoples? Though I may be attacked as anti-Marxist here, I reject this explanation as a gross simplification. It is one thing to note that the triumph of Zionism could have occurred only at the expense of another people and only by leaning on Western capitalism for support. It is another to come to understand why this movement was able to win over and lure away hundreds of thousands of European Jews, and later Jews from Arab lands—victims in their turn of the repercussions of the Zionist undertaking, of Western colonization,

and of the triumph of Arab-Muslim nationalism—who were not by vocation any more or less imperialist than others (and often, even, rather less
so). The answer, in my opinion, is beyond all doubt: Zionism triumphed
(precariously) because it was the sole movement capable of proposing to
the Jews, who were a minority everywhere, a way of becoming *the majority* somewhere. *Everything* flows from this: the "Law of Return," which is
obviously not going to be satisfactory to Palestinian peasants chased off
their land, as well as a set of institutions that often appear scandalous to us
but that were established to maintain the "Jewish" character of the State in
a world that is not Jewish and where the Jews ceased for seventeen centuries to be represented, as such, by a State.

The Zionist choice has its logic and this logic is precisely the inverse of
what had been the attitude most prevalent in the Jewish Diaspora in
Europe, and more or less also in America, during the course of the nineteenth and early twentieth centuries. Those who were, par excellence, the
excluded became those who exclude. To the anti-Semites' "No Jews
Allowed" corresponds the nonallowance of non-Jews that is the rule in
Israel. The inter-State community the Jews had formed (whence the
development of internationalism among them) has been taken over by a
"chosen Nation-State" (to cite Isaac Deutscher's phrase). Claiming to
unite Judaism in a single country, Zionism annihilates the critical function
European and American Judaism had once exercised (a function that
issued from the situation of the Jews being "both within and without"),
somewhat similar to the way the "socialism in a single country" of Stalinism has lastingly dimmed the critical function of Marxism. Of course,
Israeli socialism, which so deeply motivated the pioneers, has not escaped
this logic, either. Radek joked about "socialism in a single street." One
could speak, likewise, of "socialism in a single kibbutz." Not that I think
one should yield to the stupid fashion that presents Kibbutznik socialism
as a mere bone, thrown by the imperialists, for alienated progressives to
gnaw on. It is just as legitimate to show an interest in the kibbutzim as it
is to take a look at the aristocratic and utopian Summerhill school in
today's England. Even if some of these communities have degenerated, the
kibbutzim remain until now the only serious experiment in suppressing
the contradiction between manual labor and intellectual work. The teaching methods employed there compel admiration; the type of people they
have created gives some idea of what a democratic form of collectivism
might be. That said, it goes without saying that one cannot simply ignore
the fact that a great number of these Kibbutznik communities have been
created on stolen lands, that their military function is increasing at the

expense of their economic and social function, and that their internal democracy is no guarantee against chauvinism and a brutal certitude that one is always right. The drama of the situation is that the kibbutz cannot live without the State, that the State even furnishes it with its members, and that it is, for the moment, more a cog in an almost fully integrated society than a catalyst that serves to contradict that society.

One has to have visited a kibbutz set up on post-1967 occupied territory and observed the incredible lack of awareness on the part of those who, as recent arrivals, practice the "socialism" of conquerors in order to see how far ideology can go to cover up the most glaringly apparent realities. Need it be added, however, that Israel holds no monopoly on this kind of perversion? The "socialism" of the Syrian Baath party, which treats the Kurds in nearly the same way as the Israelis have treated the Palestinians—but in the name of Arabization, not to mention a Stalinist "socialism" that was not adverse to deporting entire peoples—highly reduces Israel's originality in this domain.

The Zionist undertaking has thus culminated in a tragically contradictory result. The effort to gather into a single country "the Jewish people" has succeeded in grouping in Palestine approximately one-fifth of this "people." It is true that the Israelis differ profoundly from the humiliated Jews of the ghettos and the mellahs; that, at an extremely heavy price, some forms of alienation have been eliminated; that a democratic society, infinitely more egalitarian than any Western society, has been created, so that this society closely resembles, in some respects, the pioneer democracy Tocqueville observed in America. The lifting of these forms of alienation has nevertheless entailed the appearance of other ones, the most evident of which is a sort of idolatry of the State that one cannot help but compare to the image of the Prussian State as the supreme incarnation of Reason in history, characteristic, it is said, of Hegel's thought at the end of his life.

While, by its very existence, Israel appears to a great number of Jews as a potential place of refuge, a sort of insurance policy against a new Auschwitz—and this sentiment is very deeply held—the very fact that Israelis believe that they are threatened with extinction (whatever may be the actual seriousness of this threat) by itself signals that Zionism has failed to "resolve" the Jewish problem. What, then, has been created in Israel? Indisputably, it is a nation whose level of integration, favored by war, is rather astonishing and striking, even to the most forewarned of outside observers. Under the circumstances, it matters little that this nation has been constituted by men and women who come from one hundred and two different countries. The United States of America, whose character as a nation no one would dream of questioning, was constituted under somewhat similar conditions. In particular, it should be pointed out that all the speculation about a possible rupture between Jews of "Oriental" origin and "European" Jews is a complete illusion. Not that such opposition is absent. Within the framework of the national struggle, however, the Israeli ruling class, which is certainly not the stupidest bourgeoisie in the world, has learned how to adopt the measures required to favor the process of integration, notably by the use of the country's educational system to help "Oriental" children gradually face up to the competition of their "Western" counterparts. Moreover, the increasing number of mixed marriages attests to the fact that, on this level, the effort has been a successful one.[5] Nevertheless, the illusion, widespread both within Israel and without, that this country might be a potential pole of regional development in the underdeveloped Middle East (somewhat as the Piedmont region was for Italy at the time of the Risorgimento or Prussia in Germany at the time of the Zollverein) should be denounced. With the aid of American Judaism, Israel is an enormous force for development and modernization, for the integration into the modern world and into "industrial society" of populations that had not penetrated there before, as well as for rationalization and acculturation. Yet, for structural reasons having to do with the logic of Zionism, all these "benefits" are reserved for the Jews alone. The Arabs of Israel have themselves "benefited" from these processes only in a quite relative way, and the undertaking can be extended to the region as a whole only under the form of colonization (which is what is tending to happen in the occupied territories) or neocolonialism. Inevitably, therefore, the national conflict will be combined with a conflict between classes, with each process reinforcing the other.

Zionism began with the affirmation that a "Jewish power" was needed in the world. Psychologically speaking, this affirmation closely resembles the demand in America for "black power." As we know, among American blacks the theme of a *return* to Africa did not fall entirely on deaf ears, either, and those who mock the idea of restoring Hebrew as Israel's national language ought to ask themselves why Swahili is being taught in New York City. Zionism soon risks becoming caught in an Algerian- or South African-style logic. We have become, an Israeli historian told me, the modern Sparta, a nation of two and a half million "Equals" reigning over a million "helots."

Since the 1967 war, the major fact has certainly been the appearance in the Arab world of a force that genuinely contests the Israeli undertaking.

The Palestinians, who hitherto were held in check by their Egyptian, Jordanian, or Syrian protectors, have become, or at least are becoming more and more each day, an autonomous force. The military impact of this force certainly remains extremely weak, and any comparison with the Vietnamese National Liberation Front or even with the Algerian NLF would be flawed. Even those Israelis who have become aware of the reality of the Palestinian nation keep their eyes trained much more on the Suez front than on the united command headquarters of the Palestinian Resistance. Nevertheless, its political significance is obvious. As an autonomous force, it is capable right now, at the very least, of threatening the political and social equilibrium of Israel's neighbors. If there is a people for whom the "wretched of the Earth" is a fitting label, a people that "has nothing to lose," it is without any doubt the Palestinian people. It is therefore entirely natural that the combat of this people, whose very existence has been and is still denied, should be understood and, when need be, supported by those for whom internationalism still retains some meaning. It does not follow, however, that this necessary struggle has to be conducted with the weapons of ideological illusion and soothing mystification. In particular, I feel that it should be pointed out with the greatest clarity and with total frankness that those who spread the idyllic illusion of a "secular and democratic" Palestine, whether unitary or binational, are seriously mistaken both about the present objectives of the Palestinian movement and about the real possibilities of implementing such a solution. On the contrary, what makes the Israeli-Palestinian conflict so profound, so total, is that it is not, for the moment, a conflict over lines of sovereignty. It is a conflict between two peoples over one and the same territory. One of these two peoples, being developed, employs and, when the need arises, forces support from the Jewish communities in the capitalist West and from the West as a whole. The other, being underdeveloped, situates itself within the context of an "Arab revolution" that aims to reconquer its pulverized national identity and that holds out a promise, perhaps in the long term, of autonomous development, but that is located on an entirely different level than that of revolutionary and socialist combat—which, as May 1968 has demonstrated, can still occur in a developed country.

In fact, Palestinian demands appear to be exactly symmetrical to the very movement that provoked these demands, by which I mean the establishment of the Zionist State. This may strikingly be seen in the text that, until now, most clearly expresses the official position of the Palestinian revolution, the "Palestinian National Covenant" (a text that was adopted at the First Palestinian Congress, held in Jerusalem in May 1964, and that has been modified and amended at the Fourth Congress, held in Cairo in July 1968, but that could not be voided, for the moment, simply by declarations imposed by passing circumstances). Article Four of this text reads as follows: "The Palestinian personality is an innate, enduring character that cannot disappear and that is transmitted from father to son." Keeping in mind that in the Arab-Islamic tradition descendance is patrilinear and that in the Jewish tradition it is matrilinear, what we have here, as the Israeli general and Arabist Yehoshafat Harkabi has observed with ferocious lucidity (*Maariv*, December 12, 1969),[6] is precisely the Palestinian counterpart to the Israeli "Law of Return." Thus, the quality of being "Palestinian" does not result from any sort of contractual arrangements (any more than would the quality of being an Israeli Jew, the potential beneficiaries of which are all sons of Jewish mothers) but is transmitted exclusively by birth.

Article Six of this same document specifies that the "Jews" who lived in Palestine on a permanent basis before the beginnings of the Zionist invasion "will be considered Palestinian." Since the "beginnings of the Zionist invasion," it turns out, are set in 1917 (the Balfour Declaration), one can easily draw the likely consequences. True, recent declarations have corrected these statements and the latest Al Fatah publications[7] mention the possibility of a Palestine made up of all the country's actual or potential inhabitants—Jews, Arabs, Israelis, persons living in the occupied territories, exiles, or refugees—but these texts have never had the solemn character of the 1968 "National Covenant." A very small Palestinian organization, the "Democratic Front," tried at the 1969 Palestinian Congress to have a serious study made of the possibility of a democratic State in which the two peoples would coexist, but these proposals, so far as I know, have been rejected. Moreover, all one need do is reflect on one simple detail: a unified Palestine of that sort could see the light of day only within the framework of a total victory over the Israelis. It is difficult to see how, under such conditions, the most democratic of intentions would be able to resist the logic of victory, which entails the destruction of one's adversary. There are also some Zionists who proclaim it to be their intention, too, to establish a binational State, or at least a State where Jews and Arabs would have the same rights. We know what happened after the 1948 war. We know, too, by way of comparison, in what a frightful fashion the restoration of a unitary and democratic Nigeria was achieved.[8]

One can escape this logic only by supposing, along with our comrades from Matzpen who are courageously trying to put their principles into action, that a revolutionary force might develop in Israel, capable of contesting the status quo and willing to cooperate eventually with Palestinian forces that themselves would recognize the Israeli people's right to self-determination. Beyond the fact that such forces have not yet really made themselves known, the possibilities for such a development in Israel appear extraordinarily problematic, to say the least. As I have already said, Israeli society is one of the most integrated societies in the world. It is, for the moment, the very model of a "one-dimensional" society. A profound transformation would appear conceivable only if Judaism in the Diaspora were to cease to lend its aid—which would entail a fall in the standard of living and a resumption of the movement toward emigration (which had already made itself felt in 1966)—or if a long period of peace were to allow the contradictions which this society, like all others, conceals to develop freely. Both these hypotheses are, for the moment, extremely improbable.

Of course, everyone is free to think that the only possible reparation for the profound injustice done to the Palestinians resides in the departure of the Israelis. Some have made up their minds and say so. "I know quite well how it will end up," a Jewish comrade of mine told me one day. "In New York." This hypothesis is still too optimistic and it forgets that, faced with those who have nothing to lose, the Israelis themselves having *every-thing* lose. It forgets, too, that the Israelis will do anything, and I really mean anything, if the military situation turns against them (in case, for example—though this possibility is for the moment highly unlikely—the American oil companies, whose interests do not lie in Israel, were to impose their views upon Washington and Soviet or Chinese aid were to become directly military in nature). Each is free to imagine the liberation of Palestine being achieved upon the ruins of Cairo, Alexandria, Beirut, and Damascus, not to mention Jerusalem or Tel Aviv—and I pass over the fact that liberation of this sort would inevitably be based, and to a certain extent already is based, upon the most retrograde anti-Semitic forces, whether this anti-Semitism be "Christian" or "socialist." For my part, I find this prospect neither satisfying nor, moreover, plausible. But what really needs to be understood is that, in the scenario of a total liberation of Palestine, there is no other one. The guerrilla forces do not have the slightest chance of defeating a modern State that is based on an integrated society. To be more precise, the guerrilla war would have a real chance of success only if the Israelis were to incorporate within their "borders" two or three times as many Arabs as are contained there at present. There is little likelihood that they will commit this irremediable error.

Under these circumstances, I see no need to hide the fact that, as lame as it might be and whether it takes the form of an Arab "Brest-Litovsk" or a self-interested intervention on the part of the "great powers," a compromise that would, at the very least, force the evacuation of the territories occupied since 1967 seems to me, of all imaginable solutions (the "good" ones not being "possible"), probably the least bad. Contrary to what has occurred before the present time, the Palestinians have now made sure that such a compromise could no longer be made entirely at their expense. The worst of hypocrisies, of course, would be to preach in favor of this compromise without at the same time trying to take some action in this direction. To the extent that we can take action here, we should do so in such a way as to ensure that this compromise will be as favorable as possible to those who have been the principal victims of three wars as well as of the very establishment of the State of Israel. Such action cannot do without at least a minimum of lucidity and truth. And this critical spirit, I fear, is what until now has so sorely been lacking.

17 | Return to Israel

Is It Another Battle of Algiers?

This trip to Israel, which took place between March 28 and April 11, 1982, is my third. In 1970, as a guest of Tel Aviv University, as I am again today, I tried to reflect on the "chances for contestation" that might break the unanimity of Israeli society with regard to the Palestinian problem. In 1975, a guest that time of the University of Jerusalem, I tried to reflect on the "invisible border," the one that separates, within Israel itself, two kinds of people, full-fledged citizens and Israeli Arabs, a border duplicated by the famous "green line" lying between pre-1967 Israel, on the one hand, and the West Bank and Gaza, on the other. I also tried to understand how the Palestinian leaders, at least those who still remained, saw the prospects for peace.[1] Nevertheless, the problems raised today by the "settlements"—which reproduce a miniature but decisively important Israel in the midst of the Palestinian people—had already become apparent at that time.

The Israel I have just visited, from the extreme north in the annexed and besieged Golan Heights to the Jordanian border and across the "territories" that themselves are also on the way to annexation, is an Israel that is hastening to complete its evacuation of the Sinai peninsula, but it is also the one now being confronted on the West Bank by a new Palestinian revolt. Arriving two days before the Day of the Land (March 30), which commemorates the murder on March 30, 1976, of six Israeli Arabs, I left the country the very day shots were fired inside the Al Aqsa mosque.

Retour en Israël" originally appeared in the April 23, 24, and 25–26, 1982, issues of the Paris daily *Libération*. Reprinted in *JMP*, pp. 465–83.

Events determined, to a great extent, what I would try to explore for my investigative report. They also determined the limits. I could not, for example, go to Yamit.

One cannot help but compare the images being shown on television during the second half of March—soldiers forcibly opening closed shops in Ramallah and Nablus—with Algiers between January 28 and February 4, 1957, that is to say, the insurrectionary general strike, along with the French paratroopers' response. Between French Algerian War General Jacques Massu and Israeli Minister of Defense Ariel Sharon, there is more than one resemblance. Not everyone, however, is in agreement: the latter is a Massu but with more intelligence, say some of my Israeli interlocutors; others grant only the first half of this formula.

Is it, then, another battle of Algiers?

Jerusalem, March 29, at Bet Agron, the press headquarters, in the western part of the city. I am attending a press conference about the repression. The speakers (two of them are Israeli Jews, members of Rakakh, Mr. Uzi Burstein and Ms. Felicia Langer) denounce in forceful terms what is taking place on the West Bank: a battle of bullets versus stones. Israel had accustomed us, says Mr. Agazarian, a history professor of the (once again closed) Bir Zeit University, to a more refined sort of behavior. It is now reinventing the most vulgar forms of colonialism. One is also reminded, not incorrectly, of the fate of the Jews in the Russian Empire who were forbidden to leave a strictly defined geographical zone. The target of the press conference? Professor Menahem Milson, head of the "civilian administration" implanted in "Judea and Samaria." The last speaker is the passionate Raymonda Tawil, the author of *Mon Pays, ma prison* (My country, my prison).[2] I meet her again, along with a few other Palestinian leaders, at 10 Saladin Street in the eastern part of the city, the headquarters of the Palestine Press Services which publishes each day a bulletin for the local and the international press. Raymonda Tawil speaks in violent terms, before a Spanish television camera, of what the Day of the Land (March 30) will be like in Israel and the occupied territories. The headline of *Al Fajr* ("The Dawn"), an English-language supplement to a Palestinian daily published in Jerusalem, reads: "Bloody Week in the Occupied Territories. Seven Killed. 31 Wounded by Bullets. 100 Arrests. 3 Mayors Dismissed. 1 City Council Dissolved."

For someone who has lived through the Algerian War and knows how much press freedom existed at the time in Algiers, these scenes and these headlines give off a somewhat surreal impression. What is deplorable is that the facts being reported at the press conference are themselves quite real: arrests, violence, bullets.

Is the freedom real, too? Tuesday, March 30, in the afternoon, at Taiyiba, a large town on the Plain of Sharon. Approximately two thousand people, a great majority of them Arab, commemorate the Day of the Land. One of the speakers, who is Jewish, is strongly applauded. The two most remarkable speeches are that of a poet, Samir el Kacem, who seems to combine in a marvelous way lyricism and irony—"This country has seen numerous emperors pass by. I am thinking not only of Sharon but also of Napoleon"—and that of a former Communist deputy, Émile Habibi, whose presentation centers around criticism of purist nationalists. The name Yasser Arafat is pronounced calmly. It is, moreover, applauded. Not the slightest incident will occur. Things will not be the same at Nazareth, where the mayor, a Communist deputy, Tewfik Zayyad, whom I met in 1975, insists upon solidarity between the Arabs of Galilee and the West Bank. Some people will be wounded and there will be numerous arrests. Yasser Arafat will then salute Arab Galilee.

I have never felt the need to joke about formal freedoms. I know only real freedoms. In Israel proper, freedom and death may coincide. And in the territories? Let us look a little closer. There are three Arabic dailies in Jerusalem: the pro-Jordanian *Al Quds* ("The Holy City": i.e., Jerusalem), as well as two pro-PLO papers, *Al Fajr* ("The Dawn") and *Al Chaab* ("The People"). For these newspapers to continue to be distributed in the occupied territories, the Israeli authorities have formulated the following requirements: a censorship officer must be present at all times at the editorial offices; this officer decides not only what appears but also the place in which it can be published (on page one or on page three, not to mention anything about type size); he can also decide what can be distributed in Gaza and what can be distributed on the West Bank. As East Jerusalem is supposedly part of Israel, here the problems are different. In each city the military governor reserves the right to block distribution. *Al Quds* tried this experiment. The other two gave it up. They are therefore forbidden on the West Bank and in Gaza, authorized in Jerusalem and in Nazareth, and obviously are allowed to sell as many copies as they wish in Tel Aviv, where they have as many chances to find readers as a Chinese newspaper would have. Beyond any doubt, what is occurring is an attempt at strangulation.

Will these measures directed against press freedom reach Israel proper? Some fear so. Israeli television enjoys a very high reputation. On

Friday, April 9, for example, it broadcast a gripping report on the Golan Heights: the Druze threw down a blanket of identity cards after the state of siege was lifted. Others are distrustful; to check whether they are getting true information about this or that news event, they watch Jordanian television, which broadcasts in Hebrew, in English, and in French—not to mention Arabic, of course. Here geography comes to the aid of freedom, and it is unclear what the authorities would gain by attacking the latter. For the moment, then, citizens have a right to freedom, but the helots are losing it a little more each day. In this area, the policy of the Begin government appears perfectly clear and deliberate. There are no Palestinians, there is no Palestinian national community. There are some Arabs in Eretz Israel: some individuals, some families, some villages, and scarcely any towns. Whence the emphasis placed on the "villagers' league," to which large sums are granted in the hope that its program will be "each in his own village." Even that plan, however, seems to be failing: in order to gain a minimum of respectability, the head of this group, Mustapha Dudein, has felt obliged to declare that he is a good patriot . . . of Jordan, and not a collaborator.[3] When I left Israel, he had just been hospitalized . . .

Reality on the West Bank is certainly complex. Some towns that were declared to be on strike actually were not so. Hebron, for example, was rather lively when I passed through there on March 29 in the afternoon. The fact remains, however, that in 1976 the Israeli government organized elections whose democratic character it proclaimed out loud, and not unjustly. These elections marked the victory, in all the large towns, of slates closely associated with the PLO. The Israeli government now tells us, and I have heard its arguments repeated by sincere people, that these elections were characterized by a PLO reign of terror. This is a strange terror, indeed, that now obliges the occupation authorities to practice authentic terrorism. At Ramallah, on the Gaza Strip, and now in Jerusalem, one shoots and one kills. Not always, not continuously, but often.

There is nevertheless one area where the failure is patent: the recently annexed Golan Heights. This plateau which dominates upper Galilee is above all a military zone. Conquered in the midst of battle in June 1967, at each turn one comes across another commemorative monument. Barracks and military posts are equally numerous. They shelter a telecommunications network that facilitates, when need be, a quick regrouping of the defense forces. All this is explained to us—four Frenchmen—by an Israeli lieutenant-colonel, a member of the General Staff who is engaging and intelligent. Strategically speaking, his presentation is brilliant. But what about the inhabitants? Nothing but the foundations remain of the surrounding Arab villages. Like so many others, they have been razed. Four Druzean villages are still standing. On this Thursday, April 1, at three in the afternoon, we travel through one of them: Massaada. The barbed wire cordoning off entrance and exit points is lifted for us. The entire population, however, is indoors: it is curfew time. The Druze living here had viewed the coming of the Israelis without rancor. Other Druze in Israel are rather well integrated. Some have attained positions of high rank in the army. For the Druze of the Golan Heights, to accept the identity card the government wanted to foist upon them would have meant that they would have had to change their identity. They said "No," and the operation failed. Tomorrow, their "No" will perhaps extend to the Druze of Israel . . .

Still further north, near Metulla, is the "good border" with the "good Lebanese," those under Commandant Haddad. A majority of them are Shiite Muslims, we are told. Signs and arrows indicate an overlook point along the good border. In sight of the television broadcasting truck of Commandant Haddad is a quotation, in Hebrew and in English, from the prophet Isaiah (2.4): "And they shall beat their swords into plowshares and their spears into pruning-hooks." A building handles border transits—which allows, notably, certain Lebanese to benefit from Israeli medical equipment. Under the Lebanese flag and the Israeli flag, there is a place for two chairs and two officers. But only the Israeli chair is occupied.

There are some good Lebanese. There are also some bad ones, and some Palestinians who have taken refuge in Lebanon. The "good border" may tomorrow become an invasion route.

A Mortal Embrace

During my first voyage, in 1970, the two societies, Palestinian and Israeli, remained fundamentally separate. This was true even in Jerusalem. It was true despite the presence in Israel of an Arab minority that certainly felt frustrated with the Israeli majority but that was more prosperous than the populations of the West Bank and Gaza, with their huge refugee camps. One did not have to be a rocket scientist [*grand clerc*] to guess, in June 1967, that in a Palestine reunited by the Israeli victory, the "New Zion" risked becoming, to borrow an expression from Jacques Berque, a "new Mitidja," the backcountry south of Algiers. I also rediscover in a text I wrote in 1970[4] the following statement: "There is . . . an enormous risk that Palestine will be transformed into a new Algeria or a new South Africa, with some people treated as full-fledged citizens and some people

treated as foreigners in their own country. This is the danger that threatens most at the present hour."

Between Israelis and Palestinians on the West Bank and in the Gaza
Strip, the confrontation can only be unequal. Certainly, the Palestinian
population is, intellectually speaking, the most developed in the Arab
world. It numbers more university graduates and students with advanced
degrees than any other Middle East country except Israel. Most of these
graduates, however, are forced to live elsewhere, and they work in the
Arab world or as far away as the United States. Faced with a traditional
society, the Israelis do not have merely a military advantage. They are a
modern society, founded, like the United States, by individuals, and it is
precisely this intermingling of individual adventures that makes Israel, for
the outside observer, such a passionately interesting country. Theirs is a
democratic society and democracy has often meant in history, whether in
ancient Athens or in Tocqueville's America, initiative and imperialism.
America was able to integrate some Russians, it was not capable of integrating the Indians. Israel can endow itself with subjects, it cannot create
Jews, and this is a country made for Jews and for them alone. In her marvelous book *L'Un meurt, l'autre aussi* (One dies, so does the other),[5] perhaps the best reportage ever written about Israel because it explores all
the extreme situations in the country, and God knows there are some,
Rachel Mizrahi offers the following aphorism that summarizes so many
things: "It is tough being Jewish, especially when one isn't." Add to this the
fact that there is an active minority: the religious "zeal" that was expressed
on these lands long ago is being reignited by the modern "zealots" of Gush
Emunim (Block of Faith), just as the Puritan pioneers of America set their
zeal in motion, though with better prospects. They, too, take themselves
to be a new Israel. Is it Algeria? Imagine an Algeria that begins five minutes away from the country's capital, an Algeria whose every place has a
name in your language and plays a role in the history book on which your
education is based. Judea and Samaria, realities as imaginary as the border
separating Israel and Jordan, now appear to be within one's grasp.

Economically speaking, the West Bank and the Gaza Strip have been
placed under complete Israeli domination. Certainly, this has resolved a
certain number of problems and lowered unemployment. But the traditional economy has been destroyed. Israel has in its colonies an outlet for
its industries. The agricultural produce of the West Bank takes, rather, the
road to Jordan. Very little of it penetrates into Israel, save through individual initiative. Dietary rules,[6] for example, prevent Palestinian wines
(which, by the way, are excellent) from penetrating to any great extent

into Israel. They are not found in the supermarkets. Palestine provides Israel with unskilled and semiskilled workers. Leaving their homes in the morning, they must return home at night. When a curfew is declared somewhere, the authorities take great care to ensure that workers will be able to depart and to return home again.

Anyone in Israel will tell you the following story, which I came across again in Rachel Mizrahi's book:

> Grandfather takes his grandson for a walk in Tel Aviv. "You see this road?" the grandfather asks the grandson. "It was I who paved it, with my very own hands, when I was young." They continue their walk. "You see this house?" the grandfather asks the grandson. "It was I who built it, with my very own hands, when I was young." They arrive at the port. "You see this breakwater?" asks the grandfather, "Well, it was I who laid the bricks when I was young. What do you think?" The grandson looks at him, perplexed. "But grandfather, when you were young, were you an Arab?"

Two societies are joined together, each is inextricably involved with the other, and yet they maintain a fundamentally inegalitarian relationship. An infinitesimal number of Israelis (though some do exist; Amnon Kapeliouk is one example) have ventured out of their world to encounter the Arab world. Many have "their Arab" who sells them tomatoes or bananas. Prices remain lower on the West Bank. Those on the West Bank have discovered Israel, whose existence is for them as evident as that of their own towns and countryside. Many have learned Hebrew. Many, including the women, have been modernized as a result of this contact. That Raymonda Tawil is a recognized spokesperson of the Palestinian movement is a remarkable fact. The Israeli press is an enormous source of information for this movement. Many articles are translated into Arabic, for what they say or for what they reveal. Thus, for example, *Al Fajr* reprinted an interview with the ultra-Right rabbi Meir Kahane, who has just completed a tour of military duty on the West Bank and wants to chase all the Arabs from the country. Not everyone has reached that point. An Israeli friend says: "They [her compatriots] do not want to kill Arabs, they do not want to chase them away, they want them to disappear." But how is one to bring about the disappearance of those whose work force one employs?

For Mr. Begin, there are no occupied territories. There is, as he has said repeatedly, only "liberated territories," an expression that appeared in 1967 and not only on the Right. What a posthumous triumph for Vladimir

Jabotinsky, whom Ben-Gurion called Vladimir Hitler and who was the first to conceive in its full breadth the problem of two-way displacement: Jews toward Palestine, Arabs out of Palestine.[7] The victory of his ideology has long been masked, save in a few lucid minds such as Hannah Arendt's. Today the triumph is total. Look at the hierarchy of bank notes (favored, it is true, by inflation): Herzl is worth only ten shekels, Ben-Gurion fifty, and Jabotinsky one hundred.

Liberated territories? An imaginary Judea and Samaria are embodied today in a network of colonies—so many small fortresses, so many acropoleis. Indeed, the Israelis of today seem to be acropolis-obsessed. These acropoleis begin in Jerusalem at the university acropolis on Mount Scopus, with its improbable architecture (Stalinist say some, fascist say others) which has brought about the near-total abandonment of the wonderful Givat Ram campus in the western part of the city. There are acropoleis, too, in the form of public housing projects, luxurious sometimes and reserved for Jews, that surround the Arab part of the city. They continue in the territories. Let us go up one of these acropoleis. Elazar, not far from Hebron, is a small set of units inhabited by twenty-one families. Many homes are still empty. An armed colonist guards the settlement, which is surrounded by barbed wire. The majority of the inhabitants are at Yamit. We encounter, nonetheless, a very young woman with her baby. She is a newly arrived American. She explains to us that the community is strictly religious and that only families who have decided to lead a religious life are granted admission here. She thinks that here, more easily than in America, she can lead a religious life and experience happiness. She thinks she has the right to live here and does not worry overly much about her Arab neighbors. Tensions, it appears to her, moreover, are being exaggerated by the newspapers. That this country has been made by a decree of the Lord God to help resolve the psychological problems of a young American Jewess seems to her as clear as day.

These acropoleis are growing. I had seen Kiryat Arba, above Hebron, in 1975. It was then a fortified camp dominating the Arab city, controlling its electrical power and its telephone system. Today it is a real city that has now swarmed into the heart of the Arab town. Does one need much imagination to form an idea of how much hatred these settlements engender? "We had become accustomed," says Raymonda Tawil, "to make distinctions among the Israelis. Now . . ." This expansion contrasts with the crisis Israel and Zionism are experiencing within its former borders. "Next year in New York" is a watchword, lacking in all ideology, that is now on the lips of numerous families. The number of *Yordim* (emigrants) clearly exceeds the number of *Olim* (immigrants).

Of course, these West Bank colonists are not numerous: around 24,000 persons. Not all are motivated by religious passions. Beyond the responsibility borne by the Gush Emunim, one must lay the blame on government policy itself, which is seeking to create an irreversible situation. If one can, as Zeev Sternhell, an Israeli historian of French nationalism, informs me, buy a villa for the price of a two-room apartment in Tel Aviv, or an apartment at a quarter of its value in Jerusalem, one will be tempted to live in a settlement without needing to appeal to any biblical memories.

On the West Bank there are not only colonists. There is also the army. And as the colonists are armed and they sometimes happen to "target shoot" on the Arabs without it creating for them the least problem, one cannot always easily distinguish between the two. Contrary to what I saw in 1970 and again in 1975, the military presence (which consists of very young, often panicky, kids) is now massive. The old "liberal occupation," which was a reality, is now dead. The army is trigger-happy, and for numerous young people it is today a school for crime. Some rabbis teach, without being contradicted by other rabbis, that it is permissible to treat the Arabs as one long ago treated the Amalekites, who were the object of an exterminatory anathema. Amnon Rubinstein, a centrist deputy, recounts this with indignation in the April 7 issue of *Haaretz*, and he brings to light the fact that a rabbi who was questioned about the right Jews may have to kill Arab civilians responded that the danger was—if, for example, one threw a grenade—that one might also hurt some Jews.

Under these conditions, what, according to the Begin government, is the right of the Palestinians to autonomy, the autonomy envisioned in the Camp David Accords and in the treaty signed in Washington? It goes little beyond the right of each Palestinian, taken separately, to choose freely what he will have for breakfast, provided that the Israeli government sees nothing therein that might prevent it from prolonging its stay. And what do the Palestinian leaders themselves say? On Thursday, April 8, I met in succession Karim Khalaf, the dismissed mayor of Ramallah who has been assigned to forced residence in Jericho, and Bassam Chaka, the dismissed mayor of Nablus who is shut inside his house, not knowing if the troops watching at his door will authorize him to go into town. Both have been victims, in June 1980, of bomb attacks. Khalaf lost a foot, Chaka his two legs. Both point out that these crimes have not even begun to be investigated. Neither one has even been questioned. Both are notables, Chaka being by origin and by temperament more working class. Indeed, the two

men are very different. As an Israeli female friend observes, Khalaf is a
rather handsome eastern Mediterranean type. He has a tendency to use
somewhat facile slogans: "Jew and Arabs, we are all brothers. Did we not
welcome Mr. Begin here during the War?" Chaka is a politician who is
cheerful, lively, and optimistic, despite the handicap he now suffers. Concerning the possibility of a political solution, both say that a Palestinian
State must be created on the West Bank and in the Gaza Strip whose capital would be Arab Jerusalem and which would coexist with Israel. For
them, the question of the recognition of Israel does not even pose a problem. As for the Palestinian Covenant, a topic about which I question them,
their retort is that negotiations will ipso facto settle this question. That
said, neither one has any illusions about the possibility of starting this
negotiation process with a government that has already seized a large portion of the soil of the West Bank.

Chaka offers some striking details about what the military government's
policy on this matter has been. The military government does not recognize
that he has a right to discuss any problem that lies beyond the city limits.
Does he want to talk about a settlement close to town? That does not concern him. Has he been called to the University of Nablus to settle a conflict
situation? He is told that the university is none of his business. He also provides some gripping details about the kind of moral degradation the occupation engenders. "If you do not do what I order you to do," an Israeli general told him one day, "don't be surprised if you find yourself being insulted
by the soldiers." There is now a policy of insult and humiliation. And also
this: on the day in June 1980 when his car exploded, while Chaka was being
taken to the hospital, an Israeli lieutenant, spotting in the car Chaka's missing leg, said to the mayor's seventeen-year-old daughter: "Take that to your
father, he might need it." Alas, he was not talking about surgery. What, then,
has become, a friend asks me, of the morality of the Jewish people?

   "A people that oppresses another cannot be a free people"? Alas! In the
course of history, the freedom of some has only too often been based upon
the reduction of others to a state of slavery or upon their exploitation. But
in any case, it is better for the morality of the nation that the oppressed
people not be your next-door neighbor.

Opponents Without an Opposition

No one can harbor the least illusion about the nature of Mr. Begin's policy. The "territories" no longer can be presented—as long had been done,

notably in the circles of a very "respectable" Left—as bargaining chips Israel keeps on the table while waiting for peace to arrive. In 1968 the Union of Jewish Students of France said, "The Israelis are occupying territories like workers occupy the factories, to force discussion."

No one can understand Israeli policy if they fail to realize that, for successive governments, it is not a question and it never seriously has been a question of letting Israel *and* Palestine coexist. Instead, these governments have posed an alternative: Israel *or* Palestine. It is because, deep down, they feel that they have built their country *on* Palestine ("Under Israel, Palestine," as the title of a book by Ilan Halévi says) that the Israeli leaders do not want to hear any talk about a Palestinian State.[8] Jordanian Palestinians have sometimes *profaned* synagogues and Jewish cemeteries. Israeli policy has tried to *erase* Palestine. The Israeli rulers are today all the more resolute in their effort to prevent any kind of process that might lead to the creation of a Palestinian State since they themselves know perfectly well, through experience, how a State is constituted. "Go set up a settlement in Tel Aviv, then," one of them said one day to the mayor of Ramallah!

Nor can one understand what is going on in Israel if one fails to realize the following fact: Israel is conducting a great-power policy with the arms of a medium-sized power and the anxieties of a small one. But of course, those who direct policy and those who feel the anxieties are not the same people. The Israeli political game resides in the alliance between cynical leaders like Begin or Sharon and the popular masses who remain deeply insecure. That Begin today has behind him the backing of a majority of popular opinion, and an enlarged majority at that, is beyond doubt for everyone. During the last elections, the working-class neighborhoods inhabited by Jews who originally came from Arab countries gave him a large majority, while the bourgeois neighborhoods of Jerusalem and Tel Aviv gave a majority to the center-Left Maarakh (the Alignment). As for the future, there is no lack of disturbing signs that point toward the establishment of a colonial world, such as the fact that the young are further to the Right than their elders. The student associations are controlled to a great extent by the Right and the extreme Right. "We are a democracy without an opposition," my friend David Asheri, a professor at the Hebrew University, told me in 1970. Is this still the case? In Israel one finds some wonderful and astonishing opposition figures, such as Benjamin Cohen, the Roman historian from Tel Aviv who was my sometime guide, or Daniel Amit, a physics professor at the University of Jerusalem who has been a pillar of support at Bir Zeit University. Scarcely had the Golan Heights been opened to civilians when he rushed in to meet with the Druze. There are also a few young people who refuse to serve in the territories and a picturesque character, mentioned by Rachel Mizrahi, who, like the hero in Aristophanes' play, has concluded a separate peace and no longer is willing to get mixed up in anything.

Let us take a closer look at a character who does not easily fit into any classic mold. Very well known in Israel, and even popular in certain academic circles, Yeshayahu (Isaiah) Leibovitz is a retired biologist who taught at Hebrew University. In physical appearance, this striking old man resembles a rabbi from Amsterdam as painted by Rembrandt. He is a religious man, a Calvinist of Judaism some of his friends say. He has only contempt for the ceremonies that take place at the Western Wall (in Hebrew: *kotel*), which we call the "Wailing Wall," and which he, speaking with a lovely bit of irreverence, calls the *Diskokotel*. He is a Zionist, and he explains to me that for him Zionism is something quite simple: "We have had enough of being governed by the *goyim*." He does not believe in peace and deems that the hatred between Israelis and Palestinians is entirely natural. He does not demand peace, he demands the total evacuation of the occupied territories, independent of any agreement. For years now he has denounced the nationalistic and chauvinistic delusions that have transformed Israel into a people who have become master over the destiny of one and a half million Arabs. A man of the Left? He does not have enough sarcasm for "this mean old lady" who started all the evil.

Today, the most urgent task is to *separate* the two societies so that the process of domination now under way will be blocked. Such a settlement, which would also involve the partition of Jerusalem, could be imposed only from without. I also ask him about the political usage that is made here of the great massacre that occurred during the Second World War. Has not Mr. Begin invoked what happened at Auschwitz and Treblinka to justify the bombardment of Beirut? "That is something so horrible," says Leibovitz, "that I refuse to respond." Nahum Goldmann has spoken on this topic of a *Chilloul ha-Shem*, a "profanation of the Name."[9]

Is this to say that only individuals are opposed to the suicidal policy that today is Israel's? I do not think so, and I have taken the risk of putting down in print my opinion that, since 1975 and thanks especially to the victory of the Right in 1977, the movement in favor of peace has profoundly been reinforced instead of weakened.

Certainly, this opposition is condemned to remain in the minority, and by far. It is weak among two large sectors of the Israeli population: Jews originally from Arab countries, the *Sepharadhim*, many of whom have the mentality of petty *pieds-noirs* (the former Algerian colonists of French ancestry), and Soviet Jews, who most often are close to the extreme Right (both on account of their anti-Communism and as a result of the nationalistic and chauvinistic habits they acquired in their former fatherland). On Saturday, March 27, at the call of Shalom Archav (Peace Now), twenty-to-thirty thousand people marched in Tel Aviv to shout in favor of an end to the occupation. On the scale of a country of three and a half million inhabitants, this is a demonstration of considerable size. Mr. Begin called the demonstrators "rotten" and flared up in anger at the presence, in the march, of twenty-six Maarakh deputies, that is to say, members of an opposition whose majority is nevertheless still pro-annexationist. During my stay, there have been numerous demonstrations, press conferences, and meetings, especially in Tel Aviv. The press, notably the very serious daily *Haaretz*, has heaped acerbic criticism upon the government. The *Jerusalem Post* itself, long characterized by its crushing conformism, has now joined the fray.

Has there really been a breakup of the old national union? And if so, what are its limits? After the assassination in Paris, on April 3, of the Israeli diplomat Yacov Barsimantov, the Israeli government immediately made known that it held this murder to be a violation, on the PLO's part, of the cease-fire agreement. This plainly meant that it considered itself to be freed from its own obligations.

On April 6, Begin met with the leaders of the Labor party, the principal partner of Maarakh. What was discussed, obviously, was the formation of a government of national union (a prospect Shimon Peres rejects for now, but not in principle) or at least opposition support for military action in southern Lebanon.

Friday, April 9. In the afternoon, everyone in Jerusalem was convinced that an attack was imminent. As we now know, it was temporarily[10] and partially blocked by leaks organized by Washington—and without Washington's support, no serious war is possible—and immediately resumed by Israeli radio, as well as by Jordanian television, although one should also note public opposition to the possibility of war from two former chiefs of staff, "Motta" Gur and Chaim Bar-Lev, the latter being, moreover, the general secretary of the Labor party. As for Shimon Peres himself, the old accomplice of Max Lejeune, Bourgès-Maunoury, and Guy Mollet during the Suez operation remained silent. And Rabin, who finds it quite natural to give speeches at the Military Academy of Argentina, where one of the most anti-Semitic regimes in the world rages out of con-

trol, also kept quiet. A lucid observer like Elie Barnavi, the author of a
good book on Israel in the twentieth century,[11] thinks that Maarakh must
split up so that a part of it, centered around people such as Yossi Sarid and
a portion of Mapam, might finally play the role of a real opposition.

Yet something more than that would also be required. The newspapers,
it is true, are filled with biting attacks against Mr. Begin. An Israeli friend,
Michel Harsgor, a professor at Tel Aviv University, tells me: "This government is, above all, comic." May he forgive me if I do not find it comic, or
not only comic. For my part, I am persuaded that, given the popular consensus, this government is capable of leading Israel into a tragic disaster in
the Greek sense of the term. In the Greek sense, I say, because, as in
Herodotus, as well as in Greek tragedy, the opportunities to choose the
path to safety present themselves repeatedly and yet, without fail, those
in positions of responsibility choose the path of catastrophe. For a real
opposition to have some chance of putting its mark on the fate of the
country and of changing the direction in which the country is heading, it
would have to translate this opposition into a refusal to furnish the government the military means it needs to carry out its policy. I was told by
a very good source that, during the bombardment of Beirut last summer,
some pilots considered the possibility of disobeying orders. Many of these
pilots are Left *kibbutznikim*. Should such a movement take on some real
breadth tomorrow, the opposition, too, will become real. A quite small
minority of Israelis is now aware of this.

How should we conclude? Israel's worst enemies—they are numerous
and they are quite far from being motivated by altruistic feelings—can
only desire that the present situation and today's policies continue. From
perversion (in which some undoubtedly see the triumph of the "normalization" of the Jewish people) to disappearance, the evolution may take a
long time, but it seems to me that it is in this direction that, according to
the logic of the moment, things are heading. I was struck to see that more
than one Israeli now sees things proceeding in this direction. Israel's
strategic position is not that of the Union of South Africa.

More than fifteen years ago, I debated with the Arab journalist Loftal-
lah Soliman. He concluded our discussion (this was right after the Six Day
War) as follows:[12]

> The Palestinian entity has been reconstituted. Palestine exists at
> present, whereas before it was torn asunder. Now something will
> happen within its borders. . . . Something is going to emerge inside

Palestine. Will it be South Africa? Algeria? For my part, I say that, in any case, some progress has been made in comparison with what went before. . . . The Arab people of Palestine, living under the conditions of a colonized people, are going to attain political consciousness and conduct a war of national liberation. I hope that on both sides we shall witness the emergence of people who want to find a solution together, within the framework of an independent Palestine. In the end, I believe that there is no longer any escape for Israel, absolutely none. In reaping a lightning victory, Israel has done what the Germans did. Qua Israel, it has rushed victoriously into the grave.

This analysis shocked me at the time. I continue to see its false side. In the last analysis, the Palestinian war of national liberation has not taken place, has not yet taken place. But how can one deny that what was built up with so much ardor, and sometimes so much heroism, under the tragic conditions of the rise of Nazism and the Second World War, is today being put into question? An unbearable idea, certainly, an idea that must be combated by pointing out that the tiny Palestinian people, too, risk disappearing in the catastrophe, a victim as it already has been both of Israeli settlement policy and of the policy of the Arab States of the region which have, to a large extent, helped maintain this people in their condition of helots. An unbearable idea, but is the idea of a Jewish State in which the army shoots at children and opens fire in a Mosque bearable?

The worst is not always certain, says the proverb that served as a subtitle for a play by Claudel. It is not unthinkable that the great powers will possibly find it in their interest to impose a compromise and to force the separation of these two mortally intertwined nations.

During the war, in Warsaw, in the ghetto, the following story, an echo of which can be found in Ringelblum's *Chronicle*, was told: Is it possible, a rabbi was asked, to chase the Nazis out of here? Here is the response: "There are two possible methods, one supernatural, the other natural. The supernatural method would be for the Allies to land. The natural method would be for God to send a host of angels to drive out the exterminators."

The Allies landed, all the same—somewhat late, it is true.

18 | "Inquiry Into a Massacre" by Amnon Kapeliouk

In the world that is ours, every event—when event there be—transpires twice: at the moment it occurs, accompanied by the media (as little as the latter might want to seize upon it), and then a few months later, sometimes a few years later, at the moment when reflection and analysis are brought to bear upon it. Books are one of the major forms of critical analysis. But such analysis might also express itself, for example, in the medium of film.

Sometimes the event and the book become confused. The flames of the May 1968 barricades had hardy died down when the first books appeared. "Commercial co-optation" the students in revolt said, and they were not mistaken.

The problem raised by the Sabra and Shatila massacres is somewhat different. From the sixteenth until the eighteenth of September, 1982, these massacres took place under the light of Israeli rockets but without the presence of the press or television cameras. It was only on the evening of the eighteenth that the drama was revealed. For a few weeks, the massacres, followed by the Israeli reactions, the establishment of the commission of inquiry, and the first meetings of this commission were front-page

"'Enquête sur un massacre' d'Amnon Kapeliouk," a review of Amnon Kapeliouk's *Sabra et Chatila: Enquête sur un massacre* (Paris: Seuil, 1982), originally appeared in *Le Monde Diplomatique*, January 4, 1983. Reprinted in *JMP*, pp. 484–87. [T/E: Kapeliouk's book appeared in English as *Sabra and Shatila: Inquiry into a Massacre*, trans. from the French by Khalil Jahshan (Belmont, Mass.: Association of Arab-American University Graduates, 1983). The quotations in the text are my translations from the original French.]

news, before disappearing into the common grave of forgetfulness, where massacres are buried.

Nevertheless, the ideologues are at work. You can be confident of that. Certain ideologues conjure away the facts, in somewhat the same fashion that the Hitlerian genocide (to which I am in no way comparing the crimes of Sabra and Shatila) is made to vanish under the pens of the "revisionists." It wasn't a matter of massacres, you see, but of battles; the numbers of dead are in reality ridiculously small and, to the extent that there was a massacre, it should be imputed not to the Lebanese Phalangists,[1] not to Israel, but quite simply to the KGB.[2] The fact that the third point contradicts the first is not of the sort to bother the ideologues in question.

Others felt the initial shock but today endeavor to forget it. So behaves Arnold Mandel, who wrote on September 29: "While refusing to participate in the chorus of invectives that is presently being cast from all sides upon Begin, I cannot myself subscribe to the argument being attributed to him in this case: *Goyim* have massacred other *goyim* and we are the ones being accused. The *goyim* engaging in this massacre have all the same been a little bit, under the given circumstances, *shabbessgoyim*, and it is this that is grave."[3] Reading what this same author has written since then, one gets the impression that he has in fact forgotten his first, quite salutary reaction.

One more word on another problem. It is true that the Sabra and Shatila massacres are not an isolated phenomenon in the region. The Syrians have massacred at Hama many more Syrians than the number of Palestinians the Phalangists massacred under Israeli control. It is equally true that those with impure motives can seize upon massacres for which the Jews are responsible. To all that, one is tempted to respond with the saying of a famous Jew from the first century of our era: "Each will be judged according to the law he has known." Israeli democracy states that it is the heir to the Jewish tradition and to the hopes of the prophets. That entails some duties and responsibilities.

Amnon Kapeliouk's book will benefit, no doubt, from the remnants of the September scandal, but in no way is this a book of co-optation. It is, rather, a cold and implacable chronological narrative of these days as they unfolded first in Beirut, then in Israel, from Tuesday, September 14, the date of the assassination of Bechir Gemayel, to Monday, September 20, the date when the Israeli daily *Haaretz* headlined its front page with an article by Zeev Schiff entitled: "War Crime in Beirut."

No narrative is innocent, and Amnon Kapeliouk, whom the readers of *Le Monde Diplomatique* know well and whom I, for my part, have known and have held in high esteem for a dozen years, is a man of commitment. He is also, however, though one does not hinder the other, a journalist of absolute integrity. I have seen him at work often enough to know that he never writes anything that cannot be backed up with an abundance of confirmations. His book is based upon a meticulous investigation. Oral and written testimony, site visits, etc.: nothing is lacking. I doubt that it can be challenged on the level of the facts. Perhaps someone who has followed in the international press what has been published about these events will not learn much that is new. There is one piece of information, however, that is of capital importance: as early as Thursday the sixteenth at midnight, the leader of the Phalangist troops who had entered Shatila sent a report to the Israeli general who was in command of the city of Beirut: "So far, three hundred civilians and terrorists have been killed." Amnon Kapeliouk adds: "This report was communicated immediately to the General Staff, and more than twenty senior officers had it in their hands in Tel Aviv." Is it possible that none of these officers spoke to their superiors? No one believes that to be the case.

Kapeliouk's account leaves no doubt about the depth of the Israeli involvement in this affair. That Mr. Begin and General Sharon might "not have wanted that," to use the hallowed expression, is possible, even likely. They probably would have been content with a small massacre and instead found themselves with a big one on their hands. Why a massacre? Here is what Kapeliouk writes: "From discussions between Israeli and foreign journalists and Phalangist officers, it emerges that the (initially maintained) thesis, according to which the massacre and the ensuing destruction resulted from an explosion of anger and spontaneous vengeance caused by the assassination of Bechir Gemayel, is erroneous. This massacre very well seems to have been premeditated. Its goal was to provoke a mass exodus of Palestinians from Beirut and from Lebanon. The cruelty of the crime—bodily lacerations, the severing of limbs, the drawing and quartering of children, the smashing of babies' heads against walls—are thus explicable within the context of a will to terrorize."

This is a hypothesis. If it is confirmed, Sabra and Shatila will be the repeat of Deir-Yassin, the 1948 massacre that caused so many Palestinians to flee. But will one ever know?[4]

19 | The Anti-Peace Colonists

T here is hardly any need to introduce Amnon Kapeliouk to the readers of *Le Monde Diplomatique*, since he is one of this monthly journal's most faithful correspondents. To dispel any misunderstandings, however, let us recall that this journalist, a *sabra* who loves his country deeply, usually lives in Jerusalem when he is not on assignment somewhere around the world. Let us also recall that, while mobilized for duty on the West Bank during the 1967 war, he discovered a Jordanian document that ordered the occupation of an Israeli village and the killing of its inhabitants (which, quite fortunately, did not occur). What does his new book, which comes after a volume on Israel[1] and after *Sabra and Shatila: Inquiry into a Massacre*,[2] tell us? It is devoted to the twenty-fifth of February 1994. On that day, in the mosque-synagogue of Hebron, a doctor—a "brilliant young man," we are told—massacred twenty-nine people who were praying in the room that contains the Tomb of the Patriarchs. He also wounded many others. Was this a simple case of one individual overcome by fit of madness? That is what has been decreed by a commission headed by the Chief Justice of the Israeli Supreme Court, Mr. Shamgar. A quite exceptional and encouraging fact is that this commission included an Arab judge among its members. The report's conclusions nevertheless were made in haste. Amnon Kapeliouk shows that the hypothesis of a second man cannot truly be ruled out and that some murky areas remain concerning whether the assassin might have benefited from others' help.

"Les Colons contre la paix" was originally published in *Le Monde Diplomatique*, October 1994, as a review of Amnon Kapeliouk's book *Hébron: Un Massacre annoncé* (Paris: Arléa/Seuil, 1994).

Baruch Goldstein was not an isolated individual. He belonged to a group of religious and racist fanatics, the kind the Jewish extremists of New York regularly send to Israel in the name of the "Law of Return." For the inhabitants of the Jewish colony of Kiryat Arba, he is a genuine hero. In fact, since his death he is now worshiped there as one. One must, as I have, see Kiryat Arba in order to believe it. It is a fortress, an acropolis that dominates the Arab town and serves as a relay station for another colony located in this town, the one founded by Rabbi Moshe Levinger. Are the inhabitants of this fortress religious fanatics? One is reminded of a satirical anticlerical song written by Pierre Jean de Béranger:

Dark men, where do you come from?
We come from down under the ground.
Half foxes, half wolves . . .

The songwriter's Jesuits are choir boys, however, when compared to these men who think that they are the direct interpreters of the will of God and the legitimate owners of all Palestine. Hebron is a sensitive area, the site of a pogrom that occurred in 1929, as Amnon Kapeliouk has not neglected to remind us. He also shows, however, how successive Israeli governments, whether Laborite or composed of representatives of the Likud, share responsibility for the development of these colonies (which I would dare describe as cancerous), especially this one, which is able to exist only in and through the expression of hatred. If the average Israeli, a member of the Likud, reminds one of the most violent Ulster Protestants, comparisons much worse than that come to one's pen when thinking of the inhabitants of Kiryat Arba.

Amnon Kapeliouk shows us that this massacre was foreseeable. It was foreseeable both because Baruch Goldstein made no mystery of his plans (his wife had tried to dissuade him from carrying them out before he committed the crime) and because the instructions given to the Israeli armed forces—never fire on a Jew who is firing—could not help but favor the occurrence of a massacre. Since then, by mid-October, candidates hoping to take over where Baruch Goldstein left off have appeared, but they have been intercepted in time by the Israeli secret services.

This criminal operation had an explicit goal: to interrupt the peace process which was inaugurated by the September 1993 Oslo agreement and which was reinforced thereafter by the handshake in Washington and the Cairo Accords. But beyond thinking about the string of events the author has reeled off for us, his story obliges us to reflect in more depth upon the accords themselves. Indeed, two readings of these accords, two logics, can be given.

The first reading, or logic, is that of an open process leading toward genuine peace. It entails the creation of a Palestinian State that, quite naturally, would be free to federate with Jordan, even with Israel. Such a development, which the most clear-headed Israelis wish for with all their might, inevitably presupposes the evacuation of the colonial settlements and a resolution to the problem of Jerusalem. One cannot see how the Palestinians could be asked to give up their capital, even if it is also the capital of Israel.

The other solution is to create another Bantustan. That is to say, one could attempt to implement the solution that failed so utterly in South Africa. Under this interpretation, the accords would have to be seen as an effort to bind the Palestinians hand and foot while granting Yasser Arafat some flattering tokens of prestige that would serve all the better to hem him in. The truly dangerous point in the Oslo agreement, as Amnon Kapeliouk has rightly shown, is found in the article of the treaty that allows discussion of the settlements question only after the expiration of a two-year waiting period.

These settlements, he reminds us, are inhabited by three sorts of colonists: pioneers of the old school, people attracted by low-cost housing, and fanatics. It would be rather simple to reduce the numbers of those representing the first two categories. One need only offer them some prospect of settlement elsewhere. Yet nothing has been done so far in this direction. As for the fanatics, those colonists who treat the Arabs like dogs, only direct confrontation will bring them under control. The Rabin government has exhibited courage. Will it know how to choose the logic, the only logic, that leads to peace?

PART FIVE

Conclusion

20 Recollections of a Witness: Protestants and Jews During the Second World War in France

For Alain Finiel

Mr. President and my dear friend, Ladies and Gentle-men: In coming here at Jacques Bompaire's request to speak to you about what I might know of the rela-tions between Protestants and Jews during those dark years, I feel as if I am repaying a debt. Some of the reasons for my feeling this way will become clear during my presentation, but there are also reasons that touch more generally upon my craft, which is that of historian. It happens, for example, that from my sophomore to my senior year in high school—that is to say, during the years when I decided upon my vocation—with but a single exception, all my history teachers (Messrs. Beucler and Paul and François-Georges Pariset at the Carnot High School, Alba, Fourniol, and Diény at Henri IV High School, and Charles Carrière in Marseilles) were members of the Reformed Church community. I have always thought that there was a certain spiritual affinity between the study of his-tory and the Reformation, if only because Protestantism encouraged a

"Protestants et Juifs pendant la Seconde Guerre mondiale en France: Souvenirs d'un témoin" was presented May 15, 1990, to the Société de l'histoire du protes-tantisme français (Society for the History of French Protestantism) and was pub-lished in the Society's *Bulletin* 136 (1990). For reasons that will become clear upon reading the text, I have (except for some very minor details) retained the original oral form of this lecture. I have simply corrected a few errors pointed out to me by Mr. Pierre Bolle, who kindly sent me in advance a copy of his article, "Les Protes-tants et leurs Églises devant la persécution des Juifs en France," *Études théologiques et religieuses* 2 (1982): 185–208. I have, in addition, borrowed a few passages from my article "Si Dieu le fit . . . ," which appeared in *Esprit* 134 (January 1988). Reprinted in *JMP*, pp. 359–80.

critical reading of the Bible. Even if Richard Simon was an Oratorian and Spinoza an excommunicated Jew, there was, after all, Pierre Bayle. I am not claiming that all these teachers of mine were admirable, and there are those on this list whom I "ragged" on. At least two of them, however, André Alba and Charles Carrière, played an absolutely decisive role in my choice of vocation. Now, Charles Carrière was not just a Protestant, he had been a missionary instructor in Cameroon. These history teachers taught me to have a critical mind and they even, if I dare say so, gave me a taste for insolence and disrespect.

This homage that is owed having been rendered, I must now set forth what I am going to say to you. As the title I have chosen with Jacques Bompaire for this presentation suggests, you will not be receiving a scholarly lecture of the kind you are accustomed to hear. I shall not tell you, along with Pierre Bolle, how the Protestant churches armed themselves against the perversion of National Socialism with Karl Barth's theology, or about what the uneven relationship was between the Federation of Protestant Churches and the Vichy authorities concerning the Jewish question. As you know, while the Protestant Churches protested against the Vichy statute on Jews, they demanded not its abrogation but its rewriting. Nor shall I, following Monsieur Poujol, resume the description of the refuge provided in the Cévennes,[1] and I shall not enter here, apropos of Chambon-sur-Lignon,[2] into the quarrel surrounding the role of Major Schmähling, a quarrel I happened to have participated in on a previous occasion.

I present to you here not the results of a historical investigation but the eyewitness account of a child who was ten years old in 1940 and who, between 1940 and 1944 and later on, too, was led by circumstances to come into close contact with people in Protestant circles, notably in the Protestant-based Unionist Scouts of France [Éclaireurs unionistes de France], the EUF, and to live for some time in two villages that had a strong Protestant presence: Saint-Agrève in the Ardèche and Dieulefit in the Drôme. Still, the import of this testimonial must be made explicit. The person speaking to you is obviously not the child of 1940. My recollections have been reclassified in terms of what I have lived and learned since then, and specifically in terms of my profession as a historian who has become accustomed to handling texts and testimony. Every recollection is reconstructed and bears as much upon the present as upon the past. I have arrived here neither with the freshness of a Rousseau, the Rousseau of the beginning of the Confessions, nor, moreover, with his arrogance.

Let me take two examples. The first lies at the heart of my topic here. The other is connected to it indirectly, but in a profound way all the same. Did I know during the war of the famous letter Pastor Boegner wrote to the Grand Rabbi Isaiah Schwarz, his much circulated letter of March 26, 1941? It is possible, likely even, but I have a much less confident recollection of it than of Paul Claudel's letter to the same Grand Rabbi or the pastoral letters from a certain number of bishops which were written in 1942.[3] The second example is a bit more complex. My entire life has been marked by the tale my father told me in late 1941 or early 1942 about the Dreyfus Affair. There is no doubt something strange about dwelling on an injustice done to an individual at a time when the outrage being committed was collective. But it is also through the Affair that not only my political but also my moral and historical education was formed. Now, everyone knows that in the Affair the role of Protestants was immense. One need only mention the names of Scheurer-Kestner, Gabriel Monod, Louis Leblois, Charles Rist, Francis de Pressensé, or Pastor Raoul Allier. It was so immense that certain narrators have on occasion enlarged it further still. Thus, in the first version of his *Souvenirs sur l'Affaire*, Léon Blum made of Colonel Picquart an Alsatian Protestant, even though Picquart was a Catholic. In my memory, however, I find nothing of all this that dates back to 1941 or 1942. I learned of it later. Every eyewitness account supposes—and this is what Marc Bloch had done in *Strange Defeat*,[4] his eyewitness account of 1940—a presentation of the one who testifies and, consequently, a presentation of that person's life history and personal subjectivity. This is indispensable, if only to indicate the limits of such testimony.

On both my grandfathers' sides I belong to a Jewish bourgeois family that came from Carpentras via Montpellier and Marseilles. We have heard Carpentras spoken about recently, due to the desecration of Jewish grave sites in that town. Starting from a very modest background, my family, like so many others, experienced upward social mobility during the second half of the nineteenth century and the beginning of the twentieth. Both my grandmothers, however, came from a different social setting: Odessa in the case of my paternal grandmother, Alsace via Paris in the case of my maternal grandmother. The first of my direct ancestors to pass the baccalaureate was my paternal grandfather, who was a lawyer, as was my father and as is the case, too, with my brother. I was born on Rue de Varenne, therefore in a fashionable quarter of Paris—not the neighborhood of Aragon (the sixteenth *arrondissement*) but rather the area around Saint-Germain Boulevard.

My family was French, patriotic, and in favor of the Republic—which no doubt is lacking in originality. It was French, despite a grandmother who was a native of Odessa and a great-grandmother born in Rio de Janeiro of parents who were, moreover, from Bordeaux and even were, it was said in the family, related to Michel de Montaigne. I say "French," and not "assimilated," expressly, for the latter word was, for us, totally meaningless. To us, Zionism naturally was an entirely alien concept. Patriotism, the idea that France was the most beautiful and the noblest country in the world was a part of our heritage. A maternal uncle, whose first name I bear, had been killed in 1917 at Chemin des Dames while an officer-candidate, and his photo, ornamented with the text of his citations, was a place of worship in the house of my grandparents, the Valabrègues. At the dramatic moment France fell in 1940, my father, who was mobilized for service at the time, recounts in his journal that, while passing in front of the Cathedral of Chartres, he uttered Edgar Quinet's cry, "O France, Christ of Nations." I also said that the family members were republicans. As a republican, my great-grandfather had been a victim of the repressive laws of the Second Empire. His correspondence from a besieged Paris in 1870–71 with his wife, who had remained in Montpellier, leaves no doubt about his feelings concerning what he called "that whole race of kings and emperors." We looked at these letters during the war. The family's republicanism quite naturally became even more pronounced during the anti-Semitic crisis at the end of the nineteenth century. My grandfather and my great uncle became very involved in the Dreyfus Affair (which was not always the case—far from it—among the members of the Jewish bourgeoisie). My father certainly did not vote for the Popular Front in 1936. Indeed, in our part of town, the seventh *arrondissement*, such a vote would have been totally useless. He was, at the Palace of Justice, the colleague of Millerand who already for many years no longer was the socialist he had been in his earlier days. In 1942 my father wrote to Léon Blum to tell him that he regretted having misjudged him, but he still thought that Blum had been wrong to have wanted to cooperate with the Weimar Republic. He told me during the war: "Believe me, one must be of the Left," and I have benefited from this advice. He followed this principle himself, however, only with extreme moderation.

What about religion in all this? We knew that we were Israelites, as one said at the time, but we were not completely PIAFs (French Anti-Semitic Israelite Patriots). We knew that the Jewish religion was, according to an adage I heard a hundred times, the mother of all religions. It was understood, to cite another adage, that God is the same for all men. We did not practice religion, and I went for the first and practically the last time to synagogue in Marseilles, in July 1940, for the Office for the War Dead. In matters of religious education, I received only a few lessons of sacred history dispensed to me by a schoolteacher and I unfortunately did not learn a word of Hebrew. This nonobservance dates back a long time. My great-grandfather asked his wife not to tell his mother that he had written to her on Yom Kippur, which we called the day of the Great Pardon. My grandfather, who died in 1936, had declared that if a rabbi appeared at his funeral, he would rise from his coffin to strangle the man. A few traces of religious observance, Yom Kippur and Passover, remained, but only on my mother's side. And while the Easter meal certainly was made with unleavened bread, it was not in any way a Seder. In fact, it was not until I happened to be in Israel in the 1970s that I participated in my first Seder. As for French anti-Semitism, before the war I noticed few traces of it. One day, while playing in a park on Boulevard des Invalides, a boy slightly older than I called me a son of Abraham. I went home to get an explanation. Another time, the governess attending me indignantly pointed out that on a poster protesting against the group fine imposed upon the German Jews after *Kristallnacht*—I suppose it was a LICA (International League Against Anti-Semitism) poster—someone had added in front of the amount listed: "It's not enough."

That is all and it is not much. My father was certainly more aware of anti-Semitism, and he knew that, as a Jew, he could never be the first secretary of the Conference of Lawyers of the Paris Bar. He was content to help arrange for his best friend, Jacques Millerand, to be chosen a few years later. Yet he wrote in his journal in 1942: "I feel as a Frenchman the insult that has been done to me as a Jew."

What did Protestantism represent for the child I was in 1939? Naturally, I knew that in France there were Catholics and Protestants. A Protestant family, the Baumgartners, lived beneath us. During the war, the Nazis demanded to know if they were Jews. There were, in the service of my mother, her sister and my uncle, Protestants from Alsace and Lorraine. One of these women remained with us during the entire war and beyond, proudly wearing a silver Cross of Lorraine. Nevertheless, I do not hesitate to add that, for me, Protestantism meant first of all *England*. This was so for a whole series of contingent reasons. In our house lived an Anglican, rather "High Church" English governess who was very proud of the fact that she had one day met the Archbishop of Canterbury. Also, in 1939 I was bilingual. I had hung above my bed a portrait of George VI and the Queen and I knew that the king was *defensor fidei*. Above all, however, I knew in a more or less confused way that the English were our potential allies against the Germans, and well before the defeat we had adopted the habit, in our family, of listening to the news on the BBC. The fact that the Germans were themselves also in their majority Protestant was left in a dark area of our field of vision. The hope we placed in England was so strong that in 1940, after the defeat, I heard my mother say that if the war were won and we escaped alive, we would convert to Anglicanism.

I said that we were a French, patriotic, and pro-republican family. A French family: like many other Jews, my father corresponded with the archivists of Bordeaux, Montpellier, and, especially, Carpentras in order to establish that our French national roots were centuries old. I should also add that, as early as 1940, our family supported the Resistance and Gaullism. My own patriotic education was such that, even though I was not yet ten, I experienced the June 17, 1940, armistice, much more than the fall of Paris, as a national humiliation. I said, apropos of Pétain, and I remember it as if it were yesterday: "The coward!" When my father was able, after many adventures on our part and his, to rejoin us in Marseilles following the defeat, the armistice, and the exodus, he could only provide violent reinforcement to the feelings I myself harbored. In fact, my father belonged, as early as 1940, to the clandestine network of the Musée de l'Homme, but that, of course, was something I did not know at the time.

A Parisian headed for the Montaigne Junior High School, I found myself instead in Marseilles at Périer Junior High School, which soon became Field Marshal Pétain Junior High School, and I entered seventh grade there at the start of the 1940–41 school year. It was there that I truly became aware of anti-Semitism and that I immediately, as a child of ten, found myself pitted against classmates who treated me as a "dirty Jew," adding blows and various forms of humiliation to their words. I will not linger over these images, which nevertheless remain very vivid in my mind. The Vidal-Naquets were highly well known in Marseilles as Jews, and my classmates—often the offspring of the upper bourgeoisie—singled me out immediately. True, I put in my own two cents with a certain amount of provocative fervor, for my brother, my sister, and my cousin Jacques Brunschwig, with whom I was raised, experienced less lively forms of persecution. I was a provocative child—not in the name of Judaism, but rather in the name of Gaullism. Old ladies pointed their fingers at me: "That's the one who doesn't like the Field Marshal." With the support of only one other Jewish classmate, I refused, in 1941, to do a homework assignment on the Chief of State's visit to Marseilles. I was again the lone student to refuse to write a ritual letter to Pétain, though this did not stop me from proclaiming everywhere, in the face of the evidence, that in France 98 percent of the people were Gaullists.

It was at the end of 1940, I believe, that I came into contact with Marseilles Protestantism, for the most part families who came from the Cévennes region (the Finiels, the Cordesses, the Fraissinets, the Arnals) but also some from Alsace (the Kellers, the Stamms, the Leenhardts, the Walters). I did so quite simply by becoming a cub scout and then a boy scout in the Grignan den and troop, which later divided in two to create the Paradise den and troop and which was connected with the Grignan Street Church, over which reigned several pastors, notably Pastor Roux, but also Pastor Cuche, first name Armand, who became the butt of countless jokes. This involvement with scouting continued throughout the war, not only in Marseilles but also at Dieulefit, and even after the war since, after the Liberation, I belonged for some time to the Roquépine troop. This was not the result of chance but stemmed, rather, from a family decision. My brother and two of my cousins also were cub scouts, boy scouts, or explorers. One of my friends, a nephew of Jules Moch (a Socialist minister in Blum's second cabinet and a member of the Resistance who joined the Consultative Assembly of Algiers), joined the cub scouts with me. Why this choice, which was basically my mother's? At the time, the Israelite Scouts of France, which later became the core of a Resistance group, enjoyed a legal status. In my family, however, nothing was to be avoided so much as anything that might smack of a ghetto. Another group, the Scouts of France [Éclaireurs de France], whose ideals were secular and whose sentiments were close to my family's, also existed, but for reasons that now seem clear my family chose to send me to the Unionist Scouts of France. Here, obviously, was one minority seeking the protection of another minority that was not being persecuted as such and that appealed to the God of Israel. Let me add that scouting, and especially Protestant scouting, was a movement that was English in origin. Its founding father was General Baden-Powell. And, by and large, its mythology was borrowed from an English writer: Rudyard Kipling. The ideal wolf cub was Mowgli, the well-known character from *The Jungle Book*. When, in July 1943, I turned thirteen, which among Jews corresponded to the age of majority, my boyhood friend Alain Michel brought me a *History of England* by the same Kipling, thinking that this present would please me, and he was right. But, on the Protestant side, there was also an open and deliberate policy of welcoming outsiders. We know today that there were pressures coming from Vichy to convince the Protestant youth movements to refuse to accept foreign children, whether Jewish or not. To their great honor, the EUF responded with a categorical refusal to follow this injunction. My experience was that the Catholic-based Scouts of France [*scouts de France*] proved more respectful of authority and that the Protestants stood out against the orthodox Vichyism of the Marseilles Catholic Church and its leader, Monsignor Delay.

Why this association, and even alliance? On the Protestant side, memories of persecution are often invoked as an explanation. I remember a worship service conducted during a Sunday outing. We sometimes attended services, sometimes, more rarely, Sunday school, and the den mother explained to us on this particular occasion that Protestants ought to be prepared for a return to the days of persecution and that, while relations with the Government were satisfactory for the moment, one had to be prepared to face up to difficulties, if need be. We know that even a man like Field Marshal Pétain's adviser René Gillouin, who had described himself as an official state anti-Semite, wrote to Pétain: "The revocation of the Edict of Nantes is a picnic compared to our laws on the Jews, Monsieur Field Marshal." I know the value of the argument about the effect previous persecutions can have, but I now have some doubts. The Greek Orthodox Church, too, had experienced violent persecutions under the Turkocracy, but that did not prevent it from being violently anti-Semitic. Nor does what is happening today in Eastern Europe, with the liberation of these countries' Churches, always inspire optimism.

I also wish to mention a more recent personal recollection. During the summer of 1959, my wife and I visited the French Museum of the Protestant Wilderness. We found there, of course, something to mark the Second World War, a copy of the famous inscription of Marie Durand at the Tower of Constance, "Resist," and a lively description of the Camisard maquis. We were in the midst of the Algerian War at the time, and I was, as Jacques Bompaire has just recalled, deeply engaged in the struggle against this war and the repression that accompanied it. The analogy was strikingly obvious to us, but it was clear, according to the conversations we overheard, that no one else around us was making this connection.

More serious, I believe, is the argument concerning the influence of the biblical tradition, and notably Protestantism's Old Testament roots. The examples we read during services came as often from the Old Testament as from the New. Of course, things were in principle the same for the Catholics, as Pope Pius XI had recalled when he stated his opposition to all forms of Marcionism and Gnosticism. But this was a time, a half century ago, when Catholics (in any case, young Catholics) did not read the Bible. And while I, personally, read it in the (rather mediocre) translation of Louis Segond, it was thanks to my Protestant educators that I did so. I still recall the small collection of psalms my mother gave me at an EUF party; in it I read for the first time "By the Rivers of Babylon."

That said, I still do not believe that we have touched here on the essential point, which is, I believe, sociological in nature. I am speaking of the encounter and the solidarity between two minorities whose actions have often, especially since the nineteenth century, converged. Of course, the Protestants had made their way into political society well before the Jews did. Guizot had been the de facto if not de jure president of the Council [of Ministers] nearly a century before Léon Blum. It is clear, however, that Protestants and Jews together had contributed to making France the secular democracy it little by little had become. It was the Guizot law of 1833 that established state-sponsored primary-school education. It was a Naquet law, if you will permit me this family mention, that in 1884 reestablished divorce in France. And it was yet another Protestant, Félix Pecaut, who was the great organizer under the Third Republic of the primary-school educational system, just as it was Méjan who was the principal architect of the separation between Church and State.[5] It is as if the two minority groups were aware that they had a mutual interest in creating a space for freedom and neutrality. Moreover, it happened that, under Vichy as well as under the Third Republic in the time of Maurras, both groups were lumped together for purposes of insult and outrage. I recall the insult directed at my cousin Jacques Brunschwig, in 1943, by a boy who has since married the daughter of a brilliant anti-Semitic author, Jean Anouilh: "You Protestant Jew!" The two communities had other traits in common, such as an interest in individual social advancement—what mean-spirited tongues call *arrivisme*—or a concern for scholarly excellence, which is characteristic of many minority groups. I will add that the fact that one belongs to a minority group may facilitate the development of theologies built around the theme of the "remnant of Israel," each group naturally deeming itself to be this deserving remnant. This provides the group with a potential source of self-justification.

If you will permit me, we shall return now to a concrete example that lies at the heart of this presentation, that is to say, what I lived and experienced. Protestant scouting had certain traits in common with scouting as a whole that did not clash to any great extent with the model being upheld by the Vichy regime: authoritarianism and, sometimes, a cult of leadership. This model was being propagated beyond the confines of the scouting movement; to the "Scouts, be prepared" motto corresponded the "Boys, be prepared" injunction that was being foisted on us at Field Marshal Pétain Junior High School. This was the time of the jingle: "A flower in one's cap, a song on one's lips, joy and sincerity in one's heart." It would be too much to say that I was always happy in my cub scout den and then among the boy scouts, but some of this was my fault. While I encountered—rather less than elsewhere, it is true—a certain number of anti-Semites (whom our den mothers and scoutmasters reprimanded), I, especially, was afflicted with a variety of nicknames on account of my extraordinary awkwardness. It must not have been pleasant to watch me attempting to light a fire; while I learned, like everyone else, how to tie a "bowline on a bight" and other such knots and while I could tap out Morse Code passably well, the rest, I must admit, was rather a disaster.

A late 1942 report card, which I read with a foolish sense of pride, offered the following judgment on me: "Already represents, despite his young age, the very type of the perfect intellectual who is totally lacking in practical sense." What is more, I was a rather terrible young member of the bourgeoisie. In our den and in our troop, there were some members of High Protestant Society, the HSP—the Fraissinets, for example, or the Cordesses—who were not all very likable. There were also some boys from quite modest family backgrounds, and in particular some orphans from the Marie orphanage, a Protestant establishment on Paradise Street. One of my most terrible feelings of remorse dates back to a camping trip we took during the summer of 1941 at Pellegrin near La Londe. I made fun of the parents of certain cub scouts who made spelling errors. The idea that one might be an adult and not know how to spell correctly was, for me, unthinkable. All the same, the world of scouting in the Grignan and then the Paradise troop was rather unique. Our den mother, Amy Walter, was a pastor's daughter, and the scoutmaster (who incidentally, I learned much later, manufactured false papers for Jews in trouble) was named Jean Contandriopoulos. How did this hapax—a Protestant Greek who is still today the Protestant chaplain at the Baumettes prison after having abandoned a very lucrative career in a brokerage firm—ever come about? Their marriage on May 30, 1942, after a year of solemn engagement, was for us a quite memorable ceremony. The marriage itself helps to explain this rarity. Naturally, Jean Contandriopoulos was raised as a Greek Orthodox. His parents had sought to enroll him in a Catholic school which refused their request. The Protestants were more open, and among them he encountered both scouting and love. Pastor Roux, who was to perish in the Nazi camps to which his wife was also deported, presided over their wedding at the church on Grignan Street.

This life among my Protestant friends nevertheless posed a problem for me. At a solemn ceremony, one had to promise to serve not only one's country but God. During the summer of 1941, my father had explained to me that God's existence was, to say the least, problematic. I made it through the ceremony with the help of one of those sophisms one can concoct at any age: in promising to serve God, I was promising *in petto* to serve the Ideal. But I was not very proud of this maneuver, and it is not a recollection I return to with any pleasure. On the other hand, the "Scout's Pledge" posed so few problems that, in the boarding school to which I was exiled in Megève for five months, Jacques Brunschwig and I recited it out loud every evening. That said, it should be added that I knew Christianity infinitely better than the religion of my ancestors, to the point that I was startled when a den mother told me that we the Jews did not believe that the Messiah had arrived in the person of Jesus Christ. I responded that there was nothing of the sort, and she told me right then: "You must really be some pretty queer Jews." And she was not completely wrong. I should add, however, that I never witnessed any attempts at conversion.

I nevertheless would not want to leave one with the impression that these encounters with Protestants constituted the main part of my life in Marseilles, where I lived, except for five months in the Haute-Savoie, until May 18, 1944. The Protestants were a minority in Marseilles—larger, no doubt, than the Jewish minority, but a small minority all the same. The Protestants represented for me, if I dare risk conveying this image, Sunday school. The rest of the time I led an almost normal life—with an awareness, all the same during the last months, that lightning could strike at any moment. That is to say, I was a junior high school student who did not spend all his time getting knocked around. A palpable change in attitude on the part of my schoolmates, even the pro-Vichy and anti-Semitic ones (and not all those who were pro-Vichy were anti-Semitic), occurred after the free zone was occupied and the Germans arrived in Marseilles. I had teachers of varying opinions and talents. One of them found it deplorable that someone who had performed a heroic feat was in fact English. The only Nazi was a narrow-minded pedant, a veteran covered with medals who on occasion would exclaim that only Jews and Communists were capable of being rowdy, which was quite an exaggeration. With this one exception, I never heard on the part of any of the teachers the least in the way of anti-Semitic remarks. At the very most, our eighth-grade history professor, somewhat peculiar in that he was an ardent supporter of the Japanese (this was after Pearl Harbor), exhibited a certain amount of complacency when he drew a map of an imaginary medieval city with its ghetto. The strongest personality was Léon Augé, who taught us Latin in seventh grade, French, Latin, and Greek in ninth

grade. He was, and fortunately still is,[6] a mustachioed anarchist—madly
patriotic, too—who labeled Caesar a "Kraut" [*Boche*] responsible for the
massacres of women and little children. Every once in a while he would
give me a package to take directly home without opening it. Most often,
it contained brochures from *Les Cahiers du Témoignage Chrétien*, a publication in which Protestants spoke out, although it was put together mainly
by Jesuits from Lyon, Reverend Father Chaillet and Reverend Father De
Montcheuil, who was a friend of my father.

It turns out, however, that I had the opportunity to live in two places
where Protestants were much more than a small minority, and in those
places I was to a very large extent integrated into their way of life. I am
alluding, as I have already announced, to Saint-Agrève and Dieulefit.
These were two small villages situated on opposite sides of the Rhône. I
stayed in Dieulefit three times, in August 1943, at the time the Allies were
in Sicily and the Red Army was retaking Kharkov, then during Passover
vacation in 1944, at a time when many said "You believe in the Allied landing" as others said "You believe in Santa Claus," and, finally, in September
and early October 1944, at the home of my grandmother, my aunt, and
my cousins, the Brunschwigs. It is from there that we returned to Paris in
a truck so that I could resume normal studies. My brother and I arrived at
Saint-Agrève a few days after the June 6, 1944, Allied landing. We had to
pass through a sort of border crossing at Lamastre, after which we were
in the liberated zone. No German dared to venture any longer into that
area. Although a rumor spread one day that some troops were coming to
sack everything (there was no lack of massacres and arrests in this region),
this particular rumor quite fortunately turned out to be false. During the
early days of September, the French army completed the liberation of the
area. There my brother and I rejoined my sister and my younger brother,
who was less than six months' old and who had, by a bit of a miracle,
escaped the Gestapo. They had found refuge with my maternal grandmother, my aunt, and my mother's sister, whose husband (my father's
brother) had joined the army of French Africa. My brother and I were
placed in the boarding house of an old Protestant spinster named Octavie
Jouve who was rather aggressively Protestant in her views and who madly
believed in the art of "self-healing."

Both Saint-Agrève and Dieulefit were villages divided between
Catholics and Calvinists. Added to this division, on the Protestant side,
was the existence of a dissident group, the "Darbyists," who were bigger
in Saint-Agrève than Dieulefit, though in the latter village the bookseller,
a very important personality, belonged to this latter community. Saint-

Agrève was located six miles from Chambon-sur-Lignon, to which we rode on bikes, crossing the continental divide between the Rhône and the Loire, the Mediterranean and the Atlantic, without taking any particular notice. This was the Chambon of Pastor Trocmé. It was at Chambon that I met again this nephew of Jules Moch who had entered the cub scouts with me and it was there, too, that my sister attended the Cévennes Junior High School during the first trimester of the 1944–45 school year. Saint-Agrève does not have Chambon's reputation as a place of refuge. Nevertheless, many Jews found asylum in this village, for example Jules Isaac, who wrote there, I believe, *Les Oligarques*,[7] an "essay in partial history" that transposes to the Athens of the Thirty Tyrants the conflict between Vichy and the Republic. Also living at Saint-Agrève while I was there was Paul Reuter, the eminent jurist and one of the resistance leaders of the Uriage School team, who, while himself a Catholic (though an austere and scholarly one), was married to a Jewish woman, one of my far-removed cousins. My family became completely integrated into the Protestant community, and my young cousin, Alain Vidal-Naquet, was the best student in Sunday school. My aunt had removed the second half of his last name, which had provoked some conflict with my father, for whom anything resembling dissembling constituted a sort of mortal sin.

One need not have read André Siegfried, whose study of the political geography of the Ardèche appeared several years after the events in question, to understand that deep political divisions can manifest themselves through religious differences. To say that the political sphere or the religious sphere has priority boils down to asking which came first, the chicken or the egg. With Catholics and Protestants, it was less a matter of Right and Left than of Reaction in the most total sense of the term (and, ultimately, of the royalist "Fleur de lys") versus the Republic. Naturally, this opposition also encompassed the conflict between collaboration—or, at least, Vichy—and the Resistance. The deputy elected from the area to the Chamber in 1936, Xavier Vallat, was Vichy's first Commissioner on Jewish Questions. His electoral agent at Saint-Agrève, the owner of the village's main hotel, was, of course, an ardent supporter of the Field Marshal, although he never, to my knowledge, turned anyone in. As a matter of fact, after Pierre Laval announced at the end of June, to our immense joy, the death of State Secretary for Information Philippe Henriot, it was Xavier Vallat who replaced him. He addressed his electors directly to warn them against the white underground, that of Lamastre, that is to say, the "Secret Army," which was in his view as dangerous as the red underground, that of the *Francs-Tireurs et Partisans*. Social conflicts naturally came to graft themselves onto political conflicts: one evening, beaming with joy and excitement, the pastor's young fiancée came to my aunt's house to announce that "Tutu" Faurie, the immensely wealthy owner of a café who was also a supporter of the Vichy regime, had signed a statement in which he renounced all his worldly possessions. Naturally, this decision lasted only the length of one summer.

At Saint-Agrève, I associated mostly with the Protestants, of course, though a Catholic industrialist who lodged at the same boarding house as I, and whom Mademoiselle Jouve warned me against because of his "fleur de lys" opinions, took the time to explain to me that all forms of socialism were self-contradictory. I also made the acquaintance of an austere and mystical lady from Dieulefit who belonged to a famous family of pastors, the Atgers. She explained to me at length that the ten tribes of Israel had spread across the world, including Denmark, as its name, which came from the tribe of Dan, proved.[8] This was my first brush with this celebrated myth, which enjoyed immense currency during the sixteenth and seventeenth centuries, especially after the discovery of America, and concerning which I have since had occasion to do some work. At Saint-Agrève, I also engaged in a little of what a sociologist would call participatory observation. That is to say, on Sundays I attended church services, alternating between the Catholics, the Protestants, and the Darbyists. It was the last group, I should add, that impressed me most. No pastor, and consequently no authority. All those who had something to say stood up, one after another, to speak. The atmosphere was at once democratic and prophetic, even apocalyptic, words which I naturally would not have employed in 1944 but which come to me now in thinking once again about this experience.

As one might expect, intercommunity relations in Saint-Agrève were very bad, to the extent that each community accused the other of being responsible for the death, during the Wars of Religion, of the village's eponymous saint. With the help of my colleagues Luce Pietri and Brigitte Baujard, I later undertook an investigation of my own, and it turns out to be quite obvious that Agrippanus—who is said to have been Bishop of Puy-en-Velay and to have been decapitated at Chiniac, which has since become Saint-Agrève, in 650—was a victim neither of the Reformation nor of the Catholic Church. The only true thing in all this is that a portion of his relics were scattered during the Revolution. Since a majority of the revolutionaries in this region were Protestants, it was natural for them to be blamed for this crime. This story, as it was recounted to me, is obviously a fine example of a self-justifying myth.

At Dieulefit tensions were much lower, but the two communities were clearly separate, to the extent that each one had, as is quite natural, its own place of worship, but also, for example, its own doctor. I noticed that on the day my aunt was suffering from nephritic colic and we could not get the Protestant doctor, Monsieur Deransart, to come for a house visit, we called the Catholic doctor, Dr. Préault, which provoked a minor revolution. He was, it turns out, a man who had rendered many services to the maquis.

Much more than Saint-Agrève, Dieulefit was a place of refuge. This was the case for the Jews, who were quite numerous in this village, some keeping their name, even if it left no doubts (like Mr. Abramowicz, who taught in the local secondary school, La Roseraie), others concealing it. For the most part and as far as I could tell, while the Jews of Dieulefit came from all over, including central and eastern Europe, like the painters Wols or Willy Eisenchitz, they were not generally religious Jews, and still less nationalistic Jews, but Jews fitting into the republican mold of the "abstract citizen" who dreamt of receiving or regaining all the rights the Vichy statutes had taken away from them. This was the case, for example, with the engraver Pierre Guastalla who bears a name well known to Hellenists. Also present at Dieulefit, and a student at La Roseraie, was the granddaughter of the president of the League of the Rights of Man, Victor Basch, the eminent representative of the Dreyfusard tradition who was assassinated, along with his wife, by the Vichy militia under circumstances of which you are well aware.

Let us leave aside the case of some Jews who, facing the most clear-cut threats, had taken refuge eight miles away in Bourdeaux, a village marked even more, if that is possible, by Protestantism. When rumors foretold of a Nazi raid (which fortunately proved untrue), a number of Resistance intellectuals made of Dieulefit a tiny "capital of the spirit." There were musicians like the great pianist Yvonne Lefébure, who lived at my aunt's house; writers and journalists like André Rousseaux, Andrée Viollis, and Emmanuel Mounier, who wrote there his *Traité du caractère*;[9] poets like Noël Mathieu, who taught mathematics and philosophy at La Roseraie and who is better known under the name of Pierre Emmanuel. Among the names I have just mentioned are those of several eminent Catholics, all of whom were determined opponents of the Vichy regime. The couple that ran La Roseraie, Paul and Madeleine Arcens, were Catholic, too, but were not Dieulefit natives. I recall my great surprise when I learned that they were Catholics: they were members of the Resistance; naturally, therefore, they were Protestants, I thought. You see, at Dieulefit, as at Saint-

Agrève, the local Resistance was composed mostly of Protestants. Of course, things offered less contrast in reality than in my childhood impressions. Jacques Brunschwig had remarked to me one day in 1943 when, passing a farm, we heard the radio from London, that the farmers must be Protestants. He informs me today that the mayor, Colonel Pizot, who, because he was an ardent supporter of the Field Marshal, wrongly passed in my family's view for a Catholic, purposely closed his eyes to the forged documents shop operating in the town hall. The woman who ran this shop, Jeannette Barnier, was the mayor's secretary, and she belonged to the town's Huguenot community. I believe I know, moreover, that this forgery operation weighed upon her conscience and that she unburdened herself to Pastor Eberhard, who offered her his complete reassurance.

This Dieufitois Protestantism radiated from two hearths. The first was the Eberhard family. Pastor Eberhard no longer exercised his duties at Dieulefit, but in Lyon. Nevertheless, he often returned to his native village where he continued to enjoy considerable influence. Like so many others, he experienced, someone has written me, some Vichyite temptations around the theme of a return to the land, but he quickly freed himself therefrom and he always combated anti-Semitism. Pastor Eberhard was the author of the first political pamphlet I ever read, a critical reflection on how to put the Liberation to good use. His sisters ran a "musical high school" that made of Dieulefit a sort of regional capital of music, Yvonne Lefébure lending assistance. Another pastor, Philippe Debû, whose style was that of a "fellow traveler," organized the first political meeting I ever attended in my life, in early September 1944, the very evening I arrived in Dieulefit. The other "hearth" was the Beauvallon boarding school run by Marguerite Soubeyran, the celebrated "Aunt Marguerite," famous for her educational innovations (Beauvallon was a part of the "new schools" network) but also for the asylum she extended to many Jewish children. One of the "Frères Jacques," a Soubeyran brother, belonged to this famous family.

All this was, perhaps, normal. A few days ago, my friend Élisabeth Labrousse quoted to me the following response of a peasant woman from Chambon-sur-Lignon: "So what? Why make such a fuss [*pourquoi faire tant d'histoires*]? We did what we ought to have done, that's all." It remains the case, however, that not everyone was so piously faithful to this austere sense of duty. The Protestants as a whole were. There were, of course, some exceptions. I have already said why I do not think that such an accomplishment of one's duty resulted from any sort of essence of Protestantism. After all, Luther had made some violently anti-Semitic statements in his day. Nor am I certain that in Alsace, where the Protestants' situation was not that of a small minority, their behavior was exactly the same. I also have already mentioned briefly that the conduct of the leaders of the Reformed Church was not always absolutely unequivocal. Like so many others, they wanted to distinguish between French Jews and foreign Jews who, they thought, constituted a problem and whom they viewed as being the beneficiaries of too hasty a naturalization. Such feelings also were extant among a number of French Jews. My father, who had nothing foreign about him, protested in 1942 in his journal against this too-widespread sentiment.

Ladies and gentlemen, by pure chance it happens that the date chosen for me to make this presentation is for me a very significant anniversary, since today is forty-six years to the very day after the Gestapo's arrest of my parents in Marseilles. My parents had for several months a secure refuge awaiting them at Dieulefit in a house quite close to that of my grandmother, my aunt, and my cousins, the oldest of whom had joined the underground forces. Still, my father, who wrote in his journal that he could never resolve to hasten his step when he felt he was being followed, could not resolve to leave Marseilles, either, despite the presence in our very house of the Nazi occupiers. He would have considered this departure to be a form of flight. Nevertheless, he had also given us formal instructions not to try to rejoin our parents in case of difficulties.

That day, my sister and I were at school, which was still named, for a little more than three months' time, after Field Marshal Pétain. My two brothers, aged twelve and a little less than four months, respectively, were at home. I do not know how my mother succeeded in convincing the men of the Gestapo to leave the baby with the neighbors. She also had the extraordinary presence of mind to help my other brother escape. He fled by a back door into the garden and then bounded into the street under the watchful eyes of a young member of the HSP, who probably did not know what made him laugh. Children then, like now, shared the loves and the hates of their parents: a few weeks earlier, when I tore down near our house a Nazi poster, a child much younger than I had threatened to tell on me to the Gestapo, who were located on Paradise Street, some two hundred yards from my house. My escaped brother and the house cook sounded the alarm at the school. My sister was still there and thus could be prevented from going home. I myself had gone into town after leaving school for the day in order to see an exhibition, as my classmates knew. My homeroom teacher, Pierre-Jean Miniconi, a very secular socialist who later taught Latin at the University of Montpellier, organized a small commando team of friends in order to prevent me from returning home. There were four of them and they have all remained my friends. In fact, they make up a good cross section of French society: Robert Bonnaud, a Marxist theoretician of history[10] who came from a working-class family of Communists; Gérard Hervé, also a nonreligious person who, after many adventures, now teaches computer sciences and economics at the Lannion Technical Institute; Alain Michel, today a colleague of Jacques Bompaire at the Sorbonne who comes from a family of conservative Catholics.

In violation of alphabetical order, I have delayed naming until last the fourth member of this commando team. He grabbed his bicycle and rode around the neighborhood, passing in front of our house to make sure that I had not escaped from the surveillance operation that had been mounted near the school. He approached the Gestapo car in which my parents had been placed; the dignity of my mother's bearing struck him in particular. Taking him for me, the Germans arrested him, but my mother calmly declared, in German, that he was not hers. This boy, who, in taking this risk, might ultimately have died in my place, was Alain Finiel, my "peer leader" in the cub scout den I had joined in 1940. Thank you.

Notes

Preface to the English-Language Edition

1. See "Flavius Josèphe ou du bon usage de la trahison," my introduction to *La Guerre des Juifs*, trans. Pierre Savinel (Paris: Minuit, 1977). This introduction was published in a more developed form in Italian as *Il Buon Uso del tradimento: Flavio Guiseppe e la guerra guidaica*, prefaced by Arnaldo Momigliano (Rome: Riuniti, 1982).
2. See Jean Levi, "Histoire, massacres, vérité, convenances," *Communications* 58 (1994): 75–85. [Translator/Editor (hereafter, T/E): In this context, a "negationist" is someone who denies the existence of the great systematic massacre of Jews, Gypsies, Soviet citizens, and others by Hitler's followers during the Second World War.]
3. [T/E: The death toll climbed slightly higher in the days after the bombing.]

PART ONE: ORIGINS AND HISTORY

1. Forms of Political Activity in the Jewish World, Principally Around the First Century C.E.

1. This paper was first read in French at the Martin Buber Institute (Brussels) in November 1977 and, in a slightly different version, a year later at the University of Warsaw. For the English text, I am once more indebted to Maria Jolas who prepared the text read at Princeton and Harvard universities in March 1979. My readers will pardon my leaving this text in the oral form in which it was first presented. [T/E: In retranslating this essay, I have followed the French text, "Formes d'activité politique dans le monde juif principalement aux environs du Ier siècle de notre ère," as it appears in *Les Juifs,*

la mémoire et le présent (hereafter, *JMP*), pp. 23–45, but I also have made extensive use of Maria Jolas's fine translation work ("Interpreting Revolutionary Change: Political Divisions and Ideological Diversity in the Jewish World of the First Century A.D.," *Yale French Studies*, 59 [1980], pp. 86–105) and have restored, with the author's consent, a few phrases found in Jolas's translation that did not appear in the *JMP* version.]

2. Tacitus *Histories* 5.12. [T/E: I have restored in brackets the incorrect information about John, which was (quite correctly) left out of the translation I used: Kenneth Wellesley's (Harmondsworth and Baltimore: Penguin, 1975).]

3. Flavius Josephus *The Jewish War* 5.255. [T/E: I have used the G. A. Williamson translation of *The Jewish War*, rev. ed. E. Mary Smallwood (London: Penguin, 1981), but altered it, when need be, to conform to Pierre Savinel's French translation (*La Guerre des Juifs* [Paris: Minuit, 1977]), which Vidal-Naquet cites and uses. As indicated below (note 8), Vidal-Naquet is the author of an extensive and in-depth introduction to Savinel's translation that addresses many of the same issues treated in the first three essays of the present volume.]

4. *Jewish War* 5.71–97 and 5.278.

5. *Jewish War* 5.433.

6. Ernest Renan, *L'Antéchrist* (1873), in *Oeuvres complètes* 4:1421 (Paris: Calmann-Lévy, 1949).

7. David Rhoads, *Israel in Revolution, 6–74 C.E.: A Political History Based on the Writings of Josephus* (Philadelphia: Fortress, 1976).

8. Yitzhak Baer, "Jerusalem in the Times of the Great Revolt," in *Zion* 36 (1971): 127–90, in Hebrew with English-language summary; I return to this study several times in my introductory essay ("Flavius Josèphe ou du bon usage de la trahison") to Pierre Savinel's translation *La Guerre des Juifs*.

9. I owe this observation to G. Nachtergael, whose major thesis on the Delphic *Sōteria* has since been published as *Les Galates en Grèce et les Sôteria de Delphes* (Brussels, 1977); see the remarks of Arnaldo Momigliano, *Alien Wisdom: The Limits of Hellenization* (London and New York: Cambridge University Press, 1975).

10. Heinz Kreissig, *Die Sozialen Zusammenhänge des Judäischen Krieges: Klassen und Klassenkampf in Palästina des I. Jahrhunderts v. u. z.* (East Berlin, 1970), pp. 63–64.

11. Flavius Josephus *Jewish Antiquities* 20.219–22; trans. Ralph Marcus (Cambridge: Harvard and London: Heinemann, 1958).

12. Kreissig, *Die Sozialen Zusammenhänge des Judäischen Krieges*, p. 141.

13. *Jewish War* 4.231.

14. *Jewish War* 4.236–82.

15. *Jewish War* 4.273.

16. *Jewish War* 4.276.

17. *Jewish War* 4.310, 4.311.

18. *Jewish War* 6.380.

19. *Jewish War* 1.6.

20. *Jewish Antiquities* 20.17–96.

21. *Jewish War* 2.388.

22. *Jewish War* 2.447, 2.520, and 6.357.

23. Joachim Jeremias, *Jerusalem in the Time of Jesus: An Investigation into Economic and Social Conditions During the New Testament Period*, trans. from the German F. H. Cave and C. H. Cave (Philadelphia: Augsburg Fortress, 1975).

24. Acts of the Apostles 6.1.

25. See Philo of Alexandria's *De Iosepho* and my development of this point in "Du Bon Usage de la trahison," pp. 61–63.

26. Or "sub-Asiatic"; here I am alluding to Fernando Belo's *A Materialist Reading of the Gospel of Mark*, trans. Matthew J. O'Connell (Maryknoll, N.Y.: Orbis, 1981).

27. *Jewish Antiquities* 14.113.

28. *Jewish Antiquities* 12.138–44; see Elias Joseph Bickerman's classic article, "La Charte séleucide de Jérusalem," in *Revue des Études Juives* (1935): 4–35.

29. The texts do not concur; see *Jewish War* 1.53 and 7.421–25, and *Jewish Antiquities* 12.387–88 and 13.62–73.

30. I am critical of the demonstration by Martin Hengel, *Judaism and Hellenism: Studies in Their Encounter in Palestine During the Hellenistic Period*, trans. John Bowden, vol. 1 (London, 1974), pp. 272–75 [now available from Philadelphia: Fortress, 1992].

31. *Jewish War* 8.44–45.

32. *Jewish Antiquities* 12.186–236. [T/E: A "novel of acculturation" (*roman d'acculturation*) is a play on "*roman d'éducation*," the French translation of *Bildungsroman*.]

33. As Hengel has rightly written: "Here the 'zeal' for education in Jewish wisdom and the Hellenistic world come together" (*Judaism and Hellenism* 1:132).

34. W. R. Farmer, *Maccabees, Zealots and Josephus: An Inquiry into Jewish Nationalism in the Greco-Roman Period* (New York, 1956), now available from Greenwood Press (Westport, Conn., 1973).

35. See Martin Hengel, *The Zealots: Investigations into the Jewish Freedom Movement in the Period from Herod I Until 70 A.D.* (1976), trans. David Smith (Edinburgh: T. and T. Clark, 1989).

36. 1 Maccabees 2.23–24, in *The Apocrypha and Pseudepigrapha of the Old Testament in English*, vol. 1 (Oxford: Clarendon Press, 1913).

37. 1 Macc. 2.25. The entire episode is modeled on Numbers 25.6–9.

38. 1 Macc. 2.45–48.

39. See Arnaldo Momigliano, "The Date of the First Book of Maccabees," in *L'Italie préromaine et la Rome républicaine: Mélanges offerts à Jacques Heurgon* (Rome: École française de Rome, 1976), pp. 657–66.

40. 1 Macc. 2.39–40; Jerusalem already had been taken by Ptolemy on a Sabbath day: see *Jewish Antiquities* 12.4.

41. 1 Macc. 2.42.

42. 2 Macc. 12.14–16.

43. *Jewish Antiquities* 13.257–58.

44. 1 Macc. 13.11; see also 1 Macc. 12.34, *Jewish War* 1.50, and *Jewish Antiquities* 13.180.

45. Édouard Will, *Histoire politique du monde hellénistique: 323–30 av. J.-C.* (1967), 2d rev. ed. (Nancy: Presses Universitaires de Nancy, 1979–1982), vol. 2, p. 285.

46. 1 Macc. 7.13–16, *Jewish Antiquities* 12.396.

47. *Jewish Antiquities* 13.288–98; this falling out goes unmentioned in the rabbinical tradition, which places the break at the time of his successor Alexander Jannaeus (Talmud B *Qiddushin* 66a).

48. *Jewish Antiquities* 12.379.

49. *Jewish Antiquities* 13.171–73, which summarizes *Jewish War* 2.119–66.

50. *Jewish Antiquities* 14.41, Diodorus 40.2.

51. See Geza Vermes, *The Dead Sea Scrolls*, 3d ed. (Sheffield, Eng.: JSOT Press, 1987), pp. 279–82.

52. Daniel 1.7; see my remarks in Claude Nicolet, ed., *Rome et la conquête du monde méditérranéen*, vol. 2, *Genèse d'un empire* (Paris: Presses Universitaires de France [hereafter, PUF], 1978), pp. 854–57.

53. Suetonius *Claudius* 25.

54. In *Jewish Antiquities* 14.116.

55. See Claire Préaux, "La Signification de l'époque d'Evergète II," in *Actes du Ve Congrès international de papyrologie* at Oxford (Brussels, 1938), pp. 345–54.

56. Philo of Alexandria *Legatio ad Gaium* 361.

57. *Legatio ad Gaium* 194.

58. Philo of Alexandria *De Congressu eruditionis gratia*.

59. *The Life and Confessions of Asenath, the Daughter of Pentephres of Heliopolis, Narrating How the All-Beautiful Joseph Took Her to Wife* (London: P. Wellby, 1900).

60. *Aristeae Ad Philocratem epistula*.

61. See the text, translation, and commentary of V. Nikiprowetzky, *La Troisième Sibylle* (Paris and The Hague, 1970) and John Joseph Collins, *The Sibylline Oracles of Egyptian Judaism* (Missoula, Mont.: Society of Biblical Literature, 1974).

62. *Jewish War* 2.398–99.

63. *Legatio ad Gaium* 281–83.

64. See A. Alföldi, "Redeunt Saturnia regna," in *Chiron* (1973): 131–42 (Jewish influences on coinage), and, in general, Harry Joshua Leon, *The Jews of Ancient Rome* (Philadelphia: Jewish Publication Society of America, 1960).

65. Acts 7.

66. Acts 8.26ff. The text plays on the meaning of two neighboring verbs, one of which means "to read" and the other "to understand," and on the meaning of another verb that means "to guide," in the physical and spiritual senses of the word.

67. Isaiah 53.

68. John 18.36.

69. Acts 1.6.

70. *Jewish War* 3.399–408.

71. Vidal-Naquet, "Du Bon Usage de la trahison," pp. 86–95.

72. See S. G. F. Brandon, *Jesus and the Zealots: A Study of the Political Factor in Primitive Christianity* (Manchester, Eng.: Manchester University Press, 1967), a book that can be traced back to a much older tradition.

73. Geza Vermes and Pamela Vermes, *The Dead Sea Scrolls: Qumran in Perspective* (Philadelphia: Fortress, 1977), p. 125.

74. See my "Du Bon Usage de la trahison," pp. 67–68.

75. See my study, "Flavius Josephus and Masada," the next essay in the present volume.

76. Sanhedrin 9.6; naturally, the primary meaning of the word *zealot* here is religious in character.

77. Renan, *L'Antéchrist* (1873), in *Oeuvres complètes* 4:1421.

78. Gershom G. Scholem, *Major Trends in Jewish Mysticism*, 3d ed. rev. (New York: Schocken, 1954), pp. 349–50.

79. [T/E: The French for "tell the story" (*raconter l'histoire*) could also be translated "recount the *history*." I have adopted in this case a compromise translation.]

2. Flavius Josephus and Masada

1. G. W. Bowersock, "Masada," in Moses I. Finley, ed., *Atlas of Classical Archaeology* (London: Chatto and Windus, 1977), pp. 228–29. For the recent bibliography, see Louis H. Feldman, "Masada: A Critique of Recent Scholarship," in J. Neusner, ed., *Studies for Morton Smith at Sixty* 3:218–48 (Leiden: Brill, 1975), which mentions numerous works that are difficult to locate.

2. It probably ended in April 74 C.E. For this date, see Emil Schürer, *The History of the Jewish People in the Age of Jesus Christ (175 B.C.–135 A.D.)*, new rev. ed., Geza Vermes and Fergus Millar, eds. (Edinburgh: Clark, 1973), p. 512. The classic date is 73. [T/E: See ch. 3, n. 60 of the present volume.]

3. According to Reverend Father Félix-Marie Abel's 1938 *Géographie de la Palestine* 2:380 (3d ed.; Paris: J. Gabalda, 1967), Masada is "one of the mesas or isolated rocks or escarpments where David wandered in the En Gedi desert (1 Samuel 24.1)."

4. Published by New York: Random House, 1966; and London: Weidenfeld and Nicolson, 1966. To my knowledge, apart from the publication of manu-

scripts Yadin has published no other scientific account of his excavation than a "Preliminary Report" that appeared in the *Israel Exploration Journal* 15, nos. 1–2 (1965): 1–120. I shall refer to this "Report" by name. This text also exists as a separate brochure. [T/E: A "Final Report" has been published at last, more than a decade after the initial publication of Vidal-Naquet's seminal and influential article and five years after Yadin's death in 1984; see *Masada: The Yigael Yadin Excavations, 1963–1965: Final Reports*, 3 vols. (Jerusalem: Israel Exploration Society and the Hebrew University of Jerusalem, 1989–1991).] See Mireille Hadas-Lebel, *Masada, histoire et symbole* (Paris: Albin Michel, 1995), p. 158.

5. Yadin, *Masada*, pp. 202–3.

6. Maurice Halbwachs, *La Topographie légendaire des Évangiles en Terre Sainte: Étude de mémoire collective* (1941; 2d ed., Paris: PUF, 1971).

7. Little matter that neither the site and the date of the foundation of the Chinese Communist Party nor the number and identity of its founders are known; one nevertheless is shown "a room furnished austerely with a table and twelve chairs; on the table there is a teapot and twelve cups; on the wall, a portrait of Mao as a young man" (Simon Leys, *Chinese Shadows* [New York: Viking, 1977], pp. 90–91).

8. See Moses I. Finley's "Schliemann's Troy—One Hundred Years After," the second appendix to *The World of Odysseus* (Harmondsworth: Penguin, 1979), pp. 159–77, whose remarks, alas, could again be updated.

9. Félix-Marie Abel, who published the second volume of his "Geography of Palestine" in 1938 (see n. 3, above), makes no allusions to the significance of the site for the Jewish world and is interested principally in the most visible vestiges, which were then the Roman camps and a Christian chapel. But this author himself was Christian. On the development of the Masada myth in the modern era, see B. Kedar, "The Masada Complex" (in Hebrew), in *Haaretz*, April 22, 1973, a translation of which my friend B. Cohen furnished me; Bernard Lewis, *History—Remembered, Recovered, Invented* (Princeton: Princeton University Press, 1976), pp. 3–41, with a comparison to Cyrus's fate in the Iran of the last Shah (a study I learned about thanks to the kindness of Lucette Valensi), and, more recently, B. R. Shargel, "The Evolution of the Masada Myth," in *Judaism* 28 (Spring 1979): 357–71, of mediocre quality for Antiquity, but very well informed as concerns the contemporary era. See also Hadas-Lebel, *Masada, histoire et symbole*.

10. Yadin, *Masada*, p. 201.

11. Ibid., p. 239.

12. Flavius Josephus *Jewish War* 7.252–407. I have used Pierre Savinel's translation, *La Guerre des Juifs* (Paris: Minuit, 1977). Permit me to refer to my introductory essay to this French translation, which is entitled "Flavius Josèphe ou du bon usage de la trahison"; on Masada, see pp. 109–12, where the themes of the present study are sketched out. [T/E: I have used the

1981 Penguin (London) revised translation, *The Jewish War*, modifying this
translation whenever it diverges significantly from Savinel's (which translation Vidal-Naquet obviously values since, as he has just noted, he wrote a
long introduction to it).]

13. Yadin, *Masada*, p. 15.

14. Let us note, in contrast, the prudence—on this specific point—of Geza
Vermes and Fergus Millar on p. 511 of Emil Schürer's work (n. 2, above).
The same does not go for Bowersock on p. 229 of the book edited by Finley
(n. 1, above).

15. Let it suffice to refer here to Martin Hengel's book, *The Zealots: Investigations into the Jewish Freedom Movement in the Period from Herod I until 70 A.D.*
(1976), trans. David Smith (Edinburgh: T. and T. Clark, 1989), and, for continuity between the era of the Maccabees and that of the "Zealots," to W. R.
Farmer's *Maccabees, Zealots, and Josephus* (New York, 1956), now available
from Greenwood Press (Westport, Conn., 1975).

16. *Jewish War* 4.161

17. *Jewish War* 5.98–105. On the "Zealots" in Josephus's work, see Hengel, *The
Zealots*, pp. 6–16. Their social underpinnings have been an object of controversy: see V. Nikiprowetzky, "Sicaires et Zélotes: Une reconsideration," in
Semitica 23 (1973): 51–63. Nikiprowetzky shows that, at the very least, the
leaders of the Zealots belonged to the Jerusalem priesthood.

18. For the details, see Hengel, *The Zealots*, pp. 46–49.

19. Flavius Josephus *Jewish Antiquities* 18.23.

20. Mark 12.13–17, Matthew 22.15–22, Luke 20.20–26.

21. *Jewish War* 2.434.

22. *Jewish War* 2.444–48.

23. Yadin, *Masada*, pp. 108–9 and 170–71.

24. See Henri I. Marrou, "La Querelle autour du *Tolle Lege*," in *Revue d'histoire
ecclésiastique* (1958): 47–57, apropos of what Saint Augustine heard.

25. *Jewish War* 7.337–38.

26. Roland Barthes, "The Reality Effect" (1968), in *The Rustle of Language*,
trans. Richard Howard (New York: Farrar, Straus, and Giroux, 1986), pp.
141–48.

27. *Jewish War* 7.398–99. The first Latin translation of Josephus, that of pseudo-
Hegesippus, eliminates the second woman. A sole woman survivor reveals
everything to the Romans. The text insists on the fact—unknown to Josephus—that the fanaticism of the wives was not inferior to that of their husbands: "Without trembling, the women offered themselves to be struck
down and, to safeguard their honor, they adopted the same resoluteness as
their husbands" (Pseudo-Hegesippus *Histories* 5.53 [Vienna: V. Ussani,
1932]). [T/E: I have simply translated the French here.] Under these conditions, educated women no longer were required.

28. *Jewish War* 7.403–4.

29. See the rightly pessimistic conclusions of Moses I. Finley, " 'Progress' in Historiography," in *Daedalus* (Summer 1977): 125–42; a partially reprinted, revised version appeared in *Ancient History: Evidence and Models* (London: Chatto and Windus, 1985), pp. 1–6.

30. Ernest Renan, *L'Antéchrist* (1873), in *Oeuvres complètes* 4:1446 (Paris: Calmann-Lévy, 1949).

31. Félix-Marie Abel, *Histoire de la Palestine depuis la conquête d'Alexandre jusqu'à l'invasion arabe* 2:42 (Paris, 1952).

32. Schürer, Millar, Vermes, *The History of the Jewish People*, pp. 511–12.

33. Yadin, *Masada*, p. 12.

34. Claire Préaux brought to my attention this *topos* of ancient historiography at the time I made an oral presentation of the present essay. Since then, I have been able to fill out this point, thanks to information provided to me by D. Ambrosino, P. Goukowsky, and P. Moraux. In general, see J. Bayet, "Le Suicide mutuel dans la mentalité des Romains," in *L'Année sociologique* (1951): 35–89. To limit myself to two authors, narratives similar to that of Josephus are to be found in Livy 21.14 (taking of Saguntum), 28.22–23 (taking of Astapa), 31.16–17 (assault on Abydus), and in Diodorus 17.28 (suicide of the Marmaraeans of Lycia during Alexander's campaign), 18.22 (taking of Laranda in Isauria), 25.15 and 25.17 (taking of Saguntum and of Victomela in Spain). For Saguntum see also Appian *Ibērikē* 12 and *Hannibalikē* 3; for Numantia, see Appian *Ibērikē* 95–97. Of course, the repetition of a *topos* in no way excludes a real repetition of events—is this not the case with the Nazi massacres?—but it is not easy to establish the connection between the *topos* and the event. One example: Polybius (16.29–34) is the source for Livy's narrative of the taking of Abydus by Philip V (200 B.C.E.), but he tells us nothing of the sort apropos of Hannibal's taking of Saguntum. Now, at 31.17.5, Livy as a matter of fact compares the episode at Abybus to the one at Saguntum: "They were overcome by a Saguntian rage" (*ad Saguntinam rabiem versi*).

35. Evidence for such an intermediary will not be found in the rabbinical tradition—not at all because, as has been suggested, the authors feared the Romans, but because they were hostile to the Sicarii. At most it may be noted that the Midrash of the Song of Songs alludes, in connection with the Roman attack on Jerusalem, to a split between Menahem and Hillel. Hillel, a contemporary of Herod, obviously has no bearing here, but this allusion might possibly concern the split between the Sicarii and the other defenders of Jerusalem, the Sicarii reaching Masada after the murder of the leader. See *Midrash, Shir Hashirim, Zuta, in fine*, cited by Feldman (in "Masada: A Critique of Recent Scholarship," p. 228), who adds some interesting philological suggestions, and *Jewish War* 2.447. [T/E: The "labor of the work" refers to Claude Lefort's monumental study of Machiavelli, *Le Travail de l'oeuvre Machiavel* (Paris: Gallimard, 1972).]

36. For the date, I follow here Heinz Schreckenberg, *Die Flavius-Josephus-Tradition in Antike und Mittelalter* (Leiden: Brill, 1972), p. 62, and, especially, D. Flusser, "Der lateinische Josephus und der hebraische Josippon," in Otto Betz, Klaus Haacker, and Martin Hengel, eds., *Josephus-Studien: Untersuchungen zu Josephus, d. antiken Judentum u. d. Neuen Testament: Otto Michel z. 70 Geburtstag gewidmet* (Göttingen: Vandenhoeck und Ruprecht, 1974), pp. 122–32; I have used the Hebraic edition with the Latin translation of J. F. Breithaupt (Gotha, 1707); since I first wrote these pages, a critical edition by D. Flusser of the *Josippon* has been prepared, the first part of which has appeared in Hebrew (Jerusalem, 1978).

37. See Vidal-Naquet, "Du Bon Usage de la trahison," p. 94, where one will find the key references.

38. This name change testifies, undoubtedly, to an ancient confusion between *resh* and *dalet*, according to Maxime Rodinson's suggestion.

39. See Henri I. Marrou, *De la connaissance historique*, 6th ed. (Paris: Seuil, 1975), p. 299.

40. Yadin, *Masada*, p. 15.

41. *Jewish War* 7.389–400.

42. Yadin, *Masada*, pp. 196–97.

43. Ibid., p. 197. During the course of a visit guided by D. Asheri and M. Amit, both of whom are professors at the Hebrew University of Jerusalem, I gathered at the site a variety of oral information. Nothing more concerning this point will be found in the "Preliminary Report," pp. 90–91; in the *Encyclopaedia Judaica* 11:1090 (Jerusalem, 1971), Yadin stipulates that the skulls are of the same type as those discovered in the caves of Bar Kochba at Nahal Hever.

44. Yadin, *Masada*, p. 201. These "eleven ostraca" were perhaps twelve; see Hadas-Lebel, *Masada, histoire et symbole*, p. 112.

45. Yadin, *Masada*, p. 191.

46. Yadin, "Report," p. 113, no. 100.

47. *Jewish War* 3.341–42.

48. *Jewish War* 3.344; here there may be, Maria Daraki thinks, a narrative symmetry.

49. *Jewish War* 3.353–54.

50. *Jewish War* 3.359.

51. *Jewish War* 3.290.

52. *Jewish War* 7.350. For a summary of all the Greek sources, see W. Morel, "Eine Rede bei Josephus," in *Rheinisches Museum* 75 (1926): 106–14.

53. *Jewish War* 3.362.

54. *Jewish War* 3.376.

55. See, in general, Helgo Lindner, *Die Geschichtsauffassung des Flavius Josephus im Bellum Judaicum: Gleichzeitig ein Beitrag zur Quellenfrage* (Leiden: Brill, 1972), pp. 33–40, and V. Nikiprowetzky, "La Mort d'Éléazar fils de Jaïre et

les Courants apologétiques dans le *De Bello Judaico* de Flavius Josèphe," in *Hommages à A. Dupont-Sommer* (Paris: Maisonneuve, 1971), pp. 461–90.

56. The Idumaean Simon nonetheless delivers a speech against the second highest priest Jeshua, part of which Josephus provides (*Jewish War* 4.270–82).

57. *Jewish War* 5.375.

58. *Jewish War* 5.419. [T/E: My translation of the French translation.]

59. *Jewish War* 5.391–93. [T/E: The end of the last sentence is my translation of the French translation.]

60. I do not believe that this attempt has ever before been made. For example, F. J. Foakes Jackson's major book, *Josephus and the Jews: The Religion and History of the Jews as Explained by Flavius Josephus* (London, 1930; rpt., Grand Rapids, Mich.: Baker Book House, 1977), does not even mention the existence of apocalyptic literature.

61. See, notably, on this topic, Harold Henry Rowley, *The Relevance of Apocalyptic: A Study of Jewish and Christian Apocalypses from Daniel to the Revelation* (1950; 3d rev. ed., New York: Association Books, 1964); D. S. Russell, *The Method and Message of Jewish Apocalyptic, 200 B.C.–A.D. 100* (London and Philadelphia: Westminster Press, 1964); J. Barr, "Jewish Apocalyptic in Recent Scholarly Study," in *Bulletin of the John Rylands University Library of Manchester* 58, no. 1 (1975): 9–35. Quite useful is the anthology edited by Louis Monloubou and Henri Cazelles, *Apocalypses et Théologie de l'espérance* (Paris: Cerf, 1977); see, in particular, the articles by M. Delcor, P. Grelot, P. M. Bogaert, and J. Stiassny.

62. I am thinking of the book by Joshua Bloch, *On the Apocalyptic in Judaism* (Philadelphia: Dropsie College for Hebrew and Cognate Learning, 1952); naturally, the apocalypse did not disappear from Jewish thought in 135 C.E. The work of Gershom Scholem (*The Messianic Idea in Judaism and Other Essays on Jewish Spirituality* [New York: Schocken, 1971] and, especially, *Sabbatai Sevi: The Mystical Messiah* [Princeton and London: Princeton University Press, 1973]) has shed much light on modern returns of the apocalypse.

63. See, in general, Harald Fuchs, *Die Geistige Widerstand gegen Rom in der antiken Welt* (Berlin: Walter de Gruyter, 1938) and, especially, Samuel Kennedy Eddy, *The King Is Dead: Studies in the Near Eastern Resistance to Hellenism, 334–31 B.C.* (Lincoln: University of Nebraska Press, 1961). On the *Oracle of the Potter*, see F. Dunand, "*L'Oracle du potier* et la formation de l'apocalypse en Égypte," in *L'Apocalyptique: Études d'histoire des religions de l'université des sciences humaines de Strasbourg* (Paris, 1977), pp. 41–67.

64. Jeremiah 25.11–12.

65. Dan. 9.24–26.

66. See John Joseph Collins, "Pseudonymity, Historical Reviews and the Genre of the *Revelation* of John," in the *Catholic Biblical Quarterly* 39, no. 3 (1977): 329–43; the most complete study is that of Martin Hengel, "Anonymität, Pseudepigraphie und Literarische Fälschung in der Jüdisch-Hellenistischen

Litteratur," in *Entretiens de la Fondation Hardt*, vol. 18, *Pseudepigrapha*, no. 1
(Vandoeuvre-Geneva, 1972), pp. 229–308.

67. See John Joseph Collins, *The Sibylline Oracles of Egyptian Judaism* (Missoula,
Mont.: Society of Biblical Literature, 1974).

68. See Collins, *The Sibylline Oracles*, pp. 12–15, where another Egyptian apocalypse is mentioned, the Demotic Chronicle. One will note, moreover, that
the theme of replacement of the foreign king by a king from the country
(which might be called "simple reversal"—see Jean-François Lyotard, "La
Place de l'aliénation dans le retournement marxiste," in *Dérive à partir de
Marx et Freud* [Paris, 1973], pp. 78–166) appears in Jewish literature as well
as in Egyptian apocalyptic literature; one could even almost literally connect
certain passages from the *Oracle of the Potter* with the third book of the
Sibylline Oracles (see Collins, ibid., pp. 40–41). The *Oracle of the Potter*, in
turn, went on to have a certain influence over texts written in Egypt, a
Coptic apocalypse notably, that of Elijah; see Dunand, "L'Oracle du Potier,"
pp. 54–59, but it does not seem that these texts traveled beyond the boundaries of Egypt.

69. In the Book of Daniel, succeeding one another are four beasts of greater
and greater monstrosity who nevertheless—like the statue made of the four
metals, but with feet of clay—all are intrinsically fragile. These four beasts
symbolize the succession of Empires, a succession that should not be overly
historicized (Dan. 7.3–8, 2.31–33; see D. Flusser, "The Four Empires in the
Fourth Sibylline and in the Book of Daniel," in *Israel Oriental Studies 2*
[1972]: 148–73). Succeeding the four beasts, in this apocalyptic vision, are
the "Ancient of the Days" (i.e., God) and the "Son of Man," whose "dominion" is built upon the ruins of the Empire of the beasts and the death of the
last of them. "And there was given him dominion and glory, and a kingdom,
that all peoples, nations, and languages, should serve him: his dominion is an
everlasting dominion, which shall not pass away" (Dan. 7.13–14). Through
exegesis, it is granted that this "Son of Man," who is living and is immortal
when the beasts have died and been dominated, should not be identified
with the Messiah, whom the "Son of Man" will become, but with the people
of Israel, to whom sovereign rule is promised (see A. Caquot, "Les Quatre
Bêtes et le 'fils d'homme' (Daniel 7)," in *Semitica* 17 [1967]: 37–71).
According to Geza Vermes ("The Present State of the 'Son of Man' Debate,"
Journal of Jewish Studies 21 [1978]: 123–34), the Evangelic Son of Man signifies only "he who speaks to you"; there nonetheless was a moment when this
expression took on a messianic meaning.

70. Elias Joseph Bickerman, *From Ezra to the Last of the Maccabees*, 6th ed. (New
York: Schocken, 1975), p. 77.

71. Isa. 53.6–8. "All we like sheep have gone astray; we have turned every one
to his own way; and the Lord hath laid on him [the "servant" of Yahweh] the
iniquity of us all. He was oppressed, and he was afflicted, yet he opened not

his mouth: he is brought as a lamb to the slaughter, and as a sheep before her shearers is dumb, so he openeth not his mouth. He was taken from prison and from judgment: and who shall declare his generation?"

72. The Jew Mordecai son of Jair, one of the Babylonian captives, an important (*mēgas*) man and minister of the king, has, like a hero in Greek tragedy, a dream. In the midst of cries and tumult, "two great dragons came forward, each ready for the fray, and set up a great roar. At the sound of them every nation made ready to wage war against the nation of the just. A day of darkness and gloom, of affliction and distress, oppression and great disturbance on earth! The righteous nation was thrown into consternation at the fear of the evils awaiting them, and prepared for death, crying out to God. Then from their cry, as from a little spring, there grew a great river, a flood of water. Light came as the sun rose, and the humble were raised up and devoured the mighty" (Esther 1.3–10) [translation from *The Jerusalem Bible* (Garden City, N.Y.: Doubleday, 1966)]. On the date and the significance of the Greek text of Esther, see Elias Joseph Bickerman's 1944 and 1951 studies, which are reprinted in *Studies in Jewish and Christian History* (Leiden: Brill, 1976), pp. 225–75; on the prologue, see pp. 264–65, where Bickerman makes some justifiable comparisons to Greek tragedy, though not to Jewish apocalypse; in another connection, H. Bardtke comments on Mordecai's dream at the end of his translation of the Greek *addenda* to the text of Esther, published in the *Jüdische Schriften aus hellenistische-römischer Zeit* 1:32–34 (Gütersloh, 1973). I have found nothing there, however, that pertains to the problems of interest to me here.

73. An expression to be found again elsewhere; see, for example, *Oracula sibyllina* 3.219.

74. See John Joseph Collins, "Jewish Apocalyptic Against Its Hellenic Near Eastern Environment," in *Bulletin of the American School of Oriental Research* 220 (December 1975): 27–36. A. Caquot ("Sur les quatre bêtes de Daniel 7," *Semitica* 5 [1955]: 5–13) has shown that the first three beasts of Daniel were borrowed from astrological chorography, from what is called the *dodēkaoros*, a duodecimal division arranged with astrological symbols under the signs of the Zodiac. A less well-known example is that of the Testament of Abraham, a Palestinian text of the first century C.E. that was reworked in Egypt sometime during the following century. F. Schmidt has shown that, when old Abraham is transported to the Zenith by Thanatos (the Greek way of departure from life, taking over from the Archangel Michael), who tries to convince the patriarch to die, the world is arranged before his eyes in accordance with the schema of "Achilles' shield" in the eighteenth book of the *Iliad*; see F. Schmidt, "Le Monde à l'image du bouclier d'Achille: La naissance et l'incorruptibilité du monde dans le Testament d'Abraham," *Revue de l'histoire des religions* (1974): 122–26.

75. This is what Christ says in a famous and long-misunderstood passage from

the Gospel according to Luke: ἡ βασιλεία τοῦ θεοῦ ἐντὸς ὑμῶν ἐστιν does not mean "the Kingdom of God is within you," or "among you," as it is currently translated, but "the Kingdom of God is within your reach," as a comparison with the Greek of the papyri establishes. On Luke 17.21, see C. H. Roberts, "The Kingdom of Heaven," *Harvard Theological Review* 41 (1948): 1–8, cited by E. G. Turner, *Greek Papyri* (Oxford: Oxford University Press, 1968), p. 151. "Among us" is the translation of the *Jerusalem Bible*. I thank S. G. Pembroke for having brought this point to my attention.

76. *Jewish War* 6.285.

77. See Vidal-Naquet, "Du Bon Usage de la trahison," pp. 93–95.

78. See Lindner, *Die Geschichtsauffassung*, pp. 33–39, and O. Michel and O. Bauerfeind, in vol. 2, part 2, pp. 276–78, of their edition of the *Jewish War* (Darmstadt, 1959–69), which describes Eleazar as "preacher of death for the Jewish people" (*Todesprediger für das jüdische Volk*).

79. *Jewish War* 7.323, 7.327, 7.329. [T/E: The translation of 7.323 is my translation of the French translation.] The theme of the "remnant of Israel" comes from Isa. 10.22.

80. *Jewish War* 7.262.

81. 2 Macc. 14.37–46, a text to which V. Nikiprowetzky has drawn my attention. To situate this example within a series of other texts, see Hengel, *The Zealots*, pp. 262–64, though I cannot accept his interpretation of Eleazar's speech.

82. *Jewish War* 7.359–69 and 7.375–79.

83. *Jewish War* 7.351–57 [translation altered to follow the French].

84. See Philo *Quod omnis probus* 93–96 and *De Abrahamo* 182. In Madeleine Petit's recently published edition of *Quod omnis probus* (Paris, 1974), pp. 92–136, one will find a set of references relating to self-immolatory suicide in Jewish and Greco-Roman literature; on Calanus, see pp. 93–96; citing Aristotle, Josephus himself speaks of "philosophers called *calanoi*" (Flavius Josephus *Contra Apionem* 1.179).

85. Cf. the astonishment expressed by Lindner, *Die Geschichtsauffassung*, p. 38.

86. *Jewish War* 7.376.

87. It is only fair to add that this demonstration has not convinced Arnaldo Momigliano; I refer the skeptical reader to his preface to my *Il Buon Uso del tradimento*, pp. 19–20.

3. Flavius Josephus and the Prophets

1. For the overall context in which this text is situated, see my "Les Juifs entre l'État et l'Apocalypse," in Claude Nicolet, ed., *Rome et la conquête du monde méditerranéen*, vol. 2, *Genèse d'un empire*, 2d ed. (Paris: PUF, 1989), pp. 846–82, and, for the bibliography, pp. 528–39 and xxxii–xxxix.

2. See Édouard Will and Claude Orrieux, *Ioudaïsmos-Hellenismos, essai sur le judaïsme à l'époque hellénistique* (Nancy: Presses Universitaires de Nancy, 1986).

3. P. Kessel and G. Pirelli, *Le Peuple algérien et la guerre* (Paris: Maspero, 1962).

4. Louis H. Feldman, *Josephus and Modern Scholarship, 1937–1980* (Berlin: De Gruyter, 1984).

5. That of David Goldenberg, presented in Philadelphia at Dropsie University in 1978.

6. Among the recent works: Tessa Rajak's *Josephus: The Historian and His Society* (London: Duckworth, 1983; and Philadelphia: Fortress, 1984) and H. W. Attridge's update, "Josephus and His Works," in Michael E. Stone, ed., *Jewish Writings of the Second Temple Period* (Assen, Netherlands: Van Gorcum, 1984; Philadelphia: Fortress, 1984), pp. 185–232. Also to be noted is the new translation *Josephus, The Jewish War* (Grand Rapids, Mich.: Zondervan, 1982) under the direction of Gaaylahu Cornfeld, which includes an abundance of commentary and places things in their archaeological context. [T/E: I am informed by Zondervan that this translation is now out of print.]

7. This is one of the principal themes of my essay "Flavius Josephus ou du bon usage de la trahison," published as an introduction to Pierre Savinel's translation of the *Bellum Judaicum, La Guerre des Juifs* (Paris: Minuit, 1977), then, in a separate and more developed form, in Italian: *Il Buon Uso del tradimento* (Rome: Riuniti, 1980). Arnaldo Momigliano's explicit endorsement of this analysis may be noted in the nevertheless critical preface he wrote for this book; against this thesis, see Rajak, *Josephus*, p. 109.

8. Comparing the *War* and the *Vita* is a classic exercise: see, now, the book of Shaye J. D. Cohen, *Josephus in Galilee and Rome: His Vita and Development as a Historian* (Leiden: Brill, 1979), which may be criticized for its having missed the ideological dimension of its subject.

9. *Contra Apion* 1.37–38, in *"The Life" and "Against Apion,"* trans. H. St. J. Thackeray (New York: Putnam's, 1936; and London: Heinemann, 1936). This connection has been made recently; see the contributions of D. Barthélemy, H. P. Rüger, and J. D. Kaestli in the anthology edited by J. D. Kaestli and O. Wermelinger, *Le Canon de l'Ancien Testament: Sa formation et son histoire* (Paris: Labor et Fides, 1984), pp. 7–102, and the first chapter of Gershon Weiler's book, *Jewish Theocracy* (Leiden: Brill, 1988).

10. *Contra Apionem* 1.40.

11. *Contra Apionem* 1.41.

12. *Contra Apionem* 1.46.

13. Need I mention here André Neher's classic work, *The Prophetic Existence*, trans. from the French by William Wolf (South Brunswick, N.J.: A. S. Barnes, 1969)?

14. *Jewish Antiquities* 1.154. [T/E: The last phrase has been altered to conform more closely to the French translation from the Greek.]

15. See J. Blenkinsopp, "Prophecy and Priesthood in Josephus," in *Journal of Jewish Studies* 26 (1975): 239–62, and, on Isaiah, p. 242.

16. For example, Leon Bernstein, in the conclusion to his book *Flavius Josephus: His Time and His Critics* (New York: Liveright, 1938).

17. *Jewish War* 5.391–93 [T/E: I have again used G. A. Williamson's translation, *The Jewish War*, rev. ed. E. Mary Smallwood (London and New York: Penguin, 1981)]; for more details on the Josephus/Jeremiah comparison, see D. Daube, "Typology in Josephus," *Journal of Jewish Studies* 31, no. 1 (1980): 18–36.

18. The basic reference work on this topic is now Will and Orrieux, *Ioudaïsmos-Hellenismos* (see n. 2, above).

19. See J. Reiling, "The Use of *Pseudoprophetes* in the LXX, Philo, and Josephus," in *New Testament* 13 (1971): 147–56.

20. The word is found, for example, in Herodotus 4.69, Aeschylus *Agamemnon* 1195, Sophocles *Oedipus at Colonus* 1097, Euripides *Orestes* 1667.

21. Jer. 6.13.

22. For the proof of this assertion, see the previously cited study by J. Reiling (n. 19, above).

23. 1 Kings 13.11 and *Jewish Antiquities* 8.236; in the parallel passage (1 Kings 13.11), the Septuagint speaks of an "old prophet," the Targum and the Old Latin speak of a "false prophet."

24. Acts 21.38 and *Jewish War* 2.261–63.

25. Talmud B *Berakhot* 210. The text then adds, in a commentary on Jer. 23.28: "Just as one cannot find wheat without chaff, so is it impossible for dreams not to contain a few meaningless elements." [T/E: I have simply translated the French here.] On dreams as a variety of prophecy, see also the Midrash of Genesis (*Berechit Rabba*) 17.5.

26. These pages had already been written when I learned of an article by A. Mosès, "Enjeux personnels, enjeux collectifs dans la *Guerre des Juifs*," *Bulletin de l'Association Guillaume-Budé* (June 1986): 186–201.

27. Flavius Josephus shares this quasi-prophetic ability with a certain number of other characters, almost all of them Essenian, whom he mentions in his work: Judas the Essene (*Jewish War* 1.78–80 and *Jewish Antiquities* 13.311–13), Menahem the Essene (*Jewish Antiquities* 15.373–79), Simon the Essene (*Jewish War* 2.113), the Essenians in general (*Jewish War* 2.59), Jeshua son of Ananias (*Jewish War* 6.300–309).

28. *Jewish War* 3.351–54. [T/E: At certain points, I have followed here Vidal-Naquet's French translation which, Vidal-Naquet notes, corrects Savinel's translation.]

29. *Jewish War* 6.312. See Tacitus *Histories* 2.78 and 5.13 (with, in addition, the introduction of an oracle of the Mount Carmel God) and Suetonius *Vespasian* 4. There have been innumerable discussions of this topic. See, for example, the in-depth study of F. Lucrezi, "Un'ambigua profezia in Flaviu

Guiseppe," *Atti dell'Academia di Scienze Morali e Politiche* 90 (1979), and my critical remarks in *Antiquité classique* 51 (1982): 411–12. For what would be the biblical sources from Gen. 49.10, Num. 24.17, and Dan. 7.13–14, see A. Mosès, "Enjeux personnels, enjeux collectifs," p. 198.

30. See the classic study of William Bedell Stanford, *Ambiguity in Greek Literature* (Oxford: Oxford University Press, 1939; rpt., New York: Johnson Reprint, 1972), and Jean-Pierre Vernant's analysis, "Tensions and Ambiguities in Greek Tragedy," in Jean-Pierre Vernant and Pierre Vidal-Naquet, *Myth and Tragedy in Ancient Greece*, trans. Janet Lloyd (New York: Zone, 1990), pp. 29–48.

31. Lucrezi, "Un'ambigua profezia," p. 17.

32. Vidal-Naquet, "Du Bon Usage de la trahison," pp. 86–95.

33. *Jewish War* 3.399–402.

34. Suetonius *Vespasian* 4, Appian 3.10, Schweighäuser (Zonaras 11.575). I thank P. Goukowky for having brought this text to my attention.

35. See *Jewish War* 4.623: "In one place after another a succession of omens had foretold his reign: he specially remembered the words of Josephus, who while Nero was still alive had dared to address him as Emperor."

36. *Jewish War* 4.601–4.

37. Tessa Rajak (*Josephus*, pp. 187–88) compares in an amusing way the announcement made to Vespasian to the prediction Ibn Khaldun made to Tamerlane, in 1401, which the Arab historian recounts in his *Autobiography* (Walter J. Fischel, ed., *Ibn Khaldun and Tamerlane: Their Historic Meeting in Damascus, 1401 A.D. (803 A.II.); A Study Based on Arabic Manuscripts of Ibn Khaldun's "Autobiography" with a Translation into English and a Commentary* [Berkeley and Los Angeles: University of California Press, 1952], pp. 35–36). Beyond the fact that Tamerlane already held supreme power, it should be added that Ibn Khaldun is even more cynical than Josephus. Although he mentions astrological predictions announcing the triumph of a great rebel nomad, he adds, "I composed in my mind some words to say to him which, by exalting him and his government, would flatter him." He is supposed to have said to Tamerlane: "May Allah aid you—today it is thirty or forty years ago that I have longed to meet you."

38. The rabbinical texts mentioning this episode have been gathered together, translated, and commented with much candor by S. Schalit, "Die Erhebung Vespasians nach Flavius Josephus, Talmud und Midrash: Zur Geschichte einer messianischen Prophetie," in *Aufstieg und Niedergang der Römischen Welt* 2, no. 2 (1975): 208–327. H. Möhring responded in a judicious way to this analysis in his study on Flavius Josephus as Jewish prophet and Greco-Roman historian in ibid., 2, no. 21 (1984): 864–969. The main rabbinical texts may be found in the *Ethics of the Fathers*, *Avot* A, ch. 5, and *Avot* B, chs. 6 and 7. We must insist upon the fact that, contrary to Josephus, the authors of these texts show not the least complacency toward Vespasian and Titus.

Mireille Hadas-Lebel has well focused her attention on the connections between the Josephinian tradition and the rabbinical tradition in "La Tradition rabbinique sur la première révolte contre Rome à la lumière du *De bello judaico* de Flavius Josèphe," *Sileno* 9, nos. 1–4 (1983): 155–72.

39. For Daniel, I have consulted F. Michaeli's Pleiade edition of the Bible, using André Lacocque's commentary, *The Book of Daniel* (1976), trans. David Pellauer, rev. ed. (Atlanta: John Knox Press, 1979), prefaced by Paul Ricoeur. I have also made use of two studies by Arnaldo Momigliano published in his *Settimo Contributo* (Rome: Edizioni di Storia et Letteratura, 1984): "The Origins of Universal History," pp. 77–103, and "Daniele e la teoria greca della successione degli imperi," pp. 297–304. [T/E: For the translation of Daniel into English, I have simply relied, as usual, on the Authorized (King James) Version, comparing this version with the French.]

40. I follow here closely André Lacocque, *The Book of Daniel*, pp. 13–14, who in turn bases his views on the remarks of Otto Plöger, *Das Buch Daniel* (Gütersloh: Gerd Mohn, 1965), pp. 26–27. Of course, these remarks bear only on the text of Daniel, properly speaking, not on its Greek additions.

41. Dan. 2.4.

42. For having defended this idea in "Les Juifs entre l'État et l'Apocalypse" (in Nicolet, ed., *Rome et la conquête de monde méditerranéen* 2:854–57), I was criticized by J. Mélèze-Modrzejewski, in J. Hassoun, ed., *Juifs du Nil* (Paris: Sycomore, 1981), p. 24, but I continue to hold to it and I affirm it once again. See, now, Will and Orrieux, *Ioudaïsmos-Hellenismos*, p. 115.

43. It first appears in Herodotus 1.95.

44. Dan. 2.44.

45. Dan. 7.3.

46. Dan. 11.30.

47. On Flavius Josephus and Daniel, see F. F. Bruce, "Josephus and Daniel," *Annual of the Swedish Theological Institute* 4 (1965): 148–62; A. Paul, "Le Concept de prophétie biblique: Flavius Josèphe et Daniel," *Recherches de sciences religieuses* 63 (1975): 367–84; and the decisive remarks of Arnaldo Momigliano in his preface to my *Buon Uso del tradimento*, pp. 18–19.

48. *Jewish Antiquities* 10.209; I follow closely here Julien Weill's translation.

49. Dan. 2.34–35.

50. *Jewish Antiquities* 10.210.

51. *Der Tag wird kommen* (The day will come) is the title of the third volume of the trilogy Lion Feuchtwanger has devoted to Flavius Josephus.

52. *Jewish Antiquities* 10.276–77. We must note, nevertheless, that this passage (and book ten) ends with an uncommon statement of modesty and tolerance: "Now I have written about these matters as I have found them in my reading; if, however, anyone wishes to judge otherwise of them, I shall not object to his holding a different opinion."

53. *Jewish Antiquities* 10.250.

54. *Jewish Antiquities* 10.268.
55. *Jewish Antiquities* 10.264.
56. *Jewish Antiquities* 10.267–68.
57. Pierre Vidal-Naquet, "Flavius Josèphe et Masada," in *Revue historique* 260 (1978): 3–21, which has been reworked and supplemented on many occasions, notably in *Il Buon Uso del tradimento* (see n. 7, above); in the previous essay in the present volume; and, more recently, in Hebrew, in the Israeli review *Zemanim* 13 (1983): 67–75.
58. For an overview, see Feldman, *Josephus and Modern Scholarship*, pp. 763–90 and 964–67.
59. In his study, cited in n. 38, above.
60. I had at first been convinced by an argument, based on the discovery of the epigraphical record of the cursus of L. Flavius Silva, that displaced the fall of Masada to the year 74. Since then I have read G. W. Bowersock's review of the English reissue of Schürer's handbook, "Old and New in the History of Judaea," *Journal of Roman Studies* 65 (1975): 180–85; his arguments in favor of the traditional date lead one to reflect further on the matter.
61. *Jewish War* 7.252–406; the book ends at 7.455.
62. In my study, cited above, n. 57 of the present essay.
63. C. Saulnier (with the collaboration of C. Perrot), *Histoire d'Israël*, vol. 3, *De la conquête d'Alexandre à la destruction du Temple* (Paris: Cerf, 1985), p. 332. If one is faithful to a narrative, one should remain so all the way to the end: Flavius Josephus mentions 960 dead and seven survivors (*Jewish War* 7.399–400), which makes 967 persons.
64. *Jewish War* 7.399.
65. Louis H. Feldman, "Masada: A Critique of Recent Scholarship," in J. Neusner, ed., *Studies for Morton Smith at Sixty* 3:218–48 (Leiden: Brill, 1975). I cite pp. 244–45.
66. Feldman, *Josephus and Modern Scholarship*, p. 776.
67. In a small book published in Hebrew at Tel Aviv in 1966 and translated into numerous languages, including English: *Masada: Herod's Fortress and the Zealot's Last Stand*, trans. Moshe Pearlman (New York: Random House, 1966; London: Weidenfeld and Nicolson, 1966). [T/E: See also my comment at ch. 2, n. 4.]
68. See Filippo Coarelli, *Il Foro Romano*, vol. 1, *Periodo arcaico* (Rome: Quasar, 1983), pp. 7–8, whose remarks are of general import.
69. For example, by Gaaylahu Cornfeld and the editors of the *Jewish War* translation, with commentary (see n. 6, above), who, without expressing the slightest reservations concerning Yadin's argumentation, nor indeed concerning Josephus's narrative, reproduce on p. 500 of the said book the ostracon bearing the name "Ben Ya'ir."
70. For example, by Tessa Rajak, *Josephus*, p. 200n93: "The excavators are accused, sometimes unjustly, of treating their finds as a confirmation of

Josephus' story, by P. Vidal-Naquet." For a much more radical judgment that challenges the historical method itself, see Jean Levi, "Histoire, massacre, vérité, convenances," *Communications* 58 (1994): 75–85.

71. See S. D. Cohen, "Masada: Literary Tradition, Archaeological Remains and the Credibility of Josephus," *Journal of Jewish Studies* (1982; issue devoted to Yadin): 385–405. On p. 398n42, this scholar makes his own my 1978 argument concerning the ostraca.

72. On this point, it is difficult to avoid having recourse to "oral sources." Is it true, for example, as was told to me in Israel by qualified specialists, that Yadin, who is now deceased but who, at the time I was writing, played a predominant role in Israeli archaeology, systematically neglected during the Masada excavations all Hasmonaean documentation so as to stick with Herod and the combatants, since here Josephus's testimony is of capital importance?

73. Trude Weiss Rosmarin, "Masada, Josephus, and Yadin," in *Jewish Spectator* 32, no. 8 (October 1967): 2–8 and 30–32, as well as other articles and letters that are listed in Feldman's *Josephus and Modern Scholarship*, p. 772; it is clearly not by chance that this polemic resurfaced soon after the Six Day War.

74. At Claire Préaux's suggestion, I have provided a few indications (see ch. 2, n. 34 of the present volume). In his article cited in n. 71, above, S. D. Cohen provides a much more searching analysis, based upon sixteen examples ("Masada," pp. 387–89). The problem has been taken up again in a chapter of Pierre Ellinger's thesis. [T/E: See Pierre Ellinger, "Recherches sur les 'situations extrêmes' dans la mythologie d'Artemis et la pensée religieuse grecque" (thesis, École des Hautes Études en Sciences Sociales, 1988, Paris), ch. 7.]

75. The oldest example in the series is that of the Lycians of Xanthus who faced the Persians in 540 (Herodotus 1.176).

76. C. Le Roy, who directs the excavations at Xanthus, told me outright that, in his opinion, Herodotus's narrative should be taken seriously.

77. As Livy (28.22–23) would have it.

78. 2 Macc. 14.37–46.

79. I had the privilege of attending in 1984 a seminar on these questions that was given by Maurice Kriegel at the École des Hautes Études en Sciences Sociales (Paris, France).

80. See Louis Marin, *Le Récit est un piège* (Paris: Minuit, 1978).

81. David J. Ladouceur, "Masada: A Consideration of the Literary Evidence," *Greek, Roman and Byzantine Studies* 21 (1980): 245–60.

82. *Jewish War* 3.361–82.

83. *Jewish War* 3.368.

84. Compare 3.372–73 (where the theme of the soul as a trust given by God, as well as that of the fugitive slave, appears) to Plato *Phaedo* 61b–62a.

85. From W. Morel's study, "Eine Rede bei Josephus," *Rheinisches Museum* 75 (1926): 106–14, to that of M. Luz, "Eleazar's Second Speech on Masada and Its Literary Precedents," in ibid., 126, no. 1 (1983): 25–43.

86. *Jewish War* 7.329. It is passages like this one that seem to me to make it impossible for one to view, along with V. Nikiprowetsky, the speech of Eleazar son of Jairus as a direct apology for Judaism (*Hommages à A. Dupont-Sommer* [Paris: Maisonneuve, 1971], pp. 461–90).

87. *Jewish War* 3.354.

88. *Jewish Antiquities* 20.259–60 and *Jewish War* 5.365–68.

89. *Jewish War* 7.359.

90. *Jewish War* 7.340 and 389. [T/E: For the French translation's "beau" I use the word *dazzling*, taken from 340 of the Penguin translation (it does not appear again at 389), and then *beauty* for "beauté."]

91. The key passage is *Jewish Antiquities* 18.23–25. The bibliography is of colossal proportions. See an analysis of it in Feldman, *Josephus and Modern Scholarship*, pp. 655–67. The main book to read is that of Martin Hengel, *The Zealots: Investigations into the Jewish Freedom Movement in the Period from Herod I Until 70 A.D.* (1976), trans. David Smith (Edinburgh: T. and T. Clark, 1989). As for the "Fourth Philosophy," this sect was so named by a comparison with the three traditional sects, the Sadducees, the Pharisees, and the Essenes.

92. See his preface to *Buon Uso del tradimento*, pp. 19–20.

93. Feldman, *Josephus and Modern Scholarship*, p. 779.

94. *Jewish War* 6.285.

95. On the silence of the Talmud, see Feldman, *Josephus and Modern Scholarship*, pp. 769–72.

96. On the *Josippon*, see ibid., pp. 57–74. [T/E: See also ch. 2, n. 36 of the present volume.]

97. Samuel Kennedy Eddy, *The King Is Dead: Studies in the Near Eastern Resistance to Hellenism, 334–31 B.C.* (Lincoln: University of Nebraska Press, 1961), and Ramsay MacMullen, *Enemies of the Roman Order* (Cambridge: Harvard University Press, 1966). Characteristically, these two classic works are not even cited in Louis H. Feldman's mammoth collection, which only goes to show that a bibliography is never complete. Naturally, I also refer the reader to Arnaldo Momigliano's *Alien Wisdom: The Limits of Hellenization* (London and New York: Cambridge University Press, 1975). The problems I am dealing with here lie at the heart of Will and Orrieux's *Ioudaïsmos-Hellenismos* (already cited several times in the present essay).

98. See the beautiful study of F. Dunand, "L'*Oracle du potier* et la formation de l'apocalypse en Égypte," in *L'Apocalyptique: Études d'histoire des religions de l'université des sciences humaines de Strasbourg* (Paris, 1977).

99. See, for example, A. Paul, *Le Fait biblique* (Paris: Cerf, 1979), pp. 105–8.

100. E. Le Roy Ladurie, *Les Paysans de Languedoc* 1:615 (Paris: SEVPEN, 1966).

101. The classic studies of Norman Cohn, notably his *The Pursuit of the Millen-*

nium: Revolutionary Millenarians and Mystical Anarchists of the Middle Ages, rev. ed. (London: Maurice Temple Smith, 1970), constitute an initial approach to the subject.

102. They were derisively called by this name on account of their cries in honor of Christ the King.

103. The Cristeros have been studied by Jean A. Meyer in a monumental thesis which unfortunately has been published only in Spanish in Mexico, and in two more summary works, *Apocalypse et révolution au Mexique* (Paris: Galli-mard-Julliard, 1974) and *The Cristero Rebellion: The Mexican People Between Church and State, 1926–1929*, trans. Richard Southern (Cambridge: Cambridge University Press, 1976).

104. Meyer, *Apocalypse et révolution au Mexique*, p. 223.

105. Yadin, *Masada*, p. 201.

106. For the history of the myth in the contemporary period, see Bernard Lewis, *History—Remembered, Recovered, Invented* (Princeton: Princeton University Press, 1976), the first part of which (pp. 3–41) includes a comparison with the myth of Cyrus in the Iran of the Pahlevis; B. R. Shargel, "The Evolution of the Masada Myth," in *Judaism* 28 (Spring 1979): 357–71; and other references in Feldman, *Josephus and Modern Scholarship*, pp. 880–83, and in Hadas-Lebel, *Masada*, p. 47n4.

107. For the trial "conducted against" Josephus in France in 1941 by activists of the Irgun, see Claude Vigée, *La Lune d'hiver* (Paris: Flammarion, 1970); in March 1943 a play entitled "The Trial of Flavius" was mounted in Vilna. The person being aimed at was Jacob Gens, the leader of the ghetto; see Isaiah Trunk, *Judenrat: The Jewish Councils in Eastern Europe Under Nazi Occupation* (New York: Macmillan, 1972; London: Collier, 1972), p. 212.

108. J. N. Svoronos, *L'Hellénisme primitif de la Macédoine prouvé par la numismatique et l'or du Pangée* (Paris: Leroux, 1919).

109. See the essential anthology edited by Orest Ranum, *National Consciousness, History, and Political Culture in Early-Modern Europe* (Baltimore and London: Johns Hopkins University Press, 1975); on the particular case of Atlantis, see my articles, "Hérodote et l'Atlantide: entre les Grecs et les Juifs. Réflexions sur l'historiographie du siècle des Lumières," *Quaderni di Storia* 16 (July–December 1982): 3–76, and "Atlantis and the Nations," trans. Janet Lloyd, in *Critical Inquiry* 18, no. 2 (Winter 1992): 300–26.

110. See Roberto Sallinas Price, *Homer's Blind Audience: An Essay on the Iliad's Geographical Prerequisites for the Site of Ilios* (San Antonio, Tex.: Scylax, 1983, and Belgrade: Izdanvačka and Tanjug, 1985).

111. See Adile Ayda, *Les Étrusques étaient des Turcs (Preuves)* (Ankara: Ayyildiz, 1985). I thank A. Javiello for having brought this work to my attention and F. Četinič—for having found for me its Yugoslavian parallel, which is mentioned in the preceding note.

112. I know of Kamal Salibi's book only through a lengthy analysis of it pub-

lished in *Libération* (October 2, 1984, with a response by E. M. Laperrousaz on November 2, 1984). In vain did I try to prevent the publication of this bit of delirium. The book, alas, has since been published: *La Bible est née en Arabie* (Paris: Grasset, 1986) [T/E: and in English as *The Bible Came from Arabia* (London: Jonathan Cape, 1985)].

113. Maurice Halbwachs, *La Topographie légendaire des Évangiles en Terre sainte: Étude de mémoire collective* (1941; 2d ed., Paris: PUF, 1971). See, now, the book edited by Pierre Nora, *Les Lieux de la mémoire*, vol. 1 (Paris: Gallimard, 1984).

114. G. W. Bowersock, "Ancient History and Modern Politics," in *Grand Street* (Fall 1984). Regrettably, Bowersock has mixed into this polemic a somewhat idealized view of the Roman province of Arabia; responses have been published, and the debate has been pursued in the Spring 1985 issue. I thank B. Isaac for having drawn my attention to this debate.

115. These observations were made on the occasion of a trip to Israel in 1985, a trip largely devoted to archaeological matters.

116. A thesis on the formation of these myths is now being prepared in France by Dan Bitar.

117. The publication, by *Zemanim* 13 (1983), of the Hebrew translation of my study on Masada has, I have been told, played a role in this challenge to nationalist archaeology. It is at the very least a sign thereof.

118. *Jewish War* 4.1–83.

119. *Jewish War* 4.79–80.

120. *Jewish War* 4.81–82.

121. See Anonymous (H. Shanks?), "Gamla: The Masada of the North," *Biblical Archaeology Review* 5 (January–February 1979): 12–19.

122. See, under this admirable title, the little book by Yosef Hayim Yerushalmi, *Zakhor: Jewish History and Jewish Memory* (Seattle: University of Washington Press, 1982), which is devoted to the question of the (dangerous) weight of Memory in the Jewish tradition. See my review of the French translation in the next essay of the present volume.

123. Among the works published since these pages were written, one should mention notably I. Villala I Varneda's *The Historical Method of Flavius Josephus* (Leiden: Brill, 1986) and two books by Mireille Hadas-Lebel: *Flavius Josephus: Eyewitness to Rome's First-Century Conquest of Judea* (1989), trans. Richard Miller (New York: Macmillan, 1993), and *Jérusalem contre Rome* (Paris: Cerf, 1990), pp. 77–107 (on Flavius Josephus).

4. Apropos of *Zakhor*

1. Jorge Luis Borges, in *Labyrinths: Selected Stories and Other Writings*, ed. Donald A. Yates and James E. Irby (New York: New Directions, 1962), p. 65. Simon

Leys, too, cites this novella in his book, *L'Humeur, l'honneur, l'horreur: Essais sur la culture et la politique chinoises* (Paris: Robert Laffont, 1991), p. 30.

2. Aharon Megged, "Yad Vachem," in Mireille Hadas-Lebel, ed., *Anthologie de la prose israélienne* (Paris: Albin Michel, 1983).

3. See P. Gibert, *La Bible à la naissance de l'histoire* (Paris: Fayard, 1979).

4. Joseph Ha-Kohen of Avignon, *Vallée des pleurs* (1561; Centre d'étude Don Isaac Abravenel, 1981).

5. See Annette Wieviorka and Itzhok Niborski, *Les Livres du souvenir: Mémoriaux Juifs de Pologne* (Paris: Gallimard-Julliard, 1983).

Part Two: Emancipation and History

5. The Privilege of Liberty

1. I borrow this expression from a course given by Georges Duveau which I followed in 1954.

2. I borrow this expression from Alfred Willener's book *L'Image-action de la société ou la politisation culturelle* (Paris: Seuil, 1970). The few references I shall provide in this preface pertain almost without exception to works whose existence was unknown to Jacob Katz, either because those works were not of direct concern to him or simply because they were published after his book was completed (March 1972).

3. See G. Weill in B. Blumenkranz, ed., *Histoire des Juifs en France* (Toulouse: Privat, 1972), pp. 179–81.

4. See François Delpech, in ibid., p. 278.

5. The Israeli historian Ran Halévi also has worked on this topic. See his *Cahier des Annales*, "Les Loges maçonniques dans la France d'Ancien Régime: Aux origines de la sociabilité démocratique" (Paris: Armand Colin, 1984); see also his key article on the topic of concern to me here, "Généalogie d'un discours moderne," *H. Histoire* 3 (1979): 9–40.

6. During the past few years, some significant studies have been devoted to these communities, works Jacob Katz could not have known: G. Nahon, "Communautés judéo-portugaises du Sud-Ouest de la France" (Bayonne and the surrounding area), a doctoral thesis at the École Pratique des Hautes Études, Sixth Section of the University of Paris, 1969, 2 vols. (available in typescript form at the Sorbonne Library), which was partially recast in *Les "Nations" juives portugaises du sud-ouest de la France (1634–1791)* (Paris: C. Gulbenkian Foundation, 1981); and R. Moulinas, *Les Juifs du pape en France* (Toulouse: Privat, 1981).

7. This document may be found in P. Hildenfinger's *Documents sur les Juifs à Paris au XVIIIe siècle: Actes d'inhumation et scellés* (Paris: Champion, 1913), p. 43. E. Szapiro concludes his contribution to the Blumenkranz volume (*Histoire des Juifs en France*, pp. 252–53) with a citation of this text. On the special case of

Jews living in Paris, see A. Burguière, "Groupe d'immigrants ou minorité religieuse? Les Juifs à Paris au XVIIIe siècle," *Revue de la Haute-Auvergne* (1985): 355–72.

8. See Moulinas, *Les Juifs du pape en France*, pp. 172–78.

9. Ibid., p. 176.

10. Memorial of the Jews of Saint-Esprit (Bayonne) to the Constituent Assembly (1790), cited by Nahon, *Les "Nations" juives portugaises*, p. 323.

11. See Nahon, "Communautés" 1:62–71. All the other "foreigners" present at Saint-Esprit were "Portuguese."

12. Jaladon, in his published *Mémoire pour les héritiers d'Abraham Vidal*, cited by Hildenfinger, *Documents sur les Juifs à Paris*, p. 43.

13. I take this information from the 1979 University of Paris-VIII doctoral thesis of S. Kerner, which is devoted to the Jews of Metz in the eighteenth century.

14. See Maxime Rodinson, "Antisémitisme éternel ou judéophobies multiples?," in *Peuple juif ou problème juif?* (Paris: Maspero, 1981), pp. 264–327.

15. No one has posed the problem with more perspicacity than Hannah Arendt in the first part of her *Origins of Totalitarianism*, new ed. (New York: Harcourt Brace Jovanovich, 1973), ch. 2, pp. 11–53.

16. See Nahon, *Les "Nations" juives portugaises*, pp. 322–27.

17. See M. de Certeau, D. Julia, and J. Revel, *Une politique de la langue: La Révolution française et les patois* (Paris: Gallimard, 1975).

18. See Gershom Scholem's masterpiece, *Sabbatai Sevi: The Mystical Messiah* (Princeton: Princeton University Press, 1973).

19. Gershom Scholem, *Du Frankisme au jacobinisme: La vie de Moses Dobruška alias Franz Thomas von Schönfeld alias Junius Frey* (Paris: Gallimard–Le Seuil, 1981). Naturally, Scholem renders homage in his book to the findings of Jacob Katz.

20. Scholem exonerates Frey from the charge of espionage and concludes, on the basis of several documents—notably Frey's last letter to his son—that he remained a sincere Jacobin. However, a document Scholem could not have known argues against this thesis. Fabre d'Olivet, himself a sect founder, recounts in his recently published *Souvenirs* a dinner he had at Frey's a few days before the latter's arrest. The upshot very well seems to be that Frey was a British agent. See Fabre d'Olivet, *Mes Souvenirs, 1767–1825*, ed. G. Tappa and C. Boumendil (Nice: Belisane, 1977), pp. 226–30. I have verified this text with the original manuscript which is preserved at the Bibliothèque d'Histoire du Protestantisme.

21. In Gotthold Ephraim Lessing, *Nathan the Wise: A Dramatic Play in Five Acts*, trans. Bayard Quincy Morgan (New York: Ungar, 1955).

22. On all this, see D. Bourel's introduction to the French translation *Jérusalem*, by Moses Mendelssohn, with a preface by Emmanuel Lévinas (Paris: Les Presses d'Aujourd'hui, 1982), pp. 31–41.

23. "Rejection of Conversion" (Letter to Johann Caspar Lavater), in *Moses*

Mendelssohn: Selections from His Writings, ed. and trans. Eva Jospe (New York: Viking, 1975), p. 134; cited by Bourel, in the introduction to Mendelssohn's *Jérusalem*, p. 36. [T/E: *Phaedon: Or, On the Immortality of the Soul* also can be found in this collection of Mendelssohn's writings, on pp. 186–204.]

24. Cited by Bourel, in the introduction to Mendelssohn's *Jérusalem*, p. 33. [T/E: see Mendelssohn's *Gesammelte Schriften* 19:119 (Berlin: Friedrich Frommann, 1974); I have translated Bourel's French translation here.]

25. See Moulinas, *Les Juifs du pape en France*, p. 183.

26. See the thesis of S. Kerner cited in n. 13, above.

27. See the collection of tales, published for the first time in Hebrew in 1814, in its English version, *In Praise of the Baal Shem Tov*, trans. and ed. Ben Amos and Jerome R. Mintz (Bloomington: Indiana University Press, 1970), pp. 169–70, no. 147.

28. I base my observations here mainly on French examples, first because this is in my area of competence, next because the German example has been developed very adequately in Jacob Katz's book. The bibliography is immense, and I shall limit myself to citing a few current and recent works: P. Girard's *Les Juifs de France de 1789 à 1860, de l'émancipation à l'égalité* (Paris: Calmann-Lévy, 1976), which is based on secondhand sources but is vibrant and even-handed; the posthumous collection of François Delpech, *Sur les Juifs, études d'histoire contemporaine* (Paris: Presses Universitaires de Lyon, 1983), which brings together a number of important writings, notably the author's contribution to Blumenkranz's *Histoire des Juifs en France*; D. Cohen, *La Promotion des Juifs en France à l'époque du second Empire*, 2 vols. (Aix: Université de Provence, 1980), which is a bit diffuse and fails to provide a synthesis but which offers a very great wealth of documentary material. There are also a number of works in progress along the lines of Michael R. Marrus's *The Politics of Assimilation: A Study of the French Jewish Community at the Time of the Dreyfus Affair* (Oxford: Clarendon Press, 1971) which extend their investigations further back into the nineteenth century, notably the research work being undertaken by Dominique Schnapper and J.-M. Chouraqui. Finally, Annie Kriegel's book, *Les Juifs et le monde moderne* (Paris: Seuil, 1977), contains the best and the worst, genuine historical analyses along with ideological passion at its purest.

29. Document reproduced in Cohen, *La Promotion des Juifs en France* 1:146.

30. I have before me a small brochure written by the historian Paul Raphaël: *La France, l'Allemagne et les Juifs: Antisémitisme et pangermanisme* (Paris: Alcan, 1916), which responds to the analogous German pamphlets. On such brochures and on the themes they developed, see the *Autobiographie* of Nahum Goldmann (Paris: Fayard, 1969), pp. 59–60, who was at the time one of these propagandists.

31. Arno J. Mayer, *The Persistence of the Old Regime: Europe to the Great War* (New York: Pantheon, 1982).

32. See Léon Poliakov, *History of Anti-Semitism*, vol. 3, *From Voltaire to Wagner*, trans. from the French by Miriam Kochan (London: Routledge and Kegan Paul, 1985), pp. 429–57; on German nationalism and the Jews, there are a few striking pages in Pierre Sorlin's *L'Antisémitisme allemand* (Paris: Flammarion, 1969), pp. 42–55.

33. Against the very idea of a Judeo-German symbiosis, what Gershom Scholem has written (in *On Jews and Judaism in Crisis: Selected Essays*, ed. Werner J. Dannhauser [New York: Schocken, 1976], pp. 61–92) appears to me to be excessive and, ultimately, ruled by passion; it was, in a sense, the very example of such a symbiotic relationship.

34. Let us recall here the classic work of Barrington Moore Jr., *The Social Origins of Dictatorship and Democracy* (Boston: Beacon, 1966).

35. See Cohen, *La Promotion des Juifs en France* 2:416–33.

36. This fact has been analyzed very well by Moulinas, *Les Juifs du pape en France*; see, also, Claude Mossé's preface to this work.

37. I quote these documents from the study written by Émile Appolis, "Les Israélites de l'Hérault de 1830 à 1870," in the Modern and Contemporary History section of the *Actes du quatre-vingt-quatrième congrès national de sociétés savantes* (Dijon, 1959; rpt., Paris: Imprimerie Nationale, 1960), pp. 481–99.

38. See Appolis, "Les Israélites de l'Hérault," pp. 488–91, with, on p. 491, an error in Gustave's first name (the incorrect "Gaston"), which I have found repeated several times, for example in Moulinas, *Les Juifs du pape en France*, p. 478.

39. I have already evoked this character in my preface to Michael Marrus's book (see n. 28, above), which was reproduced and developed as "Les Juifs de France et l'assimilation," in *JMP*, pp. 75–90 [T/E: not included in the present abridged translation].

40. As concerns the Reinach family, I have borrowed from the unpublished thesis written at the École des Chartes in 1982 by Corinne Casset (Corinne Touchalay), "Joseph Reinach avant l'affaire Dreyfus: Un exemple de l'assimilation politique des Juifs de France au début de la Troisième République." I thank the author of this thesis for having transmitted it to me via Madame France Beck, Joseph Reinach's granddaughter.

41. A few nonnumerical indicators are given in Cohen, *La Promotion des Juifs en France* 1:523–33.

42. Casset, "Joseph Reinach avant l'affaire Dreyfus," p. 66, where, moreover, such picturesque details abound.

43. Ibid., p. 69.

44. On the 1870s as a turning point in Vienna's history, see Carl E. Schorske's wonderful book *Fin-de-siècle Vienna: Politics and Culture* (New York: Knopf, 1980; rpt., New York: Vintage, 1981).

45. For the figures, see Nathan Glazer, *American Judaism*, 2nd ed. (Chicago and London: University of Chicago Press, 1989), pp. 22–24.

46. There were at this time in France approximately ninety thousand Jews; see the statistical table provided by Cohen, *La Promotion des Juifs en France* 1:64.

47. See ibid., 2:533–45, which provides the bibliography for the preceding period, and Delpech, *Sur les Juifs, études d'histoire contemporaine*, pp. 127–30.

48. See, in addition to the book of A. Chouraqui, *L'Alliance israélite universelle* (Paris: PUF, 1965), Delpech's *Sur les Juifs, études d'histoire contemporaine*, pp. 133–36.

49. *The Turning Point: The Jews of France During the Revolution and the Napoleonic Era* is the title of a 1981 brochure from the Museum of the Jewish Diaspora in Tel Aviv.

50. A picture of such a lamp is reproduced in the above-cited brochure.

51. An expression I borrow from François Furet, *In the Workshop of History*, trans. Jonathan Mandelbach (Chicago and London: University of Chicago Press, 1984), p. 224.

52. See the anthology edited by Maurice Freedman, *A Minority in Britain: Social Studies of the Anglo-Jewish Community* (London: Vallentine and Mitchell, 1955), which was reviewed by Maxime Rodinson in *Année Sociologique*, 3d ser. (1953–54; published in 1956): 298–99. It is hardly necessary to add that this example can, in large part, be transposed to France.

53. See Anahide Ter Minassian, *La Question arménienne* (Roquevaire: Parenthèses, 1983), p. 49 (which first appeared as an article in *Esprit*, April 1967), as well as my text, "And By the Power of a Word . . . ," essay 12 in part three of the present volume.

54. See Hélé Béji, *Désenchantement national: Essai sur la décolonisation* (Paris: Maspero, 1982).

55. The formula I quote figures on the back cover of *Raison Présente* 67 (July–September 1983). The theme of the relationship between the Marquis de Sade and the Baron d'Holbach is treated in this issue by J. Deprun.

56. See, especially, the important book by Arthur Hertzberg, *The French Enlightenment and the Jews* (New York and London: Columbia University Press, 1968), a book Jacob Katz uses and cites, and the works of Léon Poliakov: *History of Anti-Semitism*, vol. 3 (cited in n. 32, above); *Le Mythe aryen* (Paris: Calmann-Lévy, 1971), pp. 151–81; and "Le Fantasme des êtres hybrides et la hiérarchie des races aux XVIIIᵉ et XIXᵉ siècles," in the anthology edited by the author himself, *Hommes et bêtes: Entretiens sur le racisme* (Paris and The Hague: Mouton, 1975), pp. 167–81.

57. See the measured and balanced work of Michèle Duchet, *Anthropologie et Histoire au siècle des Lumières* (Paris: Maspero, 1971).

58. Including in de Sade, whom Poliakov, on the strength of G. Lély, curiously absolves in this matter (*History of Anti-Semitism* 3:90–91); see, for example,

the 1795 pamphlet entitled *Français, encore un effort si vous voulez être républicains*, passim.

59. I have attempted a sketch of this subject in an article entitled "Hérodote et l'Atlantide: entre les Grecs et les Juifs. Réflexions sur l'historiographie du siècle des Lumières," in *Quaderni di Storia* 16 (July–December 1982): 3–76. On the topic of national substitutions, Poliakov's book *Le Mythe aryen* (cited in n. 56, above) contributes much in the way of interesting information.

60. The references are innumerable; some can be found in Hertzberg, *The French Enlightenment and the Jews* (see, in Hertzberg's index, Voltaire), as well as in Poliakov, *History of Anti-Semitism* 3:86–99.

61. Poliakov sketches a picture of it in *History of Anti-Semitism* 3:175–89, but see, especially, the extremely fine analysis of Elisabeth de Fontenay, "Sur un soupir de Kant," in Maurice Olender, ed., *Pour Léon Poliakov: Le racisme, mythes et sciences* (Brussels: Complexe, 1981), pp. 15–29.

62. Napoleon was to backtrack on this point and create consistories that set religious boundaries for the Jews and allowed their surveillance by rabbis.

63. I refer here again to Ran Halévi's article (cited in n. 5, above).

64. See Élise Marienstras, *Les Mythes fondateurs de la nation américaine* (Paris: Maspero, 1976).

65. Furet, *In the Workshop of History*, p. 215, who bases himself on Annie Kriegel ("Révolution française et judaïsme," in *L'Arche*, March 1975).

6. Dreyfus in the Affair and in History

1. Letter preserved in the Waldeck-Rousseau Papers at the Bibliothèque de l'Institut, no. 4576. I will henceforth cite these papers by the initials WR, followed by the number of the file. On these papers, see Pierre Sorlin, *Waldeck-Rousseau* (Paris: Armand Colin, 1966), pp. 497–509.

2. WR 4576. Picquié had been the director of the "depot" at Saint-Martin-de-Ré. He regularly frequented the penitentiary population.

3. Julien Benda, review of *Cinq Années* in the *Revue Franco-Allemande*, August 1901, pp. 471–78 (the quotation I use comes from p. 471). Benda recounts the same anecdote in his 1937 book, *La Jeunesse d'un clerc* (Paris: Gallimard, 1968), p. 117.

4. Benda, *Revue Franco-Allemande*, pp. 472–73; Dreyfus responded August 20, 1901, to Benda: "Yes, I have a tendency toward objectivity . . . but you push your argument much too far" (letter cited by J. Kayser, *L'Affaire Dreyfus* [Paris: Gallimard, 1946], p. 272).

5. They were entrusted to me by Dr. Jean-Louis Lévy, the grandson of Alfred Dreyfus, whom I thank very heartily.

6. Another example: one learns, at left, that Dreyfus's military friends, notably Captain Boullenger, avoided responding to "indiscreet questions" Dreyfus had asked them "about secret or confidential matters." Dreyfus's response:

"The indiscreet question posed by Captain Dreyfus to Captain Boullenger when he met him was the following: 'What's new at the Fourth Bureau?'!"

7. Joseph Reinach, *Histoire de l'affaire Dreyfus*, vol. 2, *Esterhazy* (Paris: Fasquelle, 1903), p. 152n2.

8. Mathieu Dreyfus, *L'Affaire telle que je l'ai vécue* (Paris: Grasset, 1978), p. 22.

9. The key document on this affair is Ernest Crémieu-Foa's book, *La Campagne antisémitique: Les Duels, les responsables* (Paris: Alcan-Lévy, 1892).

10. Michael R. Marrus, *The Politics of Assimilation: A Study of the French Jewish Community at the Time of the Dreyfus Affair* (Oxford: Clarendon Press, 1971), p. 214; I will refer here just once to this work for everything it offers concerning the "French Israelites" of this era. My preface to the French translation of this work was reprinted in *JMP*, pp. 75–90. [T/E: Vidal-Naquet's preface could not be included in the present abridged translation.]

11. Maurice Paléologue (*An Intimate Journal of the Dreyfus Affair*, trans. Eric Mosbacher [New York: Criterion, 1957], pp. 50–51) notes with insistency that the Grand Rabbi of Paris, Dreyfuss, was a character witness for the Captain in 1894; this fact is mentioned, very briefly, by Reinach in his *Histoire*, vol. 1: *Le Procès de 1894* (Paris: Revue Blanche, 1901), p. 429 and n. 1.

12. Reinach, *Histoire* 2:134.

13. Re: Clemenceau, see the texts gathered by Léon Poliakov, *The History of Anti-Semitism* 4:63–65 (Oxford: Oxford University Press, 1985); re: Labori, see, for example, the judgment this lawyer delivers on Reinach's *Histoire de l'affaire Dreyfus* ("a work basically inspired by the Semitic mind") and on the "pure idealism" of "sincere and clairvoyant Aryans" such as himself, in Marguerite-Fernand Labori, *Labori, ses notes manuscrites, sa vie* (Paris: Victor Attinger, 1947), pp. 346 and 349.

14. *Dreyfus: His Life and Letters*, by Pierre Dreyfus, trans. Dr. Betty Morgan (London: Hutchinson, 1937); now available as *The Dreyfus Case by the Man—Alfred Dreyfus[—]and His Son—Pierre Dreyfus*, trans. and ed. Donald C. McKay (New York: Howard Fertig, 1977), pp. 253–76.

15. *The Dreyfus Case*, pp. 261–63. Leafing through the book edited by Pierre Birnbaum, *Histoire politique des Juifs de France* (Paris: Fondation Nationale des Sciences Politiques, 1990), especially the article of Dominique Schnapper, one can easily be convinced that, in Dreyfus, this trait is more a sociological than an individual one.

16. This letter belongs today to the Hebrew University of Jerusalem. Dr. Jean-Louis Lévy, who for his part also has made use of the letter, sent me a photocopy of it.

17. Charles-Pierre Péguy, *Notre jeunesse* (Paris: Cahiers de la Quinzaine, 1910), p. 114.

18. See Nicole Loraux, "L'Oubli dans la cité," *Le Temps de la Réflexion* 1 (1980): 213–242.

19. I am basing myself here on an unpublished document. The case of the Audin

Affair took much longer to settle, due to a judicial error regarding the court's competency and thanks to the pugnacity of the civil party. For the details, see Pierre Vidal-Naquet, *L'Affaire Audin, 1958–1978* (Paris: Minuit, 1989), pp. 168–73.

20. Reinach rallied retrospectively to the amnesty, which he had fought in *Le Siècle*. See *Histoire de l'affaire Dreyfus*, vol. 6, *La Révision* (Paris: Fasquelle, 1908), pp. 1–158.

21. See Jean-Pierre Peter, "Dimensions de l'affaire Dreyfus," in *Annales: Economies, Sociétés, Civilisations* (1961), pp. 1141–67, and, for the study of intellectual circles, C. Charle, *La Crise littéraire à l'époque du naturalisme* (Paris: Presses de l'ENS, 1979), pp. 157–88, and from the same author, *Naissance des "intellectuels," 1880–1900* (Paris: Minuit, 1990).

22. Madeleine Rebérioux, *La République radicale? 1898–1914* (Paris: Seuil, 1975), p. 38. See this entire volume, esp. pp. 4–56.

23. On which, see Zeev Sternhell, *La Droite révolutionnaire, 1885–1914: Les origines françaises du fascisme* (Paris: Seuil, 1978), a book that has occasioned much discussion, as it ought to, but which offers much information.

24. See Mathieu Dreyfus's account, *L'Affaire*, pp. 251–78, and the papers of Labori published by his wife, Marguerite-Fernand Labori, *Labori*, notably pp. 241–67 and 313–32.

25. Blum, *Souvenirs sur l'Affaire* (Paris, 1935), p. 169.

26. This question of the diverse stakes involved in the Dreyfus Affair has been broached in an interesting way by Hannah Arendt in the first part of her *Origins of Totalitarianism*, new ed. (New York: Harcourt Brace Jovanovich, 1973), pp. 117–20, but unfortunately on the basis of incomplete information.

27. On "connivance" and "rupture," see J.-M. Vergès, *De la stratégie judiciare* (Paris: Minuit, 1968), whose account of the Dreyfus Affair, on pp. 162–76, is unfortunately full of mistakes concerning the details of the matter. Vergès had previously contributed to an anthology in which these same notions were first worked out: *Défense politique* (Paris: Maspero, 1961).

28. Mathieu Dreyfus, *L'Affaire*, p. 222.

29. Reinach, *Histoire de L'Affaire Dreyfus*, vol. 5, *Rennes* (Paris: Fasquelle, 1905), p. 519, citing a September 7 letter.

30. *Rapport sur les cas de cinq détenus des îles du Salut*, presented by Joseph Reinach for the Ligue française des droits de l'homme et du citoyen (Paris: Stock, 1899). The presence in the Dreyfusard camp of certain personalities who created an awkward impression played a role in slowing the entry of certain intellectuals, notably Jean Jaurès, into the battle; see Madeleine Rebérioux, "Zola, Jaurès et France: Trois intellectuels dans l'Affaire," in *Cahiers naturalistes* 54 (1980): 266–81.

31. The World's Fair of 1900, which opened in Paris in April.

32. On the (very strong) reaction of Dreyfus and his kin to the reading of this editorial, see *The Dreyfus Case*, pp. 153–56. The Waldeck-Rousseau Papers

(WR 4568 R), moreover, have preserved for us an extremely violent letter from Reinach to Jean Dupuy, dated October 2. The indignation of the Dreyfuses and of Reinach was all the more vehement since other journals, notably *Le Figaro*, had presented the *Petit Parisien* article as semiofficial in character. "If, therefore, the note of *Le Petit Parisien* is not denied in the most formal terms, I will recount, come what may, the incidents that occurred on Monday, September 11. I will say and I will prove, evidence in hand, that the withdrawal of the petition was demanded of Dreyfus by the Government." In fact, no formal denial was forthcoming.

33. Fernand Labori, "Le Mal politique et les partis," in *La Grande Revue*, November 1, 1901, pp. 265–310; I am quoting pp. 271–72.

34. Jaurès, "L'Article de Labori," in *La Petite République*, November 9, 1901; see *The Dreyfus Case*, pp. 176–77. Bernard Lazare, too, responded to Labori. In the *Écho de Paris* of November 30, 1901, he remarked: "As for the person pardoned, he was not the master, and Waldeck, of course, was greatly mistaken not to have consulted him" (see Nelly Wilson, *Bernard Lazare* [Cambridge and New York: Cambridge University Press, 1978], p. 179).

35. Dreyfus's reaction to this article may be found in *The Dreyfus Case*, pp. 177–79.

36. I have done no more than take some soundings, but *Le Petit Parisien*, *Le Temps*, *Le Siècle*, *La Petite République*, and *L'Aurore* constitute a rather representative selection. I certainly should have read other dailies, notably *Le Figaro*, but one cannot do everything.

37. This article is reprinted in Joseph Reinach, *Les Blés d'hiver* (Paris: Stock, 1901), pp. 115–20; in his *Histoire de L'affaire Dreyfus* 5:544–46, Reinach recounts how the article was drafted and how it was received.

38. The article was written on the twelfth and Gérault-Richard knew quite well that the pardon had already been decided upon in principle.

39. The article was written on September 11; Dreyfus decided on the twelfth to withdraw his petition.

40. The "uhlan letter" was a letter written by Esterhazy to Madame de Boulancy, his mistress, in which he imagined himself "captain of the uhlans . . . cutting down the French with a saber." Its publication in the *Figaro* of November 28, 1897, had created a bit of a stir. Lauth was Colonel Henry's deputy. An excellent Hellenist, Clemenceau alludes to the gesture of Tydeus—the most furious of the *Seven Against Thebes*—who devoured the skull of Melanippus.

41. This is the text that appears at the end of *Five Years*. No one knew at the time that it had been drafted by Jaurès at the Ministry of Commerce on the evening of September 11. A reproduction of the manuscript appears in Léon Blum's *Souvenirs*.

42. Bibliothèque Nationale, Manuscripts, New French Acquisition no. 13,582, pp. 327–75; hereafter, "Récit" [narrative]. The manuscript was bound along

with an outline of the great *Histoire de l'affaire Dreyfus*. This extraordinarily vibrant account ought to be published. Its existence was brought to my attention by Pierre Sorlin in his *Waldeck-Rousseau*, p. 525. The text now appears in *JMP*, pp. 316–38. [T/E: This "Journal de Joseph Reinach" could not be included in the present abridged translation.]

43. They are used by Joseph Reinach in volume 6 of his *Histoire*, which was published at that time. First partial publication in R. Gauthier, *Dreyfusards!* (Paris: Julliard, 1965); complete publication, with a preface by Jacques Millerand, by Grasset (Paris, 1978).

44. Reinach, *Histoire* 5:535–66.

45. Reinach, "Récit," pp. 329–30; cf. *Histoire* 5:545.

46. Reinach, "Récit," pp. 332–34; cf. *Histoire* 5:545–46.

47. Reinach, "Récit," pp. 335–41; cf. Mathieu Dreyfus, *L'Affaire*, pp. 238–39, and Reinach, *Histoire* 5:549, where the statements attributed to Waldeck-Rousseau are slightly different.

48. Jacques Millerand, preface to Mathieu Dreyfus, *L'Affaire*, p. 12.

49. Reinach, "Récit," pp. 346–47; this phrase of Millerand's is not repeated in the *Histoire*.

50. Reinach, "Récit," pp. 347–48; cf. *Histoire* 5:352.

51. Reinach, "Récit," p. 363; this statement was related neither in the *Histoire* nor by Mathieu, who was present.

52. Reinach, "Récit," p. 363.

53. It is then that Jaurès wrote the declaration that was to be published by Dreyfus.

54. Reinach, "Récit," pp. 370–75; cf. *Histoire* 5:559–65, and *L'Affaire*, pp. 242–46. Mathieu Dreyfus indicates that he was asked to take his brother out of the country, which he refused to do; see also Alfred Dreyfus, *The Dreyfus Case*, pp. 141–43.

55. "Récit," p. 365, *Histoire* 5:561. Barrès provides an echo of these hesitations on Loubet's part and offers some unverifiable information concerning the role Rouvier might have played in the final decision; see Barrès, *Mes Cahiers* 2:167 (Paris: Plon, 1930).

56. The main files (see n. 1, above) are WR 4567, 4568, and 4576. Accessible since 1955, they have been used by Pierre Sorlin (*Waldeck-Rousseau*, pp. 410–15), who treated "The Liquidation of the Affair" with his usual concise precision. May the dedication I set below the heading to these pages be recognition enough for what I owe to this book and to its author.

57. Deposition before the Criminal Chamber of the Supreme Court, June 11, 1904, cited by L. Leblois, *L'Affaire Dreyfus: L'iniquité, la Réparation; les principaux faits et les principaux documents* (Paris: Quillet, 1929), p. 895.

58. Ibid., pp. 896–97, discussing the matter with Attorney Mornard.

59. See Pierre Sorlin, *Waldeck-Rousseau*, p. 411, who quotes some revealing texts.

60. Undated letter, WR 4567 G. It is in this same file that are found all the Galliffet letters from which I will be quoting.
61. Pierre Sorlin, *Waldeck-Rousseau*, pp. 411–12. Waldeck-Rousseau had advanced quite far in his secret contacts with Germany, obtaining from the imperial government evidence, turned over by Esterhazy, that demonstrated Dreyfus's innocence; cf. M. Baumont, *Aux Sources de l'affaire Dreyfus d'après les archives diplomatiques* (Paris: Les Productions de Paris, 1959), pp. 246–51.
62. Letter to Waldeck-Rousseau, WR 4567 G.
63. Notably by Reinach, *Histoire* 5:579–81.
64. In these letters, the words and expressions given emphasis are those underlined by their author.
65. The date indicated on this letter poses a difficult problem. Is it really from the evening before?
66. In fact, it was only on the nineteenth, at 1:00 P.M., therefore after the Council of Ministers meeting, that Attorney G. Brunschvicg, secretary to Attorney Mornard, advised the president of the council that the petition had actually been withdrawn. Confidence did not reign supreme (WR 4576.12).
67. This theme returns like a shooting pain. It also figures in his "official" letter to Waldeck-Rousseau (Reinach, *Histoire* 5:581–82), which, on September 13, proposed the pardon.
68. This is Galliffet's only reference to that political current.
69. The text (preserved in WR 4576) is not dated, but it is beyond doubt that, in studying "the consequences of the verdict," it was prepared for the council meeting of the twelfth. Certain of its preambulatory points render even more astounding Galliffet's incoherencies concerning the withdrawal of Dreyfus's petition.
70. The words emphasized are underlined by Waldeck-Rousseau himself.
71. Preserved among his letters in WR 4567 G.
72. This document, which is preserved in the file WR 4576.12, has never been, to my knowledge, published or used.
73. For example, the "judgment" of the Court-Martial becomes, correctly, a "sentence" [*un "arrêt"*].
74. Reinach, *Histoire* 5:555. [T/E: New Year's presidential pardons are an annual affair in France.]
75. Georges Sorel, *La Révolution dreyfusienne* (Paris: Rivière, 1909), p. 41.
76. It is reproduced in a small book by P. Boussel, *L'Affaire Dreyfus et la presse* (Paris: Armand Colin, 1960), p. 227.
77. Marcel Thomas, *L'Affaire sans Dreyfus* (1961), 2d ed. (Paris: Cercle du Bibliophile, 1971).
78. The two images are partially reproduced in Boussel's *L'Affaire Dreyfus*, pp. 258–59; I was able to see a complete copy of the second at the Bibliothèque du Musée Social.

79. See Pierre Nora, "Ernest Lavisse: Son rôle dans la formation du sentiment national," *Revue historique* 3 (1962): 73–106.

80. Ernest Lavisse, "La Réconciliation nationale," in *Revue de Paris*, October 1899, pp. 648–68; the phrases I have quoted appear on pp. 659 and 648.

81. I know this text only through a long quotation of it given by Alfred Dreyfus in *Souvenirs et correspondence* (Paris: Grasset, 1936), pp. 275–78. [T/E: This quotation does not seem to have been included in the English translation, *The Dreyfus Case*.] He dates this lecture May 9. Lucien Mercier suggests to me that it might in reality be a class he gave on the historian Michelet at the "Solidarity" popular university in the thirteenth arrondissement of Paris, as mentioned in the May 9, 1900, issue of *La Petite République*.

82. See the fine article by Madeleine Rebérioux, "Histoire, historiens et dreyfusisme," *Revue historique* 2 (1976): 407–32.

83. Rebérioux, "Histoire, historiens et dreyfusisme," p. 409.

84. Ibid., citing his death notice, written by C. Bémont for the 1921 *Revue historique*: "Journalist, diplomat, highly cultured statesman." Concerning Joseph Reinach, we now have a thesis by J. El Gammal, "Joseph Reinach et la République" (University of Paris—X, 1982).

85. Rebérioux, "Histoire, historiens et dreyfusisme," p. 420.

86. Jean Jaurès, *Les Preuves* (Paris: La Petite République, 1898) has recently been republished with a preface by Madeleine Rebérioux (Cergy: Le Signe, 1981).

87. Benda, *La Jeunesse d'un clerc* (1968 ed.), pp. 119–20.

88. See *L'Humanité*, November 3, 1949, cited by M. Winock in his *Histoire politique de la revue "Esprit"* (Paris: Seuil, 1975), p. 308. [T/E: Lászlo Rajk, a Communist leader in Hungary, was tried in September 1949 for "Titoist" deviationism and executed.]

89. Benda, *La Jeunesse d'un clerc*, p. 118.

90. See the research (already cited in n. 21, above) of Charle, *La Crise littéraire*, pp. 171–73, and *Naissance des intellectuels*; see also C. Prochasson, *Les Années électriques, 1880–1910* (Paris: Découverte, 1991).

91. "Henri Dutrait-Crozon," *Précis de l'affaire Dreyfus, avec un répertoire analytique* (Paris: Nouvelle Librairie nationale, 1909); cf. Pierre Vidal-Naquet, *Assassins of Memory: Essays on the Denial of the Holocaust*, trans. Jeffrey Mehlman (New York: Columbia University Press, 1992), p. 54.

92. Mathieu Dreyfus, *L'Affaire Dreyfus*, pp. 48–51; cf. Rebérioux, *La République radicale?*, pp. 29–31.

93. Jean-Pierre Peter, "Dreyfus (Affaire)," *Encyclopaedia Universalis* 5:794 (1969).

94. To take a measurement of the torrents of ink that have flowed on this subject, see Joseph Reinach, *Histoire* 6:206–48, where one can begin to retrace the path, step by step, through the previous volumes.

95. "Dutrait-Crozon," *Précis de l'affaire Dreyfus*, p. 423 and passim.

96. Raoul Allier, *Le Bordereau annoté* (Paris: Bellais, 1903), a reworked version of articles published in *Le Siècle* between April 12 and May 4, 1903.

97. Allier, *Le Bordereau annoté*, pp. vi–vii [T/E: and see the following note concerning this tiara].

98. The "tiara of Saitaphernes," a work by a Russian silversmith that was contemporary with the Dreyfus Affair, was bought in 1896 by the Louvre as an object of Antiquity. It can still be found there.

99. At the time, some serious people believed in its existence. For example, Italy's ambassador to Paris, Tornielli, wrote to his ministry on September 5, 1898, as follows: "These strange documents exist, it seems, in the archives of the War Ministry" (Baumont, *Aux Sources de l'affaire*, p. 217). The Imperial forgery played an important role in Paléologue's account, *An Intimate Journal*, but naturally it never actually appears.

100. Allier, *Le Bordereau annoté*, p. 62; see also, for the memorandum, Reinach, *Histoire* 6:272. Let us compare this comment with what, in an entirely different context, Simon Leys writes concerning a famous document from the history of Chinese calligraphy: "By a remarkable paradox, it was only *after* it definitively disappeared into the imperial sepulcher that this work . . . began to exercise its greatest influence, through various indirect copies of uncertain origin" (*L'Humeur, l'honneur, l'horreur: Essais sur la culture et la politique chinoises* [Paris: Robert Laffont, 1991], p. 39).

101. See, for example, Reinach, *Histoire* 6:319–22.

102. François Mauriac, "L'Affaire Dreyfus vue par un enfant," in *Cinq Années de ma vie* (Paris: Fasquelle, 1962), pp. 11–21.

103. P.-V. Stock, *Mémorandum d'un éditeur*, vol. 3, *L'Affaire Dreyfus anecdotique* (Paris: Stock, Dalamain, Boutelleau, 1938), p. 176.

104. Ibid., pp. 176–77.

105. In order to resituate these pages within the context of the overall history of the Dreyfus Affair, see Jean-Denis Bredin, *L'Affaire* (Paris: Julliard and Fayard, 1993); Michael Burns, *Dreyfus: A Family Affair* (New York: Harper-Collins, 1991); M. Drovin, ed., *L'Affaire Dreyfus de A à Z* (Paris: Flammarion, 1994); Pierre Birnbaum, ed., *La France de l'Affaire Dreyfus* (Paris: Gallimard, 1994).

7. Jewish Prism, Marxist Prism

1. Michael Löwy, *Redemption and Utopia—Jewish Libertarian Thought in Central Europe: A Study in Elective Affinity*, trans. Hope Heaney (Stanford, Calif.: Stanford University Press, 1992).

2. Karl Marx, "La Question juive," in *Annales d'histoire révisionniste* 5 (Summer–Fall 1988): 5–29. For the context, see my book, *Assassins of Memory: Essays on the Denial of the Holocaust*, trans. Jeffrey Mehlman (New York: Columbia University Press, 1992).

3. J. Molitor's translation, cited by Traverso, was republished in 1968 by Éditions 10/18 (Paris), along with a translation of Bauer's essay. It is erro-
neously indicated in this edition that the translator is J.-M. Palmier. [T/E:
The English translation of Traverso's book (see the publication note at the
beginning of the present essay) cites the Lawrence and Wishart *Collected
Works'* English translation of Marx's review of Bauer's book, *On the Jewish
Question*; this English-language edition also cites the same French "10/18"
translation of Bauer's work.]

4. See Arno J. Mayer's book, *Why Did the Heavens Not Darken? The "Final Solution" in History* (New York: Pantheon, 1988). I do not share all the postulates
of this important book, but I am convinced by a number of his basic analyses. See my preface to the French edition (essay 11 in part three of the present volume).

5. The Bund was the General Jewish Workers' League of Poland, Lithuania, and
Russia; it was the largest force in the Jewish, Marxist, anti-Zionist workers'
movement.

6. "According to Jewish custom." This oath was sworn in synagogues in the
presence of the rabbi and the justice of the peace of the canton. It was abolished by a decree of the French Supreme Court on March 3, 1846.

7. Alphonse Toussenel, *Les Juifs: rois de l'époque: Histoire de la féodalité financière*
(Paris, 1845); the book was republished in 1846 and then again (by Marpon
and Flammarion) in 1886, after the initial successes of the anti-Semitic
French writer Édouard Drumont.

8. See, in chapter 7 of Traverso's book (pp. 161–62) the 1939 analyses of
Arnaldo Momigliano, which were cited sympathetically by Antonio
Gramsci.

9. Here, I am using Michael Graetz's *Les Juifs en France au XIXe siècle*, trans. from
the Hebrew by Salomon Malka (Paris: Seuil, 1989), pp. 122–23.

10. Beilis was a Jewish resident of Kiev who was accused of committing a ritual
murder in 1911; he was eventually acquitted.

11. This was a current of the eastern European Jewish workers' movement that
stood opposed to Zionism (that is, to the choice of Palestine) but still
favored a rebirth of the Jewish nation on a territorial basis.

12. Primo Levi, *If Not Now, When?*, trans. William Weaver, introduction by
Irving Howe (New York: Summit, 1985), p. 67.

13. Ernest Renan, *Histoire du peuple d'Israël* (1891), in *Oeuvres complètes* 6:715
(Paris: Calmann-Lévy, 1953).

14. They have been studied in Michael Löwy's book, cited in n. 1, above. See
also in *JMP*, pp. 262–64, my article "Sur une réédition." [T/E: In this article,
which originally appeared in *Esprit*, June 1982, pp. 174–75, Vidal-Naquet
discusses the republication of Bernard Lazare's *L'Antisemitisme, son histoire et
ses causes* (Anti-Semitism, its history and its causes). Lazare's book was reissued by Éditions de la Différence in a series edited by Pierre Guillaume; on

Guillaume and his "tiny abject band," La Vieille Taupe (The Old Mole), see Vidal-Naquet's *Assassins of Memory*, esp. pp. 116–19.]

15. See Walter Benjamin and Gershom Scholem, *The Correspondence of Walter Benjamin and Gershom Scholem, 1932–1940*, ed. Gershom Scholem, trans. from the German by Gary Smith and André Lefevere, introduction by Anson Rabinbach (New York: Schocken, 1989); and Scholem's own book, *Walter Benjamin* (New York: Leo Baeck Institute, 1965).

16. This is the postulate on which Michael Waltzer's book, *Exodus and Revolution* (New York: Basic Books, 1985), rests.

17. An American cultural review published in New York, which at first was radical, but later became very reactionary, notably under Reagan.

18. Franz Neumann, *Behemoth: The Structure and Practice of National Socialism, 1933–1944*, 2d ed. (New York: Octagon, 1972); this edition clearly distinguishes between the 1942 text and the 1944 appendix.

19. Raul Hilberg, *The Destruction of the European Jews*, rev. ed., vol. 1 (New York and London: Holmes and Meier, 1985); see pp. 249–55.

20. Abram Leon [Abraham Léon], *The Jewish Question: A Marxist Interpretation*, introduction by E. Germain (New York: Pathfinder, 1970), p. 262.

21. As late as 1989, Henri Alleg, in his book *L'URSS et les Juifs* (Paris: Messidor, 1989), p. 158, was still citing Lenin's quotation of Naquet without gauging the abyss that separates the French Jews from those of the Russian Empire.

22. See Renée Poznanski's translation from the Russian (with introduction and critical apparatus): Simon Doubnov [Dubnow], *Lettres sur le judaïsme ancien et nouveau* (Paris: Cerf, 1989), and my own introduction to the new edition of the *Histoire moderne du peuple juif* (Paris: Cerf, 1994).

23. On the thought of Georges Sorel and his connections with Marxism, see notably Shlomo Sand, *L'Illusion du politique: Georges Sorel et le débat intellectuel (1900)* (Paris: Découverte, 1985) and Jacques Julliard and Shlomo Sand, eds., *Georges Sorel et son temps* (Paris: Seuil, 1985), as well as Larry Portis, *Georges Sorel: Présentation et textes choisis* (Paris: Maspero, 1982; rpt., Paris: La Brèche, 1989). Portis's book offers a somewhat optimistic view of Georges Sorel's thought. For an analysis of Sorel's changing attitudes toward the Jewish question, see Shlomo Sand, "Sorel, les Juifs et l'antisémitisme," *Cahiers Georges Sorel* 2 (1984): 7–36.

24. It is difficult to speak of the Polish Socialist party (PPS) without knowing Polish, and of Romanian and Bulgarian Marxists without knowing their respective languages.

25. Their participation is evoked in novelistic fashion by Schalom Asch in his trilogy, *Pétersbourg, Varsovie et Moscou*, published by Belfond (Paris) between 1986 and 1989.

26. Jewish self-hatred.

27. See Jacques Le Rider, *Le Cas Otto Weininger: Racines de l'antiféminisme et de antisémitisme* (Paris: PUF, 1982).

28. Traverso, *The Marxists and the Jewish Question*, p. 193.

29. See ibid., p. 200.

30. See Henri Alleg's book (cited in n. 21, above), where the author continues to hunt down the Bund as if nothing had happened in the world since 1903.

31. Of course, the mere fact that one is in the minority does not necessarily make one intelligent and lucid.

PART THREE: DESTRUCTION, MEMORY, AND THE PRESENT

8. The Hero, the Historian, and Choice

1. Pierre Vidal-Naquet, "Treblinka et l'honneur des juifs," in *Le Monde*, May 2, 1966, p. 17.

2. "One limited oneself to poking sorrowfully over the cold ashes of the International," a formula invented by Raymond Lefebvre for his *L'Éponge de vinaigre* (Paris: Clarté, 1921), p. 5, was long famous in France when it came to recalling the disarray experienced by internationalists after the outbreak of the First World War.

3. *Archivum Ringelbluma: Getto Warszawskie lipiec 1942—styczen 1943* (Warsaw: Panstwowe Wydawnictwo Naukowe, 1980).

4. Ibid., p. 8.

5. The others were Mordecai Anielewicz of the Ha-Shomer ha-Za'ir, Michal Rojzenfeld of the PPR (Communist Party), Yizhak Cukiermann (of the Hekhalutz pioneer movement), and Hersz Berlinski of the (left-wing) Po'alei Zion. Three of the five were therefore Zionists, the two others either anti-Zionist or alien to Zionism. Another center of insurrectional activity, the Jewish Military Association, was in its majority made up of right-wing (revisionist) Zionists.

6. Notably in France in *L'Express*, May 5, 1975. Solec is the name of a street located in a working-class district of Warsaw.

7. Michel Borwicz, *L'Insurrection du ghetto de Varsovie* (Paris: Julliard, 1966); K. Moczarski, *Entretiens avec le bourreau* (Paris: Gallimard, 1979); Emmanuel Ringelblum, *Notes from the Warsaw Ghetto: The Journal of Emmanuel Ringelblum*, ed. and trans. Jacob Sloan (New York: Schocken, 1974); and the novel of John Hersey, *The Wall* (New York: Modern Library, 1967).

8. The first part, "The Ghetto Struggles," was published in Lodz in 1945, the second, "Overtaking God," in Warsaw in 1977. [T/E: I have simply translated the French titles as they have been provided by Vidal-Naquet.]

9. May I be forgiven for this violently subjective outburst. On the "tiny abject band," its origins, and its ramifications, see my book, *Assassins of Memory: Essays on the Denial of the Holocaust*, trans. Jeffrey Mehlman (New York: Columbia University Press, 1992).

10. Moczarski, *Entretiens avec le bourreau*, p. 190.

11. See Borwicz, *L'Insurrection du ghetto de Varsovie*, pp. 96–103.
12. April 19, 1943, the day that marked the beginning of the uprising.
13. Adolf Rudnicki, *Les Fenêtres d'or* (Paris: Gallimard, 1966), p. 7.
14. See, for example, P. Joutard, *La Légende des camisards: Une Sensibilité au passé* (Paris: Gallimard, 1977). Among the rare scholars who reflected in depth on the theme of memory was Ignace Meyerson.
15. I return to *Shoah* in another text, "The Shoah's Challenge to History," later in the present volume.
16. Rudnicki, *Les Fenêtres d'or*, p. 93.
17. Henri Bergson, *Creative Evolution*, trans. Arthur Mitchell (London: Macmillan, 1954), pp. 287–314; I am summarizing here some formulations given on pp. 308–11.
18. Isaac Deutscher, "The Jewish Tragedy and the Historian," in *The Non-Jewish Jew* (Oxford: Oxford University Press, 1968), p. 164.
19. See A. Donat, ed., *The Death Camp Treblinka* (New York: Holocaust Library, 1979), p. 164 (a book that was brought to my attention by Arnaldo Momigliano). For the itinerary of F. Stangl, who was the head of Treblinka, see the major work by Gitta Sereny, *Into That Darkness* (New York: Random House, 1983).

9. The Historian and the Test of Murder

1. Raul Hilberg, *The Destruction of the European Jews*, rev. ed., 3 vols. (New York and London: Holmes and Meier, 1985). [T/E: Hilberg's book had just appeared, in a French translation by Marie-France de Polmera and André Charpentier, as *La Destruction des Juifs d'Europe* (Paris: Fayard, 1988). Page citations in the present essay refer to the consecutively numbered pages of the three-volume English-language edition.]
2. Franz Neumann, *Behemoth: The Structure and Practice of National Socialism, 1933–1944*, 2d ed. (New York: Octagon, 1972). Let us recall also Martin Broszat's fundamental book, *The Hitlerian State: The Foundation and Development of the Internal Structure of the Third Reich*, trans. from the German by John Hiden (White Plains, N.Y.: Longman, 1981), which also was translated into French in 1986.
3. Hannah Arendt, *Eichmann in Jerusalem: A Report on the Banality of Evil* (New York: Penguin, 1964, 1978).
4. Besides Raul Hilberg's book, another indispensable work that should be translated into French is Isaiah Trunk's *Judenrat: The Jewish Councils in Eastern Europe Under Nazi Occupation* (New York: Macmillan, 1972; London: Collier, 1972).
5. All this has been analyzed in the book by historian Arno J. Mayer, *Why Did the Heavens Not Darken? The "Final Solution" in History* (New York: Pantheon, 1988), which I discuss in "On an Interpretation of the Great Massacre: Arno

Mayer and the 'Final Solution'" (essay 11 in the third part of the present volume).

6. By way of example, I refer the reader to an issue of Pierre Bourdieu's review, *Actes de la Recherche en Sciences Sociales* 62–63 (June 1980), and in particular to the studies of Michael Pollak, one of which is called "La Gestion de l'indicible" (The management of the unsayable); this study was revised and developed in his book *L'Expérience concentrationnaire: Essai sur le maintien de l'identité sociale* (Paris: A.-M. Métailié, 1990).

7. Margaret Buber-Neumann, *Déportée en Sibérie*, trans. Anise Postel-Vinay, afterword by Albert Béguin (Paris: Seuil, 1986); *Déportée à Ravensbrück*, trans. Alain Brossat (Paris: Seuil, 1988). Let us also recall, from the same author, her *Milena*, trans. from the German by Ralph Mannheim (New York: Seaver, 1988).

8. Germaine Tillion, *Ravensbrück*, followed by *Les Exterminations par gaz à Ravensbrück* by Anise Postel-Vinay and *Les Exterminations par gaz à Hartheim, Mauthasen et Gusen*, by Pierre-Serge Choumoff (Paris: Seuil, 1988). [T/E: See, now, Pierre Vidal-Naquet's "Réflexions sur trois *Ravensbrück*," in Claude Habib and Claude Mouchard, eds., *La Démocratie à l'oeuvre: Autour de Claude Lefort* (Paris: Esprit, 1993), pp. 345–58.]

10. The Shoah's Challenge to History

1. See *Assassins of Memory: Essays on the Denial of the Holocaust*, trans. Jeffrey Mehlman (New York: Columbia University Press, 1992), p. 99.

2. Thucydides 3.82–83. [T/E: I use here the translation of Rex Warner, *History of the Peloponnesian War*, introduction by Moses I. Finley (Harmondsworth: Penguin, 1972).]

3. Thucydides 3.81–83.

4. This is one of the most important words in the Greek political vocabulary. Its meaning oscillates between domestic conflict and violent revolution. Nicole Loraux is preparing a comprehensive work on *stasis*. She has already published a number of preliminary studies on this topic over the past few years.

5. Thucydides 4.80.1–4. [T/E: Here I have translated R. Weil's French translation, which Vidal-Naquet makes use of here, so as to retain the word "disparaître" (disappear).] A young researcher, Mr. Roger-Vasselin, has written a detailed study of this strange and relatively neglected passage. See, provisionally, Vidal-Naquet, *Assassins of Memory*, pp. 99–102.

6. The date is in fact uncertain. The episode in question may have occurred much earlier, Thucydides citing it for its exemplary quality. The date of 424 is the one most often given, sometimes without the least hesitation, for example, by G. E. M. de Sainte-Croix in *The Origins of the Peloponnesian War* (London: Duckworth, 1972), p. 93.

7. Book three ends with an eruption of Mount Etna. The connection between

the Peloponnesian War and great natural catastrophes is made very explicitly at 1.23.

8. Thucydides 3.82.2. [T/E: The French translation is more detailed: these bad situations "increase or abate or change form with each variation in the circumstances."]

9. We are greatly aided here by Jean Ducat's *Les Hilotes de Sparte*, a book I was able to read in manuscript form. It now appears as a supplement to the *Bulletin de Correspondance Hellénique* 18 (1990).

10. François Furet, ed., *Unanswered Questions: Nazi Germany and the Genocide of the Jews* (New York: Schocken, 1989).

11. The latest attempt at a direct historical synthesis of which I am aware is Arno J. Mayer's *Why Did the Heavens Not Darken? The "Final Solution" in History* (New York: Pantheon, 1988). Mayer's book is, as it should be, both a narrative account and an interpretive assessment. [T/E: See the next chapter of the present volume for Vidal-Naquet's discussion of this book.]

12. Olga Wormser-Migot, *Le Système concentrationnaire nazi* (Paris: PUF, 1968).

13. See my review of the French translation, *La Destruction des Juifs d'Europe*, essay 9 in part three of the present volume.

14. Philip Friedman, *Roads to Extinction* (New York and Philadelphia: Conference on Jewish Social Studies, 1980).

15. Mayer, *Why Did the Heavens Not Darken?*, ch. 7: "Conceiving Operation Barbarossa: Conquest and Crusade."

16. See her February 25, 1972, article in *Le Monde* and the conclusion to her book, *The Theme of Nazi Concentration Camps in French Literature* (Paris and The Hague: Mouton, 1973).

17. Henry Rousso, *The Vichy Syndrome: History and Memory in France since 1944* (Cambridge: Harvard University Press, 1991). I do not always agree with the details of this book (I challenge, for example, his judgment on *Shoah*, pp. 237–39) or with its basic outlook, that is to say, its chronological parameters, but I do not see how one can challenge the question it raises.

18. Michael R. Marrus and Robert O. Paxton, *Vichy France and the Jews* (New York: Schocken, 1983); Serge Klarsfeld, *Vichy-Auschwitz: Le rôle de Vichy dans la solution finale de la question juive en France, 1942–1944*, 2 vols. (Paris: Fayard, 1983, 1986).

19. One will find a dossier on this affair in the January–March 1982 issue of *Le Mouvement social*, pp. 101–2.

20. To savor this saying, it is helpful to recall that the last two volumes of that great interwar undertaking, the *Géographie universelle*—that is, the volumes devoted to France, which were published in 1948 under the direction of Albert Demangeon, the famous geographer and father-in-law of Aimé Perpillou—presented the country in its 1939 state, which occasioned numerous protests.

21. See Arno J. Mayer's protest in the "Personal Preface" to his latest work.

22. This was not the case in the 1982 colloquium, where I was asked to present

some "theses on revisionism." These theses may be found, with a few modifications of detail, in Vidal-Naquet, *Assassins of Memory*, pp. 79–98.

23. Pierre Pachet, "Pas d'excuses à l'ignorance," in *La Quinzaine Littéraire*, November 1–15, 1987.

24. "Henri Dutrait-Crozon," *Précis de l'affaire Dreyfus, avec un répertoire analytique* (Paris: Nouvelle Librairie nationale, 1909). This work followed upon a "revision" of the history of the Dreyfus Affair: Joseph Reinach's *Histoire de l'affaire Dreyfus*.

25. A point made by François Hartog during his seminar at the École des Hautes Études en Sciences Sociales.

26. Paul Ricoeur, *Time and Narrative*, trans. Kathleen Blamey and David Pellauer, vol. 3 (Chicago and London: University of Chicago Press, 1988), p. 154. [T/E: the emphases of Ricoeur's original French have been restored.]

27. A difference in degree, responds Arno J. Mayer, *Why Did the Heavens Not Darken?*, p. 362, and on this point I separate myself from him.

28. Hans Laternser, *Die andere Seite im Auschwitz-Prozess 1963–1965: Reden eines Verteidigers* (Stuttgart: Seewald, 1966), pp. 185–86.

29. On the basis of an entirely different analysis, Arno J. Mayer also makes the end of 1941, the failure to take Moscow, a decisive turning point in the war, the turning point that allowed the "Judeocide" to occur.

30. Michel Deguy, "Au Sujet de *Shoah*," reprinted now in the collection of the same name. [T/E: See the footnote at the beginning of this essay.] Indeed, this article should be cited in its entirety.

31. See "The Hero, the Historian, and Choice," essay 8 in part three of the present volume.

32. The problem is posed in a different way by Paul Ricoeur in *Time and Narrative* 3:127–43.

11. On an Interpretation of the Great Massacre: Arno Mayer and the Final Solution

1. Hannah Arendt, *Eichmann in Jerusalem: A Report on the Banality of Evil* (New York: Penguin, 1964, 1978).

2. Because it is so archetypical, I shall refer here only to one of these critical attacks, Lucy S. Dawidowicz's "Perversion of the Holocaust," in *Commentary*, October 1989. Worth noting is the fact that the real negationists were not themselves deceived. In the *Journal of Historical Review* 9, no. 3 (Fall 1989), one will find a venomous review by Arthur R. Butz, the only negationist who has written the *semblance* of a historical study—by which I mean a rather well-packaged lie.

3. François Furet, ed., *Unanswered Questions: Nazi Germany and the Genocide of the Jews* (New York: Schocken, 1989); François Bédarida, ed., *La Politique nazie d'extermination* (Paris: Albin Michel, 1989).

4. For a historiographical perspective on Mayer's book, see Enzo Traverso, "Auschwitz, l'histoire et les historiens," in *Les Temps Modernes*, June 1990.

5. It is only fair to point out that Claude Lefort protested in advance against this monolithic vision in *Socialisme ou Barbarie* 14 (1956): 2. See, now, the translation, "Totalitarianism Without Stalin," in his *Political Forms of Modern Thought*, ed. John B. Thompson (Cambridge, Eng.: Polity Press, 1986), pp. 52–53.

6. See Fritz Stern, *The Politics of Cultural Despair: A Study in the Rise of Germanic Ideology* (Berkeley: University of California Press, 1961; rpt., Garden City, N.Y.: Anchor, 1965), which has just recently been translated into French.

7. Jacques Le Rider, *Modernité viennoise et crises de l'identité* (Paris: PUF, 1990), pp. 223–348.

8. Stern, *The Politics of Cultural Despair*, p. 93.

9. See Y.-M. Bercé, *Le Roi caché. Sauveurs et imposteurs: Mythes politiques populaires dans l'Europe moderne* (Paris: Fayard, 1990).

10. Philippe Burrin, *Hitler and the Jews* (New York: Routledge, 1994).

11. The precise reference for this document, which exists in microfilm form in Paris, may be found in Burrin, *Hitler and the Jews*, p. 194nn26–27. J. Stengers has drawn my attention to this text in a detailed and still unpublished review of Burrin's book, to appear in *Annales: Economies, Sociétés, Civilisations* 4 (1991). [T/E: This review did indeed appear in the above-mentioned issue, pp. 865–69.]

12. The principal documents are presented in Ernst Klee et al., eds., *The Good Old Days: The Holocaust as Seen by Its Perpetrators and Bystanders*, trans. Deborah Burnstone (New York: Free Press, 1991). The French translation by C. Métais-Bührendt is rather shoddy, so I have consulted the original of one of these documents, using a text sent to me by Anise Postel-Vinay.

13. Here again, I am inspired by J. Stengers's review of Burrin's work, which I cited in n. 11, above.

14. Concerning this history-film, one should now refer to the volume entitled *Au Sujet du "Shoah,"* ed. Bernard Cuau et al. (Paris: Belin, 1990).

15. Jean-Claude Pressac, *Auschwitz: Technique and Operation of the Gas Chambers* (New York: Beate Klarsfeld Foundation, 1989). One would hope that this book, written in French, will be published in French in the near future. [T/E: While this book has not been translated into French, a French version now exists of another, more recent work by Pressac: *Les Crématoires d'Auschwitz* (Paris: CNRS, 1993), whose publication in an English-language edition, I am informed, has been held up.]

16. Jean-Claude Pressac's book highlights very well the responsibility of the managerial personnel of the manufacturing company J. A. Topf & Sons of Erfurt, and in particular the engineer Kurt Prüfer, the builder of the crematoria and gas chambers. The proceedings instituted against this very respectable firm never led to a judgment. One of its top officers committed

suicide May 31, 1945. See Pressac, *Auschwitz*, pp. 93–104. [T/E: In a
Reuters dispatch, the *International Herald Tribune* of September 1, 1994,
reports that "the heirs of the German company that built the crematoriums
at Auschwitz and other death camps will not get the factory site in Eastern
Germany back, a regional government office said Wednesday. However, the
claims by the heirs of J. A. Topf & Söhne for restitution of private assets are
still under consideration, the spokesman for the Office for Outstanding
Property Questions in Thuringia said. . . . [U]nder laws introduced after
Germany's unification in 1990 . . . [t]he Topf heirs are seeking restitution for
property seized by the Communist government of East Germany."]

17. See Anise Postel-Vinay's study in Germaine Tillion's *Ravensbrück*, 3d ed.
(Paris: Seuil, 1988).

12. And by the Power of a Word . . .

1. These resemblances sometimes involve strange confusions; thus, Annie Besse
(Kriegel), in wanting to contrast the Rothschilds to the "symbol of the pro-
letariat of Jewish origin," cited Manouchian in the *Cahiers du communisme*,
February 1953, p. 242: "Over and above the *ad hominem* attacks, I cited
Manouchian as the symbol of the proletariat of Jewish origin" (p. 777 of her
memoirs, *Ce que j'ai cru comprendre* [Paris: Laffont, 1991]).

2. Anahide Ter Minassian, *La Question arménienne* (Roquevaire: Parenthèses,
1983), p. 21.

3. Michael Arlen, *Passage to Ararat* (New York: Farrar, Straus, 1975), p. 59.

4. On this date and its significance, see Yves Ternon, *The Armenian Cause*, trans.
Anahide Apelian Mangouni (Delmar, N.Y.: Caravan, 1985), pp. 170–71.

5. See the discussion on "Hitler's Little Statement," in Ternon, *The Armenian
Cause*, pp. 145–47. We know that Hitler said in 1939: "Who still mentions
today the massacre of the Armenians?"

6. This fact is naturally more evident in the case of Nazi Germany, a technological power, than in the case of Turkey in 1915, but one must not forget that,
while those who carried out the orders in 1915 were "underdeveloped" people, those from the Union and Progress committee, who had overthrown
Abdul-Hamid II in 1908, were modernists whose accession to power had
favorably been greeted as "progressive," even by the Armenians' leaders.

7. "Arménie: Le droit à la mémoire" (Armenia: The right to remember) is the
title of the April 1984 issue of *Esprit*. Forthcoming is a special issue of *Les
Temps Modernes* (July–September 1988) entitled "Arménie-diaspora,
mémoire et modernité" (Armenia/Diaspora: memory and modernity).
[T/E: This issue appeared as nos. 504–506.]

8. See, on this point, Ternon, *The Armenian Cause*, pp. 151–59, and Gérard
Chaliand and Yves Ternon, *The Armenians: From Genocide to Resistance*, trans.
from the French by Tony Berrett (London: Zed, 1990), pp. 84–97, from

whom I borrow a few quotations [T/E: See the following note]. On the authenticity of other, slightly more direct telegrams read in Berlin in 1921 at the trial of Teilirian, who had killed Talaat, there is, to say the least, reason to be highly cautious. Yves Ternon places the various genocides in perspective in *L'État criminel, les genocides au XXe siècle* (Paris: Seuil, 1995).

9. It is by error that I, in the version of the present text that was published by Flammarion and in the wake of other authors, attributed this phrase to the future Ataturk. See, on this problem, the clarification written by James H. Tachjian, "On a 'Statement' Condemning the Armenian Genocide of 1915–1918, Attributed in Error to Mustapha Kemal, Later 'The Ataturk,' " in the *Armenian Review* 25 (Fall 1982): 227–44. [T/E: It turns out that the quotation from this Kurdish Mustapha Kemal also had to be corrected in the English translation of Chaliand and Ternon's book (see p. 152 of *The Armenians: From Genocide to Resistance*). I have used this corrected, and still quite damning version in the quotation reproduced in the text of the present essay. The quotation from Inonu, also reproduced below in the present text, appears on pp. 153–54 of the same book.]

10. Nadine Fresco, "Les redresseurs de morts," *Les Temps Modernes* (June 1980): 2111–2180. The *witz* may be summarized as follows: A is accused of having returned broken a cauldron that he had borrowed from B; in his defense, he says: "I didn't borrow a cauldron, it was already broken, I returned it intact."

11. The Turkish arguments are summarized by Yves Ternon, and also by M. Marian in *Esprit* (April 1984): 80–85; thanks to Adnan Bulak, Turkish ambassador to France, a perfectly clear presentation of these arguments may be found in the May 2, 1983, issue of *Le Monde*. The most elaborate "scholarly" version of the Armenian "file," which was prepared under the auspices of the Turkish Historical Society, is contained in Kamuran Gurun's book, *The Armenian File: The Myth of Innocence Exposed* (New York: St. Martin's, 1986).

12. This issue sometimes poses a problem in the Armenian argument, to the extent that, among the Armenians, there exists a tradition that presents them as the defenders, against Islam, of Western and Christian values. See, for example, the testimony of Ms. Kilndjan, in *Les Arméniens en cours d'assises* (Roquevaire: Parenthèses, 1983), p. 36: "My father and my uncle were, like all Armenians, forced into the military."

13. Richard Marienstras, "Un Génocide dans le sens de l'histoire," in *Être un peuple en diaspora* (Paris: Maspero, 1975), pp. 205–13.

14. A resolute opponent of the American war in Vietnam, I had nevertheless intervened at the time with one of the judges, Laurent Schwartz, to try and prevent this designation from being applied in this case, as it appeared to me improper.

15. Anahide Ter Minassian, *La Question arménienne*, p. 8n3: I have solicited on this point the testimony of Laurent Schwartz, and it is from him that the detail about the Pakistani judge was gathered.

16. Edwy Plenel, in *Le Monde*, June 19, 1984.

17. See, most recently, Maxime Rodinson's article, "Quelques idées simples sur l'antisémitisme," *Revue d'études palestiniennes* 1 (1981): 5–21.

18. In 1981 this university's Senate adopted a resolution justifying the deportation of the Armenians. Apropos of the great massacre, it spoke of a "calumny."

19. There exists among Faurisson's associates at least one person, Vincent Monteil, who—for love of Islam—is a denier of the genocide of the Armenians. See his book, *Les Musulmans d'Union soviétique*, 2d ed. (Paris: Seuil, 1981), and his contribution to the anthology entitled *Intolérable intolérance* (Paris: Différance, 1981).

20. To use the title of the famous work by Joseph Ha-Kohen of Avignon, which was completed in 1560, two generations after the Spanish exile (1492).

21. [T/E: From "Liberté," a Resistance-era poem on freedom by Paul Éluard.]

13. A Wonderful School . . .

1. *Memorial to the Jews Deported from France, 1942–1944: Documentation of the Deportation of the Victims of the Final Solution in France* (New York: Beate Klarsfeld Foundation, 1983). The figures provided there allow us to correct those given by Nadine Heftler.

2. See Marc Klein's account, admirable on every point, in the anthology entitled *De l'Université aux camps de concentration: Témoignages strasgbourgeois* (Paris: Belles Lettres, 1954), pp. 429–55.

3. To be absolutely complete, let me add that two errors of substance have been corrected in the text: Adolf Hitler's birthday, which was the occasion for a better meal than usual, has been reestablished as April 20 (instead of the twenty-fourth) and the exact name of the commandant at Drancy, Aloïs Brünner, has been reestablished instead of and in the place of "Kramer," the head of the Nazi centers whose name Nadine Heftler might have heard at Auschwitz or at Ravensbrück.

4. Annette Wieviorka, *Déportation et génocide: Entre la mémoire et l'oubli: le cas des juifs de France* (Paris: Plon, 1992).

5. For example, the account of Suzanne Birnbaum, *Une Française juive est revenue: Auschwitz, Belsen, Raguhn* (Maulévrier: Hérault Éditions, 1989), a narrative that offers more than one parallel with that of Nadine Heftler.

6. Permit me to refer here to my "Réflexions sur trois *Ravensbrück*," in Claude Habib and Claude Mouchard, eds., *La Démocratie à l'oeuvre: Autour de Claude Lefort* (Paris: Esprit, 1993), pp. 345–58.

7. Nadine Heftler's account offers us some hitherto unknown information concerning this convoy. We do not have a list of the men and women who were on it.

14. The Harmonics of Szymon Laks

1. *If this is a man*, trans. from the Italian by Stuart Woolf (New York: Orion, 1959), p. 102, emphasis added on "musicians."

2. Annette Wieviorka, "Les déportés ont-ils témoigné?" *Bulletin trimestriel de la Fondation Auschwitz* 27 (January–March, 1991): 7–23, an article that takes up themes dealt with in more detail in a text published in *Pardès* 9–10 (1989): 23–59. Beginning in 1988, General Rogerie, who was himself at Auschwitz, took the initiative to reprint via Hérault Éditions (Maulévrier) a number of eyewitness accounts dating from 1945.

3. Primo Levi, *The Drowned and the Saved*, trans. from the Italian by Raymond Rosenthal (New York: Summit, 1988); the Italian edition dates from 1986.

4. Ibid., p. 69; Primo Levi had just mentioned Chaim Rumkoski, the lord of the Lodz ghetto.

5. In particular, an interview granted in 1987 by Pauline Laks, Szymon's widow, to Molly McCoy, the author of a University of Texas Ph.D. thesis on Simon Laks's vocal music.

6. Korab, *L'OEil de Dayan*, stories translated from the Polish by Simon Laks (Paris: Robert Laffont, 1974). Korab was the pseudonym for the Polish writer Yosef Hen.

7. Simon Laks and René Coudy, *Musiques d'un autre monde*, preface by Georges Duhamel (Paris: Mercure de France, 1948). [T/E: Despite the obvious similarity in title, *Music of Another World* (see the footnote at the beginning of this essay) is the English-language version of the book called in French *Mélodies d'Auschwitz*, not of *Musiques d'un autre monde*.]

8. Claude Lévi-Strauss, *The Raw and the Cooked*, trans. from the French by John and Doreen Weightman (New York and Evanston: Harper and Row, 1969). The book is dedicated "To Music," on a theme by Emmanuel Chabrier, and includes, for example, a "sonata on good manners."

9. Before being translated into French as *Mélodies d'Auschwitz*, this book was published in 1979 in Polish and in 1989 in English. *Music of Another World* was published by Northwestern University Press in Evanston, Ill., that is, the press of the university where Arthur Butz teaches. Butz is the master thinker and master writer for the French "revisionists," the only difference being that *he* is a *talented* forger. Thus can truth and freedom be reconciled in a fragile synthesis. Freedom would not be freedom were it not also the freedom to lie.

10. See Germaine Tillion, *Ravensbrück*, 3d ed. (Paris: Seuil, 1988) and, specifically, Anise Postel-Vinay's study, presented on pp. 305–30 of this book.

11. Thucydides 3.81.

12. I read this passage to Raymond Weil, the editor and translator of Thucydides, simply suppressing the word *camp*. He responded immediately: "Thucydides."

13. "To organize," in camp lingo, meant "to steal."

14. Meaning "The singer."

15. Zofia Posmysz, "Sängerin," in *Contribution à l'histoire du K.L. Auschwitz* (Auschwitz: State Museum of Auschwitz, 1968), pp. 143–67.

16. Dante *Inferno* canto 26.142. [T/E: I have used W. S. Merwin's translation, in *Dante's Inferno: Translations by Twenty Contemporary Poets*, ed. Daniel Halpern (Hopewell, N.J.: Ecco, 1993), p. 122]; cf. the chapter entitled "The Canto of Ulysses," in *If this is a man*, pp. 127–34.

15. Presentation of a Document: The Journal of Attorney Lucien Vidal-Naquet

1. See *L'Arche* 44 (September 1960) and 46 (November 1960).

2. *Carnets du pasteur Boegner, 1940–1945* (Paris: Fayard, 1992); and Charles Rist, *Une saison gâtée: Journal de la guerre et de l'Occupation, 1939–1945*, ed. J.-N. Jeanneney (Paris: Fayard, 1985).

3. R. R. Lambert, *Carnet d'un témoin*, ed. R. Cohen (Paris: Fayard, 1985).

4. Marc Bloch, *Strange Defeat: A Statement of Evidence Written in 1940*, trans. from the French by Gerard Hopkins (New York: Octagon, 1968). [T/E: This book begins with a chapter entitled "Presentation of a Witness," to which Vidal-Naquet alludes in the present essay.]

5. Marc Bloch to Étienne Bloch, *Lettres de la drôle de guerre*, ed. François Bédarida and Denis Peschanski, *Cahiers de l'IHTP* 19 (December 1990).

6. They met for the last time on October 8, 1939, in Charleville. That day, a photo of Raymond Aron and Georges and Lucien Vidal-Naquet was taken. The most military-looking of the three is the last mentioned. Raymond Aron appears entirely alien to the uniform he was wearing.

7. Pierre Birnbaum, *Les Fous de la République: Histoire politique des Juifs d'État, de Gambetta à Vichy* (Paris: Fayard, 1992).

8. The establishment of the Millerand Cabinet inspired from him the following commentary (letter of January 21, 1920): "What is more remarkable is the quantity of names missing. I noticed that we—and by 'we' I mean Papa— don't know anyone there, except for the nice president himself." It was, according to Lucien Vidal-Naquet, a "business cabinet." An amusing detail: the Minister of Finances of this business cabinet, F. François Marsal, was to become, at the end of the thirties, Lucien Vidal-Naquet's principal client.

9. Association amicale des secrétaires et anciens secrétaires de la Conférence des avocats à Paris, *Annuaire* 49 (1954): 237–53; see p. 242. The entry concerning Lucien Vidal-Naquet was written by Paul Arrighi. It is unfortunately not free from some errors of detail.

10. It was Jean Vidalenc who made this sobriquet known to me.

11. Letter from Désiré Oono, November 12, 1991, to Pierre Vidal-Naquet.

12. Bloch, *Strange Defeat*, p. 175.

13. Card to Margot Vidal-Naquet, April 16, 1942.

14. *Journal*, October 10, 1942; see *L'Arche* (September 1960).

15. On my thirteenth birthday, July 23, 1943, my father told me that this age corresponded, among the Jews, to the age of religious majority . . . and as it also did for the kings of France. But when I tried to relate this fact to my friend Alain Michel, he cut me off immediately.

16. "Marc Bloch et l'U.G.I.F.," in *Étrange défaite*, new ed., with a preface by Stanley Hoffmann (Paris: Gallimard, 1990), pp. 305–21. [T/E: This appendix does not appear in the English translation, *Strange Defeat*, cited in n. 4, above.]

17. Bernanos's *Le Message* (which consists of excerpts from his *Lettre aux Anglais*) was found in Lucien Vidal-Naquet's room on May 15, 1944, the day of my parents' arrest). [T/E: Georges Bernanos, *Plea for Liberty: Letters to the English, the Americans, the Europeans* (New York: Pantheon, 1944).]

18. This unpublished letter is in my possession.

19. Under the date of November 9 one reads in the *Journal*: "Our High Command, our *haute bourgeoisie*, and a few of their political lackeys have preferred the defeat of France to the victory of the Republic. The latter will yet be reborn. And these men covered with mud will return to the stream, with a bit of blood, but not enough to wash away their infamy and our shame."

20. The Communist deputy had asked: "Can we let bygones be bygones?" The answer was in the affirmative.

21. Henry Morgenthau, *Ambassador Morgenthau's Story* (Garden City, N.Y.: Doubleday, 1918).

22. On Pierre Masse and Jacques Frank, see the entries written by Marcel Héraud and Maurice Alléhaut for the *Annuaire* of secretaries and former secretaries of the Paris Conference of Lawyers, pp. 138–61 and 220–236, respectively.

23. *Journal*, January 25, 1943: "I never understood, as today, what tragedy can be contained in the simple word 'terror.' " On this event, see Christian Oppetit, ed., *Marseille, Vichy et les nazis: Le temps des rafles, la déportation des Juifs*, published for the Amicale des déportés d'Auschwitz et du camp de Haute-Silésie, Section Marseille-Provence (Boussens, Switzerland: Edisud, 1993).

24. I thank Gérard Brunschwig for having communicated this letter to me.

25. French National Archives, AJ 38.146.

26. Claude Singer, *Vichy, l'Université et les Juifs* (Paris: Belles Lettres, 1992), p. 262.

27. In 1927, as secretary of the Conference, Lucien Vidal-Naquet had been awarded the Liouville Prize.

28. Paul Arrighi, p. 249, of the entry cited previously (n. 9, above). I shall give here an example of his reaction in 1940, which I obtained thanks to Raymond Weil. While attending a "tea" in November 1940, he heard Gen. Alphonse Weyler (himself Jewish) explain at length France's defeat by

attributing responsibility for it to schoolteachers. His riposte: "Well, dear
general, we have heard a lot about the responsibility of the schoolteachers.
And now, what if we talked a bit about the responsibility of the generals?"

29. Ibid., p. 246. Raymond Aron gathered an echo of this audacity in his
    Mémoires (Paris: Julliard, 1983), p. 162. Aron speaks there of Lucien Vidal-
    Naquet's "almost excessive courage." [T/E: The English edition—*Memoirs:
    Fifty Years of Political Reflection*, trans. from the French by George Holoch
    (New York and London: Holmes and Meier, 1990)—omits this passage
    on p. 112.]

30. Maurice Alléhaut, p. 232, of the entry on Jacques Frank, cited previously
    (see n. 22, above).

PART FOUR: HISTORY, MEMORY, AND THE PRESENT

16. Reflections at the Margins of a Tragedy

1. This article—which, like the previous one [T/E: "La Contestation en Israël,"
   Le Nouvel Observateur 285 (April 27, 1970): 26–28; reprinted as "Israël: Les
   chances d'une contestation (1970)" in *JMP*, pp. 139–48], was written upon
   my return from a trip to Israel—appeared at the end of an issue of *Partisans*
   devoted to "The Palestinian People on the March." By and large, the readers
   of *Partisans* shared the extremist "Palestinianism" that then reigned in the
   revolutionary Left. This text, like Gérard Chaliand's *La Palestine n'est pas le
   Viêt-nam* (Palestine is not Vietnam), was aimed at "sowing some doubt"
   among the members of this public, as the introductory paragraph (not
   reproduced here) had indicated.

2. Abram Leon [Abraham Léon], *The Jewish Question: A Marxist Interpretation*,
   introduction by E. Germain (New York: Pathfinder, 1970). See the debate
   around this book in *Israc* 5 (January–March 1971).

3. This was an exaggeration. See now, on these questions, P. Korzec's *Juifs en
   Pologne* (Paris: Presses de la Fondation Nationale des Sciences Politiques,
   1980).

4. That is, during the antistudent and anti-Semitic crisis of 1968.

5. [T/E: Vidal-Naquet here refers the reader to note 2 of the previous text
   reprinted in *JMP* (on this text, see note 1 above): "On the whole, I must say
   that I was wrong to have spoken so categorically, both here and in other
   pages of this collection. Even though it has not challenged state structures
   or brought Arabs and Israelis closer together, the Sephardic explosion
   really did occur; see 'Le Second Israël,' in *Les Temps Modernes* 394 'bis'
   (May 1979)."]

6. And now in Yehoshofat Harkabi, *Palestinians and Israel* (New York: John Wiley,
   1974; Jerusalem: Keter, 1974), pp. 52–53.

7. El Fath, *La Révolution palestinienne et les Juifs* (Paris: Minuit, 1970).

8. An equally excessive statement.

17. Return to Israel

1. These two reports, both of which were published in *Le Nouvel Observateur*, were reprinted in *JMP*. [T/E: Vidal-Naquet is referring to "Israël: Les Chances d'une contestation" and "Israël-Palestine: La Frontière invisible," which appeared in issues 285 (April 27, 1970) and 574 (May 5, 1975) of *Le Nouvel Observateur* and which were reprinted in *JMP*, pp. 139–48 and 166–73. Neither one could be included in the present abridged translation.]
2. Raymonda Tawil, *Mon Pays, ma prison* (Paris: Seuil, 1982).
3. Statement in the *Jerusalem Post*, April 4, 1982.
4. In *Éléments* 5–6 (1970).
5. Rachel Mizrahi, *L'Un meurt, l'autre aussi* (Paris: Hachette, 1982).
6. For a wine to be kosher, the entire harvesting and wine-making processes must be performed by Jewish hands.
7. Let us be fair; it should be noted that Jabotinsky also had a more acute understanding of the Hitlerian danger than his political adversaries.
8. I have rightly been reminded that a desire to wipe Israel off the map has not been lacking on the Arab side. This helps to explain the reverse situation that prevails today, but it does not eliminate what I said in 1982. [Note added in 1991. T/E: The title *Sous Israël, la Palestine* (Under Israel, Palestine) recalls the famous May 1968 slogan *Sous les pavés, la plage* (Under the paving stones, the beach) of the French students who, while digging up paving stones for purposes of building barricades and throwing projectiles at the police, found sand—"the beach," symbolic of their playful revolution— below.]
9. Nahum Goldmann, in *Jewish Chronicle*, September 27, 1981 (reprinted as "The Dangers Facing World Jewry," in *New Outlook*, December 1981, pp. 8–15).
10. The Israeli attack was finally unleashed, as we now know, on June 7, 1982.
11. Elie Barnavi, *Israël au XXe siècle* (Paris: PUF, 1982), reissued as *Une Histoire moderne d'Israël* (Paris: Flammarion, 1988).
12. The debate was published in the review *Trois Continents* 3 (July–September 1967).

18. "Inquiry Into a Massacre" by Amnon Kapeliouk

1. Whose leaders—and in particular Eli Hobeika, the person principally responsible for the massacre—will not suffer as a result any disruption of their political careers. For the specifically Lebanese context, see I. Makhlouf, *Beyrouth ou la fascination de la mort* (Montreuil: Éditions de la Passion, 1988), pp. 80–90.

2. See Annie Kriegel, *Israël est-il coupable?* (Paris: Robert Laffont, 1982), pp. 149–80.
3. See *Traces* 5 (Fall 1982). A *shabbessgoyim* is a non-Jew who, on behalf of the Jews, performs certain work that Jews are forbidden to perform on Saturdays (the *shabbath*).
4. This affair became the object of an official commission of inquiry (the Kahan Commission), the conclusions of which were published in February 1983. These conclusions were in turn criticized, notably by Uri Avnery, whose analysis, published by *Ha-Olamazeh*, February 16, 1983, was translated into English for *Israleft*, March 4, 1983.

19. The Anti-Peace Colonists

1. Amnon Kapeliouk, *Israël: La fin des mythes*, preface by Jacques Fauvet (Paris: Albin Michel, 1975).
2. Amnon Kapeliouk, *Sabra and Shatila: Inquiry into a Massacre*, trans. from the French by Khalil Jahshan (Belmont, Mass.: Association of Arab-American University Graduates, 1983). [T/E: See the previous essay in the present volume.]

PART FIVE: CONCLUSION

20. Recollections of a Witness: Protestants and Jews During the Second World War in France

1. See, on this topic, the texts collected by P. Cabanel, P. Joutard, and J. Poujol, in *Cévennes, terre de refuge, 1940–1944* (Montpellier: Presses du Languedoc, 1987).
2. Pierre Sauvage's film, *The Weapons of the Spirit*, attributes to Major Schmähling, commandant of the Puy-en-Velay garrison, a protective role with regard to the Jews who had taken refuge at Chambon, even though no historical document known to me allows any verification of this claim. For this reason, I joined the protest published in *Le Monde Juif* 130 (April–June 1988), under the title "Le Mythe du commandant SS protecteur des Juifs" (The myth of the SS commandant, protector of the Jews).
3. See Serge Klarsfeld, *Vichy-Auschwitz: Le Rôle de Vichy dans la solution finale de la question juive en France, 1942–1944*, 2 vols. (Paris: Fayard, 1983, 1986).
4. This testimonial, *L'Étrange défaite*, written in 1940 and published after the war along with his *Écrits clandestines*, was republished by Gallimard (Paris) in 1990. [T/E: Marc Bloch, *Strange Defeat: A Statement of Evidence Written in 1940*, trans. from the French by Gerard Hopkins (New York: Octagon, 1968).]
5. Lucie-Violette Méjan, *La Séparation des Églises et de l'État: L'OEuvre de Louis

Méjan, dernier directeur de l'administration autonome des cultes (Paris: PUF, 1959).

6. He has since died, at age ninety.

7. Jules Isaac, *Les Oligarques* (Paris: Minuit, 1946), reprinted by Calmann-Lévy (Paris) in 1989.

8. See, in particular, Francis Schmidt's contribution ("Naissance d'une géographie juive," pp. 13–30) to the anthology *Moïse géographe*, ed. A. Desreumaux and F. Schmidt (Paris: Vrin, 1988).

9. Emmanuel Mounier, *Traité du caractère* (Paris: Seuil, 1946).

10. Robert Bonnaud, *Le Système de l'histoire* (Paris: Fayard, 1989).

Index

Other Books by Pierre Vidal-Naquet in English

Assassins of Memory: Essays on the Denial of the Holocaust (1992), translated with a foreword by Jeffrey Mehlman

The Black Hunter: Forms of Thought and Forms of Society in the Greek World (1986), translated by Andrew Szegedy-Maszak

Cleisthenes the Athenian: An Essay on the Representation of Space and Time in Greek Political Thought from the End of the Sixth Century to the Death of Plato (1995), Pierre Vidal-Naquet and Pierre Lévêque; with a new discussion of the invention of democracy, by Pierre Vidal-Naquet, Cornelius Castoriadis, and Pierre Lévêque; translated and edited by David Ames Curtis

Economic and Social History of Ancient Greece (1978), Pierre Vidal-Naquet and M. M. Austin; translated and revised by M. M. Austin

The French Student Uprising: An Analytical Record (1971), Pierre Vidal-Naquet and Alain Schnapp; translated by Maria Jolas

Myth and Tragedy in Ancient Greece (expanded ed., 1988), Pierre Vidal-Naquet and Jean-Pierre Vernant

Politics Ancient and Modern (1995), translated by Janet Lloyd

Torture: Cancer of Democracy (1963)